FIXING GOD'S TORAH

Fixing God's Torah

The Accuracy of the Hebrew Bible Text in Jewish Law

B. Barry Levy

OXFORD
UNIVERSITY PRESS

2001

OXFORD
UNIVERSITY PRESS

Oxford New York
Athens Auckland Bangkok Bogotá Buenos Aires Cape Town
Chennai Dar es Salaam Delhi Florence Hong Kong Istanbul Karachi
Kolkata Kuala Lumpur Madrid Melbourne Mexico City Mumbai Nairobi
Paris São Paulo Shanghai Singapore Taipei Tokyo Toronto Warsaw

and associated companies in
Berlin Ibadan

Published by Oxford University Press, Inc.
198 Madison Avenue, New York, New York 10016

Library of Congress Cataloging-in-Publication Data
Levy, B Barry
Fixing God's Torah : the accuracy of the Hebrew Bible text in Jewish law / B Barry Levy
p. cm.
Includes index.
ISBN 0-19-514113-X
1 Masorah. 2. Bible. O.T.—Canon.
3. David ben Solomon ibn Abi Zimra, fl. 1513–1573—Views on Masorah. I. Title.
BS718 .L388 2001
221.4'46—dc21 00-055775

9 8 7 6 5 4 3 2 1

Printed in the United States of America
on acid-free paper

For

David, and Karen, and Sarah Tova

and

Jonathan, and Meredith, and Judah Israel

and

Daniel

Preface

Contemporary interest in the state of the Torah's textual precision lags far behind the more widespread and better-known concerns about its historical accuracy. Yet the textual integrity of every biblical book should be extremely important to those interested in either the Hebrew Bible or classical Jewish thought. Indeed, it is one of the many Bible-related issues discussed in numerous tractates of the Talmud, books of midrashic Bible interpretation, mystical writings of the medieval and postmedieval kabbalists, Bible commentaries, works of Hebrew linguistics, guidebooks for Torah scribes, and exacting codes and essays that are integral parts of the halakhic literature (the formal and binding system of Jewish religious law). These authoritative works reflect and in some cases control the consonantal text of the Torah and of other hand-copied Bible scrolls, which, for our purposes, must be differentiated from the similar but more detailed copies of the masoretic text (including most printed Bibles) that also contain the vocalization and cantillation signs and often one or more sets of detailed textual notes, known collectively as the Masorah.

Comparison of these two complementary corpora—scrolls on the one hand and texts containing all or part of the Masorah on the other—offers no evidence of the recensional variations that have emerged from studies of some prerabbinic Bible manuscripts, but neither does it produce one completely uniform text. In fact, these corpora and the rabbinic discussions of them do provide important data that augment the story of the Bible text's evolution from antiquity to the present.

Most text critics, whose attention is focused on the ancient prerabbinic evidence, devote little attention to these rabbinic works. Indeed, one often hears them claim that no significant textual variants are found or discussed in rabbinic literature and that one should not even expect to find the problem addressed by writers who doubted the very possibility of variations in a divinely revealed and perfectly transmitted text. Concomitantly, some students of rabbinic literature have concluded that the rabbis' many precise statements about textual details assume letter-perfect accuracy as well as unanimous agreement of all testimonies to all related textual matters, whatever their apparent significance. In certain religious circles, the existence of disagreements over textual details, particularly spelling, is actually deemed impossible, and consideration of the problem is judged to be inappropriate or foolish, at best, if not downright heretical.

Premodern Jewish discussions of the Bible's accuracy were based almost exclusively on the scriptural texts transmitted by Jews and the many related rabbinic teachings, some of which suggest that the rabbis' Bibles contained wordings or spellings that differed slightly from those now in use. The evidence from the Samaritan Pentateuch and the Septuagint, for example, was either unavailable or largely disregarded, because rabbinic leaders did not take seriously the possibility that someone other than their forebears could have preserved the correct text. But significant nonmasoretic variants do appear in rabbinic literature; the rabbis did recognize variants in their own textual traditions; and they did discuss the Septuagint and the Samaritan Pentateuch on occasion. In fact, rabbinic material, early and late, is far from irrelevant to reconstructing the history of the Bible text.

But even had the rabbis been willing to consider the possibility that these other texts were correct (in isolated cases, if not globally), popular and mystical Jewish sentiments strongly opposed this stance. In addition, and in some contexts even more significantly, the pressing realities of anti-Jewish polemics, motivated in part by a strong desire to discredit both the Hebrew Bible text and the Jews' faithful transmission and interpretation of it, militated against making any such concessions. Naturally, documents like the Dead Sea Scrolls, many of which date from pre-Christian times but became known only in the recent past, had no impact on the development of this literature; to the best of my knowledge, they still do not.

As additional nonreceptus texts continued to become available, scholars of the past few centuries rapidly moved beyond the limitations imposed by the selective use of only Jewish (or, in some cases, Jewish and early Christian) source material and, in the process, came to ignore the discussions of their rabbinic contemporaries, who were thought to be uninterested in the issue, if not entirely hostile to it. Because the minor differences emerging from these rabbinic observations are less spectacular than the so called recensional variations recovered from some earlier witnesses, rarely if ever are they discussed in the scholarly literature about the evolution of the text. Because they trouble certain religious interests, popular Jewish writings about the Bible also avoid them.

Indeed, the virtually universal decision of contemporary rabbinic teachers and writers not to explore this subject on a popular level, and, even more so, their failure to address it in many contexts of advanced learning, have created an intellectual vacuum that allows all sorts of silly notions to catch the public's fancy, the latest and most widespread manifestation of which is the the "decoding" craze.

Basing themselves on the erroneous assumption that the text is letter-perfect, dozens of latter-day aficionados, including some respected mathematicians, are decoding the Torah and other biblical books. To do this, they position the text in grids of varying sizes, thereby juxtaposing letters originally found at recurring, often very extensive intervals. This positioning creates new combinations of letters that, when read frontwards, backwards, or diagonally, can be interpreted as words. Counting every nth letter from various arbitrary starting points seemingly reveals allusions to Napoleon, AIDS, Israeli and American politics, the Holocaust, and other medieval, early modern, and contemporary figures and events. In like manner, Christians are decoding Hebrew Bible texts and finding references to Jesus and to christological themes. They are also decoding the New Testament, as are Muslims the Qur'an.

Decoding generates limitless letter combinations, some of which resemble words, but attributing meaning to them requires accepting many dubious assumptions. First, one must be convinced that such decodings cannot be mere random coincidences. Also, one must agree that, when the Torah text was formed, detailed knowledge of the future was possible, available, and actually encoded in it—that is, that some higher intelligence intended what is perceived as encoded information; that transmission of the Torah text has been so accurate that these messages are still intact; and that the decoded combinations of letters are valid representations of the people, dates, and events with which they are associated. Despite the simplicity and clarity attributed to the decoding process, making sense of the alleged messages often requires no small amount of ingenuity and subjectivity.

God is often assumed to be the encoder (indeed, the results of the decoding effort are often used to suggest or to confirm a belief in a text's divine authorship). This notion reinforces the Torah's sanctity and authority and may sound quite pious to some readers, but a philosophy predicated on such extensive predestination is far from a universally accepted idea among traditional Jewish thinkers. Even Jewish religious law does not support the decoders' claims, because it cannot sustain belief in a letter-perfect text; indeed halakhic authorities often claim just the opposite, which is demonstrated conclusively by many of the texts discussed in this book. Despite the halakhic preference that all Torah scrolls be identical, a universal text containing 304,805 letters—one preferred form—exists only among preselected exemplars. All copies are not identical; they are only very nearly so. In fact, the past 2,000 years have witnessed numerous rabbinic debates about hundreds of spelling variations in the Torah and thousands throughout the Bible.

The discovery of allegedly encoded meanings in mechanically generated letter combinations taken from the Bible ignores all this and, instead, shares much with ancient and medieval textual manipulations that originated as pious play and with now discredited notions regarding the movements of the stars, the shapes of human skulls, and the palm lines on one's hands. Because of being associated with some scientifically accurate information, such thinking has often been confused with science, but eventually serious study helped to debunk it.

Despite the popular, pious-sounding assumption that the Torah text is letter-perfect, frequent and extensive discussions by highly respected rabbinic leaders demonstrate that they, in some measure similar to modern scholars, were concerned about its true textual state; some of them even tried to clarify known textual doubts and to eliminate many troublesome inconsistencies. Basing their discussions on a series of passages from ancient and early medieval rabbinic documents that explored the significance of pentateuchal variations—usually in contexts about writing, reading, or correcting Torah scrolls—many famous halakhic authorities entertained serious doubts about the letter-perfect accuracy of the Torah and, by extension, the rest of the Bible. In all likelihood, rabbinic literature would contain even more such discussions, but many have been avoided out of frustration at the lack of a definitive solution. Often this silence has led to misunderstandings and mistakes, but it should not be interpreted as simple acceptance of otherwise indefensible positions on textual uniformity.

My present efforts attempt to clarify the nature and extent of some of these doubts and how they were dealt with, particularly between the thirteenth and sixteenth centuries. In addition to providing extensive evidence of the subject's universal importance, they demonstrate that the rabbinic writers of the past were far more aware of textual inconsistences in the Bible than is usually acknowledged by today's rabbinic writers, that they appreciated the legal and interpretative implications of this evidence, and that their overall reactions were, in many cases, far from what they are often imagined to be.

Acknowledgments

It is a great pleasure to thank the many people and institutions that have helped me during the preparation of this study. In the early stages of my work, the courtesy of Professor Isadore Twersky, of blessed memory, provided me with access to the Harvard University Libraries; this was renewed and expanded in 1994–1995 with my being named a Harry Starr Fellow in Judaica at Harvard, where much of the research was completed. My dear friend and former McGill colleague, then Director of the Center for Jewish Studies, Professor Ruth Wisse, showed me every possible courtesy during my stay in Cambridge, and to her, to Professor Twersky, to Professor Jay Harris, to Professor James Kugel, and to Visiting Professor Uriel Simon, as well as to the other Harry Starr Fellows of that year, I owe deep thanks for their interest in my work, their encouragement, and their suggestions.

The support of the Social Sciences and Humanities Research Council of Canada and the McGill University Faculty of Graduate Studies research grants program enabled me to consult various libraries, including the National Library of Canada, the National Library in Jerusalem, the British Library, and the libraries of Yeshiva University, the University of Pennsylvania, Princeton University, Harvard University, and the University of Toronto.

On various occasions Mr. Brad S. Hill, formerly of the National Library in Ottawa, subsequently the British Library, and now Oxford University, assisted with my use of the Lowy Collection of rare Hebraica in Ottawa and the wonderful resources of the British Library. Dr. Dan Shute has placed Presbyterian College Library's early and rare Bible editions at my disposal. Dr. Benjamin Richler of the Institute for Hebrew Manuscripts of the National Library in Jerusalem has continually guided me to its riches. Professor Hayyim Zalman Dimitrovsky graciously shared his vast knowledge of the related medieval responsa literature, and I have received additional help and encouragement from other students, colleagues, and friends too numerous to mention. As always, Mr. Joel Linsider has helped sharpen the legal dimensions of my presentation and improved its style. It is impossible to describe the many ways in which his friendship, erudition, and interest have contributed to my work.

Generous SSHRC support has enabled me to utilize the talents of many of my students as research assistants. To Debbie Abecassis, Jill Borodin, Jonathan Clenman, Leah Cohen, Lesleigh Cushing, Leah Fima, Jason Kalman, Zvi Ish Shalom, Ari Kaplan, Gila Pollack, and Dan Rand go my sincere thanks for the many large and small ways in which they have helped. Shawn Aster and Zvi Birnbaum deserve special thanks for their work on translations of some of the texts cited; Shawn also helped with the transliterations. Daniel Levy provided important assistance with many biblical references. Dr. Barbara Galli, through her careful attention to the details of presentation, helped eliminate many problems. Appreciation is also expressed to *The Canadian Jewish News* for permission to use reworked materials first published there. Special thanks to Menachem Silber, whose erudition challenged and broadened many of my observations, and to Jason Kalman and Jacqueline du Toit, who prepared the indices. Of course, any errors that remain are mine alone. Finally, I am pleased to acknowledge the invaluable assistance of Mr. Robert Milks of Oxford University Press and the copyeditor, Ms. Ilene McGrath. Their careful reading has helped improve numerous passages.

During 1999–2000 I enjoyed serving as the Shoshana Shier Distinguished Visiting Professor of Jewish Studies at the University of Toronto. My deep appreciation goes to the university; to Professor David Novak, the head of the Jewish Studies Program; and to the Shier family for the opportunity to share my research with the students in Toronto. I also thank my McGill colleagues who afforded me the chance to spend every Monday in Toronto and away from the pressures of my deanship. Ultimately, it was unencumbered research time at University College that enabled me to complete the project at this time.

Most of all, I owe an indescribable debt to my wife, Cooki, and my sons, David, Jonathan, and Daniel, for the many sacrifices they made in order that I could spend my 1994–1995 sabbatical away from home, working on this and several other projects. Their commitments in Montreal made it impractical to spend the year with me, and I can do no more than acknowledge the myriads of ways in which the opportunity to escape to Cambridge advanced my work while it made their lives more difficult. Without their sacrifices, my efforts would not have been fruitful; without the four of them, it would have no meaning. I shall be eternally in their debt.

To my daughters-in-law, Meredith and Karen, whose joining the family since that year has provided the most wonderful distractions imaginable, my blessings and thanks for all the pleasure they have added to our lives. We all rejoice over the recent birth of Sarah Tova, daughter of Karen and David, the first girl born into the Levy family in many generations, and more recently, the arrival of Judah Israel, son of Meredith and Jonathan.

Contents

A Note On Transliteration xv

Abbreviations xvii

1. Fixing God's Torah 3

2. Ibn Zimra's Responsum A: The Zohar, the Talmud, and Fixing the Torah Text 42

3. Ibn Zimra's Responsum B: The Masorah and Fixing the Torah Text 67

4. Ibn Zimra's Responsum C: The Talmud, the Torah Scrolls, and Fixing the Torah Text 89

5. Ibn Zimra's Responsum D: Logic and Vocalizing the Torah Text 97

6. The Literary Background of Ibn Zimra's Responsa: Rabbi Solomon Ben Adret and the Medieval Sefaradi Halakhic Literature 102

7. Ibn Zimra, Ben Adret, Ibn Adoniyah, the Masorah, and Fixing the Torah Text in the Sixteenth Century 137

8. Fixing God's Torah Since the Sixteenth Century 156

Notes 177

Topical Index 225

Source Index 233

A Note on Transliteration

Attempting to reflect the specific requirements of different contexts in the simplest way whenever possible, I have used several complementary transliteration systems. Bibliographic references are rendered as in modern Hebrew, with diacritical marks added to the consonants occasionally to aid in pronunciation, e.g., *Sheʾeilot uTeshuvot HaRambam*, *Nodaʿ BiYehudah*, *Parashat Beshalaḥ*. In the body of the book, when orthography is important (as it often is), Hebrew letters are transcribed in a one-to-one correspondence to English letters that relies on diacritical marks but leaves them unvocalized, e.g., *šlwm*, *ʿbry*, and *ḥkm*. Otherwise, transcription is done as simply as possible. In vocalized passages, spirantized b, d, g, k, and t are underlined; f is used instead of p̱. Prefixes are joined with hyphens rather than doubled letters, e.g., *ha-malʾaḵ*, not *hammalʾaḵ*. Vocalization is intended to aid the reader and not to represent accurately the complexities of classical notation; most accents are omitted.

Abbreviations

A.Z.	Avodah Zarah
B.B.	Baba Batra
Ber.	Berakhot
BT	Babylonian Talmud
Chron.	Chronicles
Deut.	Deuteronomy
Ecc.	Ecclesiastes
Eruv.	Eruvin
Est.	Esther
Ex.	Exodus
Ezek.	Ezekiel
Gen.	Genesis
Gen. Rab.	Genesis Rabbah
Git.	Gittin
Hag.	Haggigah
Heb.	Hebrew
Hul.	Hullin
Is.	Isaiah
Jer.	Jeremiah
Josh.	Joshua
Jud.	Judges
Lev.	Leviticus
Lev. Rab.	Leviticus Rabbah
M.	Mishnah
Mac.	Maccabees
Meg.	Megillah
Men.	Menahot
M.Q.	Mo'ed Qatan
M.S.	Ma'aser Sheni
Ned.	Nedarim
Neh.	Nehemiah
Nid.	Niddah
Num.	Numbers
Num. Rab.	Numbers Rabbah
Pes.	Pesahim
Prov.	Proverbs
Ps.	Psalms
PT	Palestinian Talmud
Qid.	Qiddushin
R.H.	Rosh HaShannah
Sam.	Samuel
San.	Sanhedrin
Shab.	Shabbat
Sheq.	Sheqalim
Shev.	Shevuot
Sof.	Soferim
Sot.	Sotah
Suk.	Sukkah
T	Tosefta
Ta'an.	Ta'anit
Tos.	Tosafot
Yad.	Yadayim
Yev.	Yevamot
Yom.	Yoma
Zech.	Zechariah
Zev.	Zevahim

FIXING GOD'S TORAH

Fixing God's Torah

It is clear, indeed, how we take most seriously the very letters [of our holy texts], for, although such a long time has already passed [since their having been recorded?], no one has dared to add anything, or to remove anything, or to change anything.

Josephus Flavius (fl. first century C.E.)
Against Apion I, 42

The Problem: Can One Find or Establish a Letter-Perfect Torah Text?

Introduction

The Bible Text in Historical Perspective The accepted scholarly notion that the consonantal text of the Hebrew Bible was set at the latest by the first or second century of the Common Era derives from the study of the Qumran, Wadi Murabbaʿat, and Nahal Hever manuscripts and other so-called Dead Sea Scrolls; from some early Bible citations and translations; and from various dicta culled from rabbinic literature.[1] But regardless of the extent to which this reconstruction may describe the evolution of the consonants, it surely does not apply to all letters that serve as vowel indicators.[2] In point of fact, many questions about these *matres lectionis* and their failure to exhibit complete consistency were raised over the centuries in the vast literatures that contain rabbinic interpretations of the Bible and the Talmud and that debate and codify their relevant parts into the binding system of rabbinic law. Extensive discussions of these matters were recorded during and after medieval times; the sixteenth century, in particular, witnessed a mushrooming of concern about them. Interest was stimulated then by the newly developed art of printing and by the need to correct and standardize mass-produced texts issued by different editors or publishers,[3] but since antiquity, much attention had been directed to both the accuracy of hand-copied Torah scrolls and the halakhic priorities for determining the correct spellings of the words in them. This concern necessitated the preparation of text-editing guidelines for correcting divergent copies, be they scrolls, codices, or printed books. The fact that these issues were under discussion and contributed to changes in the Hebrew Bible demonstrates that the process of fixing that text—

whether in the sense of establishing it or of correcting it—continued throughout these centuries, as it still does today.[4]

The popular assumption that no changes were ever introduced into copies of the Bible during rabbinic times or under rabbinic auspices simply does not accord with the facts.[5] For most of the centuries under discussion, no single, authorized, and officially registered Bible text (or Torah text) existed, and therefore it is meaningless to claim that Jews either did or did not alter it.[6] Many copies of biblical books circulated, especially the Torah, and as far as we can tell, the most that can be said is that their texts varied from each other much less than do, say, witnesses to the textual traditions of Euclid, Galen, and the Talmud. Bible manuscripts contained variations from what might today be considered textual norms, and some of them did suffer changes; and these variations and changes are no less real simply because the variations were relatively minor in comparison to those generally found in nonbiblical texts, while the changes were usually accidents or restorations, theoretically made in conformity with a majority of available texts but more often through reliance on a few carefully chosen witnesses.

Rabbinic treatments of the Torah usually focus on its masoretic forms, which include the text plus the supplementary vocalization, cantillation marks, various scribal niceties, and a series of highly detailed textual notes. But the rabbinic tradition insists that originally the scrolls lacked these helpful additions—collectively known as the Masorah, though the textual notes alone often bear that designation. To be sure, many writers believed that all or most of these elements originated at Sinai, and a way of pronouncing the words and parsing the sentences must be as old as the texts themselves; but the rabbinic tradition as a whole differentiated between the letters in the Torah scrolls and the other signs now found almost exclusively in Masorah manuscripts and in some printed books. (For now, we shall ignore the exceptional diacritical marks in the scrolls—such as superlinear dots and inverted *nuns*—and irregularly shaped letters.)

A *Fixed Bible Text with Flexible Interpretations* Beyond even this earlier, less developed image of the Torah text that consists essentially of letters and spaces is one that moves away from the scribally produced, masoretically controlled, ink-on-parchment form. In the Palestinian Talmud (e.g., Sheq. 6:1, 49c–d), and subsequently in the writings of Rashi (e.g., commentary on Deut. 33:2), Nahmanides (introduction to Torah Commentary), and many others, one meets the notion that the original Torah, like other heavenly objects, consisted of fire, in this case black fire written on white. While this ethereal presentation does not imply textual uncertainty, it does suggest an elusive, flickering, constantly resonating text, and various medieval treatments reinforced this less than concrete image. Rabbinic writers were sometimes asked why it was prohibited to write the universally accepted vowel signs, supposedly of Sinaitic origin, in Torah scrolls. One popular response observed that they controlled the reading and thereby limited the virtually infinite number of possible meanings allowed by an unpointed text.[7] Obviously, in the minds of some medieval writers, the potential of the Torah text to convey many meanings ranked higher than the need for it to offer one unequivocal message.

The exegetical flexibility imposed by the vast and creative midrashic literature, which originated in antiquity but continues *mutatis mutandis* today, must be seen, in large measure, as a complementary effort to manipulate the Bible text into an almost infinite number of shapes and to establish the hermeneutical dynamics needed to ensure a permanent commitment to this process. Chronologically, midrashic interpretation both preceded the introduction of the vocalization and cantillation signs and survived the attempt of medieval philologists to have these systems of dots and dashes define or control the text's simple meaning. To some extent, these signs may have been introduced in order to limit midrashic excesses, though occasionally they exhibit clear influence from that very corpus. The tradition of including in Bible manuscripts many of the masoretic rubrics, which listed regular and irregular spellings and word patterns and perhaps originally were intended as a sort of scribal guide, actually stimulated some midrashic interpretation.[8]

Whatever the cause or the broader implications, early rabbinic thinking had accommodated itself to a fluid rather than a static and inflexible image of the Torah. Subsequently, kabbalistic teachings about the Torah's virtually infinite number of possible interpretations carried the idea even further. Perhaps most radical was the notion of Rabbi Isaac Luria (1534–1572), who attributed a unique interpretation of every word, if not a unique hermeneutical system, to each of the 600,000 adult male Israelites who reportedly left Egypt with Moses—and thereby, in effect, to each Jew. This number was increased by his student Rabbi Hayyim Vital (1542–1620), who accredited each individual with a unique version of the four-part medieval system of interpretation, PaRDeS—usually defined as *Peshat* (literal), *Remez* (philosophical-allegorical), *Derash* (midrashic), and *Sod* (mystical). Unique application of these four classes or literatures of interpretation by each of the 600,000 who left Egypt produced a theoretical number of 2,400,000 distinct interpretations.[9]

Despite the relatively late mystical context in which these pluralistic teachings were developed and circulated, the general attitude underlying them may actually derive from a passage that appears near the original end of Mishnah Avot, which in some settings may have concluded the Mishnah. The routinely printed and popularly known version of Ben Bag Bag's teaching (Avot 5:32 in some editions, the end of Avot in the Kaufmann manuscript) recommends investigating the Torah from every angle, *hafok̲ bah we-happek̲ bah*. The wording of the reason for doing so varies from text to text and falls into one of three general patterns, though other variations exist as subsets.

In the first pattern, the rationale behind Ben Bag Bag's teaching says (or includes) *de-k̲ola' b̲ah*, "because everything is in it," meaning that all subjects in all times and places can be addressed by careful study of the Torah; subsequent words found in the next two patterns are omitted. This reading is exemplified by many vulgar Mishnah texts, as well as Paris Manuscript 328–329, Parma Manuscript C (De Rossi 984), and the 1482 edition of the Mishnah published in Naples. It also appears in at least one Mishnah fragment found in the hoard of medieval manuscripts whose discovery in the Cairo Genizah by Solomon Schechter approximately one century ago has revealed so much about the history of Judaism and its classical religious literature.

A second version of the statement is *hafok̲ bah we-happek̲ bah de-k̲ola b̲ah we-kolak̲ bah*, "because everything is in it, and all of you is in it." This reading was published by W. H. Lowe in his edition of the Mishnah underlying the text of the Palestinian Talmud, and it is even more specific than the first one. It suggests that the Torah has anticipated all subsequent personal situations: "all of you is in it," that is, you need only look in the right place in the right way to find the guidance you seek.

Most interesting, however, is the third pattern, the wording in the Kaufmann manuscript: *hafok̲ bah we-happek̲ bah de-k̲olah bak̲ we-k̲olak̲ bah*, "because all of it is in you, and all of you is in it."[10] Though the published facsimile of this manuscript has smudge marks and marginal notes, suggesting the possibility that this reading resulted from a later emendation, as presented it anticipates (or reflects) the medieval mystical multiplication of interpretations and even some postmodern ones. This last formulation virtually equates the reader's understanding with the text's meaning and thus approximates the mystical notion described above. Note the similar teaching of Johann Albrecht Bengel (1687–1752), *Te totum applica ad textum, rem totam applica ad te*, "Apply yourself totally to the text; apply it totally to yourself."[11] In all its versions, this mishnaic teaching contrasts sharply with other, more exclusive postures on interpretation that emerge from the reading of other mishnaic passages.[12]

To be sure, this version of Avot was more an exegetical position than a textual one, but the two were opposite sides of the same coin. Though many medieval rabbis were haunted by the fear of having "two *toro*t̲," by which they sometimes meant inconsistent wording or spelling of the Torah texts, and they did everything in their power to ensure that all copies of their scrolls were as nearly identical as possible, others were convinced that such agreement was unattainable. Some kabbalistic writers accommodated themselves to the reality of textual inconsistencies; they acknowledged the existence of differences in presentation and provided respectable homes for pentateuchal textual variants (see chapter 2). In their minds, the Torah was dynamic, not static; in some ways, that dynamism extended to the text.

Because there existed no one official text to change or to replicate—only some amorphous ideal text that no one possessed, from which all differing copies theoretically descended, to which they were theoretically compared, and against which they were theoretically standardized—the process of adaptation and restoration was always incomplete. Of course, wanton changes were forbidden—a prohibition that was highly respected—but restoration or correction of faulty texts was not only permitted but required, and the range of possible errors was fairly broadly construed: paragraph spacings, shapes of the letters, large and small or otherwise unusually formed letters, dotted letters, textual layout, and, most important, spelling (see, for example, Maimonides' legal formulation, translated in chapter 8). Model texts often influenced popular ones; widespread acceptance of the spelling of a particular word often became an ideal to be emulated.

This situation reflects a difference between what might be called the Aristotelian and Platonic notions of the reality of text. The former would see all copies of the Torah as the physical manifestation of the only true text, a theoretical one; the latter would extrapolate the theoretical model from the common qualities of all extant exemplars. In Islam, for example, earthly copies of the Qur'an are often taken as mere manifestations of the heavenly one, perhaps in imitation of early rabbinic texts that treat Moses' Torah this way (a notion at least as old as Jubilees, usually dated in the second pre-Christian century).

The halakhic and masoretic works on which the following chapters are based are more practical than philosophical and do not dwell on this distinction, but, given the opportunity, most writers probably would have professed commitments to both positions. In practice, the principle of restoration according to majority testimony regularly received the sanction of Torah law. An excellent example of this process is David Ibn Zimra's responsum, translated in chapter 2, in which Ex. 23:2—which, according to rabbinic interpretation, requires following the majority—is applied to making such textual decisions. Many other examples from responsa and halakhic handbooks are discussed in chapter 6.

The Ancient Story Reported in Tractate Soferim and Its Implications: Should One Base the Torah Text on Torah Scrolls or on Codices?

Soferim 6:4: Three Scrolls in the Temple Court Many medieval discussants found in the post-talmudic tractate Soferim a precedent for correcting texts to follow majority testimony. The passage, though attributed to a third-century Palestinian rabbi, describes a situation from Second Temple times (i.e., from before 70 C.E.).[13]

> Said Rabbi Shimon ben Laqish:
>
> Three scrolls were located in the Temple court, *Sefer "M'wn," Sefer "Z'ṭwṭy,"* [and] *Sefer "Hy'."*[14]
>
> In one they found written *m'wn 'lhy qdm*, "the dwelling place of the ancient God," and in two they found written *m'wnh 'lhy qdm* (Deut. 33:27); and they established [the reading in the] two and invalidated [the reading in the] one.
>
> In one they found written *wyšlḥ 't z'ṭwṭy*[15] *bny yśr'l*, "and he sent the youths of the Israelites," and in two they found written *wyšlḥ 't n'ry bny yśr'l* (Ex. 24:5); and they established [the reading in the] two and invalidated [the reading in the] one.
>
> In one they found "she" spelled *hy'* eleven times, and in two they found it spelled *hw'* eleven times; they established [the reading in the] two and invalidated [the reading in the] one.[16]

According to this version of the report, which also appears in slightly different forms in cognate rabbinic texts,[17] three scrolls in the Temple were found to contain inconsistencies ranging from the fairly innocuous spelling of the third person feminine singular pronoun *hi'* (as *hy'* instead of the common consonantal form, *hw'*) to the substitution of the otherwise nonbiblical and non-Hebrew *z'ṭwṭy* for the common Hebrew *n'ry*. In each case, the texts were compared, and what appeared in two of the three scrolls was validated. This both applied and reinforced the principle of resolving textual inconsistencies according to majority testimony.

Soferim 6:4: Interpretations and Implications Many questions have been raised about the story in Soferim 6:4 and what it may reveal about specific scrolls of Second Temple times, about what other textual deviations may have existed, about the extent to which it describes the general state of that era's Bible texts, about the role of Temple scrolls in standardizing them, about the process of comparing ancient texts in the search for inconsistencies, and even about what these scrolls were doing in the Temple. One scholarly opinion has challenged the claim that there were three scrolls in the Temple at all. (For example, *nimṣṣe'u ba-ʿazara*, which appears in some versions of the story and was translated above as "were located in the Temple court," may mean either that the scrolls were housed in the Temple or that they once happened to be there at the same time; *maṣe'u*, "they found," another attested reading, may suggest only the latter.) As important as these studies may be, our concern here is neither to determine the validity of the story nor to deduce whatever it may hint about ancient Torah scrolls, but to examine exactly what it suggested to later rabbis about correcting divergences in the scrolls and codices they knew. Halakhic authorities who were challenged by textual inconsistencies frequently appealed to this passage as a precedent and guide. What did it teach them?

The codex—a manuscript bound in the shape of a book rather than a scroll—seems to have become available only in the first century, and though we know of early writing on rock, on metal, and on a host of other objects, including animals and humans, we have no ancient evidence of extensive copying of Bible texts on anything other than scrolls.[18] If the story in Soferim was intended to be prescriptive, an assumption suggested by its context, its primary point must have been to avoid the three errors or groups of errors discussed, possibly to establish a procedure for dealing with similar situations; if it was to be descriptive, it merely reported how the ancients dealt with variations in their texts.[19]

Of course, one might assume that the association of this story with the prerabbinic era is incorrect and that the passage, attributed to a third-century Palestinian rabbi, reflects talmudic more than Temple times. This view seems unduly skeptical, but, even if warranted, it would change the situation very little, because in both periods the primary if not the almost exclusive form in which the Bible text was copied was the scroll. The routine use of scrolls is confirmed by early rabbinic writings about the Torah text, some of which mention rolling a *sefer* or its accidental rolling (e.g., M. Yom. 7:1, Eruv. 10:3). The scroll format was so popular that one midrashic text actually applied it to the tablets of the Ten Commandments, and, in perhaps related presentations, medieval artists occasionally depicted the tablets in scroll form.[20]

The most frequently cited talmudic passage about the accuracy of the Torah text (BT Qid. 30a) recounts a discussion about the enlarged *waw* in *gḥwn*, Lev. 11:42, reputed to be the middle letter of the Torah (presumably, in a text with an odd number of letters). When Rav Joseph questioned whether it was indeed the last letter of the first half or the first letter of the second half (assuming a text with an even number of letters), the retort suggested bringing a *sefer* and checking. Even though by that time a codex theoretically could have been available, the Talmud says a scroll was procured. Upon further reflection, the rabbis found themselves unable to proceed, because "they [i.e., the ancients or perhaps other contemporary rabbis] were [or: are] expert in defective and plene spelling; we are not expert." In point of fact, checking a scroll, or at least any other scroll in their vicinity, would not produce the precise information they sought.

This statement in BT Qid. 30a implies that previously a letter-perfect text of the Torah had been available, presumably in scroll form, and that that text was an exact replica of the original, of which the scroll mentioned here was an imperfect copy. The early rabbis and, for very different reasons, some modern writers (e.g., E. Rosenmueller, who died in 1835, and P. LaGarde, who died in 1891) assumed all Torah texts to derive from a single copy, correct by definition. Others, including Rabbi Isaac Judah Yehiel Safran (1806–1874), who believed that all the variations were, in any case, of Sinaitic origin, and Rabbi Mordecai Breuer, who has published extensive studies of the masoretic text, suggested that the definitive text was produced later. M. H. Goshen-Gottstein went so far as to argue that the Aleppo Codex, produced by Aaron Ben Asher about 1,000 years ago, was in fact "the *first codex of the complete Bible* with full Masoretic annotation, exhibiting what was to be regarded as the prototype of the Tiberian Bible text."[21]

Before the production of the Aleppo Codex, all copies of the Bible were not identical and, even after it was produced, there is little likelihood that all other copies were systematically corrected to follow it, though the suggestion to maximize the attempt often was made. The generalizations of Rabbi Meir HaLevi Abulafia (ca. 1170–1244) about the need to collate the various witnesses to the Torah text demonstrate that, by the thirteenth century, either the situation that existed before Ben Asher's production of the Aleppo Codex had not changed much, or it had returned. In any case, at that point all copies of the Torah were not identical.

Abulafia, in his *Masoret Seyag LaTorah*; Rabbi Menahem ben Solomon Meiri (died in 1313), author of *Qiryat Sefer*; Yedidiah Solomon Norzi (1560–1616), author of *Minhat Shai*; Rabbi Solomon Ganzfried (1804–1886), through the rulings in his *Kesset HaSofer*; and others tried to produce the definitive Torah text, but no one has ever attempted to collate all extant Torah scrolls and thus to fulfill what might be seen as the logical requirement of the Soferim passage. Indeed, despite some halakhic protests, the popular use of computer scanning to identify for correction any deviations from one preestablished textual norm is making this task increasingly difficult by eliminating the variations, even as the technology itself allows one to anticipate the possibility of creating a data base containing the texts of all extant Torah scrolls.[22] Moreover, inconsistencies among the many seemingly trustworthy documents and sources on which such determinations might be made often thwarted attempts to rely on them, while variants supported by the authority and availability of the Talmud and the Midrashim constantly called into question the accuracy of those traditions that deviated from what appeared to be the early rabbis' certified spellings of certain words.

Nonpentateuchal texts are no less problematic; indeed, as a group they exhibit more and greater inconsistencies than do witnesses to the Torah. Norzi admitted that he did not even try to handle fully the spelling problems in the postpentateuchal books, as Abulafia had not dealt with them. The inconsistencies were too extensive for him to investigate himself (see the passage translated later in this chapter), and the strictness of the rules governing the Torah gave it a special status not held by other biblical texts.[23]

Scrolls—that is, unpunctuated and unvocalized rolls—were once the norm for those who possessed copies of any biblical books, but for many centuries such texts of the Prophets and most of the Hagiographa have been relatively rare. In most cases, medieval and postmedieval work on nonpentateuchal texts relied primarily on codices, not on scrolls, and it seems that the very existence of this extensively documented and somewhat independent tradition of the Torah text's being preserved in scrolls (which ultimately is the source of the text in the codices) has been a major factor in creating such a different situation regarding the state of its text.

Secondary works often suggest that the phenomenon of the codex is not mentioned in the Talmud; indeed, few if any early rabbinic texts refer to it, but one possible candidate is BT Meg. 27a. It differentiates between a Torah and a Torah scroll and asks a telling question about the Torah, the Prophets, and the Hagiographa: *miḵraḵ haḵi karḵinan, qa' yateḇ dappa' 'a-ḥaḇreh,* "How could we bind them, because one *daf* would repose on another?" If here *daf* means "page"—not "column of text," which is another possible meaning—this passage would be trying to avoid a situation in which the later, less holy books could sometimes rest on the earlier, holier ones. While a scroll may cause this problem, the description seems more appropriate to a codex. Also the concern for not placing single-columned pieces of parchment in a scroll (BT Men. 30a) may reflect an objection to recycling pages from a codex, though loose, unbound, one-page texts are known from Qumran, and other explanations of this prohibition do not rely on this assumption.

If the Soferim narrative had intended solely to teach a commitment to the concept of majority testimony, it might be instructive but largely superfluous. Ex. 23:2 prohibits following a multitude (*rabbim*) to pervert justice by falsifying testimony in favor of the multitude (*lo' tihye 'aḥarē rabbim le-ra'ot we-lo' ta'ane 'al riḇ linṭoṭ 'aḥarē rabbim le-haṭṭoṭ*). By separating the last three words from the rest of the sentence, the rabbis effectively coined a new injunction, *'aḥarē rabbim le-haṭṭoṭ,* which they understood to mean "follow the majority." A biblical prooftext that supported majority rule in many areas of halakhic debate, this phrase and issues of majority evidence are prevalent throughout rabbinic literature, including many textual discussions. As interpreted, *'aḥarē rabbim le-haṭṭoṭ* would require consideration of all types of evidence (not just scrolls), as would be the operative principle in legal contexts unrelated to Torah scrolls, but no other sort of Torah text was available when the event described in Soferim took place. Even if, at first glance, the story seems to legitimate a broader range of witnesses and to rely exclusively on the testimony of the scrolls because only they were available, one cannot argue that its intended purpose was to validate evidence found in kinds of texts that did not yet exist.

Only if the passage is taken to reflect a later attitude, such as a third-century context or the post-talmudic era of Soferim itself (which might have been times of competition between codices and scrolls), can one seriously consider the use of codices to be addressed. If so, because in this story the three *sefarim* on which ancient decisions were made refers to three scrolls, one could interpret the story as an anticodex sentiment and strong support for using only scrolls. Or one could argue that scrolls were used merely because only they were available and that the story has no intent to disqualify other types of evidence; but the later the presumed date, the less convincing this line of reasoning appears.

Because the story from Soferim 6:4 also appears (in somewhat different forms) in earlier rabbinic texts, one should not argue that its original purpose was to support only the use of codices. Probably it refers to scrolls because it reflects an era when only they were in use, particularly in what can be assumed to be, at least regarding this particular phenomenon, the relatively conservative context of the Temple. Medieval application of the story to codices is permitted by logical inference and simply reinforces the commitment to deriving majority testimony from whatever sources were available at the time.

Additional interpretations further limit the choice of texts, for even if Soferim intended to teach reliance solely on scrolls, it clearly did not suggest the use of all scrolls. Whereas many medieval rabbinic writers argued that the principle of majority determination derived from Soferim 6:4 or was confirmed by it, a number of more recent ones pointed out that only three scrolls, not all others in existence, were actually used, presumably because those other texts were less sacred, less accurate, and less authoritative. This observation both takes into account and simultaneously discredits many ancient Torah texts—including those now being discovered by archaeologists—for it assumes that only those scrolls housed in the Temple possessed a presumption of accuracy (even though they disagreed with each other in a number of ways).

According to some later writers, the procedure described in Soferim 6:4 applied only when the Temple was standing and its scrolls, which possessed a presumption of accuracy, were available to provide the necessary information. Since these official scrolls no longer exist, they argued, reliance on them or on the principle of majority testimony based on them is no longer possible, especially because now one must depend on the inferior texts "of our dispersion." This clever reading provides a justification for the later rabbinic use of any other scribal, masoretic, talmudic, or midrashic information, regardless of antiquity or relative popularity, to establish the correct text. It might even open the door a crack to considering some ancient scrolls discovered by modern archaeologists; but this interpretation responds to the story, it does not reflect its primary intention. In reality, the account in Soferim 6:4 relied solely on scrolls and therefore should convey support for only their use,[24] but an additional factor needs to be discussed.

At the time of the event described in Soferim, only scrolls existed, but later masoretic traditions did refer to at least one other type of contemporary evidence. The Bible speaks of recording on limed stone *kol dibrē ha-tora ha-zo'ṯ*, "all the words of this *tora*" (Deut. 27:2–8), which often was taken to refer to the entire Torah and to be reflected in the story of Joshua 4, where such recording is reported. While some medieval rabbis understood this reference in Deuteronomy to include something substantially less than the entire Torah, some medieval masoretic works refer to a copy of the Torah made from this ancient record.[25] Whatever the possible role of this copy in preserving the Torah text, the theoretical implications for the passage in Soferim are considerable. If this alternative text had been available for consultation at the time of the event described in Soferim and had been deemed authoritative, the entire context of that passage would change. One is forced to assume either that this other text did not exist then, or that the three Temple scrolls included all pertinent information from it and that they, or the process by which they were compared, obviated consulting it. This possibility too underscores the extent to which the textual information from these three scrolls—and only these three scrolls—was taken to be the exclusive authoritative witness to the text.

One modern reconstruction suggests that three types of Torah texts existed in ancient times: (1) official, corrected copies kept in the Temple; (2) accurately copied but somewhat deviant texts that were studied by people like Rabbi Meir;[26] and (3) popular, unauthoritative, and inaccurate texts used in villages or for teaching children. Unfortunately, this picture combines the situation in Temple times with that in the tannaitic era (so it probably could not have pertained fully in the second century, when Rabbi Meir lived), and it has been challenged by later scholars, whose more complex theories of textual classification derive from the ancient translations and the many copies of scriptural books found among the Dead Sea Scrolls.[27] Although the latter group of writers assumes no a priori preference for any particular class of texts, the rabbis did; and the notion of holding model texts in the Temple or using Temple texts as models accords well with the story in Soferim and with other sources that mention a group of official correctors of Temple texts (e.g., 2 Mac. 2:14–15, M. M.Q. 3:4, and PT Sheq. 4:3). It also reflects the rabbinic ideal of a uniform textual tradition, is consistent with the interpretation of a number of other statements preserved in various Hellenistic and early rabbinic documents, accommodates the many midrashic interpretations that reflect slightly different spellings, and even parallels the situation that existed later, as will be explained. Similar scribal activities seem to have been part of the procedures in other ancient Near Eastern temples as well.

The rabbinic tradition also speaks of thirteen Torah scrolls produced by Moses, one for each tribe and one either to be given to the Levites or to be housed in the Ark. Though relatively late, this story provides additional support for the notion of a centrally located, model text. In all versions of the story, the purpose of this extra, thirteenth exemplar is to protect the Torah against the introduction of both intentional and unintentional textual changes.[28]

Of course, had any of the three scrolls used in the Soferim passage been copied from one of the other two, or had any two been closely related, their value as independent witnesses would have been reduced. Therefore Rabbi Abraham ben Mordecai HaLevi (ca. 1650–1712) suggested that when the original comparison was made in the Temple, three unrelated texts were used in order to avoid validating a common error that two might have shared.[29] While Soferim in no way intimates that such things were considered, this interpretation attributes to the ancients both a relatively large collection of scrolls and a fairly sophisticated appreciation of each one's textual lineage. It also suggests an awareness of lines of transmission that may have contained consistently erroneous texts.

What Were Kiṯḇē Ha-Qoḏeš? One final point about the Soferim passage. The phrase used for these scrolls in almost all versions of this passage is *šeloša sefarim nimṣe'u ba-ʿazara*; other sources speak of *sifrē ʿazara* and *sifrē ʿezra*. The third term may be a variation on the second, but even if it is not, the second (and possibly the first as well) may suggest that at least some scrolls were known as "Temple-court scrolls," *sifrē ha-ʿazara* or the like. An additional synonym may exist.

The Hebrew term *kiṯḇē ha-qoḏeš*, which seems to be attested only in texts written after the Temple was destroyed, is mentioned several times in the Mishnah, such as in Yad. 3:2, 5, and Shab. 16:1, as well as in the Tosefta and the Talmud. Generally it is understood to be the equivalent of Hagiographa, "holy writings," the third section of the Hebrew Bible (a term found in Greek several centuries earlier), and undoubtedly it is so used in some places, but this may be a derived meaning. *Qoḏeš* is primarily a noun meaning "sanctuary" (or "the Holy One," as in the vocalized divine epithet, *ha-qoḏeš baruḵ hu'*), not an adjective, "sacred." Thus as a starting point one should assume *kiṯḇē ha-qoḏeš* means either "the writings of the Holy One" or "the writings of the sanctuary."

Many targumic passages containing paraphrases or midrashic additions render the Hebrew term *miqdaš* into Aramaic as *bai(ṯ) maqdeša*, *har ha-qoḏeš* as *ṭur baiṯ maqdeša*, and *lešon ha-qoḏeš* (often introducing the untranslated Hebrew word, *hinneni*) as *lešan baiṯ quḏša*.[30] In like manner, *ʿir ha-qoḏeš* means "the city of the sanctuary." On the other hand, *yerušalayim ha-qeḏoša* and *yerušalayim qeḏoša*, found on some coins from the time of the first uprising against Rome, refer to the city as a holy place.[31]

Thus it is entirely possible that the mishnaic term *kiṯḇē ha-qoḏeš* originally meant "Temple writings," a meaning that may be echoed in M. Shab. 16:1, which speaks of saving *kiṯḇē ha-qoḏeš* from a fire that breaks out on the Sabbath, and the PT (ad loc.), which compares them to private documents, *šeṭarē heḏyoṭoṯ*. (The loss of the Temple's documents through fire is documented from ancient accounts of the destruction of Jerusalem.) Note also the frequency with which rabbinic sources juxtapose or compare things designated as *heqdeš* and *heḏyoṭ*. It remains to be seen if or how this interpretation would affect our understanding of the status of any individual ancient Bible text, but an extensive tradition of using *miqdaš*, "Temple," as a term for the Bible has been charted by N. Weider. Possible connections with the etymology of the Greek term *hagiographa* (which also could mean "temple writings," not only "holy writings") require further consideration. As well, scrolls represented by ancient artists as housed in a shrinelike ark could qualify as *kiṯḇē ha-qoḏeš*, though the preserved representations themselves contain no such designation.[32]

Defining Sefer *and* Masoreṯ

Before proceeding, we must consider the definitions of two terms that recur throughout the literature concerned with establishing and restoring Torah texts: *sefer* and *masoreṯ*. The precise meaning of the word *sefer* (plural: *sefarim*) varies with the context. When compared with Tefillin, *sefarim* are probably copies of all biblical books (e.g., M. Meg. 1:9). When juxtaposed with Torah, *sefer* seems to refer to nonpentateuchal books (e.g., BT Meg. 26a). As was already seen in the Soferim passage, the common rabbinic term *sefer* frequently refers to a book written in the form of a scroll, often to a Torah scroll; synonymous terms include *sefer tora*, *megilla*, and *megillaṯ sefer*. *Ḥumašim* were scrolls containing one of the five pentateuchal books, as seen, for example, from discussions about binding them together (e.g., BT Git. 60a); cf. *ḥomeš*, "one fifth." When some manuscripts were changed from scrolls to bound volumes, the term *sefer* was extended to include them; *miṣḥaf*, "codex" (cf. Arabic *muṣḥaf*) was used in rabbinic writings but only much later.[33] Thus in many of the texts discussed below, *sefer* can mean either a scroll or a book. Only context can clarify which is intended, and sometimes it is impossible to tell; on occasion, I have rendered it "text" or included the transliteration, either to mark the uncertainty or to signal the reader that I have intentionally chosen one meaning over the other. Translations containing "Torah scroll" reflect the Hebrew term *sefer tora*.

The term *masoreṯ* likewise carries several almost contradictory meanings.[34] Presumably derived from the Hebrew root meaning "to transmit," *masoreṯ* is often taken as "transmission" or "tradition." As explained by Y. S. Norzi in the introduction to *Minhat Shai*, his masoretic Bible commentary, which follows the presentation of Elijah Levita (who died in 1549) in *Masoret HaMasoret*:

> It is appropriately called *masoret*, because it was transmitted (*nimsera*) to the sages, from one man to the next, until [it reached] Ezra and his assistants . . . . And from Ezra and his supporters, it was transmitted (*nimšeka*) to the sages of Tiberias, who wrote it down and called it Masorah.[35]

Practically speaking, the Masorah or Masoret includes the entire corpus of traditional teachings about the Bible text: hundreds of lists of (often obstruse) data about the text and any rare or unusual phenomena in it; comparisons of similar or identical usages, spellings, or constructions within a single book, the third of the Bible in which that book appears, or the entire Bible; tabulations of the numbers of verses in each book and the number of times each letter in the alphabet can be found; and similar material.

In addition to these more widespread and better-known meanings, some early rabbinic texts used the term *masoret* to indicate the consonantal text of the Bible. This usage appears, for example, in the talmudic term *ʾem la-masoret*, often paired with *ʾem la-miqraʾ*, where *miqraʾ* refers to the reading tradition, the vocalization or traditional pronunciation of the text, and is contrasted with the *masoret*, the written, consonantal text. In his commentary to BT Suk. 6b, Rashi (died 1105) explained *yeš ʾem la-masoret*: as "Moses wrote and transmitted (*u-masar*) in a Torah scroll to Israel; this is the main thing (*ha-ʾem we-ha-ʿiqar*), not as it is read." Rabbi Abraham Min HaHar of Montpellier (late twelfth century) was even clearer: "The *masoret* is what Moses wrote in the Torah, and he handed it over (*u-mesarah*) to Israel."[36]

The root *m-s-r* is also used to describe the process of adding the masoretic notes to the consonantal text. Bible codices sometimes refer to the full production of the text as "x *katab niqqed u-masar*," "x copied, vocalized, and masorized," or the like.[37] While this usage is undoubtedly derived from that just discussed, the potential for misinterpreting ancient descriptions of transmitting the unvocalized text this way (also described with the verb *m-s-r*) are obvious.

Perhaps the best-known early rabbinic reference to *masoret* is Rabbi Akiva's statement, *masoret seyag la-tora*, in M. Avot 3:13; this statement is missing from some witnesses to the text but, where present, it is usually taken to mean "*masoret* is a fence around the Torah." Classical rabbinic commentators offered at least two different interpretations of the phrase. Many, perhaps most—including the commentary in *Mahzor Vitry* (twelfth century), Rabbi Shimon ben Zemah Duran (fourteenth century) followed very closely by Rabbi Ovadiah Bertinora (sixteenth century), the Vilna Gaon (eighteenth century), Rabbi Israel Lipschuetz (nineteenth century), and Rabbi Baruch HaLevi Epstein (twentieth century)—saw *masoret seyag la-tora* as a direct reference to the careful control of plene and defective spellings by the Masorah and to its value as a protection against corruption of the Torah text.[38] Many authors related the passage to the use of the term *masorot* in the talmudic interpretation of Neh. 8:8, which links ancient translation and interpretation of the text to that biblical text.[39] Others, like Rabbi Isaac Magrisso (eighteenth century), contributor of the commentary to Avot in Jacob Culi's *Yalqut MeʿAm Loʿez*, took it in the more general sense of tradition that protected against violations or misinterpretations of authoritative religious teachings or beliefs.[40] In his Avot Commentary, Rabbi Menahem Meiri (who died in the early fourteenth century) cited a series of masoretic rubrics but also included the other interpretation, "tradition."[41]

Whatever the original intention of Rabbi Akiva's statement and regardless of its subsequent use to exaggerate the antiquity of some parts of the Masorah, the term *masoreṯ* came to refer to the highly detailed, accumulated teachings of a group of post-talmudic masters of the Bible text who are now known as masoretes. Eventually, this *masoreṯ* was assumed to include the letters; the vocalization signs; the cantillation signs; the various interlinear, marginal, and appended textual notes; and virtually all other comments associated with the Bible's textual state or nature, even the authorship and chronological range of each book. Thus in medieval texts, *masoreṯ* can refer either to the consonantal text of the Bible or to any of these nonconsonantal accompaniments. The plural, *masoroṯ*, is used for Masorah codices containing the Bible text along with the Masorah, for the texts containing independent masoretic lists or books, and for the lists themselves. As was suggested by Norzi, *masora* and *masoreṯ* are often interchangeable, especially when referring to the masoretic literature; *masora* seems not to have been used regularly for the consonantal text of the Bible, though one passage discussed later would be much easier to explain if it had been. As with *sefer*, only context can suggest which meaning of *masoreṯ* is intended.

The interplay of these two terms and their ambiguities is particularly troublesome in some passages. When a writer said that a certain textual problem should be solved by one's relying on a *sefer* in his possession, or on a group of *sefarim*, did he mean the scrolls or the Masorah codices; or both? If a particular spelling is attested in *sifrē sefaraḏ*, "the *sefarim* of Sefarad," or in *sifrē ʾaškenaz*, "the *sefarim* of Ashkenaz," or in *ha-sefarim šellanu*, "our *sefarim*," is it to be found in the scrolls or in the Masorah codices; or in both? This ambiguity was read into Soferim 6:4 as well. Some later writers who claimed that it suggested reliance on a majority, *roḇ sefarim*, meant a majority of the scrolls, which is what Soferim was discussing; others applied it to the Masorah texts, or to both. Similarly, instructions to follow the *masoreṯ* could have meant the consonantal text in the scrolls or the early medieval masoretic literature. This uncertainty is compounded by the fact that, unlike contemporary scholars, many medieval authors believed that the Masorah existed in pretalmudic times and associated it with the Soferim (the ancient Scribes, routinely capitalized to differentiate them from simple copyists), the Men of the Great Assembly, Ezra, or even Moses. These ambiguities also helped reinforce the impression that all of these terms were interchangeable synonyms.

An edifying example of avoiding the problem caused by this linguistic situation appears in the *Shulhan Arukh* of Rabbi Joseph Caro (1488–1575) and in some of its commentaries. The first volume of this work, which deals with, among many other things, the rules of the public Torah reading, requires that, in cases where the traditional consonantal text—the *Keṯiḇ*—has been accompanied by one of a series of variation types called *Qere*, one follow the latter exclusively in reading the text (*Orah Hayyim* 141, 8). It recounts an incident where someone read the *Keṯiḇ* in the presence of three rabbis, who strongly disapproved. The reader refused to do as instructed, was admonished appropriately, and was removed from the reading table.

The key phrase is *we-hiṯru ḇo še-yiqra' ke-fi ha-masora,* "they warned him that he should read according to the *masora.*" If, in this context, *ha-masora* meant "the consonantal text," the criticism would have been meaningless, as the reader could have claimed that he was doing precisely that, and perhaps this notion guided his behavior. Obviously in this context *ha-masora* means the oral reading tradition. Nonetheless, a number of commentators on this passage troubled themselves to clarify it further. For example, Rabbi Israel Meir HaKohen Kagan (1838–1933), in the *Mishnah Berurah* (ad loc.), noted: "according to the *masora*—that is to say, the tradition that we have received [regarding how] to read it, and that we do not follow the written text (which is called only *masoreṯ* [as in the term] *'em la-masoreṯ*)."[42]

Interpretations and translations of *sefer* and *masoreṯ* will differ depending on how one understands the passages treated later, but several points seem virtually certain. References to vowels, cantillation marks, and masoretic notations must relate to codices, not scrolls (though a passage in Soferim is often understood to refer to a scroll in which verse markers had been added). Moreover, if, for a particular purpose, a document suggests that one should not rely on the *masoreṯ,* its position is to reject the masoretic notes or lists, not the consonantal text preserved in the Torah scrolls. While some writers did articulate this other position, they expressed it unequivocally and specifically criticized the failure of the scrolls to offer a uniform text. Positive statements, on the other hand, are sometimes less certain in meaning. When writers cite both *sefarim* and *masoroṯ,* in most contexts one may assume that the former refers to the Torah scrolls and the latter to codices containing the Masorah, though this is not absolutely certain, and of course Masorah codices routinely contain both the Masorah and the text. Some writers probably thought that the consonantal texts in the scrolls and the masoretic works were identical, a notion that would eliminate the practical textual problems, even if their own intentions remain unclear; but the evidence against the validity of applying this assumption to all details in numerous specific contexts prevents its being taken seriously as a general premise.

What Constitutes the "Majority"?

The Best Available Torah Text According to the Letter of Aristeas The Bible may have mentioned the concept of following a majority, but it surely did not discuss applying the principle of majority testimony to determining its text. The earliest reference to this process may be in the Letter of Aristeas, usually dated to the second or third century B.C.E., which discusses the ancient Greek translation of the Torah prepared for Ptolemy. According to some interpretations of this epistle, the text of the Torah was in an imperfect state that required correction before the translation could be prepared; according to others, this description applied to a preexisting Greek version. In any case, an observation about the Torah's textual imperfection was followed by the request to Ptolemy to produce the translation:

> O King, if you approve, a letter will be written to the high priest in Jerusalem, that he should send elder men who have lived noble lives and who are expert in matters of their law, six from each tribe, so that, when we have examined *that agreed by the*

majority and have obtained an accurate translation, we can preserve it in a place and in a manner worthy of both the contents and your purpose.[43]

Different texts were known or assumed to exist. Of necessity, establishing the preferred version was a preliminary step to providing the king with a copy, and presumably the best results would be achieved by relying on the majority opinion of a large group of highly learned and distinguished men. It is impossible to tell if the suggested tribal representation (whatever it might have meant at that time) is purely symbolic, if it was intended to include all possible textual traditions preferred by one group or another, or if it is part of some other tradition of editorial practice. In any case, the principle of deciding textual questions on the basis of a majority was already a well-established procedure, though in this case the focus of the attention is a majority of learned men, not necessarily a majority of texts, as it is in the story in Soferim.

Majority Testimony In and Since Medieval Times The later rabbis who tried to apply Soferim 6:4 to their own situations (and in all likelihood those men described in the Letter of Aristeas who relied on a majority of people, not texts) realized that it would be impossible to consult all extant scrolls or opinions. Therefore the next determination is the practical alternative that would have been considered as valid as "majority testimony." In some contexts, the majority of scrolls available in a town was deemed satisfactory evidence, as if this choice would typify the situation everywhere and provide testimony to a theoretical majority of all extant scrolls.[44] If nothing else, this approval assured (or strove for) local consistency, but often such uniformity was difficult to attain, particularly when, as happened all too frequently (especially in the fifteenth and sixteenth centuries), exiles and migrations found scrolls produced in widely dispersed communities and in accord with varying traditions and standards, not only varying levels of workmanship, housed in a single synagogue ark and competing for liturgical attention and textual authority.

In the sixteenth century, Abraham Hasan, a Spanish refugee, was engaged by the community of Salonika to examine and correct its Torah scrolls. The number of serious problems he found, exacerbated by the zeal with which he undertook and executed the task, became cause for a major confrontation that involved a number of leading rabbis (see chapter 6.)[45]

As reported by Rabbi Hayyim Palaggi (Palache) (1788–1869), a similar but apparently less volatile situation developed in Izmir, when a certain Ashkenazi sage named Rabbi Joseph, a professional checker of Torah scrolls, arrived in town. He began to examine the local scrolls and found many mistakes—sometimes in excess of thirty—in virtually every one of them, including those that were removed from the ark for the annual recitation of *Kol Nidrei* and had been checked many times before. The only exceptions were scrolls that had been checked previously by Rabbi Israel Ashkenazi. Palaggi ruled that all Torah scrolls in the city that had not been checked and corrected by one of these two sages should be brought forward and examined. From his discussion, it seems that he never considered the possibility that commitment to a similar Ashkenazi scribal tradition lay behind the fact that this outsider found the only correct scrolls to be those checked by another Ashkenazi rabbi; whether this was, in fact, the reason, remains to be seen.[46]

Many rabbis paid homage to the principle of deciding textual questions according to a majority of witnesses, particularly a majority of the Masorah codices or masoretic compositions.[47] Others took into account a broader assortment of evidence but ultimately preferred certain categories of sources or specific documents whose reputations for containing ancient and highly accurate presentations of the text gave them greater authority than others. Many writers may have identified with Ibn Masʿud's teaching, "The one with the truth on his side is the majority, even if he is alone";[48] brief descriptions of their *modi operandi* suggest that on occasion they actually applied this principle to the selection of textual witnesses.

Rabbi Meir Abulafia's Attempt to Fix the Torah Text in the Twelfth Century The most important systematic medieval attempt to determine the halakhically correct text of the Torah in the period after the masoretes was that of the Spanish talmudist Rabbi Meir Abulafia (1170–1244).[49] The following excerpt from the introduction to *Masoret Seyag LaTorah*, his handbook of precise masoretic spelling and orthographic detail, describes both the sorry state in which he found the Torah text and some of what he did to correct it.

> And if we have come to rely on the corrected scrolls (*ha-sefarim ha-mugahim*) that we possess, even they contain many disagreements. And were it not for the Masorah texts (*masorot*) that were made a fence around the Torah [cf. M. Avot 3:13], a man would be unable to find his hands and feet because of the disagreements. Even the *masorot* were not spared the occurrence of disagreements, for disagreements are found in some places even among them, but not like the large number of disagreements among the scrolls (*sefarim*). And if someone would intend to write a Torah scroll correctly, it would be imperfect regarding defective and plene spellings; and he would find himself groping like a blind man in the darkness of disagreements, and he would not successfully achieve his purpose to find what he seeks. Furthermore, "though a wise man think to know it, yet he will not be able to find it" [Ecc. 8:17]. . . .
>
> And I . . . hurried to arm myself, and to seek, and to search for scrolls (*sefarim*) that are corrected and accurate and for accurate *masorot*, and to deal with their disagreements; and to abandon the new scrolls (*sefarim*) that have come from near [cf. Deut. 32:17], and to follow the trustworthy old ones, and, with respect to them, to follow the majority, as is the method prescribed in the Torah in all cases of disagreement, to follow the majority, as is stated, "follow the majority" [Ex. 23:2].[50]

Abulafia's theoretical commitment to the halakhic principle of majority testimony is clear, and he preferred to use the old scrolls to which he had access, but their state of disagreement precluded sole reliance on them, and exactly how he determined the "majority" in all cases is not explained. In fact, as he says in the last paragraph just cited, he used a combination of what he believed to be accurate scrolls and accurate Masorah texts, and he abandoned recently produced copies in favor of older ones brought from afar. On occasion he also cited the evidence of the early rabbinic literature. Abulafia's procedure was highly successful and his results received strong though far from universal recognition, but in a few cases even he failed to offer a definitive spelling.[51]

A complete picture of how Abulafia determined the "majority" remains a desideratum, but enough data are scattered throughout his many comments to suggest some preliminary observations. Dozens of passages in his book contain references to "accurate texts," "a majority of accurate texts," and "minority" readings, and many also refer to accurate or inaccurate *masoroṯ*. Usually he cites the Masorah only when faced with a problem of some sort—often conflicts among the scrolls or relevant masoretic traditions—and it was far from rare for him to correct *masoroṯ* on the basis of all or a majority of accurate texts, sometimes supported by other conflicting *masoroṯ*.

In at least one passage he mentions the number of exemplars included in his majority and minority determinations. Case 3 below refers to a majority of four readings and a minority of two, suggesting that he actually used six texts. Since it is reasonable to assume that with relatively little effort he could have had access to more than six witnesses, the six he used were probably preselected. In other words, his tabulations reflect not a random majority but a carefully controlled one, a procedure suggested by some rabbis to have been employed in the Temple (as reported in Soferim) and later used by Norzi, Breuer, and others.

Comparison of six texts left Abulafia with the possibility of even splits in some cases but also provided a two-thirds majority in others. Some of these doubts were resolved by reliance on the Masorah; perhaps uncertainty created by an even split also explains the few undecided cases. A relatively few references to rabbinic interpretations appear in the work, including passages from both the Midrashim and the Babylonian Talmud. In most cases of disagreement, he offers a preferred spelling; in a few, either he did not or the printed text of *Masoret Seyag LaTorah* fails to record his decisions. And in at least one, no. 6, he rules against the majority in favor of a single old and venerated text. The following sketches of some of his observations help portray his thinking. Note the many examples (nos. 9, 11–16, etc.) that cite "accurate texts," perhaps scrolls (page numbers in parentheses refer to the Florence edition of *Masoret Seyag LaTorah*).

1. *ʾznk*, "your equipment" (Deut. 23:14, 2b): This spelling is found in a majority of accurate texts; one has *ʾznyk*, and one *masora* supports it. He concludes that one must follow the majority.
2. *lʾpd*, "for the ephod" (Ex. 25:7, 6b): He refers to "all the *masoroṯ* that have come into our possession" but also mentions Masorah traditions that are different but internally inconsistent.
3. *bgblk*, "in your land" (Ex. 10:4, 13a): In discussing the various forms of *bgblk*, he refers to a minority opinion of two and a majority opinion of four, with the latter confirmed by the Masorah.
4. *dkh*, "crushed" (Deut. 23:2, 16a–b): In the process of deciding between *dkh* and *dkʾ*, he corrects the *masoroṯ* that differed.
5. *wthyyn*, "they shall be" (passim, 17b): Here too he corrects the Masorah.
6. *ḥdškm*, "your new moons" (Num. 10:10, 20b): The "majority of the texts with a presumption of having been checked" (*rubbaʾ de-nusahē de-miṯḥazeqē beḏiqaʾ*) contain the plene spelling, *ḥdšykm*, but he declares them in error, while in a "corrected" [or: "checked"] version (*mugah*) it was spelled without the *yod*. He decides the latter is correct and supports it by means of an old text (*nusaḥa ʿattiqa*) and a spelling suggested by BT Sukkah.

7. *klwt*, "completion of" (Num. 7:1, 34a): This passage is translated in chapter 2. He notes that the texts and the *masoroṯ* are divided and that a rabbinic exposition supports one of the opinions.
8. *hklywt*, "the kidneys" (Lev. 3:5, 34a): He accepts a majority of *masoroṯ* and *nusahoṯ* against a minority.
9. *hlh*, "Lo" (Deut. 3:11, 36a): He notes an error in the Masorah; most accurate texts disagree with it.
10. *tlntykm*, "your complaints" (Ex. 16:7, 36b): He corrects the Masorah.
11. *mlʾt*, "full" (Gen. 41:22, etc., 39a): "Accurate" texts read one way; a minority of texts read another, but a majority of accurate texts and *masoroṯ* disagree with the latter.
12. *mlkyṣdq*, "Melchizedek" (Gen. 14:18, 39a): In accurate texts it is written as one word; in the Masorah, as two. He rules that it must be written on one line.
13. *whkyty*, "and I will smite" (Ex. 3:20, 43a): He rejects two different *masoroṯ*, because accurate texts disagree with them.
14. *wsqlny*, "and they will stone me" (Ex. 17:4, 47b): He observes that what others have recorded here as *Qere* and *Keṯiḇ* variants are not so designated, but that the people of Sura have different *Keṯiḇ* and *Qere* readings, the former being *wsqlnw*. He rejects this, because all accurate texts have identical readings for both the *Qere* and the *Keṯiḇ*; that is, there is only a *Keṯiḇ*.
15. *ʿgt*, "loaves" (Ex. 12:39, 48b–49a): He resolves a contradiction between two *masoroṯ*; a majority of accurate texts agree with one of them.
16. *wʿmdy*, "and the columns" (Num. 3:37, 51b): He corrects one *masora* on basis of another and accurate texts.
17. *tyʿśh*, "should be made" (Ex. 25:31, 53b): He refers to the long discussion of the passage in Midrash Yelamedenu that some took as evidence of an alternate spelling. [Note also Ibn Ezra's comment, a.l.]
18. *pdhṣwr*, "Pedahzur" (Num. 1:10, etc., 54b): He notes that in accurate texts it is spelled as one word; one text has it spelled as two.
19. *hpylgšym*, "the concubines" (Gen. 25:6, 55a): (Translated in chapter 2.) He notes it to be doubly plene in all accurate texts that came into his hands; a rabbinic exposition suggests the second *yod* to be lacking.
20. *bplylym*, "by the judges" (Ex. 21:22, 55a): He notes a conflict of *masoroṯ*.
21. *whpryty*, "I will make you reproduce" (Lev. 26:9, 56a): He uses accurate texts and one *masora* to reject the spelling in another *masora*.
22. *ṣprh*, "Zipporah" (Ex. 18:2, 59b): He uses accurate texts and one *masora* to reject the spelling in another *masora*.
23. *whqmt*, "and you should erect" (Deut. 27:2, 60b): He uses accurate texts to reject the spelling in a *masora*.
24. *hqrb*, "closest" (Ex. 12:4, etc., 62b): He corrects three incorrect *masoroṯ*.
25. *wyrymh*, "and stood it up" (Gen. 31:45, 65b): He cites accurate texts and one *masora* against another *masora*.
26. *lšbr*, "to buy grain" (passim, 68b): He uses accurate texts to reject a spelling suggested by the Masorah.

27. *šbtt*, "Sabbaths of" (Lev. 23:38, 69a): He corrects an errant *masora* on the basis of accurate texts.
28. *w'śymm*, "and I will place them" (Deut. 1:13, 70a): (Translated in chapter 2.) He notes that all accurate texts spell it plene but that according to a rabbinic exposition it is defective.
29. *wlśkyrk*, "and to your hired worker" (Lev. 25:6, 71b): He notes that most accurate texts have the word plene.

Subsequent attempts to gather relevant data ranged over a much wider array of texts, which continually expanded as rabbinic interest in the problem intensified and as medieval commentators showed increased preference for associating their teachings with the orthographic details in the Bible text. Interpreters who contributed to this approach built on a legacy of midrashic interest and included Rashi (1045–1105), the Tosafists, Hasidei Ashkenaz, and especially Rabbi Jacob ben Asher, the Ba'al Ha-Turim (1270?–1340). Perhaps the most sustained effort to find significance in the *matres lectionis* or to interpret the spelling of words in the Torah is the numerological commentary of Rabbi N. Spira (1585–1633), *Megaleh Amuqot*.[52]

Of course, this approach to the text had not been universally valued, as may be seen from the comment of Rabbi Abraham Ibn Ezra (1089–1164), who preceded Abulafia by about a century and, it seems, was more opposed to the search for meaning in the spelling than to the belief in the text's accuracy. He feared that people would attempt to correct (i.e., to fix supposed errors in) the Torah text from their own generalizations about spelling:

> And I will not discuss [in my commentary] the explanations of those interested in the Masoret (*ṭa'amē 'anšē ha-masoreṯ*), why a certain word is plene [here] and [elsewhere] is defective, for all of their explanations are like the manner of *deraš*. Sometimes Scripture (*ha-kaṯuḇ*) [other texts: the writer (*ha-koṯeḇ*)] spells the word plene and clear; and sometimes it [or: he] is brief and omits a silent letter. And after they seek out a reason for the plene and defective spellings, they will show us how they would be able to write the books. Now Moses spelled *ha-šem yimloḵ* [Ex. 15:18] without a *waw*, while the transmitter of Proverbs (*ma'aṭiq sefer mišle*) [cf. Prov. 25:1] spelled it with a *waw* [in] *taḥaṯ 'eḇeḏ ki yimloḵ* [Prov. 30:22]; and many years separated them. Their explanations are good only for children.[53]

Yedidiah Solomon Norzi's Attempt to Fix the Bible Text in the Late Sixteenth Century

One of the most informative lists of the sources used to fix the Bible text was that of Yedidiah Solomon Norzi (1560–1616), who, in the introduction to *Minhat Shai*, wrote:

> And the Lord gave me the merit to see a certain book composed by the wonderful sage, Rabbi Meir HaLevi Abulafia, a bubbling river, a source of wisdom, [one who] possesses the knowledge of holy things [or: of angels (*da'aṯ qeḏošim*)], a supervisor and a master craftsman; there is no authority like him in the matters of the *masoroṯ* regarding defective and plene spellings. . . . And he called the book *Masoret Seyag LaTorah*, and therefore, he did not discuss in it all of the twenty-four [biblical] books, only the Torah. And here I acknowledge the truth that I too did not check the defective and plene spellings meticulously, except for the five books of Torah, because of the strictness of [the laws of] the Torah Scroll.

And it is said that many disagreements have occurred [in the texts of] the Prophets and Hagiographa, and the labor is great. And every place I found the words of Rabbi Meir HaLevi, of blessed memory, I relied on him and followed in his paths. And in all things I followed him, for he was a great man. . . .

I also drank with thirst the words of the elder and revered sage, Rabbi Menahem di Lonzano, a righteous man who came to my home to take refuge in the shade of my walls. And he showed me his notes that he made on the Pentateuch prior to bringing it to the printer. He called the name of the book *Or Torah*,[54] which is very useful to everyone, particularly whoever has in his possession the *Miqra' Gedolah*,[55] the second printing by Bomberg, of the year [5]308 [i.e., 1548] or the *Miqra' Qetanah*, Bomberg edition of the year [5]304 [i.e., 1544].[56] And to tell the truth, he opened my eyes to [the contents of] many texts (*sefarim*) to which he had access in Jerusalem. . . .

I did not refrain from citing a matter in the name of the one who said it, as I did, as well, from the many books of the famous grammarians that are available to us, for many people are not expert in them. For, according to their opinion, they do not see any order in them, and in every place where they need to investigate in the books of the grammarians, the matter became very weighty for them, "and they are unable to find the opening" [Gen. 19:11]. . . .[57] And also what our master, Rabbi Solomon ibn Melekh, wrote in the book *Mikhlol Yofi*,[58] which he collected from thirty-nine authors, geonim, and sages, as were listed at the end of his book. He simplified the work for the readers and took the book *Mikhlol VeShorashim* and commented on the rules of Radak, according to the order of the twenty-four holy books. . . .

In every place in which I found the words of our rabbis, of blessed memory—scattered in the Babylonian Talmud and Palestinian Talmud, Midrash Rabbah, Mekhilta, Sifrei, Pesiqta, Tanhuma, and other books of Aggadah, Sefer HaZohar, and the [Torah commentary of Rabbi Menahem] Recanati[59]—disagreeing with the Masorah texts (*masoroṯ*) and our scrolls (*sefarim*), I took them into account as much as I could . . . and I labored in some places to minimize the conflict between them as much as I was able to understand and to decide. . . .

I also included in this composition many [passages] from the Midrashim of our rabbis regarding the explanations of the plene and the defective spellings and the *Qere* and the *Keṯiḇ*, for they are part of the completeness of the Torah and the allusions hidden in its letters; and they are luminaries to open blind eyes.

I also corrected several erroneous Masorah texts (*masoroṯ*), some of them on the basis of logic and some of them from other Masorah texts in manuscript. I also cited many of them [only] to correct mistakes, for it was not my intention to copy them all.[60]

As might be expected from its appearance in a number of important Pentateuch editions and rabbinic Bibles, Norzi's masoretic commentary is the most popular work of its kind in rabbinic circles today, but the introduction to the work never achieved equal status. Though the commentary appeared in 1742, the introduction was first published in 1876 and, until the publication of the reprinted Shulsinger Humash of 1950, had never appeared together with the commentary it introduces (and then only with the parts related to the Torah and the Five Scrolls).[61] Reliance on Abulafia is clearly an important aspect of Norzi's method, but he also consulted many other early and late rabbinic works that related to his quest for the precise text, including many writers not referred to here. He often exhibited a strong allegiance to Spanish manuscripts, somewhat in contrast with the procedures of his two sixteenth-century Italian predecessors, Felix Pratensis, editor of the 1517 Rabbinic Bible, who gave somewhat greater attention to medieval Ashkenazi contributions, and Jacob ben Hayyim Ibn Adoniyah of Tunis, editor of the 1524–1525 Rabbinic Bible, who also demonstrated an affinity for some Ashkenazi authorities, though he too preferred Spanish texts.[62]

Yehudah Leib Saraval's Attempt to Fix the Spelling of "Aaron" in the Seventeenth Century An instructive example of the process of determining the spelling of a single word is the attempt to gather information about one specific *waw*, described in the letter of Yehudah Leib Saraval (died in 1617), appended to the 1750 edition of *Masoret Seyag LaTorah*.[63] Having recalled that, during his youthful work as a scribe, he was taught to spell Aaron's name plene (*'hrwn*) in Ex. 29:15, despite the generally accepted masoretic rule that in the Torah it is always defective (*'hrn*), Saraval sent letters to various communities to learn both how they spelled the word and how they decided.[64]

The rabbis of Budon in Hungary responded that Aaron should be spelled *'hrwn*, as in their ancient model codex. Their oral scribal tradition favored inclusion of the *waw*, and the oldest Torah scrolls in their possession contained it. While some of the newer ones lacked the letter, the older texts were assumed to be more accurate. Despite this preference, the report presumes that both spellings have the authority of valid traditions and that both should be allowed to stand.

The respondent from Constantinople unequivocally supported the plene spelling on the basis of *Minhat Kohen* and reported that several scrolls in which the word was spelled defective had been corrected not long before. Rabbi David Nahmias of Salonika responded that some printed texts exhibit the plene spelling, as does the Masorah, but that the expert scribes whom he consulted on the matter all use the defective spelling everywhere in the Torah. Rabbi Eliah Arbara of Ishkofia noted that they found two old Torah scrolls containing the plene spelling, but he added that both the plene and the defective spellings are authoritative and one should not erase the *waw* in question. He ruled that both are acceptable, but he seems to have preferred the plene spelling.[65]

Rabbi Menahem Azariah of Fano referred to the statement of the Tosafists admitting ignorance of some spellings and said that texts copied by experts that contain any of a series of well-known variants of this sort should not be changed. Rabbi Ben Zion Tzarfati of Venice, in whose court Saraval served as a judge, consulted both senior and junior scribes, and representatives of both groups noted that this was a long-standing problem; Tzarfati allowed both spellings to stand.

Saraval then cited a responsum often attributed to Nahmanides, actually part of a collection of responsa written by Solomon Ben Adret, his student (*She'eilot uTeshuvot HaRashba HaMeyuhasot LeHaRamban*, no. 232, discussed at length in chapter 6), which proscribed changing Torah scrolls to follow the Masorah. But in a paragraph reminiscent of one in *Beit David* by Salonika's Rabbi Joseph David, he suggested that this ruling made sense only when there were official disagreements within the Masorah, like those between Ben Asher and Ben Naftali. In a case where a Masorah presented a clear, unequivocal spelling, it can be assumed to be correct, and if no one argued against it, an extant text that agrees with it should not be changed, as concluded from his correspondence about the spelling of *'hrwn*.

The collected views of Saraval's respondents allowed him to retain the plene spelling of Aaron that he had copied in scrolls some forty years earlier and to discount Abulafia's statement that it should be spelled defective throughout the Torah (*Masoret Seyag LaTorah*, p. 2a). While researching this point, Saraval collected and subsequently presented arguments for various readings based on model codices, on oral traditions among professional scribes, with allowances for differences between junior and senior ones, on Torah scrolls, again differentiating between older and newer ones, and on one printed book. An obvious preference for old scribes and old texts over new ones stands in sharp contrast to the principle of majority rule, but even more striking is the frequency of the position that in many cases more than one acceptable spelling exists and that scrolls following any of them should not be changed.

Allowing defensible extant texts to remain unchanged is a little easier than altering them, because they possess a presumption of accuracy. But this position is, in the last analysis, a very different one from that espoused by writers whose mystical beliefs demanded a letter-perfect text, whose polemical experiences required total uniformity as a defense against the non-Jewish criticism that Jews neglected or corrupted the text, or whose halakhic reasoning told them that a lack of consistency among the scrolls meant that obviously some were unfit for ritual use. Perhaps most interesting is the fact that Saraval's summaries of the six responses never mention the concept of majority testimony. He opened and closed his piece with a reference to it based on Ben Adret's Responsum 232, but it seems to have played little or no role in his correspondents' handling of the problem, and even he limited its applicability.

In evaluating such different types of evidence, one must recognize the variations among the rules and procedures that applied to the production of Torah scrolls, Masorah codices, and other types of documents, including talmudic and midrashic texts. Of them all, the scrolls have the most exalted status in halakhah, and their production is most carefully governed by it. The almost indescribable sanctity Judaism attributes to the Torah is reflected in this care as well as in deep reverence for the scroll itself and unstinting dedication to its teachings.

Before we move on, a few additional words about Saraval's letter are in order. In discussing Saraval's text, I. Ta-Shema identified it as anonymous and attributed it to Menahem Moscatto, because it is found in the manuscript of *Masoret Seyag LaTorah* that he wrote but not in the one from which he copied.[66] Though it makes no difference in its use as an example of divergent opinions about spelling the Torah text, I find it difficult to accept fully Ta-Shema's observation. Moscatto may have incorporated this material into the text, but it is less clear that he had more than a possible editorial hand in its production.

The appendix to *Masoret Seyag LaTorah* in which it appears is composed of two separate, originally unrelated parts that share three things. Both parts report that their authors consulted rabbis in some of the same places, allow for a range of answers instead of one definitive ruling, and appear printed together. The shorter first part deals with two specific conflicts regarding paragraph spacing and concludes by noting the different practices of the communities of Constantinople and Salonika. The second, longer one, which makes no reference to the first, deals with the spelling of Aaron in Ex. 29:15.

After the relatively lengthy second question, the text continues with seven answers from a broad selection of rabbinic writers. This itself is somewhat unusual, since normative practice required seeking one final ruling from an accepted authority, not conducting an international survey. But this procedure may be understood as an attempt to find the elusive *roḇ*, the accepted practice of a majority of the world community of Torah scribes, and as an attempt to undermine the authority of *Masoret Seyag LaTorah* itself, whose spelling was challenged by the survey's results (hence its appearance as an appendix to Abulafia's book).

In any case, the last in a series of seven answers to the question, the final two of which are signed, is that of Yehudah Leib Saraval himself, and the first line of his statement refers to the answer of the previous writer, Ben Zion Tzarfati. With regard to the questionable *waw* in Aaron's name, Tzarfati said, *šeḇ we-ʾal taʿaśe ʿaḏif, we-ʾen li-šloaḥ yaḏ le-moḥaqo*, "it is better to do nothing and not to extend a hand to erase it." Saraval's paragraph begins *yafe dan ha-gaʾon ha-n[izkar] l[e-ʿel] de-ʾen li-šloaḥ yaḏ*, "the previously mentioned sage ruled well, not to send forth a hand to erase it." Since he was commenting on the previous answer, not merely providing an independent seventh response, it seems that the collection of responses is his. I should think that a letter from Tzarfati would not have required Saraval's support, nor, under the circumstances, would it have benefitted from his input, which would be the case if both answers were taken as a single statement on the subject.

Moreover, the subject of Saraval's answer corresponds very closely to the issues and language of the question itself. In fact, Responsum 232 of Solomon Ben Adret (attributed to Nahmanides), cited in the question, is identified only in this part of the answer. Either a very clever editor rewrote them this way and placed the already joined answers of Tzarfati and Saraval last in order to reflect the contents of his question, or one must conclude that at least the second of the two parts of the appendix is the result of Saraval's research and organization.

This interpretation is not possible from reading the letter as it appears in A. Jaffe's *Mishnat Avraham*, because the third of the seven responses was omitted from its correct place and added after Saraval's, which no longer concludes the text. I assume this change was an accident and that whoever is responsible was anxious to avoid recopying the text or resetting the type and was oblivious to the error's literary or historical implications. Otherwise, it would suggest that he too did not take Saraval to be the author.[67]

The Use of Tiqqunim by Torah Scribes One type of evidence not specifically mentioned in the foregoing sources was Tiqqunim, model texts often produced during training under the direction of a master scribe, from which scribes copied and corrected scrolls. In theory, Tiqqunim were more carefully controlled and therefore more accurate than the average scroll, but in reality their contents still fell short of being the ideal, letter-perfect text. In the words of Rabbi Menahem Meiri:

> And that we find Tiqqunim in the possession of the scribes—on which [or: on whom] (*ʿal pihem*) we rely in writing a Torah scroll—they are only what they found in the scrolls with a presumption of having been checked (*ba-sefarim ha-muḥezaqim ba-meḏuyyaqim*), not that the matter is so clear.[68]

Note also the seemingly more positive but still carefully worded statement of Rabbi Abraham HaLevi:

> The general conclusion is that, since the scribes before us obviously labored much over the *masorot* and made careful decisions in the matter of defective and plene spellings and the differences among the texts (*u-maḥloqot še-ba-sefarim*), when they agreed on something, they did so only because they followed the majority of texts (*sefarim*) that are worthy of being followed as the majority, according to the conditions that they wrote. Therefore, the scribal Tiqqun in our possession, that the early authorities established for us, one should not add [anything] to it or remove [anything] from it; we consider it as if it were received by us from Sinai.[69]

He treated this scribally reconstructed text as if it were the original one; he did not claim the two were identical.

The Masorah codices and the Tiqqunim remained primarily a scribal domain, though their contents often contributed to halakhic debates, where they and other types of evidence were evaluated on an ad hoc basis. Many of the most prized texts were the Masorah codices, but not all exemplars possessed equal value or authority. In a statement that superficially resembles S. Lieberman's classification of ancient scrolls and might reflect the masoretic equivalents of the three ancient types of texts he described, M. Goshen-Gottstein presented the medieval codices as another tripartite group. At the top of the ladder were "Masorah codices," precise in virtually every detail, exquisitely executed, and intended to serve as model texts. The second rung was occupied by "study codices," manuscripts without the Masorah that fell well short of the first description but whose copyists aspired to produce (and whose owners thought to have) accurate copies of the vocalized consonantal text. The third group, "listening codices," consisted largely of fragments of books, often relatively inaccurate, poorly copied, partially or ineptly vocalized, and used, he suggested, primarily to follow the Torah reading in the synagogue.

The precise nature of the production and distribution processes of these codices remains to be clarified, and Goshen-Gottstein did not discuss Torah scrolls at all. Moreover, an important distinction must be made between true model codices and Masorah manuscripts that failed to measure up to them, as his following comment suggests:

> . . . we had better remember that the rules about the fitness of Scrolls were never applicable to codices. Apart from certain rules about the Divine name, no mistake rendered a codex "unfit" (unless the scribe was so incompetent that he could not sell the codex?).[70]

This perspective is quite different from that of, for example, Rabbi Moses Aryeh Trestino, author of the Esther commentary, *Be'er Sheva'*, who gave greater credence to the evidence in Masorah manuscripts than to what might be concluded about the biblical citations in various rabbinic texts, because the former were copied by expert scribes who were extremely careful with every dot, while the latter were the work of much less proficient and less attentive copyists.[71]

Copying and Interpreting the Torah Text One of the more prominent aspects of medieval Ashkenazi Bible exposition is the association of various teachings with the orthographic details in the Torah text. The great degree of inconsistency in the use of *matres lectionis* in many of the words on which these writers comment may reflect not only legitimate variants in the locally available model texts but also their reliance on codices of the second type (and possibly even the third type) described by Goshen-Gottstein, as well as inferior exemplars in type one.[72]

Production of a Torah scroll was considered one of the 613 commandments binding on all adult males and was carried out personally by many leading rabbinic figures and by hired scribes on behalf of others.[73] In theory, a Jewish community could not function liturgically without a Torah scroll. Even though some were forced by circumstances to do just that (or to function without an accurate one),[74] in fact, Torah scrolls were relatively common. Complete manuscripts of the Bible and Masorah, on the other hand, which are less practical and more time-consuming to produce (and therefore more expensive) must have been even less readily available; few people copied or attempted to copy one, and even fewer ever saw one of the highly pedigreed model codices.[75] Tiqqunim, though less expensive, may have been even further removed from the public eye.

When people such as Meir Abulafia, Menahem Meiri, Jacob ben Hayyim, and Y. S. Norzi—and, for that matter, J. De Rossi, C. D. Ginsburg, P. Kahle, M. Goshen-Gottstein, and M. Breuer—set out to work on the Bible text, they required access to many different manuscripts. Numerous medieval and early modern reports mention sending manuscripts from one place to another, buying and selling them, and sending scribes or scholars to copy or to check them. Obviously some resources were shared by those who controlled them, but often truly special texts, like the Aleppo Codex, were not readily accessible. Various medieval and modern records tell of those who were able to examine this famous manuscript and of others who were frustrated in their attempts to consult it, to copy it, to photograph it, or even to see it. In some periods, just opening it was a major community event.[76]

Subjecting Scribal Practices to Halakhic Determinations

Ḥiluf *and* Maḥloqet̲

By allowing themselves to be drawn into the details of textual determination and by making the debates over fixing the text a halakhic issue, the medieval rabbis largely claimed (or perhaps reclaimed) this concern from the scribal domain, where it had previously resided, and they went about resolving the disagreements among the various textual witnesses as they routinely resolved nontextual conflicts in all other areas of Jewish religious practice. The spelling of the text was thus determined by rabbinic ruling, not merely by scribal convention, even if the rabbis making the decisions consulted model codices and scribal traditions.

One of the key terms in the medieval debates over the text is *maḥloqet̲*, "disagreement" or "difference," between authoritative witnesses or categories of evidence. In contrast, the masoretic literature itself often speaks of *ḥilufim*—in a sense, officially sanctioned "variants" or "alternatives." *Maḥloqet̲* refers to a conflict in law; *ḥilufim*, to differences in scribal practice, in text. The marginal masoretic note *Seb̲irin* indicates another category of formal notes, understood by some as unofficial variants and by others as attempts to avoid error or accidental correction. Despite their potential relevance to questions of the Bible's textual accuracy, generally they are not discussed in the passages from the primary texts to be considered here, and therefore they remain outside our present concern.[77]

Maḥloqet imputes authority, essentially equal authority, to the conflicting sources of evidence, but it also suggests a dialectic legal rather than a unilateral scribal approach to a solution. As the determination of the text became the subject of rational legal decisions (and was not assumed to result merely from accurate copying and faithful reliance on uniformly consistent scribal traditions), and as this deciding was done somewhat independently by many far-flung medieval and post-medieval halakhic authorities, the Tiberian Bible text continued to evolve ever so slightly. Simultaneously, the impact on it of the Babylonian Talmud, the primary source of direction in all halakhic determination, but a work produced in a land whose Bible texts and related traditions differed in some ways from those of the Land of Israel, increased.[78] In the process, the text became more flexible in a number of places, not less so, and that potential for variation has been noted in numerous contexts. One, taken from *Ginat Veradim*, is extremely candid. After referring to the Soferim text, Rabbi Abraham HaLevi says:

> And they acted according to the law by invalidating the one in the face of the two, because, according to the Torah, we must follow the majority in all matters. And even though it is possible and actual (*ʾefšar u-šeḵiaḥ*) that we are not acting in accord with the truth [he then explained how this could happen when the principle of majority determination is allowed to apply to a husband who has disappeared at sea, whose body has not been recovered, and who is presumed dead, with the results that his wife is permitted to remarry, or with sacrifices that were presumed to be internally unblemished and therefore acceptable for use on the altar, both of which may actually turn out to be other than what the majority rule would suggest], this is what the men did in the Temple court. When they found disagreements among the scrolls, they followed the majority.[79]

Thus textual determination is analogous to the outcomes of most trials, secular and halakhic, that do not purport to find the truth but reach only fair, factually based, usable approximations of it. Scribes, mystics, students of the Torah, and other idealists may seek perfection and try to recover the one "true" text; halakhists look for a legally sustainable text, even if it does not qualify as absolutely perfect.

Responding to the position in *Ginat Veradim*, Rabbi Abraham Kook (1865–1935) observed that, in a situation that the Talmud has clearly designated as an uncertainty, it is rather illogical to claim that a majority of texts can be presumed to be accurate. According to him, the passage in BT Qid. 30a places the entire matter in serious doubt, and such questions cannot be determined by majority testimony.

> Anything that requires information (*yeḏiʿa*) that is done without [that] information has a presumption of being improper (*be-ḥezqaṯ še-ʾēno ka-raʾui*) . . . Because we are not expert in defective and plene spellings, we cannot escape from the doubt of error.[80]

Over the centuries, many writers have alluded to the halakhically controlled evolution of the Torah text, but perhaps the clearest statement is that of Rabbi Yaakov Weinberg, of Yeshivat Ner Yisrael, in his discussion of Maimonides' claim about the accuracy of the received Torah text (Thirteen Principles, no. 8):

> Although the Torah itself instructs Jews to follow the majority in making a decision, one suspects that after many such occurrences, his decisions are not going to produce *absolutely* accurate reproductions of the original Sinai version. The Talmud, too, says we are no longer experts in the exact spelling of many words. . . . The words of *Ani Ma'amin* and the words of the Rambam, "the entire Torah in our possession today," must not be taken literally, implying that all the letters of the present Torah are the exact letters given to Moshe Rabbeinu. Rather, it should be understood in a general sense that the Torah we learn and live by is for all intents and purposes the same Torah that was given to Moshe Rabbeinu.[81]

When the Evidence Is Not Consistent and a Simple Majority of One Type of Witness Will Not Suffice

Types of Evidence In Temple times, Torah scrolls were assumed to contain the correct consonantal text, and questions of a textual nature were answered by recourse to them. This procedure continued for centuries and was in force at least through talmudic times. In the geonic period, the question of the Torah text's theoretical accuracy seems to have received relatively little attention or, to be more precise, I have found little interest in it among the randomly preserved geonic literature I have examined. While this lack of material may reflect the accidents of discovery, it also may suggest either that the types of problems encountered in later centuries went unnoticed or that the scribes and masoretes active during this time were in control of the situation and handled the difficulties competently and expeditiously without involving the halakhic leaders.[82]

Perhaps the greatest exception to this very tentative generalization is Tractate Soferim. It is based in large part on talmudic sources, and one of its priorities is the settling of differences between conflicting scribal practices we know to have existed in earlier rabbinic times. Still it offers no clear statements on the actual state of the text, what constitutes an error, or how textual variations were treated. In fact, its composite nature sometimes reflects conflicting rulings that derive from different traditions.

By medieval times, testimony to the presumably correct spelling of any number of questionable words was available, as well, from a number of authoritative sources, including scrolls, Masorah codices, direct or indirect statements found in early rabbinic literature, Tiqqunim, and the teachings of the medieval grammarians, lexicographers, Bible exegetes, and halakhic authorities; but the evidence derived from these sources was not always uniform, nor was the relative value of each type of document universally accepted.

It is popularly believed that all textual uncertainties that had evolved in post-Temple times were eliminated by the masoretes, but this is a gross oversimplification. Though they did standardize the text to a large extent, and though one might designate a particular Masorah codex or family of codices as the definitive version, many questions could not be laid to rest permanently. Regardless of conclusions reached, continued fluctuations in the authority or the relative values attributed to the different types of available evidence—particularly the Talmud, the Midrashim, and Rashi's Torah commentary—which often were older, better known, or more highly respected than the fairly obscure masoretic literature, continually caused certain questions or doubts to resurface.

According to early rabbinic thinking, all Torah scrolls attest to the original, correct, Sinaitic text,[83] and cases of doubtful orthography or textual detail should be corrected according to the majority of extant scrolls. But other authoritative witnesses to differences (large and small) greatly complicated this simple notion, particularly since the scrolls themselves were often found to be inaccurate or inconsistent. Thus, medieval and postmedieval rabbinic leaders and experts in the Bible text were often called upon to rank the witnesses in order to determine the correct spellings of a number of problematic words. Discussion usually centered on a limited list of cases, but the general principles employed were applicable to other passages as well. Some determinations were based on information drawn from a range of trusted sources, including scribal traditions, old and new manuscripts, masoretic treatises, halakhic works, and later even printed texts.

The following chapters focus primarily on the relative values of these types of witnesses, but some writers, such as Norzi (in the introduction to *Minhat Shai*) and Solomon Ibn Melekh (in *Mikhlol Yofi*) included also the statements of medieval grammarians, who occasionally testified to or suggested alternatives. This last group usually directed much of its attention to the vocalization, but some writers were less than supportive of their efforts. Rabbi David ben Solomon ibn Abi Zimra (sixteenth-century Egypt and Israel) often indicated his less than total satisfaction with some of their teachings, particularly their discussions of the consonantal text. One of his responsa (treated in chapter 5) is especially interesting in this respect, as it discusses a change in the vocalization of a word in the Torah proposed by a highly respected French Torah commentator from the end of the period of the Tosafists, not by a "mere" grammarian.

Rabbenu Tam's Admission of Inability to Fix the Torah Text Some writers, particularly those in medieval Ashkenaz, were content to accept a variety of testimonies and disparate texts. The most famous of them was Rabbi Jacob Tam (twelfth-century), a grandson of Rashi.[84] Rabbenu Tam's halakhic writing on Torah scrolls, often cited as *Tiqqun Sefer Torah*, had a profound and pervasive impact on numerous Ashkenazi halakhists. His work has been published as part of the *Mahzor Vitry* and from an independent manuscript.[85] Like all specialized handbooks and general codes containing the rules of Torah production, *Tiqqun Sefer Torah* deals with a wide range of issues, including the materials from which a Torah is made, its assembly, and the correct procedures for writing and correcting errors in the divine name. Most of these works devote little attention to the question of the Torah's textual accuracy, but in a relatively lengthy comment, Rabbenu Tam wrote:

> And now, pay attention to the scribal details (*diqduq soferim*) and to the shapes of the letters, because we are not expert in all the details (*be-ḵol ha-diqduq*), as Rav Joseph said in the Gemara of the first chapter of Qiddushin [30a]: "They are expert in the defective and plene spellings, but we are not expert." And [it is now] "a time to act on behalf of God, they have violated your Torah" [Ps. 119:126], therefore [we rule that] ours [i.e., our Torah scrolls] are also ritually proper.
>
> But in the places where we have received [a correct textual tradition], we study these defective and plene spellings in which we are expert; and the [extraordinary] largeness of the letters, like the Bet of *berēšiṯ* [Gen. 1:1], which is counted in the Ma-

> soret with the large letters, and their [extraordinary] smallness, like the Waw of *šalom* [Num. 25:12], "cut";[86] and their crowns (*u-be-tagēhen u-be-ziyunan*); and their [proper] formation.[87]

Somewhat before Rabbi Meir Abulafia tried to fix the Torah text, Rabbenu Tam applied to it a verse from Psalms, frequently understood as despair over breakdown in the halakhic system. He thereby acknowledged the imperfect state of its preservation, but it is far from certain if by the statement, "therefore [we rule that] ours [i.e., our Torah scrolls] are also ritually proper," he meant to concede that only Ashkenazi scrolls were hopelessly flawed or that by medieval times no one could do better. Either way, he saw these textual doubts as a series of localized problems. The proper spellings of some words could not be determined, but those of other words could be. As he said, the latter point was very much in keeping with the general Ashkenazi tendency to seek meaning in plene and defective spellings, scribal irregularities, and other unusual textual phenomena.

Particularly because it derived from such a respected authority, this candid statement played a major role in the recognition of the less than letter-perfect state of the Torah text and informed numerous Ashkenazi treatments of it that found expression in the glosses and commentaries on the *Shulhan Arukh*, as well as related responsa. Joseph Caro (1488–1575), a Sefaradi authority, ruled as follows:

> If an error was found in a Torah scroll during the reading, we take out another Torah scroll and begin from the place where the error is found, and we complete the [number of] readers, in addition to those who read in the erroneous [scroll].

To this, Moses Isserles (ca. 1525–1572), an Ashkenazi, added the following gloss:

> And this rule that we take out another [scroll] is [applicable] only when a complete error is found, but because of plene and defective spellings, one should not take out another, for our Torah scrolls are not so exact that we can say that the other will be more proper, (therefore we must make this distinction) [between complete errors and errors in plene and defective spellings]. . . . And if one Humash [i.e., one of the five books of the Torah] is complete, without error, there is reason to be lenient and read from that Humash, although there are errors in the others.[88]

Numerous other writers followed this lead, creating a full literature of halakhic authorities who assumed the presence of minor inconsistencies or flaws in the text.

The Attempts of Jacob Ben Hayyim Ibn Adoniyah and Yedidiah Solomon Norzi to Fix the Bible Text By the sixteenth and seventeenth centuries, the discussion of fixing the Bible text had been broadened to include many other types of witnesses, and the resulting confusion appeared much more serious. In 1524–1525 Jacob ben Hayyim published the first edition of a Masoretic Bible, the second Rabbinic Bible. In the introduction, included in newly typeset Rabbinic Bibles until the end of the nineteenth century and still reproduced photomechanically in some reprints, he described the situation this way:

> And after I looked at the books of the Masorah and studied them, I saw that they were utterly confused (*mebulbalim be-taklit*) and corrupt to the point where there is

no house that does not contain a corpse [cf. Ex. 12:30], that is, the verses that the author of the Masoret cited and the great confusion in them.[89]

His description of the types of confusion he found and how he dealt with them need not detain us now. Suffice it to note that, not long afterward, Norzi undertook the effort from the beginning. To cite his introduction again:

> And it came to pass, as our days in our exile lengthened, our knees weakened, and our hands loosened, and our eyes dimmed, and the wells of our wisdom were sealed, and the masters of Scripture and Mishnah . . . were no more, and the disputes and opinions multiplied, for not only did the Torah become like two *toroṯ*, it was more like an infinite number of *toroṯ*, because of the many variants that are found in the texts (*sefarim*), that are in our regions, both new and old—Torah, Prophets, and Hagiographa—there is no saying and no words that do not contain confusions (*bilbulim*) filled with errors in defective and plene spellings, cantillation signs and punctuation marks, *Qere u-Keṯiḇ*, [letters incorrectly marked with] *dagesh* and without *dagesh*, [and] penultimate and ultimate accents. And this is nothing less than a severe plague, because the teachers sin accidentally and intentionally; the light has become darkness for them . . . "the work of the Lord is fraudulent" [Jer. 48:10].
>
> Provide an antidote for their poison, for the students who come after them will drink it for generations, and they err with their tongues, and they will remain in their failure. "And a mistake, once it arises, has permanence" [BT Pes. 112a, etc.]. . . .
>
> And how do they dare to teach Scripture to others, if they still have not achieved the status of a Bible reader [i.e., of mechanical literacy]. For we say in chapter two of Qiddushin [49a] that:
>
> > One who betrothed a woman and said to her, "It [i.e., the betrothal] is on condition that I am a Bible reader," [is not betrothed] until he has read the Pentateuch, the Prophets, and the Hagiographa correctly.
>
> And I apply to them [i.e., to these illiterates] this verse: "This is their way, foolishness is theirs, and after them in their mouths they will rush forever" [Ps. 49:14]. And this is a disgrace for the Torah, because, heaven forbid, "behold it puts on a sackcloth and stands before the Holy One, Blessed Be He, and says 'Your children have made me like a song' [cf. Kallah, chap. 1]. And they are not concerned for my honor. This should not be [allowed to happen] in Israel." (Another formulation, in the language of the Targum [i.e., Aramaic]: "The Torah herself puts on a sackcloth and goes to the Holy One, Blessed Be He, and says to Him, 'Your children have made me a joke.'" This I copied from the Zohar, *Parashat Terumah*, page 144.)[90]
>
> And also the Masorah codices (*masoroṯ*) did not escape disagreement in some places, but not like the many disagreements among the scrolls [themselves]. And if one should decide to write a Torah scroll as prescribed by law, it will be imperfect regarding defective and plene spellings, and he will be found groping like a blind man in the darkness, and he will not succeed in finding what he seeks. And even if this sage seeks to know [all that he needs], he will not be able to find [it], because in every disagreement there are not *masoroṯ* to decide [the correct reading].
>
> And it is known that we do not have in the text of the Torah (*be-sefer tora*) a flaw greater than defective or plene spelling, [for] the whole Torah [consists of] the names of the Holy One, Blessed Be He [cf. Nahmanides, introduction to Torah Commentary], and one who reads from it [i.e., an incorrect scroll] damages the name of the King, heaven forbid, as is stated explicitly in the Zohar, *Parashat Mishpatim*, at the top of page 124. . . .[91]

And the value of the Masorah is very great, because from it are derived a number of substantial laws (*gufē halakot*), numerological interpretations (*gemaṭriot*), and intriguing manipulations of the text (*parparot*), and reasons (*ṭeʿamim*), and interpretations (*perušim*), simple and derived meanings (*pešaṭim u-midrašim*), symbolic meanings (*sodot*), and allegories (*remazim*).[92] And were it not for the masoretes, who placed the Torah and the [rest of] Scripture (*miqra'*) on a sure footing, a man would almost not find his hands and his feet because of the disagreements, and already the Torah would have been forgotten in Israel, and the Torah would have become like several *torot*, heaven forbid. And we would not be able to find two [copies of] books from among all the books of Scripture that were in agreement, as happened to other books of the [various] authors.

Go see the greatness of the Masorah, for we have found in several places that the Talmud disagrees with it and, even so, we give priority to the Masoret. And all the copies (*sifrē*) and Tiqqunim of Torah scrolls are produced according to it. And we learn regarding it that the Men of the Great Assembly established it, and we follow them.[93]

And I set myself to stand in the breach and to repair the destroyed altar of the Lord [cf. 1 Kings 18:30]; and to seek and explore in the science of the reading; and to take hold of the books of grammar [or: books of precise grammatical information] (*sifrē diqduq*) that are in our possession at this time; and to search after and to investigate the corrected scrolls (*ha-sefarim ha-mugahim*), and the precise Masorah texts (*masorot*), and the readings (*girsa'ot*) that are pleasant and truthful; and to examine the important and superior Torah scrolls that are worthy of being relied upon; and to follow the majority of them, as we were commanded from the Torah "follow the majority" [Ex. 23:2], and as the sages did with the three books they found in the Temple courtyard. In one they found [the text written one way, and] in two they found [it written another way], and they established [the reading in the] two and invalidated [the reading in the] one . . . , as stated in the Palestinian Talmud, [in the] last chapter of Taʿanit [4:2] and in Soferim, chapter 6;[94] and in Sifrei, *Parashat VeZot HaBerakhah* [no. 356]; and as I will write in *Parashat Naso'*, with divine assistance.

> And similarly, when the sage asked the Khazar King [article 3, paragraph 25]:
> [25] And what will you say, if a variation will be found in one book, or in two, or in three?
> [26] He answered him: They will examine the majority of texts, because the lie will not affect the majority of them, and they will ignore the individual [texts containing the incorrect version]. And likewise will the copyists (*maʿaṭiqim*) do; when a minority disagrees, they return to the majority opinion.

And likewise they said in the Palestinian Talmud of Sanhedrin, [in the] chapter [entitled] "Both the Civil Laws . . ." [4:2 (22a)]:

> Said Rabbi Yannai: If the Torah had been given decided [i.e., with definitive rulings in all cases], there would be no place for a foot to stand. What is the reason? "And the Lord spoke to Moses" [Torah, passim].
>
> He [Moses] said to Him: Master of the World, tell me what the law is.
>
> He [God] said to him: "Follow the majority" [Ex. 23.2]. If those who acquit are the majority, he is innocent; [if] those who convict are the majority, he is guilty, etc.[95]

And I abandoned new texts "that came recently" [cf. Deut. 32:17], and I relied on the old trustworthy ones, as is written, "Wisdom is among the aged" [Job 12:12]; and likewise it says, "Ask your father and he will inform you, your elders and they will tell you" [Deut. 33:7].[96]

The introductions to many works of halakhah and exegesis (both biblical and talmudic) are replete with analogous complaints about the shortcomings of the books of their authors' predecessors and colleagues, as if each new composition required a rationale for writing yet another treatment of a well-worked subject.[97] Even so, it is hard to imagine that the pitch of the complaints about the holy Bible text registered by the writers just cited was mere hyperbole mixed with a self-serving justification for undertaking their projects. Besides, by the time the introductions were written, the actual work had probably been completed, and no excuse was needed for other than publishing the results. In short, these writers perceived global consistency of the words in their Bible texts, particularly in the Torah, and chaos in many orthographic details, even in the Torah.

Notwithstanding a full history of attention to the problem—including the efforts of M. Abulafia, M. Meiri, Jacob ben Hayyim, Y. S. Norzi, other rabbis, and a host of conscientious scribes to produce accurate scrolls and model codices—the data about the state of the text included in Norzi's commentary more than justify his complaints and those of his colleagues. But however his personal resolution of the myriads of detailed problems is evaluated, the existence of these many textual questions was hardly his discovery. On occasion, they were brought to the attention of earlier halakhic authorities, whose treatments both drew on and contributed to the ongoing efforts of these men to fix the correct text. In fact, the rabbis' major concern was the halakhic need for precise scrolls, and some preferred to use only the scrolls for determining the Torah's spelling and to utilize the Masorah for other things.

Subsequent Reactions to the Foregoing Teachings Following what was taken to be pretalmudic precedent, medieval writers often argued that questionable spellings should be made to follow the majority of extant (or available) scrolls, but the sixteenth century witnessed an affirmation (or reaffirmation) of the Masorah's being the determining factor. Were the scrolls totally abandoned? If so, when and why? And when did the rabbinic debate, which at one time afforded the masoretic literature no more authority than the relatively unimportant Midrashim, ultimately come to favor it over all other types of evidence? These are some of the concerns that emerge in the chapters to come.

Were all the rabbinic authorities in agreement with this development? How did they continue to respond to the spelling variations that appeared in the different types of ancient and presumably authoritative witnesses that lay before them? The documents cited in the ongoing analysis—which are drawn from explanations of the 613 mitzvot, from Bible commentaries, and especially from the halakhic codes and responsa about writing Torah scrolls and about reading and repairing inaccurate copies, and which include statements by important and influential rabbinic spokesmen—explore these questions and their relationship to the Torah's textual integrity.

These documents reveal that highly respected rabbinic leaders of the past fifteen centuries described in detail the theoretical and practical problems confronting anyone who might attempt to produce a letter-perfect Torah scroll, and they demonstrate that many authors entertained serious doubts about the theoretical possibility of doing so. Though many rabbis gave full halakhic approval to efforts to produce a precise text, not all did; and even the former, larger group contained many who conceded the severe difficulty of the problem. When compared with the homiletical and mystical ways in which the Torah's textual state is treated in some other rabbinic writings (some of which will be translated and discussed), these candid disclosures may appear quite surprising. Indeed, some such teachings seem to have been all but forgotten, even by many rabbis who routinely rule on other matters of doctrine and practice on the basis of the very books that contain them.

Thus J. Simha Cohen's *The 613th Mitzvah,* a popular presentation of the laws and regulations regarding Torah scrolls, omits all reference to this problem, despite his detailed and learned discussions of other matters.[98] More surprising perhaps, but providing equally strong evidence either of collective obliviousness to the traditional rabbinic literature that openly considers inconsistent spellings in the Bible text, or else of unwillingness to discuss or even to annotate it, are the many cases where learned editors of rabbinic texts failed to offer the customary sources for, or the parallels to, their authors' treatments of textual problems. These include Hayyim Pardes, annotator of Rabbi Judah Loew's *Tif'eret Yisrael,*[99] and Moshe Hayyim Haraz, author of *Otzar Hayyim,* notes on Ibn Ezra's Genesis commentary.[100] A similar criticism applies to B. Sherwin, *Mystical Theology and Social Dissent: The Life and Works of Judah Loew of Prague,*[101] and to *Gilyon HaShas HaShalem,* an annotated version of Rabbi Akiva Eiger's glosses on BT Shab. 55b.[102] The English translation of the Zohar by H. Sperling and M. Simon also has omitted a key passage within a much larger unit that has not been translated.[103]

Similarly, hagiographies of the rabbis who made these seemingly unorthodox observations often largely or totally ignore this issue. See, for example, E. Katz, *Ha-Hatam Sofer,*[104] M. Burak, *The Hatam Sofer,*[105] and J. Nahshoni, *Rabbenu Moshe Sofer: HaHatam Sofer,*[106] in which I have found no discussion of Sofer's explanation of the reason for not reciting a blessing before commencing to write a Torah scroll (translated in chapter 2), an admisssion of unresolvable doubts about spellings. Hirschler's two-volume *Me'oran Shel Yisra'el: Rabbenu Aqiba Eiger* did refer to the famous passage about 21 scriptural variants in rabbinic texts from *Gilyon HaShas,* BT Shab. 55b, but only in part of a very brief footnote.[107] Even more extreme in its denial of reality is Solomon Zvi Schick's observation in his *Torah Shelemah:*

> . . . an errant student wrote these words in the margin of the Talmud [the Tosafist comment in Shab. 55b], or one of the students of "Bilaam" wrote this in the margin, and in error and ignorance the printers inserted the words among the words of the Tosafot.[108]

I have seen many otherwise learned people deny the possibility that these saintly rabbis even could have considered the idea that the Torah text is less than letter-perfect, and more than a few have been left speechless when shown the actual statements. Equally learned academic audiences accustomed to the idea that rabbinic teachings neither acknowledge nor tolerate the problem are no less surprised by what they actually say. The conventional wisdom is pervasive. Depending on context, it seems to result from simple ignorance, stereotyping, the inability or unwillingness to use rabbinic texts properly, superior ranking of some other rabbinic teaching (perhaps the assumption that an official halakhic decision assumes the authority of divine will), a conspiracy of silence engendered by fear of the implications of these admissions, or a combination of these and other factors.[109]

The operational assumption in the early Middle Ages, especially in Sefaradi circles, seems to have been that textual variations were not only improper but theoretically impossible and subject to immediate elimination; the Ashkenazi position was considerably more flexible. Today the positions may actually be reversed, as is evident from the teachings of various rabbis who lived in and since the eighteenth century. It becomes particularly apparent when one compares the thinking of Rabbi Joseph Soloveitchik and Rabbi Ovadiah Yosef, two highly respected Orthodox leaders of the late twentieth century.

The Opinions of Rabbi Joseph Dov Soloveitchik and Rabbi Ovadiah Yosef

Rabbi Joseph Dov Soloveitchik's Teaching on the Accuracy of the Torah Text The position of Rabbi Joseph Dov Soloveitchik (1903–1993), the Rav, on the accuracy of the Torah text relates to another issue that initially seems somewhat distant. Late in the last century, Rabbi Gershon Hanokh Leiner of Radzin claimed to have discovered the way *tek̲ēlet̲* was produced, and he attempted to restore the use of this blue-colored dye in the threads of the *ṣiṣit̲*, tassels placed on the corners of one's garment (cf. Num. 15:38). His contemporary—Rabbi Joseph Baer Soloveitchik (1820–1892) in the Rav's reports, as well as Rabbi Hayyim Brisker (1853–1918) in Leiner's—rejected that claim because, he argued, one could not restore such practical halakhic information once its transmission had been interrupted.[110] The discussions for and against the proposition have been preserved and continued by proponents of both sides, and the presentations of the facts and opinions do not concur fully,[111] but it is the Rav's version of the episode that engages us here, because it relates to the question of textual restoration. As reconstructed from various witnesses, it also includes his father's input.[112]

The rejection of Rabbi Leiner's innovation was based, we are told, on the assumption that there are two types of tradition, theoretical and practical—in different accounts, called *masoret̲ ha-halak̲a* or *masora šel limmud̲* and *masoret̲ ha-maʿaśe* or *masoret̲ maʿaśit̲*. The former derives from the biblical verse "and you must do according to the ruling they present you" (Deut. 17:10) and resides in the Sanhedrin; the latter is based in the people and is sanctioned by the verse "Ask your father, and he will tell you; your grandfathers, and they will instruct you" (Deut. 32:7). It is the second, "practical" tradition that identifies the objects to which one applies certain religious laws (e.g., wheat, a *lulab̲*, etc.), and if it is interrupted, its loss prevents one from positively identifying the object—in this case the *ḥilazon*, shellfish from which the dye in question was produced—and consequently from reinstituting the practice. An interruption in the transmission of such a tradition, though recoverable from study, prevents the return of a practice to the status of *masoret̲ ha-halak̲a*.

Applied to Torah scrolls, this argument assumes a theoretical base for the definition of certain scribal procedures (spacing, paragraph divisions, etc.) and a practical tradition for their correct application. Referring to the passage about the three scrolls found in the Temple (in Soferim 6:4 and parallels), Rabbi Moses Soloveitchik

(1876–1941), we are told, questioned why all Torah scrolls were not consulted to decide on the preferred reading. His answer assumes such consultations to be part of the "theoretical tradition," handed down among the early scribes, which takes precedence over matters of "practical tradition," transmitted by the people at large.

This comment suggests that in Temple times confusion about the Torah text was already so widespread that scrolls considered to be other than model texts could not be consulted, an answer that, in a sense, anticipates what we now know of the situation from the many premasoretic and nonmasoretic texts that have become available in the past six decades. The discussion concludes by arguing that only the theoretical tradition was lost, not the practical one, that is, the correct spelling or the actual half of the Torah to which the large *waw* of *gḥwn* (Lev. 11:42) belongs, and that this is what the Talmud meant in BT Qid. 30a by the statement that the rabbis were not experts in spelling. Even if a correct Torah scroll were examined, the "theoretical tradition" could not be restored from the practical one, but the tradition of how to spell the words required no restoration; it was never lost.

This analysis, which acknowledges but does not formally consider the many medieval and early modern documents that discuss inconsistencies in the Torah text, rejects the assumptions of Rabbenu Tam, Rabbi Moses Isserles, and their Ashkenazi followers mentioned earlier, and it is much more in line with what has been suggested by many medieval Sefaradi writers. Its poignancy is sharpened by its historical context, one in which archaeological discovery was emerging as a potential source of information about the ancient past—though the Dead Sea Scrolls began to be available only in 1948—but it fails to capitalize on other earlier references to archaeological discoveries (or what were imagined to be) that contradict or seem to contradict this position.

Ancient reports of the intentional burying of ritual objects from the Temple and the like, on the assumption that they will one day be discovered and restored (a process associated even with the recovery of *Sefer Tagin*; see note 25 in this chapter) suggests that archaeology's potential halakhic value is much greater than has often been recognized. Maimonides' use of historical and contextual perspectives to explain the pagan backgrounds for many of the commandments (*Guide of the Perplexed*, Book III) shows that he appreciated the potential value of information recovered from the ancient non-Jewish world; Nahmanides' treatment of the ancient coin whose discovery is reported at the end of his Torah commentary documents the extent to which he valued its halakhic implications.[113] Other examples abound.

Rabbi Ovadiah Yosef's Teaching on the Accuracy of the Torah Text Rabbi Ovadiah Yosef (born in 1920) represents the opposite process, whereby the Sefaradi rabbinate, though originally opposed, has come to recognize the existence of variations among Torah texts. Discussions prior to the twentieth century confirm the general awareness of differences among the Torah texts of various Sefaradi communities. Rabbi Abdullah Sumak (Ovadiah Somekh) of Baghdad (1813–1889), for example, categorically rejected Yemenite scrolls, known to deviate from others, though he proudly declared that Baghdad's scrolls possessed a presumption of accuracy.[114]

Rabbi Shalom Isaac HaLevi (died 1973) also discussed the matter at length[115] and defended a range of practices. By ruling that a Torah scroll written correctly according to a known Masoret should not be changed to follow another one, and that a synagogue with Torah scrolls written according to different masoretic traditions may read all of them, he laid the groundwork for Rabbi Ovadiah Yosef's position. HaLevi, himself a Yemenite, is only one of the many writers who discussed the differences between Yemenite Torah scrolls and others, now generally acknowledged to contain some nine official spelling differences, though other variants appear with more regularity than the minimalists would like to admit. The concluding page of the Deuteronomy volume of *Torat Hayyim*[116] lists nine differences between Yemenite scrolls and the standard ones:

1. Gen. 4:14—*mnś*ʾ instead of *mnśw*ʾ
2. Gen. 7:11—*m*ʿ*ynt* instead of *m*ʿ*ynwt*
3. Gen. 9:29—*wyhyw*! instead of *wyhy*
4. Ex. 25:31—*t*ʿ*śh* instead of *ty*ʿ*śh*
5. Ex. 28:26—*h*ʾ*pd* instead of *h*ʾ*pwd*
6. Num. 1:18 (17?)—*bšmt* instead of *bšmwt*
7. Num. 10:10—*ḥdšykm* instead of *ḥdškm*
8. Num. 22:5—*b*ʿ*r* instead of *b*ʿ*wr*
9. Deut. 23:2—*dk*ʾ instead of *dkh*

Only Gen 9:29 (no. 3), which substitutes a plural verb for a singular one, is of morphological significance; and seven of the other eight examples (no. 9 being the exception) are differences of plene and defective spelling, in which the standard text is plene in six cases, while the Yemenite tradition is defective. In one case (No. 7) the Yemenite is plene and the standard text is defective. Other editions or facsimiles of Yemenite texts contribute to some of the familiar debates about plene and defective spellings, such as *pylgšym*, Gen. 25:6; *klwt*, Num. 7:1; *šlwm*, Num. 25:12 (the *waw* written the usual way and so marked); *hmwl ymwl*, Gen. 17:13; and others.[117]

Rabbi Ovadiah Yosef explored this problem in *Yehaveh Da*ʿ*at*, which addresses the question of allowing non-Yemenites to recite a blessing over a Yemenite scroll.[118] He discussed a number of important statements on the accuracy of the Torah text, including Responsum 91 of Abraham Maimon, Menahem Meiri's commentary to BT Qid. 30a and the introduction to his *Qiryat Sefer*, as well as several unpublished works. Basing himself on the often disputed responsum of Maimonides, which allows the recitation of a blessing on an incorrect scroll, Rabbi Yosef concluded that anyone may recite a blessing when called to a Yemenite scroll. He then noted that, in these times, it is very difficult to find a Torah scroll that is ritually proper in the full sense of the word because, almost every time one checks, one finds improper spacing of the letters, missing letters, extra letters, and other errors.[119]

Rabbinic Learning, Nonrabbinic Bible Scholarship, and Contemporary Orthodox Jewry

Accompanying this recognition and prior to the completion of this Ashkenazi-Sefaradi reversal of positions, many Jewish and non-Jewish scholars began collecting variants from Hebrew witnesses and from the ancient versions in order to demonstrate the extent of the evidence for variations and what it could teach about the history of the Bible text. Convinced that the text was so far from letter-perfect that more than one possible version of numerous passages existed, many people became very skeptical about its overall accuracy, and the evolution of this line of reasoning eventually produced the lower criticism applied in modern scholarship.[120] Once resistance to admitting the possibility of change was overcome, emendation (i.e., the attempt to restore what was believed to have been the original text) became a routine practice, if not an overly casual and highly creative one. The propriety of discovering or generating variations in the text and of suggesting improvements in it, even when it posed no difficulty, was thus accepted as a routine part of its scholarly discussion.[121]

But rabbinic writers, whose attitudes on the Bible's accuracy derived from the masoretic text and the traditional rabbinic literature rather than from the emerging scholarly treatments, generally did not suggest or accept emendations in Bible texts,[122] a position that was given a measure of unexpected reinforcement by the discovery of texts in ancient Semitic languages cognate to biblical Hebrew that confirmed the validity of some irregular structures or otherwise unknown biblical words.[123] In fact, most rabbis could not value the emendation procedure at all, surely not as it was applied to the Torah; and many people gradually came to reject the very possibility of textual variation, even when it was supported by data preserved in traditional rabbinic sources. Many religious writers now perceive the entire matter of spelling variation as relevant only to critical inquiry and refuse to discuss or to publish discussions of any aspect of it; their impact on presentations of a more academic bent is also surprising, and high school teachers of Jewish Studies are often encouraged to follow suit.[124]

This is not to suggest that either the candid observation of the Bible's textual problems or their correction through emendation is a strictly modern phenomenon. To some extent, the work of Origen in the third century contributed to it; the early masoretes also engaged in it; and the type of paraphrase that, though not actually changing a text, interpreted it as if it were written other than as it is, was an acceptable form of correction in some medieval rabbinic circles. One of the thirty-two hermeneutical principles traditionally attributed to Rabbi Eliezer, son of Rabbi Yose HaGelili (no. 20: "From something said about this that does not apply to it but does apply to something else"), which has antecedents in the Mekhilta and, for purposes of interpretation, allowed transfer of a text from one context to another, suggests but falls short of actually being a form of emendation.[125]

Because many rabbinic writers practiced a form of Bible interpretation that was largely inductive and intuitive, they knew how to explain things as if they were written other than as they appeared, but they never assumed the right to introduce permanent, personal changes into the text. Writing the Bible had been the contribution of the ancient prophets and their inspired colleagues. The exegetes' responsibility was to unpack the text, to explain it, to find meaning and direction in it, and to deal with the foibles of its idiosyncratic preservation, but not to rewrite it. In the minds of many who were educated along these relatively conservative lines—including those willing to acknowledge that the Bible text had evolved—many modern scholars, and even more so the collective force of modern scholarship, though in principle motivated by the goal of restoration, seemed to encourage far greater intentional violence to the text than the ancients might have committed through accidental faulty transmission.

As the modern exploration of the biblical world continued, much was learned about the orthography of ancient Hebrew from newly discovered epigraphic texts. They suggest that most *matres lectionis* and the forms of the final letters, as well as the vowels and cantillation signs, could not have been original parts of most Bible texts composed during the periods whose historical period they describe. Concomitantly, many variations between the masoretic text and other ancient witnesses (e.g., the Septuagint, the Samaritan Pentateuch, and the Dead Sea Scrolls) appeared to reflect texts lacking these phenomena.[126] On the other hand, the Dead Sea Scrolls have generally confirmed the antiquity of the text in the early rabbis' Bible, of some scribal practices codified later, and even of some text-related rabbinic notions, such as the use of superlinear dots to mark errors.[127]

These observations about the nature of Hebrew spelling in biblical times, coupled with the types of variants documented among nonreceptus Bible texts, have led some scholars, in the name of restoring its theoretical, "original" state, to rewrite the Bible according to the recoverable rules of Northwest Semitic philology. The radical implications of this practice were developed by a long series of scholars and can be explored fruitfully in M. Dahood's three-volume Anchor Bible commentaries on Psalms and in a series of similar commentaries by his students and followers.[128]

Whatever its merits, this approach lies far from our present concern, which explores the consistency of the witnesses to the extant Torah scrolls, the masoretic text(s), and the related rabbinic literature, and avoids hypothetical reconstructions of premasoretic or nonmasoretic alternatives. It is even further removed from most contemporary Orthodox treatments of the text, which have jettisoned virtually all interest in the Bible's textual evolution, just as many Orthodox leaders have systematically avoided other scholarly enterprises that are analogous to what were for centuries important parts of traditional rabbinic learning.[129]

Despite what modern discoveries suggest about the transmission of the Bible text and the systematic avoidance of their implications by almost all contemporary rabbinic writers, many earlier rabbis, especially those who lived in the "pre-emendation era," acknowledged the existence of textual variations or "disagreements" and, notwithstanding their dislike for them and what they suggested about textual transmission, saw their inherent challenge as a part of the halakhic debates that had evolved for centuries. Thus, despite the avoidance of the general critical posture, some discussions of spelling variants were entertained in the religious literature of the last several centuries, even though they remained both qualitatively and quantitatively very different from most scholarly treatments.

Modern halakhic authorities have neither contributed to nor endorsed (nor even discussed) most modern textual theories,[130] and they have added virtually nothing to our knowledge of the Bible text's early evolution; but their deliberations are essential for identifying the parts of the traditional literature related to lower criticism and for what they teach about both the rabbinic beliefs regarding the accuracy of the extant Bible text and the procedures for correcting inconsistencies among the rabbinically acceptible witnesses to it. Accordingly, they are an aspect of Jewish intellectual history that holds great potential importance for a series of exegetical and doctrinal issues much more crucial to contemporary Judaism than to Bible scholarship.

If the Torah text is believed to be perfect and is found wanting only by nonbelievers, the modern, secular forces that are seen to be challenging traditional, pious ones can be dismissed as religiously irrelevant. But if the imperfection has been recognized by rabbinic leaders, indeed, if it has been a serious part of classical rabbinic learning for over fifteen centuries, the contemporary religious response must be seen in a different light. In this case, the matter cannot remain a taboo, though it may shake, even topple, religious beliefs and modes of interpretation built on the foundation of a letter-perfect text and though, in theory, it may render defenseless the bulwarks of a similarly based homiletical literature. It cannot remain a taboo, that is, unless the religious community admits to being selective in its response to earlier rabbinic teachings, or it brings some other overriding consideration to bear on the subject, thereby reducing all these other arguments to secondary status. And apparently this last option is very appealing because, despite many premodern rabbinic discussions of textual uncertainties and their implications, the alternative belief in the letter-perfect text not only existed among religious Jews throughout the past two millennia but was sometimes the preferred position, as it is in many quarters today.

Be all of this as it may, the openness that once characterized rabbinic discussions of these textual realities—however insignificant they may appear to contemporary Bible scholars—shows that many rabbis did not shy away from this issue, especially when the deliberations were internal, halakhic, and controlled. What may have helped reverse this openness, at least among many Orthodox Jews, was the fear that disclosure of the actual state of affairs might be taken to concede the truth of some centuries-old anti-Jewish polemics and thus inevitably undermine the veracity of the tradition and force the faithful into the arms of the heretics; in addition, it would raise serious challenges to any form of rabbinic teaching or authority based on an assumption of pentateuchal textual accuracy.[131] Recently proffered claims that the text, in addition to being letter-perfect, is the repository of carefully encoded secrets that are meaningful to those able to probe its spelling patterns with the aid of computers have encouraged such a seemingly faithful response.[132] In turn, these beliefs have led to further avoidance or suppression by contemporary rabbis and teachers of much of this candid rabbinic information about the text.[133]

However one perceives contemporary rabbinic handling of the subject, it is incorrect to attribute avoidance or suppression of this issue to all rabbinic leaders of the last millennium, or even to all contemporary Orthodox rabbis. Examination of their treatments of the evidence and their conclusions helps complete the story of the Bible's textual evolution; portrays what Judaism, as they knew and represented it, actually claimed about the Torah's textual accuracy; and shows how, to this day, the halakhic literature continues to refine the text transmitted throughout the ages. I leave for now any further observations, beyond those in the foregoing note, on the sociology of contemporary Orthodoxy, the ways in which its adherents have reacted to the challenges inherent in their revered rabbis' teachings, and the possible reasons for them.

Ibn Zimra's Responsum A: The Zohar, the Talmud, and Fixing the Torah Text

Said Rabbi Meir: When I arrived at Rabbi Ishmael's [place], he asked me, "What is your occupation?" I said to him, "I am a scribe." He said to me, "My son, be careful in your work, for your work is the work of heaven. If you delete one letter or add one letter, you will destroy the entire world."

Babylonian Talmud, Eruvin 13a

Four Masorah-Related Responsa of Rabbi David ben Solomon Ibn Abi Zimra

The remaining chapters of this book explore the principles that underlie medieval rankings of various types of halakhic evidence for deciding on a number of questionable spellings in the Torah text, including an important shift in ranking that received much support in the sixteenth century. They center on four responsa of Rabbi David ben Solomon ibn Abi Zimra, whose name appears in shortened form in the published responsa as both David ibn Shelomo and David ibn Abi Zimra; Arabic writers referred to him as Da'ud ibn Zamiru.[1] Popularly he is known in English as Ibn Zimra, in Hebrew as HaRaDBaZ.

Ibn Zimra served as the rabbinic head of the Egyptian Jewish community between 1517 and 1553 and as a leading religious figure in the Land of Israel during the subsequent twenty years. Eight volumes of his responses to questions from a wide range of European and Mediterranean communities and a number of his other writings have been published; these responsa include four about the accuracy of the Bible text and closely related matters.[2] Ibn Zimra devoted several responsa to other textual matters as well, namely the required shapes of the letters *heh*, *het*, and *qof* (discussed here later) and the question of whether the first set of the Ten Commandments was written in *keṯaḇ ʿiḇri*, Paleo-Hebrew script, or in *keṯaḇ ʾašuri*, square Hebrew script (III, no. 442), but they inform our present discussion only insofar as they portray him defending the antiquity of the text as he had it.

Even excluding these responsa just mentioned, the four to be analyzed in detail here do not exhaust Ibn Zimra's treatment of the Bible or of its textual matters. In fact, dozens of his responsa are devoted to explicating parts of biblical texts or issues explored in earlier exegetical works, and we shall have occasion to refer to many of them, but these four form a closely related group.[3]

The first discusses the propriety of changing a word in the Torah to conform with the spelling evidenced by the Zohar. Following the Zohar's midrashic exposition, several people had changed the spelling of the word *'tw* (*'oṯo*), "him," to *'wtw* in two places, and Ibn Zimra was asked to react. The second, which shares much with some well-known medieval polemical literature, is an important statement on the origin and authority of the Masorah and the extent to which it should be used to determine the correct spelling of biblical words. The third responsum deals with the unusual shape of the letter *waw* in the word *šlwm*, "peace," in Num. 25:12 and whether it was necessary to follow a talmudic teaching that required it be "cut." The last comments on a medieval suggestion to change the traditional reading of *hw'*, "it," in Lev. 25:33 from *hu'* to *hi'*.[4]

A careful look at Ibn Zimra's discussions and decisions offers an important glimpse into how a leading sixteenth-century rabbinic authority evaluated his predecessors' treatments of textual questions and ranked the conflicting witnesses to the spellings or orthographic irregularities of certain biblical words. It also clarifies the halakhic literature's overall approach to fixing the Bible text and reveals what appears to be a major inconsistency in Ibn Zimra's attitude toward the Masorah. The presentation includes a translation of these four responsa, an analysis of the sources and nuances of their author's arguments, and observations on the relationships between these documents and other issues and compositions of masoretic and halakhic importance.[5]

Introduction to Ibn Zimra's Responsum A

Their routine search for scriptural prooftexts often led the talmudic and midrashic rabbis to associate halakhic or homiletical observations with orthographic details in the Bible text. Among the passages that record this practice are BT Suk. 6b, which associated the number of walls in a sukkah with the spelling of *sukkoṯ*, "booths," in Lev. 23:42–43; and BT Zev. 4a, where the spelling of the word *qarnoṯ*, "horns" (Lev. 4:7, etc.), was linked with laws about sprinkling blood on the altar. Elsewhere unusual orthographic details were interpreted as signs of distinctive meanings. An example of the latter is Gen. Rab. 61, 4, where *pilagšim*, "concubines" (Gen. 26:5), was noted to be spelled defective, suggesting that only one concubine was intended, Qeturah.

Medieval students of this material occasionally noticed differences between the ways biblical citations discussed or interpreted in these passages were spelled and the spellings in their own received Bible texts, as is the case in each of these three verses and in many others. Particularly significant are places where the interpretations depended on or highlighted deviant spellings.[6] One of the numerous writers who left a legacy of such observations was Rashi (1045–1105), whose comments on several verses casually call attention to the differences between the Bible texts in general circulation and those underlying the rabbinic spellings.[7] As was observed in chapter 1, the most influential Ashkenazi writer who, in his halakhic writings, articulated serious concerns about the lack of consistent spelling of some words in the Torah was Rashi's grandson, Rabbenu Tam; but it remained for the Tosafists at large to develop a full presentation of the problem. The following statements by a number of early Ashkenazi writers, cited by Rabbi Judah ben Eliezer (the Riva) in his Torah commentary, traditionally dated to 1313, are fairly typical.[8]

> *wlbny hplgšym*, "And to the children of the concubines . . ." [Gen. 25:6]: Rashi explained, "[It is spelled] lacking a *yod*, for there was only one concubine, who was [both] Hagar and Qeturah."
>
> And this is difficult for Hizquni, because it is spelled plene in accurate scrolls (*be-sefarim meḏuyyaqim*) and according to the Masoret.[9]
>
> And Rabbi Eliakim says that Rashi's interpretation follows Genesis Rabbah, for regarding that which we say, [namely] "Qeturah is Hagar," the question is raised there:
>
> > Regarding the text, *we-li-ḇenē ha-pilagšim*, it is spelled *plgšm*, [referring to] the one who sat at the well and said to the Eternal, "See my disgrace."
>
> And in Tractate Niddah, [in] the chapter [entitled] "Daughters of Kuteans" [33a], regarding [the statement that, for purposes of purity laws,] a lower bed is like an upper one, the Tosafot explained that it is routine for the Talmud to contradict the Masoret. And there they cited a proof for their words, as it says, "And the one who carries (*whnwś'*) them should wash his clothes" [Lev. 15:10], but *whnś'* lacks the [medial] *waw*. And the Tosafot challenged [this exposition], because in the Masoret it is plene:
>
> > But we find that the Talmud disagrees with the Masoret in Tractate Shabbat [55b]. Regarding the sons of Eli, the text says *mʿbyrm*, "spread," but, in our scriptural texts, *mʿbyrym* [1 Sam. 2:24] is spelled plene.
>
> And similarly, *klwt*, "[And when Moses] finished . . ." [Num. 7:1] is expounded, "It is spelled *klt*," even though in the Masoret it is plene.
>
> And similarly, in *Parashat VaEtḥanan*, Rashi explained: "It is spelled *mzwzt* [Deut. 5:9]," even though in the Masoret it is plene, [with a *waw*] between the *zayyin* and the *taw*.[10]

This brief but compact text discusses five examples of conflict over the spelling of biblical words as suggested by the Talmud, the Midrashim, and the Masorah. But despite its rich collection of data, it fails to inform us how these differences were treated and if any texts were changed because of it.

The published text of Tosafot to BT Nid. 33a, s.v. *whnś'* actually reads:

> *we-ha-nośē'* is spelled *whnś'*, lacking the *waw*. This is surprising, because in the Masoret it is plene, but we have found that the Masoret disagrees with the Talmud in Tractate Shabbat [55b]. Regarding the sons of Eli, [the Talmud says] *maʿaḇirim* [1 Sam. 2:24] is spelled *mʿbyrm*, but in our Bibles it is spelled *mʿbyrym*, plene.

In contrast to Riva's claim, the commonly used edition of the Tosafot does not contain the statement that "it is routine for the Talmud to contradict the Masoret," even if it is.[11] It is conceivable that such a line could have been removed, but I have found no evidence of the statement anywhere in the Tosafot on the Talmud. It is also possible that a similarity between the consonantal texts, *dereḵ ha-šas la-ḥaloq ʿal ha-masoreṯ*, "it is the way of the Talmud to disagree with the Masoret," and *de-raʾinu ha-šas ḥolēq ʿal ha-masoreṯ*, "we have seen the Talmud disagree with the Masoret," led to the confusion, especially if one assumes that the first word was abbreviated.

In any case, the Tosafists were prominent in pointing out these inconsistencies, and they were followed by many other writers, particularly in Ashkenazi countries. In this light, the suggestion of S. Z. Schick that a marginal error was introduced into the text of the Tosafot by a student or an intentional forger cannot be taken seriously.[12] The extent to which these medieval works influenced the texts under discussion remains uncertain (see chapter 6), but they and others like them extended the list of troubling examples.

The Zohar also displayed an awareness of the fact that more than one spelling of a particular word may exist. In discussing *u-mi-geḇa'oṯ*, "from the heights" (Num. 23:9), and whether it should be spelled *wmgb't* or *wmgb'wt*, it observed:

> *u-mi-geḇa'oṯ 'ašurenu*, "from the heights I will see it": In the upper academy (*meṯiḇta 'ila'a*), *geḇa'oṯ* is spelled lacking the *waw*. . . . In the academy of heaven (*meṯiḇta' de-reqi'a*), [it is spelled] *wmgb'wt*, with the letter *waw*.[13]

As this example shows, the Zohar, like the Talmud and the Midrashim, occasionally associated its teachings with the plene and defective spellings of biblical words; in several cases these spellings also differed from those routinely found in the Torah scrolls.[14] Given the authority that rabbinic writers attributed to the Talmud and the Midrashim, it is not at all surprising that the halakhic codes and responsa of the past eight centuries contain a number of questions, discussions, and decisions about the propriety of these observations and whether the Torah texts should be changed to concur with their alternative spelling suggestions. And given the high regard in which the Zohar was held in many sixteenth-century circles—it largely surpassed the Midrashim (or controlled their interpretation) and in some cases challenged the Talmud[15]—it is equally understandable that minor changes to the Torah text could be introduced in its name.

Rabbi David Ibn Zimra became aware of such an incident, where two words in several Torah scrolls were altered from *'tw* to *'wtw* in order to conform to the Zohar's suggested spelling. As it now lies before us, the discussion of how he handled this situation seems to contain a question from someone who heard about the incident after the fact and sought a documented answer from the rabbi, although the questioner could have been the very person who informed Ibn Zimra of the changes and called upon him to respond. It is possible, perhaps even likely, that Ibn Zimra himself phrased the issue posed by the questioner as a way of introducing his answer, essentially the official explanation of why he acted as he did, which he wished to incorporate into one of his responsa collections.

Many of Ibn Zimra's responsa begin "You have asked me to give you my opinion on. . . ." Others, like this one, begin "Question" and require insertion of the request for information or advice at the end. The introductory paragraphs read like Ibn Zimra's summary of the question, and, were it not for the final line, one might construe it as a description of a halakhic problem, not a formal question at all. While it is far from unusual for rabbis to create questions for themselves to answer, Ibn Zimra is not suspected of doing this. On the other hand, the number of his responsa devoted to local problems and likely to have arisen in private discussion or in teaching situations is quite high and would allow him or his assistant a relatively free hand in composing the questions and organizing them within the responsa. In fact, responsa on the Bible are grouped together in II, nos. 813–818; glosses on Maimonides produced several such collections, and thematic groupings are evident in other places. Clearly some of Ibn Zimra's ongoing interest in the Bible was reflected in the organization and presentation of his responsa.

The identity of the questioner, assuming one existed, remains unknown, but the question itself reflects something of what we know of Ibn Zimra. At the very least and from the outset, it refers to the individual reported on by the uncomplimentary term *'eḥaḏ min ha-miṯhakkemim*, "one of the self-designated sages," which hints to the reader that the forthcoming response will object to whatever has been done.

The Query: Should One Correct Words in the Torah Text to Follow Spellings Suggested in the Zohar?

Question:[16]

[1] Regarding what one of the self-designated sages did, [namely] that he changed[17] all the scrolls (*sefarim*) according to the Midrash of Rabbi Shimon bar Yohai,[18] peace be upon him, who wrote with reference to the verse *'al tira' 'tw*,[19] "Do not fear him" [Num. 21:34], that it [i.e., the word *'tw*, "him," referring to Og, King of Bashan] is [written] plene with a *waw* [as *'wtw*]. [He said this] because Moses our Master, peace be upon him, feared lest the merit of Og's circumcision would protect him, for Og, King of Bashan, was a member of Abraham's household and had been circumcised. And [accordingly,] The Holy One, Blessed Be He, said to him [to Moses], *'al tira' 'wtw*, "Do not fear his sign," as in the expression "sign of the covenant."[20]

And similarly, they changed the verse *'d drwš 'ḥyk 'tw*, "until your brother seeks it" [Deut. 22:2], [to be] plene with a *waw* [as *'wtw*], because they also saw written there [in the Midrash of Rabbi Shimon bar Yohai] that it is to be spelled plene, from the word [*'wt*, meaning] "sign."

But the matter was troubling because, according to their opinion, all the scrolls (*sefarim*) that were written in the days of all of the geonim, which [or: who] existed in former times, would be unfit for ritual use. And you have asked to know my opinion.

The Spelling of 'oṯo

The question about spelling relates directly to the midrashic exposition of these two verses, in which *'tw*, "him," if spelled *'wtw*, may carry a secondary meaning of "his sign." Og, the main character in the first passage, figured in the narratives in Numbers 21, where the first correction was entered, but rabbinic lore, which often dwelled on his gigantic physical size, frequently associated him with earlier times. Some Midrashim claimed he could not fit into Noah's ark and therefore rode out the flood on its roof; others, that Abraham circumcised him during his service as the patriarch's slave or that he was the escapee of Gen. 14:13.[21]

The belief in Og's being protected by circumcision derives from its general importance as the sign of the covenant with God and the belief in its prophylactic powers. Circumcision's importance was discussed, for example, in Rashi's interpretation of Gen. 24:2, based on BT Shev. 38b and Gen. Rab. 59, 8. Kabbalistic emphasis on the sign and its location on the male sex organ gave it special significance, and passages in the Zohar discuss this belief. These include I, 93a, which states (regarding circumcised Jews) that "anyone who has this sign on him does not descend to Hell, if he guards it properly."[22] It is assumed here that Og, circumcised by Abraham, might have been afforded this type of protection, though the more prevalent midrashic position suggests that it was his longevity, not his having been circumcised, that was Moses' concern.[23]

The second passage, from Deuteronomy, obligated the finder to hold a lost object until the owner claimed it (*'tw*), though rabbinic discussions explored the claimant's need to prove ownership through the presence of some identifying mark (*'wt*).

In describing the situation with which he had to deal, Ibn Zimra referred to the offending party (i.e., the scribe[s] who changed the Torah scrolls to follow the Zohar) in both the singular and the plural. While he first mentioned "one of the self-designated sages," he soon switched to "they." The phrase *'eḥaḏ min ha-miṯḥakkemim* implies the existence of a group of like-minded people, one of whom actually emended the Torah scrolls and bore the brunt of Ibn Zimra's ire. The question also refers to "their opinion," and the answer mentions "those who change the texts," plural (A.2), as well as the one person who actually did the work (A.6). Even more telling is the reference to "scrolls that *they* changed," the situation described in this responsum, recounted in another translated in chapter 3, B.17. This repeated use of the plural points to an organized group that greatly valued the Zohar and altered the Torah text to conform to the text assumed by its midrashic suggestions.

The Characterization of Those Who Emend the Bible Text

The *hitpa'el* form of the Hebrew verb is sometimes used to express intention or falsification; thus *'eḥaḏ min ha-miṯḥakkemim* means literally "one of those who feigned being wise." The term is used extensively in the halakhic literature written in and since medieval times, usually in a pejorative way, though that connotation seems not to have been its original meaning. Ex. 1:10, *haḇa niṯḥakkema lo* means "let's outsmart them," and many of the talmudic and midrashic usages suggest a meaning of "growing wise" or "intensifying wisdom," such as *ha-roṣe še-yiṯḥakkem ya'asoq be-ḏinē mamonoṯ*, "one who wishes to grow wise should study the aspects of halakhah related to nonritual, monetary concerns (*mamonot*)" BT Ber. 63b.[24]

Negative or sarcastic usages of *miṯḥakkem* are found in many medieval works and in responsa from both medieval and later times.[25] Even closer to the usage here, in Jacob Al-Gazi's *Emet LeYa'aqov*, the term *miṯḥakkem(im)* is routinely applied to those who emend Bible texts on the authority of midrashic sources.[26] It is also used by Ibn Zimra himself in at least four other responsa: I, no. 146, and IV, nos. 107 and 299, which respond to those who had rendered improper legal decisions, and VIII, no. 3, in which he refers to an individual who, like the people criticized here, deviated from an accepted halakhic norm, in this case by placing sixteen strings in the *ṣiṣiṯ* tassels. Like A.7, this last responsum appeals to the notion of not allowing the Torah to seem like two *toroṯ*.

The data on the spelling of *'tw* are highly consistent. Rabbi Meir Abulafia said that *'tw* is always defective in the Torah, as did Rabbi Menahem Meiri and Rabbi Y. S. Norzi.[27] The spelling of this particular *'oṯo* is also defective in *The Lisbon Bible of* 1482, in the 1524–1525 Rabbinic Bible, in Leningrad B19A, and in the Spanish Pentateuch of 1241.[28] J. De Rossi skipped the verse; B. Kennicott noted two references to a plene spelling. Rabbi S. Ganzfried said it is defective, like all other cases in the Torah. S. Rosenfeld discussed the passage from the Zohar but observed that all scrolls known to him were defective.[29]

The word *'tw* in Deut. 22:2 is spelled defective in all the texts mentioned above, as well as in Cambridge manuscript T.-S. B4, 27.[30] The plene spelling was mentioned by Rosenfeld (ad loc.); the verse was skipped by De Rossi; Kennicott listed two texts with the plene spelling.

According to C. D. Ginsburg, the word *'wtw/'tw* appears 479 times throughout the Bible. Of them, 41 are plene and 438, including all 248 in the Torah, are defective. In his words, "no Massoretic School attempted to introduce the later plene orthography into this division of the Scriptures."[31]

Neither the Zohar nor its sixteenth-century adherents qualify as a masoretic school, but they do offer evidence of some variation from this norm, though usually it was rejected by masoretic writers. Note the comment of Jacob ben Asher (ad loc.), *'aḏ deroš 'aḥiḵa 'oṯo*, "that he should seek his sign (*ha-'oṯ šelo*) [meaning] he should present him with the [identifying] sign on it," which assumes a plene spelling.[32] That this plene spelling did receive widespread circulation in antiquity may be seen from its routine appearance in place of MT *'tw* in Dead Sea Scroll Hebrew, including passages from biblical texts preserved among the scrolls.[33]

In *Heikhal HaBerakhah*, a masoretic commentary on the Torah, Rabbi Isaac Judah Yehiel Safran (1806–1874) noted:

> *'wtw* [Num. 21:34]: plene *waw*, and, similarly, *'aḏ deroš 'aḥiḵa 'wtw* [Deut. 22:2], as is explained in the Zohar; but in our scrolls the *waw*[s] are lacking. And if the scribe wrote these two *'oṯo*'s plene *waw*, he need not correct them at all, and it [i.e., the scroll] is ritually fit according to law, because the *masoroṯ* do not decide definitively. The tradition of Rabbi Meir HaLevi [Abulafia], of blessed memory, is not strong enough to overrule the tradition of the Zohar. Even so, before the fact, one should write [the word] defective, as the majority of the world is accustomed to do; and both of them are the words of the living God.[34]

This complex statement respects the defective spelling in the majority of scrolls but accepts both plene and defective alternatives (cf. Saraval's research on the spelling of *'hrwn*, discussed earlier in chapter 1). It clearly ranks the Zohar's spelling above Abulafia's, despite the latter's claim to represent the "majority" in medieval times and the general acceptance of his rulings by halakhic writers.[35] It also reduces the Masorah's authority relative to those other sources.

The Reply: No

The answer, of average size by Ibn Zimra's standards, presents his own reasoning (about 50 percent of the text), followed by a similarly minded passage from a responsum by Rabbi Solomon ben Abraham Ben Adret, the Rashba (about 30 percent of the whole), and his conclusion about the local situation (the final 20 percent).

> Answer:
> [2] I am surprised at those who change the text, for is the Midrash of Rabbi Shimon bar Yohai, of blessed memory, more authoritative for them than an explicit [passage of the] Gemara in our possession? And, in it, it says:
>
> [1] [The word] *pilagšim*, "concubines" [Gen. 25:6], is spelled *plgšm*;
>
> but in all the scrolls (*sefarim*) it is plene. And similarly,
>
> [2] *w'śymm br'šykm*, "and I will place them over you," [Deut. 1:13] is spelled *w'smm*;
>
> but in all the scrolls (*sefarim*) it is spelled plene [i.e., *w'śymm*]. And similarly,
>
> [3] *wyhy bywm klwt mšh*, "and when Moses finished. . . . ," [Num. 7:1] is spelled *klt*;
>
> but in all the scrolls (*sefarim*) it is spelled plene [i.e., *klwt*].
>
> Now why have they not changed all of these [words] according to their erroneous idea that one should correct [the Torah text] to follow the Midrash? Rather the principle of the matter is, as I shall tell you, that [changes should be made only with respect to] any plene or defective spelling with which a law is associated, according to what they learned in the Gemara—like *qrnwt/qrnt*, "horns" [Lev. 4:7, etc.], and like *swkt/skt*, "booths" [Lev. 22:42–43], and like *wbn 'yn lw*, "and he has no son" [Num. 27:8]—"check it [cf. BT B.B.115a]."[36] In these and similar cases, one should correct scrolls (*sefarim*) if they are found contrary to what is written in the Gemara.
>
> But [in the case of] any plene or defective spelling that is irrelevant for a legal purpose but is only a midrash, we should not change any scroll (*sefer*) on the basis of the rabbinic exposition, or on the basis of the Masorah. Rather, we follow the majority; for this is no different from any lenient or strict laws of the Torah, about which we say "follow the majority" [Ex. 23:2]. [Therefore,] in a matter that has no bearing on a legal issue, we should correct the scrolls (*sefarim*) according to the majority of scrolls (*sefarim*).

Ibn Zimra begins his reply by referring to a series of early rabbinic teachings that bear witness to different spellings of words in the Torah but that were never used to change it. Since they are merely midrashic, he rejects their textual authority and, concomitantly, the right to change the Torah text to conform to them. He treats a second group of passages differently. Because their expositional contents are halakhic, he assumes that the rabbis checked the matter more carefully, he takes their spelling suggestions more seriously, and he rules that the scrolls should be corrected to conform to them. He then reiterates that, in general, a Torah text should be corrected not solely on the basis of the Masorah or the Midrashim, but only on the basis of a majority of scrolls.

Modern writers[37] often assume that variations in the spellings of a word are of no cognitive significance. This notion was expressed by Abraham Ibn Ezra (1089–1164) in the introduction to his Torah commentary and elsewhere (see chapter 1 here), but this idea was far from universally accepted, and many rabbinic teachings demonstrate the opposite assumption. Genesis Rabbah contains the suggestion that the defective spelling of the toponym *ṣr* (which can be read as *ṣar*, rather than the customary *ṣor*) should be understood as a reference to Rome, while the plene spelling, *ṣwr*, connotes Tyre. Similarly, the defective spelling of *tnynm*, "sea monsters" (Gen. 1:21), was understood to suggest the existence of only one such creature.[38] This type of reasoning is quite extensive in Genesis Rabbah and elsewhere, as may be seen from the discussion (ad loc.) in Rabbi Samuel Jaffe Ashkenazi's *Yefei Toʿar* and in Rabbi Yehiel Mikhal of Glogau's *Nezer HaQadosh*, and from the almost routine treatments of plene and defective spellings in other Midrashim, in the tosafist literature on the Torah, in classical interpretations of the Masorah, and in many more recent works.[39] We now return to the specific cases mentioned here and to some of the notions associated with their spellings.

pilagšim, "concubines" (Gen. 25:6): The question about the spelling of *pilagšim* is traceable to Gen. Rab. 61, 4, which contains the best-known observation on its variants,[40] and general awareness of the problem is directly attributable to Rashi's discussion of it in his Torah commentary. Even so, his exact intention is subject to question, as all logical possibilities of the spelling of *pilagšim* are attested in the various editions of his commentary: *plgšm*, *pylgšm*, *plgšym*, and *pylgšym*. Particularly interesting is the juxtaposition of the spellings published together in *Ariel: Rashi HaShalem*: (1) *hplgšm*, taken from the Venice Rabbinic Bible of 1524–1525; (2) *hplgšym*, found in Rashi's Commentary on the Torah from Rome (1470) and Regio (1475); and (3) *hpylgšm*, from the Rashi edition of Guadaljara (1476). The most useful discussion of this matter is Abraham Baqrat's sixteenth-century supercommentary on Rashi, *Sefer HaZikkaron* (ad loc.); interesting but fanciful is the opinion that the Midrash assumed a normal reading of *plgšyym* or *pylgšyym*, with two *yods* before the *mem*.[41] Including these last two, the rabbinic supercommentaries on Rashi collectively consider six different spellings.

Parallel midrashic and midrash-based exegetical statements about the spelling of *pilagšim* abound. J. Gellis has cited a passage from Vatican MS 45 that reads:

> *lbny hpylgšym*, "to the sons of the concubines": "It is written plene with two *yods*," thus far in the Masoret, and even though he had only Hagar. But [this is] because she was married to him twice, also because her name was changed, and she became pregnant by him during both the first and second marriages.[42]

The comment of Rabbi Eleazar of Worms is also telling:

> *hplgšym*, "the concubines": "One concubine, who is [both] Hagar and Qeturah"; and if it is [spelled] plene, *pylgšym*, then it [the Torah] wishes to say that there were two, Hagar and Qeturah.[43]

The citation in Gellis that follows the first passage above (p. 289, no. 2) associates the numerical value of *wlbny hplgšym* with the rabbinic teaching, "He transmitted the impure name to them."[44] This exposition offers no help in analyzing the spelling of the phrase, for it is usually associated with the subsequent phrase (*naṯan ʾaḇraham mattanoṯ*, "Abraham gave gifts"), but Rabbi Isaiah Horowitz managed to link the two by creatively dividing *plgšm* into *pelag*, "half," and *šem*, "name," taken to mean "half a name," which he associated with Samael, a synonym for Satan, half of which is profane (*śam*, "poison") and half of which is holy (*ʾēl*, "God").[45]

Grammatical justification for the midrashic interpretation of the form *p(y)lgšm* as singular was sought unsuccessfully by generations of interpreters. Many empathized with (and even copied) Rabbi Elijah Mizrahi's admission in his commentary (ad loc.), "I do not know the function of the *mem* of *plgšm*."[46] In fact, it could be explained as enclitic, analogous to the usage in Ugaritic,[47] rather than as the defective plural of *p(y)lgš*, but it is doubtful if the ancient rabbis were aware of this phenomenon, though some of their medieval successors were. Their explanation may be based solely on the absence of a letter (in this case the *yod*), which is often taken to indicate the absence of something—in this case, the regular plural concept.[48]

Of course the spellings of *pilagšim* found in the manuscripts are far from uniform. For example, British Museum Manuscript Add. 10,445, a very large and important Masorah codex dated to 1311, has *p^{h}lgš^{h}m*, doubly defective, with two superlinear *hets* (signifying *ḥaser*, "defective") above the places where the *yods* appear in other texts.[49]

kallot̲, "finished" (Num. 7:1): The case of *kallot̲* is simpler and somewhat less celebrated than that of *pilagšim*, but the situation is essentially the same. Midrashic association of *klt* (in *wa-yehi be-yom kallot̲ moše*) with "bride" derived from a defective spelling, but many witnesses, conveniently listed by Norzi, are plene.[50]

wa-ʾaśimēm, "and I will place them" (Deut. 1:13): Again, some midrashic and midrash-based sources, a full list of which is included in Norzi's discussion (ad loc.), identify *wa-ʾaśimēm* as defective, as did Rashi, but Torah scrolls reportedly spell it plene, *wʾśymm*.

Judah ben Solomon Calais, sixteenth-century author of a supercommentary on Rashi, doubted that Rashi ever wrote the note on *wa-ʾaśimēm* now found in his commentary. Because Calais knew of no evidence for this defective spelling and possessed traditions that consciously negated its existence, he declined to attribute this spelling option to a difference between the Ashkenazi and Sefaradi Torah scrolls, a suggestion he did accept in discussing *pilagšim*. Instead, he suggested that Rashi wrote only *wʾśymm ket̲ib̲*, "it is written *wʾśymm*," to differentiate between *sin* and *shin*, but someone misunderstood and added *ḥaser ket̲ib̲*, "it is written defective."[51]

The evidence from these three biblical words was rejected by Ibn Zimra, because it was not of halakhic import; the next three examples, which appear in halakhic discussions, were taken as definitive statements about how to spell the words and, in these and similar cases, Ibn Zimra himself would change the Torah text to conform with them.

qarnot: The word *qrnwt/qrnt*, "horns," occurs at least nine times in the Torah. Expositions in the Sifra to Lev. 4:7, in BT Zev. 40a, and in various parallels associate the plene spelling with various laws about sprinkling blood on the altar.

ba-sukkot: The word *bskt* is found twice in Lev. 23:42, while it is spelled *bskwt* in 23:43. Rabbinic discussion (BT Suk. 6b) associated the number of walls required for a sukkah with these variations in spelling.

u-b̲en ʾēn lo: The phrase *wbn ʾyn lw*, "and he does not have a son," occurs in Num. 27:8 and Deut. 25:5. Both deal with laws of levirate marriage, but this discussion focuses on the appearance in Numbers; see BT Qid. 4a and Rashi (ad loc.). The exposition relates to the fact that *ʾyn* is spelled with a *yod*. This reasoning is rather farfetched, because the standard spelling of the word includes the *yod*, but its association with a legal matter gives it preferred status. Ibn Zimra's later example, *mʾn blʿm*,

"Bilaam refused" (Num. 22:14), clarifies the ways in which this manner of spelling was exposited by the early rabbis (A.5).

We will return to these six words later, but more pressing than the need to find a solution to the spelling anomalies is the need to develop an appropriate strategy for doing so. One important consideration was the relative value of the witnesses; another was majority testimony.

As was explained earlier, following the majority is a hallowed halakhic principle derived from Ex. 23:2 (some would say read into it, in violation of the literal meaning assumed by the cantillation signs; cf. Rashi, a.l.). Talmudic discussion of the verse appears, for example, in Hul. 11a, and the principle was applied routinely in nontextual matters. It served in the textual domain as well, particularly together with the story about the three scrolls in the Temple, featured earlier in chapter 1. Interestingly, neither this passage nor any of its midrashic parallels cites or refers to Ex. 23:2 (conceivably this treatment of the verse postdated the event described in Soferim); the juxtaposition of the verse and the story seems to have been a medieval contribution.

Whatever its origin, our present concern lies primarily with spelling details and the principle by which they should be determined. A grave halakhic implication of these considerations is the potential need to alter all extant scrolls, should it be deemed necessary to follow Midrash-based changes. Here Ibn Zimra wished to discredit the change, so he questioned a practice that would invalidate all early scrolls; elsewhere he did nothing less. Thus he rejected, in principle, all scrolls in which the separate parts of the letters *heh* and *qof* were formed of contiguous quill strokes (a very common way of writing and a matter of constant concern in the responsa literature),[52] saying, "and even if the ancient scrolls are written that way, should the halakhah be abandoned for the sake of ignorant scribes?" (I, no. 363). He then demonstrated his reasonableness by explaining how to correct them—potentially some 30,000 letters in a single Torah scroll.[53]

More recently the observation that all Torah scrolls are ritually unfit, at least according to the Babylonian Talmud, was made by Rabbi Moses Sofer (1762–1839). Sofer was queried about the reason for not reciting a blessing on the writing of a Torah scroll. After dismissing the length of time involved and other time-related factors, he answered:

> If the sages, of blessed memory, would have been experts in defective and plene spelling, they would have instituted a blessing for [the writing of] a Torah scroll. But since [a] they themselves were not expert, as is explained in Qiddushin 30b, since they were not even expert in the verse divisions; and also [b] there are several times where the Torah disagrees with the spelling suggested by the Talmud; and [c] we write the Torah to follow the Masorah, [then] according to the Talmud, the Torah scroll is unfit for ritual use.
>
> Furthermore, it says in Tractate Niddah 33a and in the Tosafot, s.v., *we-ha-nośē'* [that *whnwś'*, "the one who carries" (Lev. 15:10)] is written defective; "check it." For we follow the Talmud in rendering halakhic decisions, but as far as writing a Torah scroll, we write it plene, with a *waw*. And even though Maharam Lonzano in the book *Or Torah* [*Meṣora'*, Lev. 15:10] tried to resolve the problem, it is still unresolved. And you cannot conclude anything from [the talmudic and tosafist discussion of the inconsistency associated with the word] *ma'abirim*, "spread" [1 Sam.

> 2:24, cf. BT Shab. 55b]; and there are many places like this. And since the situation is this way, and we learn that a Torah scroll lacking one letter is not called a Torah scroll, as is clear from the statement of the Talmud, [in] the chapter [entitled] "One Who Takes a Fistful" [Men. 30a], therefore it is impossible, in any respect, to recite a blessing. Thus it appears according to my humble opinion.[54]

Lest this position be attributed to youthful exuberance, it should be noted that Sofer was in his fifties when he wrote this responsum, and some twenty years later, in 1835, shortly before his death, he was asked a similar question and gave the same answer. Despite his ruling, however, some scribes do recite the blessing.[55]

We return to Ibn Zimra's treatment of the Zohar's suggested spellings that deviated from masoretic norms.

> [3] And, if you ask, granted that [the spelling change suggested by] "Do not fear him" [Num. 21:34] is inconsequential, because it is only a homiletical exposition (*derash*), but "until your brother seeks it" [Deut. 22:2] makes a difference in a legal issue—because we do not return a lost object unless it has signs [of ownership]—two answers [may be given] in this matter. First, that one should not rely on the Midrash in this case, because it is not mentioned in the Gemara. And [second] moreover, because, according to my opinion, the Gemara disagrees with it; for, if [we follow] the Midrash, [the need for] signs [on a lost object] would be of biblical authority, so why are we asked if [the need for] signs is biblical or rabbinic?[56] [According to the Midrash,] there would be an explicit biblical verse; *ʿad̲ deroš ʾaḥik̲a ʾot̲o* [usually translated "until your brother requests it"] would mean "until you request his sign [of ownership]." But surely the Gemara does not think the word is spelled plene.

In this section Ibn Zimra continues to buttress his argument by placing the two examples of the Zohar's spelling claims within two established categories. The zoharic suggestion to spell *ʾtw* as *ʾwtw* in Numbers is midrashic, not halakhic, and, while that in Deuteronomy is halakhic, it stands in direct conflict with the Talmud. Even though the Zohar carried halakhic weight, the operative position was that its authority was not equal to that of the Babylonian Talmud.

Reliance on Midrashim for exegetical or halakhic directives was often a source of rabbinic debate, and a vast literature on the issue has been assembled. Ibn Zimra's first argument, that the explanation is only midrashic, is similar to the statements of a number of geonim and early Sefaradi writers who felt bound by Midrashim canonized in the Talmud, but not by those preserved elsewhere. In these writers, *midraš* (from the root *d-r-š*, "expound") and *ʾaggad̲a* (plural: *aggad̲ot̲*) or *haggad̲a* (derived from a root meaning "to talk") tend to be treated in similar fashion. Technically the former term refers to rabbinic exposition of scripture, while the latter approximates the English terms "legend" or "narrative," both of which are related to Latin words meaning "to talk." Regardless of which is used, the evaluations are quite clear and uniform; note, for example:

1. Rav Hai Gaon (939–1038): Know that words of Aggadah are not like authoritative oral teachings (*šemuʿa*), but everyone expounds what occurred to him, as [if to say it is] "a possibility" or "there is room to say," not a clear-cut matter. Therefore one should not rely on them [i.e., on Aggadah].[57]
2. Rav Sherira Gaon (died in 1006): Those things derived from biblical verses and called Midrash and Aggadah are conjectures . . . therefore

"one should not rely on Aggadah"; and they [i.e., the rabbis] said, "One should not learn [i.e., derive halakhic decisions] from Aggadot. . . . We accept those correct aspects, what is reinforced by reason and the Bible, but there is no end to Aggadot.[58]

3. Rav Hai was asked: What is the difference between Aggadot written in the Talmud, from which we are required to remove errors, and the Aggadot written outside the Talmud [presumably: in which errors are allowed to remain]?

   He responded: Whatever was placed in the Talmud is clearer [or: better] (*meḥuwwar*) than what was not placed in it. Even so, if the purposes of the Aggadot written in it are not clear or they have been corrupted, one should not rely on them, because there is a general principle "one should not rely on Aggadah." But anything placed in the Talmud, which we are required to correct, we should, in fact, treat this way, because if it did not contain a [cogent] Midrash, it would not have been placed in the Talmud.

   And if we are unable to remove the error [of this talmudic material], it assumes the status of things that are not halakhah. But we do not need to the same extent those things that were not placed in the Talmud. If something is correct and appealing, we expound and teach it; but if not, we pay no attention to it.[59]

4. Samuel HaNaggid (993–1055): Haggadah is any explanation in the Talmud on any subject that is not a commandment. And you should learn from it only what makes sense. You should know that everything that the sages, of blessed memory, established as halakhah in a matter of a commandment—which is from Moses our teacher, peace unto him, which he received from God—you should not add to it or detract from it. But [as for] what they explained with regard to biblical verses, [there,] each did according to what occurred to him and what he thought. We learn those explanations that make sense, but we do not rely on the rest.[60]

Though Ibn Zimra sought to overrule the Zohar by appealing to the Talmud, his argument is weak, since the Talmud does not state a position contrary to the Zohar's or even mention the issue. Indeed, some writers tended to follow the Zohar when it did not contradict the Talmud, a position articulated in another of Ibn Zimra's responsa:

> And anywhere that you find the books of the Kabbalah disagreeing with a legal decision of the Gemara, follow the Gemara and the halakhic authorities [who presumably ruled in accord with it]. And anywhere it [i.e., kabbalistic literature] does not disagree, as in this matter [i.e., the wearing of Tefillin from home to the synagogue], which is not mentioned in the Gemara or in the [writings of the] halakhic authorities, I prefer to rely on the words of the Kabbalah. [IV, no. 1111]

Though positively inclined toward using the Zohar in halakhic debate, in this particular case Ibn Zimra declined to accept the Zohar's suggestion; hence the effort to butress his position with a second argument, which tried to demonstrate the existence of an actual conflict between the Zohar and the Talmud.

The next section of the responsum cites the first and last thirds of a responsum by the Rashba, Rabbi Solomon ben Abraham Ben Adret, the leading Spanish halakhic authority of the late thirteenth and early fourteenth centuries; except for Ibn Zimra's added discussion of the passage in the Zohar, it goes over the same ground. Ibn Zimra's formulation and language are so close to Ben Adret's that one can safely assume Ben Adret's responsum to be their source.

> [4] And it is unnecessary to deal with this at length, because the Rashba, of blessed memory, was already asked about a similar matter, and he responded (this is his language):
>
>> It is my opinion that this is the truth, [namely] that one should neither add nor delete [letters] in any place in scrolls (*sefarim*) according to the Masorah or according to aggadic Midrashim, because on the authority of their sages—who were expert in defective and plene spelling—the sages in their respective places disagreed with each other.[61] And it seems to me [that this is so] even regarding the pronunciation (*miqra'*) and regarding the tradition[al spelling] (*masoreṯ*), like the disagreement[s] between Ben Asher and Ben Naftali, and similarly between the Westerners and the Easterners, etc. Check item 70 [read?: Check it].

This attribution to Ben Adret is presented three different ways in Responsa A, B, and C. Identified as no. 232 of Solomon Ben Adret's responsa that were mistakenly attributed to Nahmanides,[62] it contains, from someone with whom Ben Adret had a prior relationship, a learned question regarding the differences between plene and defective spellings as presented in the early rabbinic and masoretic works. The complete question, which reflects a concern that resurfaced in many subsequent centuries and is of interest in its own right, is translated with the answer here and is discussed more fully in chapter 6.

In short, Ben Adret ruled that the Torah text could be changed to conform to talmudic expositions of a halakhic nature, but not to nonhalakhic ones. This apparently unprecedented distinction, which gave the Talmud control of a relatively small percentage of biblical spellings, was accepted by many subsequent writers but was challenged by Rabbi David Joseph (see later in this chapter). Ben Adret further argued that the very existence of disagreements among the masoretes precluded relying on them indiscriminately, and he therefore stated that one should not emend scrolls on the basis of Midrashim or the Masorah, but only follow the scrolls (*sefarim*). As additional evidence, he cited the passage from Soferim 6:4 which, taken together with Ex. 23:2, proved that such decisions should be based on majority testimony.

The disagreements Ben Adret mentioned between Ben Asher and Ben Naftali, a formal list of masoretic variants, deal mostly with relatively minor points of vocalization, not with major textual differences, though they include a few variations in *matres lectionis* and consonants.[63] Differences between the Westerners and the Easterners generally included more weighty matters, such as divisions of words and verses and spelling variations.[64]

Paragraph A.4 concludes with "etc.," indicating the omission of a piece of Ben Adret's answer. The deletion was the middle third, which deals with whether or not the *nun* in *mmnw* carries a *dagesh*, a difference of opinion between the eastern and western masoretes regarding the vocalization of "from us" and "from him." A discussion of this passage and translation can be found in chapter 6. After skipping this unneeded passage, Ibn Zimra continues with the final third of Ben Adret's responsum (A.5). One more item must be noted first, however.

Following the "etc." near the end of A.4, the text reads *ʿyyn symn ʿ[ayyin]*, which literally means "check item [or: section] 70." The reading is attested in all citations of the responsum, but it makes no sense in this context. M. Phillip also was stumped by it,[65] though he assumes that a different collection of responsa, of which this was no. 70, is intended, as did Rabbi Hayyim Moses Amarillio before him.[66]

This is possible, but not supported by other evidence. Perhaps the abbreviation ʿʿ, which also stands for *ʿyyn ʿlyw* ("check it"), was improperly restored as *ʿayyēn ʿayyin*, taken to be "check 70," then expanded to *ʿayyēn siman ʿayyin*. The phrase *ʿyyn ʿlyw* has implications for textual discussions, and it is cited in the subsequent paragraph, but this does not seem to be the precise intention here. Perhaps it was introduced here from a marginal note on another part of the responsum. In II, no. 696, Ibn Zimra referred to another of Ben Adret's responsa as no. 94, its actual number in the first volume of the existing edition of his responsa.

> [5] And at the end, he [Ben Adret] wrote:
>
> In any case, anything discussed in the Gemara in a matter of principle of law, like *qrnwt/qrnt* [Lev. 4:7, etc.], *bswkt/bskt*, "booths" [Lev. 22:42–43], [and] *wbn ʾyn lw*, "and he has no son" [Num. 27:8],[67] which we expound [for legal purposes], "check it," [BT B.B. 115a] since it is not written without a *yod*, like *mʾn blʿm*, "Bilaam refused" [Num. 22:14],[68] from which [i.e., from Num. 27:8] we learn that an inheritance is transferable[69] [i.e., from one relative to another], in this case, we certainly correct [the text]. But in each and every place, even with regard to defective and plene spellings, we correct the minority according to the majority, because there is an explicit biblical statement "follow the majority" [Ex. 23:2].

This key passage reiterates that one should change Torah scrolls to follow spellings suggested by halakhic passages of the Babylonian Talmud and readings suggested by a majority of scrolls. It complements A.4, which stipulates that such changes should not be made on the basis of aggadic Midrashim or the Masorah.

Ben Adret continued by recounting the story of the three Torah scrolls; Ibn Zimra presents it as a citation within a citation. Here it is attributed to Rabbi Levi, whereas Soferim presents it as the words of Resh Laqish. Responsum 144 of Rabbi Moshe Halava, presented in chapter 6, concurs with Soferim by attributing it to R[abbi] Sh[imon] b[en] L[aqish]. Undoubtedly, decoding of the common abbreviation *r- l-* has caused the confusion.[70]

> [6] And we learned in Tractate Soferim [6:4]:
>
> Said Rabbi Levi: Three scrolls were located in the Temple court, *Sefer* "*Mʿwn*," *Sefer* "*Zʿṭwṭy*," [and] *Sefer* "*Hyʾ*."
>
> In one they found written *mʿwn ʾlhy qdm*, "the dwelling place of the most high," and in two [they found] *mʿwnh* [Deut. 33:27]; they established [the reading in the] two and invalidated [the reading in the] one.
>
> In one they found written *wyšlḥ ʾt zʿṭwṭy bny yśrʾl*, "and he sent the youths of the Israelites," and in two [they found] *wyšlḥ ʾt nʿry* . . . [Ex. 24:5]; they established [the reading in the] two and invalidated [the reading in the] one.

> In one they found "she" [spelled] *hy'* eleven times, and in two [they found it spelled] *hw'* eleven times; they established [the reading in the] two and invalidated [the reading in the] one.

Thus far his [i.e., Ben Adret's] language.

Ibn Zimra continues his presentation by recounting how he restored the scrolls to their original state, and he rules that one should not change Torah scrolls to follow the spellings in the Midrashim. He further notes the importance of having textual consistency in the scrolls, because criticisms of how Jews preserved and transmitted the Torah text contained accusations that they willfully changed it. He concludes:

> [7] And even though the one who changed the text frightened me by saying that [by doing this] one of the sages[71] was [merely] restoring the Torah scroll as it had been, since before the year was over he became blind, I have not taken his words seriously. And I said:
>
> > Not for my honor, nor for the honor of my father's house, have I done so, but rather so that controversies will not multiply in Israel,[72] and so that our Torah should not become like two *toro̱t*.
>
> How much more so [is this appropriate], when we are among this nation, who say that we have changed the Torah, and added [things to it], and removed [things from it], and changed it as we wanted.[73] And what [will they say] even now, if our Torah scrolls appear in conflict with each other?
>
> Therefore, I personally went to the home of the one who changed the text and found three changed scrolls (*sefarim*); I corrected them and "restored the crown of the Torah [to its place], as it was formerly"[74] and [as it is] in the other scrolls (*sefarim*). And I decreed regarding him that he should not correct scrolls (*sefarim*) according to a Midrash, but rather according to the majority of scrolls (*sefarim*). And I have relied on Him, be He blessed, because He knows the secrets of the heart.

Ibn Zimra followed faithfully the precedent set by his Spanish predecessor, Solomon ben Adret. By doing so, he gave significant authority to the Babylonian Talmud, which he utilized several times in this passage. He also accepted as a significant sign the fact that his opponent had become blind. Here too the Talmud may be his precedent, since it considered a blind man as if dead (BT Ned. 64b). The sudden onset of blindness was taken as a very serious omen and was sometimes interpreted, especially by one's opponents, as divine retribution for some misdeed.[75] Here it is seen as vindicating Ibn Zimra's response.

Also, according to the Talmud, having "two *toro̱t*," that is, two conflicting systems of religious teachings, occurred because the students of Hillel and Shammai failed to learn from their teachers and to serve them properly (BT San. 88b, Sot. 47b). Ibn Zimra has applied the phrase to the actual Torah text, as did Norzi after him.

Fixing the Scrolls on the Basis of a Majority of Scrolls

In chapter 1 we saw that the simple meaning of the passage in Soferim suggested that corrections in scrolls should be made by comparison with a majority of scrolls and that, in later times, some writers modified this stance by including other witnesses to the text and justified the idea by reading it into Soferim. Here we find Ben Adret, as cited by Ibn Zimra, opting for the earlier position. Not only does his reference to Soferim by itself suggest the use of the scrolls; Ben Adret makes the point himself clearly and unequivocally. When queried about correcting Torah scrolls according to various external witnesses, he answers:

> It is my opinion that this is the truth, [namely] that one should never add or delete [letters] in any place in *sefarim* according to the Masorah or according to aggadic Midrashim. (A.4)

Sefarim in this passage (in contrast to the next) must be referring to Torah scrolls, because the question to Ben Adret clearly did so, and because the answer refers to changing *sefarim* according to the Masorah, which means that the *sefarim* referred to are not themselves the Masorah.

Sefarim is used differently in the subsequent middle section of Ben Adret's response, omitted by Ibn Zimra, which deals with vocalizing *mmnw* with or without a *dagesh*, depending on whether it means "than us" or "than him." Here, because the subject is a vocalized text, references to *sefarim* must be to Masorah codices; Ben Adret even refers specifically to *sifrē ha-masora,* perhaps to differentiate them from the other *sefarim* under discussion, the scrolls. The purpose of this middle section was to discredit the Masorah and to demonstrate that it was inconclusive in certain areas because of disagreements among its authoritative spokesmen. In other words, one should not use the Masorah to correct *sefarim*, that is, scrolls.

Ben Adret next returned to the original theme of correcting Torah texts according to the Talmud, which means that the *sefarim* are again the Torah scrolls discussed at the beginning. He continues: "In any case, anything discussed in the Gemara in a matter of principle of law, like *qrnwt/qrnt* . . . in this case, we certainly correct the minority."

The word *ha-miʿuṭ*, "the minority," is not found at this point in Ibn Zimra's version of Ben Adret's text but appears in the version found in Ben Adret's collected responsa and in all other citations I have found, as well as in Paris MS 411 of Ben Adret's responsa. S. Leiman and J. Penkower have suggested that *ha-miʿuṭ* here is an error (perhaps because it anticipates a similar phrase used very shortly thereafter) and should be omitted.[76] That awkwardly leaves the verb *metaqqenin*, "(we) correct," without an object, and perhaps they would consider adding *ha-sefarim*. But with or without the addition, the object must be the same as before; the question was still about corrections to the scrolls, and at this point Ben Adret still must have been speaking about scrolls. Accordingly, he continues in A.5:

> But in each and every place, even with regard to defective and plene spelling, we correct the minority according to the majority, because there is an explicit biblical statement "follow the majority" [Ex. 23:2].

There is no reason to consider any type of text other than scrolls to be a part of the discussion. At no point did anyone ask about changing any other type of text, and other than to highlight the inconsistent information provided by the Masorah, other potential witnesses were never even mentioned. There is simply no way to read the responsum as anything other than a claim that, except for the spellings of halakhic significance discussed in the Talmud, Torah scrolls should be corrected according to majority testimony of Torah scrolls, not according to the Masorah or the aggadic Midrashim.

This procedure was described earlier by Judah HaLevi (ca. 1240) in the Kuzari III, 26–27 (see chapter 1, note 95):

> (26) Said the Kuzari: So what is to be done, if a change is found in one of the manuscripts of the Torah, or in two, or more?
> (27) Said the sage: It is necessary to accept the reading of the majority of manuscripts—for the majority cannot be erroneous—and to reject the opinion of the minority. And so should one act regarding the tradition [or: *Masoret*]; in a place where the minority disagrees, one should follow the majority.

The extent to which one might go in fulfilling this type of textual comparison was demonstrated by Rabbi Hayyim Moses Amarillio (1695–1748), who reported that the form of the *waw* in *šalom*, "peace" (Num. 25:12), was checked in approximately 800 Torah scrolls in his city.[77]

In like manner, the question posed to Ibn Zimra pertained to correcting Torah scrolls. Where he cited or paraphrased the question to Ben Adret or his answer, it is clear that he used *sefarim* to refer to scrolls. In fact, because Ibn Zimra omitted the middle part of Ben Adret's answer, there is no reference in Ibn Zimra's responsum to any other type of *sefer*; all seventeen usages of the term (eleven of *sefarim*, including one in the citation from Soferim; five of *sefer*, including three from Soferim; and one of *sifrē toraṯenu*) refer to scrolls. When both men spoke of using *roḇ sefarim* as a model, they meant to use the majority of scrolls, not the Masorah codices.

As clear as this is, several later writers saw a need to specify that Ben Adret favored using a majority of Torah scrolls, not the Masorah and not the ambiguous *sefarim*, to correct questionable spellings. In the course of presenting his case for the proper way to establish the correct Torah text and to correct divergent scrolls, Abraham Hasan (sixteenth century) discussed the procedures established by Meir Abulafia, Menahem Meiri, and Ben Adret. He was devoted to Abulafia's work and strongly disapproved of the fact that neither Ben Adret nor Meiri worked according to Abulafia's principles or even used *Masoret Seyag LaTorah*. As a part of his critique, he argued that Abulafia had applied the majority principle to the best Masorah texts, and that Meiri affirmed this position, though he failed to execute it properly. Hasan also claimed that Ben Adret agreed with this position. His evidence, a short responsum discussed more fully along with a translation of his own statement in chapter 6, does not sustain the claim, but from his language it is clear that the issue in his mind was whether one should decide on the basis of a majority of *sefarim*, scrolls, or a majority of Masorah texts, *masoroṯ*: "not by any means is it possible, that what they [i.e., Meiri and Ben Adret] said [was] that [the principle] "one should follow the majority" means the majority of scrolls (*sefarim*). Rather [it means] the majority of *masoroṯ*."[78] He favored the Masorah and attributed this position to Ben Adret, but he clearly perceived the need to choose between the two options. Others went much further. Rabbi Joseph David included the following reference in his *Beit David*, a commentary on Jacob ben Asher's *Arbaʿah Turim*:

> [Regarding the] matter of correcting Torah scrolls according to the Masorah codices (*masoroṯ*) or according to the majority, see the responsa [of Ben Adret] attributed to the Ramban, of blessed memory, no. 232.[79]

Again the subject is scrolls, and the comparison of Masorah codices and the majority, *roḇ*, must mean that the latter are the scrolls.

A third example is offered by Rabbi Isaac Jacob Al-Gazi (1680–1756), who composed a very extensive anthology of laws and decisions about Torah scrolls, *Emet LeYa'aqov*. His discussion of textual variations that do or do not disqualify a scroll from public use contains a lengthy paraphrase of Ibn Zimra's responsum and of Ben Adret's.

> But [in the case of] any plene or defective spelling that is irrelevant for a legal purpose [. . .], we should not change any scroll (*sefer*) on the basis of the rabbinic exposition, or on the basis of the Masorah. Rather, we follow the majority, *the majority of Torah scrolls* . . . in a matter that has no bearing on a legal issue. [emphasis added][80]

LeDavid Emet by Rabbi Hayyim David Joseph Azulai (1724–1806) is likely based on the above and is equally explicit. The passage from which the following brief statement has been extracted will be treated shortly, but it is important for understanding the responsa presently under discussion: "And one should not correct the scrolls according to Midrashim but according to the majority of Torah scrolls."[81] Notwithstanding the clarity of the position articulated in these many texts, other documents to be discussed later seem to suggest otherwise.

Sources from the Babylonian Talmud?

A closer look at Ibn Zimra's answer highlights an interesting side problem related to the sources of the evidence he cites: talmudic expositions demonstrating divergent spellings have not been used to emend Torah texts, so surely this one from the Zohar should not be used to change the Torah text either. To prove the case, he cites treatments of three specific words (*pilagšim*, "*concubines*"; *wa-'aśimēm*, "and I will place them"; and *kallot*, "finished"). But while the relevant discussions of these words appear in various Midrashim, none of them is found in the Talmud. We are thus forced to consider at least three alternatives: the removal from the Talmud of one or more passages of great importance; an error about the origin of these sources, repeated in many places; and the existence of another meaning for the word "Gemara" in A.2, broader than "the text of the Babylonian Talmud."

In support of the notion that the passage was found in at least some texts of the Gemara, one must note that several medieval documents that will be cited and translated here repeat this attribution. The talmudic origin of this material is mentioned in the question addressed to Ben Adret (no. 232 of his responsa attributed to Nahmanides, discussed at length in chapter 6). It is also found in another of his responsa, preserved in Joseph Caro's *Beit Yosef* and in Abraham Hasan's *Iggeret HaSofer*.[82] The question may also be the first place in which all five of these verses (which frequently appear together in discussions of the problem) are so grouped, though several are joined in BT San. 4a–b and in the medieval discussions cited later. At this point it is the question to Ben Adret and not a variant talmudic text available in sixteenth-century Egypt that seems to be the source of Ibn Zimra's remark here.

At the same time, the suggestion that these passages were removed from the Talmud has been made by several writers, including Elijah ben Azriel of Vilna.[83] One possible reason for the deletion would be evidence of biblical spellings that differed from the masoretic text but, in light of the many other such contradictions that remain in the Talmud and the absence of corroborating manuscript support,[84] that idea is far from convincing.

Alternatively, one may assume that a strategically placed error, which erroneously cited a series of midrashic passages as Gemara, had more than its proper share of influence. If so, the question posed to Ben Adret could be the source of the confusion. It seems to be the earliest statement claiming talmudic support for all of these spellings, and it is possible that all the other references descend from it. This is not to suggest that the questioner necessarily made the mistake. Questions that appear with rabbinic responsa often have been reworked, and the error might have arisen later, although, because it appears in two of Ben Adret's responsa, such a suggestion would affect our understanding of the relationship between them (see further chapter 6).

Finally, one may argue that here "Gemara" refers to the entire corpus of rabbinic teachings, not just to the Talmud, and that it approximates the notion of "the rabbinic tradition," for which there is a substantial amount of support, including Responsum C.[85] Relatedly, in A.2, even Ibn Zimra attributed the material in question to "Midrash"; and in B.14, in a similar context, he referred to the "masters of the Talmud" (*baʿalē ha-talmuḏ*)—which may include the rabbis of the Midrashim and even post-talmudic rabbis, not to "the rabbis in the Talmud."

Many other medieval writers who discussed these passages also identified their sources. Rabbi David ben Samuel of Etoile (thirteenth to fourteenth century) located differences between the Bible text and rabbinic derashot in *Midrash Rabbah* but listed only two (*skt/skwt* and *ṭṭpt/ṭṭpwt*), both of which are found in the Talmud.[86] Norzi identified the sources as midrashic in *Minhat Shai*, Gen. 25:6.

Rabbi Moses (Maharam) Halava, who studied with Ben Adret toward the end of the latter's life, located the three examples of *kalloṯ*, *pilagšim*, and *wa-ʾaśimēm* "in the Gemara and the Midrashim,"[87] and this fact probably presupposes that at least one is in the Talmud, but the conjunction *w-* may also mean "or," and "Gemara and Midrashim" may serve as an hendiadys representing the entire corpus of early rabbinic literature.

In his commentary on BT Qid. 30a, Rabbi Menahem Meiri, another of Ben Adret's important contemporaries, correctly identified *kalloṯ*, *pilagšim*, and *wa-ʾaśimēm* as examples of "a disagreement between the Midrashot and the Masoret."[88] He attributed discussion of *le-ṭoṭafoṯ*, *sukkoṯ*, and *u-ḇen ʾēn lo* to the Talmud.

Another medieval writer who referred to these sources as nontalmudic was Rabbi Shimon ben Zemah Duran (1361–1444).[89] In this case the question of the correct spelling of *hmwl ymwl* (Gen. 17:13), *pylgšym* (Gen. 25:6), and *klwt* (Num. 7:1) was raised because, according to the query to Duran, Rashi's Torah commentary noted all to be defective. Duran responded that no one questions the spelling of *hmwl ymwl* and that the other two spellings are found in Midrashim (he did not cite the Talmud), but that Ben Adret already ruled that these cases are to be left plene and that only words of legal import, such as *bskt/bskt/bskwt*, or *qrnt/qrnt/qrnwt*, should be changed.

In fact, several talmudic passages may presuppose the defective spelling *hml*;[90] it is mentioned and explained in two manuscripts cited by J. Gellis in *Tosafot HaShalem*,[91] and Rashi's Torah commentary mentions the defective spellings of the two other words. Also of possible relevance is Rashi to Ex. 31:18, where the defective spelling of *kkltw*, apparently accepted by both the masoretic and midrashic sources, is discussed.

Rashi's commentary to Gen. 14:14, in the Rome edition of 1470, contains a similar problem. It suggests that the word *ḥnykyw* should be spelled defective, *ḥnykw*. Very little support for the presence of this brief passage in Rashi can be marshaled from the secondary literature (early supercommentaries and citations by the Tosafot), and the fact that the question to Duran did not mention it suggests that it was unknown to its author.[92]

Of these many writers, the closest in geographic and historical proximity to Ben Adret are Meiri and Maharam Halava. Meiri cited all of the references correctly, and Maharam Halava may have done so as well. Such contemporary evidence for the correct attribution suggests that the passages in question were not removed from the Talmud, but that one of the other explanations is preferable.

Given the nature of Ben Adret's distinctions among the types of evidence and Ibn Zimra's acceptance of it, one must differentiate among four categories that can be arrayed in a two-by-two matrix: halakhic and nonhalakhic expositions, and those found in the Talmud and those in other works. Essentially, halakhic expositions from the Talmud have been accepted by Ben Adret and Ibn Zimra as authoritative; nonhalakhic ones, whether in the Talmud or not, have been rejected. The fourth category is halakhic discussion not in the Talmud, of which the passage in the Zohar is an example. Ibn Zimra disqualified this entire category in general (A.3), but he also dismissed this particular example by arguing that in fact it contradicted the Talmud. He thus suggested at least two subcategories in the fourth box of the matrix: nontalmudic halakhic discussions contradicted by the Talmud, and those about which the Talmud was merely silent. Some later writers were more sympathetic to halakhic expositions in midrashic sources, and some objected to this entire line of reasoning, which assigned different values to Torah spellings in halakhic and nonhalakhic contexts, because every letter in the text is governed by the laws of Torah scroll production and therefore of halakhic significance.

Solomon Ben Adret's Rejection of the Masorah as an Aid in Fixing the Bible Text

As will become clear later, one of the major questions arising from Ibn Zimra's four responsa and from Ben Adret's is each authors' attitude toward the Masorah and its authority in determining the text of the Torah. In the present context, it is noteworthy that the question to Ibn Zimra mentioned the Masorah and limited its concern to the issue of spelling and whether, if the Zohar's spelling were to be accepted, it would be proper to invalidate all ancient Torah scrolls on its authority. In I, nos. 363 and 446; in II, no. 596 (where he discusses the shapes of the letters *heh*, *het*, and *qof*); and in VIII, no. 171 (Responsum C, treated in chapter 4), which deals with the "cut" *waw* in *šlwm*, Num. 25:12, Ibn Zimra issued rulings that could very well have done just that. Here he was adamant that the scrolls should not be changed, and the implications of invalidating so many other ancient scrolls seem not to have entered his mind. Rather, he acknowledged that all scrolls must be identical, related the problem to non-Jewish attacks on the accuracy of the text and its faithful transmission by the rabbis, and solved it by classifying the Zohar as a Midrash and by limiting its authority in such matters to that of the other Midrashim.

It is potentially significant that Ibn Zimra did not challenge the Zohar's assumption that Moses' feelings influenced the spelling of the word. This fact may reflect the presumed sanctity of the Zohar and the belief that this interpretation correctly presented the esoteric intentions behind this divinely inspired, irregular spelling. Alternatively, it allows for some human influence in some of the Torah's textual details.[93]

In rendering his decision, Ibn Zimra relied on the answer to a similar question posed to Ben Adret and claimed that no one had ever considered emending Torah texts on the authority of Midrashim. The question to Ben Adret does show that someone had considered making such changes, but the answer established the halakhic precedent that Ibn Zimra used in order to limit such changes to cases where the Talmud associated a law with a particular spelling; the authority for this position was based on the account in Soferim. Since the authority of the masoretic literature was not an issue, at least as the question to Ibn Zimra is now formulated, we must conclude that Ibn Zimra's discussion of the Masorah derived from Ben Adret's. The end of his answer, which summarizes the issue for the reader, also avoids the question of the Masorah's authority. In any case, Ibn Zimra concurred with Ben Adret about not emending Torah texts in such circumstances, but this statement did not exhaust his treatment.

References to and summaries of this responsum appear in numerous halakhic works, and the manner in which Rabbi Hayyim David Joseph Azulai (1724–1806) has presented it in his *LeDavid Emet*, a compendium of laws about Torah scrolls, is interesting in its own right. Part of Azulai's treatment is now translated. The bracketed restoration in (a) is virtually certain, but omission of a key phrase from (b) may suggest unfinished editing or defective copying, from which many other sections of this text also suffer.

> (a) Any plene or defective spelling on which, according to the Talmud, a law is dependent, like *qrnt/qrnwt*, *swkwt/skt*, [and] *wbn 'yn lw*, one should correct the scrolls [presumably according to the spelling suggested by the Talmud].
> (b) But [in a case of] any plene or defective spelling that makes no difference regarding a matter of law, like *'al tira' 'oṯo, pilagšim, wa-'aśimēm, be-yom kalloṯ*, etc., one should not correct the scrolls [presumably to follow the Midrashim, but possibly even the Talmud]. And *ʿaḏ deroš 'aḥiḵa 'oto*, which, according to the Midrash [i.e., the Zohar], is plene [i.e., *'wtw*], even though it is a law from the Gemara, seems to be the opposite. And one should not correct the scrolls according to Midrashim but according to the majority of Torah scrolls. . . .[94]

Given Azulai's rigor in seeking a letter-perfect text, it is unreasonable to assume that he intended to accept many deviant spellings, but this position is not clear from the wording here. Particularly curious is this mystical writer's location in the Gemara of what Ibn Zimra has carefully identified as a notion from the Zohar opposed by the Gemara. Perhaps this error derives from a phrase in Jacob Al-Gazi's *Emet LeYa'aqov*, from which Azulai took much of his presentation. Though there is no error there, in one place Al-Gazi referred to the claim that the extra *waw* in *'wtw* was made *'al pi d-r-z-l* [*derašat razal*], "according to the exposition of the rabbis of blessed memory"; Azulai perhaps took this as talmudic.

The fact that Ibn Zimra reported going and personally fixing the scrolls shows that this issue was a local matter under his personal jurisdiction. In describing his actions, he noted that he restored the three emended scrolls to their original state, which was also that of the other scrolls. In other words, the original presumption of correctness was complemented by what was essentially the testimony of the other scrolls. Tradition and testimony based on a majority of (local?) scrolls were followed; changes based on midrashic exposition or on the Masorah were eschewed.

A Formal Reinterpretation of Ben Adret's Position

Many later rabbinic leaders discussed Ben Adret's responsum and his differentiation between spellings of halakhic and nonhalakhic importance, and most agreed with the distinction. One who did not was Rabbi Joseph David of Salonika. In his *Beit David*, he expressed upset at the seemingly cavalier way in which some (mostly Ashkenazi) authorities dismissed the entire enterprise of determining the precise way to produce a correct Torah scroll; and while he acknowledged the existence of some difficulties, he rejected out of hand the notion that all scrolls contained errors and that they no longer possessed a presumption of accuracy.[95]

He then cited Ben Adret's responsum as presented by Ibn Zimra in Responsum A and qualified it by suggesting that the discussion that rejected the Masorah was to be applied only to cases in which no binding halakhic determination had been made. In cases where one had been made, obviously one is bound by them. Moreover, he added, all spellings, even in nonhalakhic contexts, are halakhically significant for the way one writes a Torah scroll; Ben Adret's distinction is therefore unfounded.

> So, even though one should not correct the scrolls (*sefarim*) according to the Masorah and the aggadic Midrashim, because we assume the [masoretic] sages disagreed with each other in their [different] locales, if in [even] one place there is a difference between the scrolls themselves—whether plene or defective, and similar things—we must correct the minority according to the majority of that locale. And we do not say, let each remain as it is, defective or plene, and assume that each was written according to some authority. And if so, why should we not say so as well about the division of paragraphs, that everywhere one should correct the minority according to the majority? All the more so, since it appears that the Rashba [i.e., Ben Adret], of blessed memory, did not say to follow the majority before us other than where we have not found halakhic authorities who decided the matter.
>
> But where we have found great authorities who checked very carefully (*diqdequ u-badequ*) and decided [that a word should be written] like a particular text, surely one should follow them, even against the majority before us. And for this too there is a clear biblical authority, "according to the Torah that they teach you"

> [Deut. 17:11]. All the more so when it is against the majority and against the authorities who have ruled that one should not say, "Let us leave it as it is written and not correct it at all, because we assume that the scribe wrote it according to some great rabbi."[96]

He discussed Ben Adret's suggestion to correct the "minority," and he continued by arguing that there is no real distinction to be made between biblical words with whose spellings laws are associated and words subjected to some nonhalakhic exposition, because, in the final analysis, any misspelled word will invalidate the Torah scroll. "And how can we sustain a Torah scroll that is ritually invalid according to our Talmud, which is primary?" (Note how different this is from Sofer's position, disussed earlier in this chapter.)

Other writers attempted to differentiate between errors and variations in certain and uncertain appearances of *aleph*, *heh*, *waw*, and *yod*; between their use to represent root letters and vowels; between words that naturally would be read as they should have been written and those that would not; between spellings whose meanings would differ from the norm and those that would not; even between those spellings preserved anonymously and those attributed to individual rabbis, in order to know which exposition on spelling reflected an individual's opinion and which was accepted by the Gemara. Each distinction carries with it certain leniencies and strictures, but all allow for some leeway from the strict ruling that believed letter-perfect accuracy to be attainable and that required it for a Torah scroll used in public reading.

A Suggestive but Opaque Conclusion to Ibn Zimra's Responsum

The concluding sentence of A.7 invites speculation. Ibn Zimra composed thousands of responsa, and clear stylistic patterns may be observed throughout them. Many, particularly the longer ones, conclude with a summary statement or a paragraph that is introduced with the Aramaic phrase *kelala de-milta*, "the summary of the matter is." In addition, hundreds are sealed with the Hebrew phrase meaning "And I have written what appears [correct] according to my humble opinion," or a close equivalent. In some places, the inclusion of this addition in many consecutive responsa may mark groups of collections of texts (*quntresim*) that may have suffered collective histories of scribal transmission and were subsequently collected into the eight published volumes. Ibn Zimra's present statement, "And I have relied on Him, be He blessed, because He knows the secrets of the heart" (*ta'alumot leb*), is quite unusual. This relatively early responsum may have been penned before the full development of the stylistic patterns noted earlier, or the conclusion may signal a special message to those familiar with Ibn Zimra's style and teachings.

One of the few parallels to this cryptic ending appears in III, no. 1029, which concludes, "and this makes sense to us; and blessed is the One who knows the truth." There is no obvious connection between the contents, sources, or analytical methods of these two responsa, and the parallel offers no help in understanding Ibn Zimra's intention. Closer to the usage here is II, no. 796, the first paragraph of which ends "for He knows the secrets of my heart (*ta'alumot libbi*) to seek the truth," the conclusion to the brief, harsh, poetic rejection of the Karaites as members of the community that preceeds his lengthy discussion of this matter. The term also occurs in II, no. 694, where he refers to God as *yoḏea' ta'alumoṯ*.

The presentation in II, no. 623, which deals with the reasons for donning Tefillin in a particular way, includes: "I have another reason, and I cannot explain it [in writing]. And the smart [reader] will understand it from my words." This statement seems to imply that Ibn Zimra wished to hint at a mystical explanation of his legal position but felt it inappropriate to put such esoteric matters in his answer. Should a similar preference underlie the statement with which he ended this responsum, one could posit that he was drawn to the spelling indicated by the Zohar but that he felt bound by the Gemara and earlier halakhic authorities and merely hinted at his frustration in this manner. Another example of his concealing some of his thoughts, again mystical matters, appears in II, no. 696. It may not be accidental that these occur in close proximity, in what once probably was a single notebook.

We have seen that many rabbinic writers were troubled to explain minor spelling inconsistencies between some words found in traditional Torah scrolls and various rabbinic witnesses to them. One of these persons was the Spanish rabbinic leader Solomon Ben Adret, who ranked such witnesses in the thirteenth century. David Ibn Zimra, himself of Spanish descent but working in sixteenth-century Egypt, followed Ben Adret's lead in affirming that, in cases of inconsistent evidence, scrolls should be corrected to follow a majority of scrolls. Halakhah-related expositions in the Babylonian Talmud that depended on spellings also could serve as a model for correcting scrolls, but under no circumstances could scrolls be corrected on the authority of midrashic witnesses or evidence from the Masorah.

Ibn Zimra's Responsum B: The Masorah and Fixing the Torah Text

> And I will not mention the explanations of the masters of the Masoret—why this [word] is spelled plene and that is defective—because all their explanations are like derash. . . . Their explanations are good only for children.
>
> Abraham Ibn Ezra (1089–1164)
> Introduction to Torah Commentary

> Moreover, we possess a mystical tradition that the entire Torah consists of the names of the Holy One, Blessed Be He.
>
> Nahmanides (1194–1270)
> Introduction to Torah Commentary

Introduction to Ibn Zimra's Responsum B

Though Responsum B shares much with Responsum A, it differs in both scope and focus. Its question, also paraphrased by Ibn Zimra, is shorter, but the answer is significantly longer and seemingly motivated more by ideological considerations than by practical ones. The questioner (who, like the first, remains anonymous) was concerned about a series of well-known problems relating to the accuracy of the Bible text and the exact nature, source, and authority of the accompanying talmudic discussions and masoretic notes.

A fair number of Christian and Muslim critics of the Jewish transmission of Scripture and a few respected rabbinic Bible interpreters who understood the tradition to include some equivocal readings had suggested that the rabbinic and masoretic traditions bore witness to a series of early changes in the text or to doubts about its accuracy. The apparently learned author of this question did some reading of these sources on his own—he may have summarized them in the question, prompting Ibn Zimra's paraphrase—and then turned to the rabbi to find out what he thought.

The Query: What Are the Origin and the Authority of the Masorah?

[Question:][1]
[1] You have requested that I tell you, in brief, my opinion on the matter of *Miqra' Soferim*, and *'Iṭṭur Soferim*, and *Keṯiḇ We-La' Qere*, and *Qere We-La' Keṯiḇ*, and *Keṯiḇ Haḵi u-Qere Haḵi*, because it appears, heaven forbid, that there is a doubt about the [accuracy of the] text (*keṯaḇ*) in our possession [i.e.,] if it was incorrect and they corrected it. And you have examined what the early authorities have written on the subject, but you are dissatisfied [with their explanations].

Because of their technical nature, the five "editorial" terms mentioned in the question, two in Hebrew and three in Aramaic, are set forth in transliterated form throughout the translation and explained shortly. At least the first four derive from a passage in BT Ned. 37b–38a, most of which is cited and discussed as part of the answer.

The ambiguous antecedent of "they corrected it" refers to the *soferim*, the pre-mishnaic Scribes, who, according to BT Qid. 30a, were so called because "they used to count all of the letters in the Torah." On the other hand, PT Sheq. 5:1 attributes their title to the fact that they grouped laws in numerical rubrics. It is not clear if the phenomena whose designations do not contain the word *soferim* should be associated with them as well, but that seems to be the assumption underlying Ibn Zimra's statement in paragraph 10.

The Reply: They Are "Halakhah to Moses from Sinai"

Ibn Zimra begins his response by citing the primary talmudic passage that deals with the question; he then moves to other considerations.

[2] You should know that all the items that appear to you to be changes[2] are Halakhah to Moses from Sinai,[3] as we learn in the chapter [entitled] "There Is No Difference Between One Who Vows. . ." [BT Ned. 37b]:

A. Said Rabbi Isaac: *Miqra' Soferim*, and *Iṭṭur Soferim*, and *Qere We-La'* Keṯiḇ, and *Keṯiḇ We-La' Qere* are Halakhah to Moses from Sinai.

B. *Miqra' Soferim*:
1. *'rṣ*, "land";
2. *šmym*, "sky";
3. *mṣrym*, "Egypt."

C. *Iṭṭur Soferim*:
1. *'aḥar ta'aḇoru*, "[eat,] afterwards travel on" [Gen. 18:5];
2. *'aḥar tēlēḵ*, "[let the girl stay. . . ,] afterwards she can go" [Gen. 24:55];
3. *'aḥar tē'asēf*, "[avenge. . . ,] afterwards you will die" [Num. 31:2];
4. *qiddemu šarim 'aḥar nogenim*, "the singers came first, afterwards the players" [Ps. 68:26];
5. *ṣiḏqaṯeḵa ke-harere 'ēl*, "your goodness is like a high mountain, [your justice is like the great deep]" [Ps. 36:7].

D. *Qere We-La' Keṯiḇ*:
1. *perat* of *be-leḵto* [i.e., "Euphrates" associated with the word "in his going"] [2 Sam. 8:3];

2. *'iš* of *ka-'ašer yiš'al 'iš* [i.e., "man" associated with the phrase "as a man asks"] [2 Sam. 16:23];
3. *ba'im* of *nibneta* [i.e., "come" associated with the word "let us build"] [Jer. 31:37];
4. *lah* of *peleṭa* [i.e., "of her" associated with the word "remnant"] [Jer. 50:29];
5. *'et* of *hugged huggad li* [i.e., *'et* associated with the phrase "it was told to me"] [Ruth 2:11];[4]
6. *'ēlai* of *ha-goren* [i.e., "to me" associated with the word "the threshing floor"] [Ruth 3:5];[5]
7. *'ēlai* of *ha-śe'orim* [i.e., "to me" associated with the word "the barley"] [Ruth 3:17].

E. *Ketib* We-*La' Qere*:

1. *n'* of *yislaḥ* [i.e., "please" associated with the word "may he forgive"] [2 Kings 5:18];
2. *z't* of *ha-miṣwa* ["this" (read: "and," Heb. *w't*) associated with the word "the commandment"];[6]
3. *ydrwk* of *ha-dorēk* [i.e., "he will draw" associated with the word "the archer"] [Jer. 51:3];[7]
4. *ḥmš* of [*u-*]*fe'at negeb* [i.e., "five" associated with the phrase "southern direction"] [Ezek. 48:16];
5. *'m* of *ki go'ēl* [i.e., "if" associated with the phrase "though a redeemer"] [Ruth 3:12].[8]

And even though our Talmud does not agree with the Masorah (not[9] that the Masorah adds or detracts), in any case, all agree that all of these [cases] are Halakhah to Moses from Sinai.[10]

This talmudic passage appears to contain at least two layers. Rabbi Isaac's statement lists the four terms, two in Hebrew and two in Aramaic, that are claimed to be of Sinaitic origin; there follow from three to seven examples of each, the Hebrew terms explained in Hebrew and the Aramaic ones in Aramaic. As preserved in BT Ned. 37b–38a, the passage concludes with a sixth unit (F), "These are written but not read," which describes only E. It is possible that the initial statement (A) was independent of the subsequent explanatory sections (B–E), which then would contain the earliest known attempt to explicate Rabbi Isaac's statement, not an integral part of it; but as we have it, the talmudic text contains a host of uncertainties. Problems in decoding it and in identifying the biblical references in standard masoretic Bibles have led many traditional commentators to propose significant emendations in the talmudic text, and numerous important variants from manuscripts and medieval commentaries have been collected.[11]

Ibn Zimra's answer affirmed that all of the alleged changes are classified as "Halakhah to Moses from Sinai," a well-known category of laws often considered to be equal in age and authority to the Torah itself. He based this claim on a key passage from the Babylonian Talmud that clearly said this about some of the terms in question, but he extended the category to include others not found there. He also discussed, as we shall see, why some of these phenomena are associated with the relatively late Scribes, if they derive from Mosaic times.

It is clear that the Babylonian Talmud and the Masorah disagree on the contents of the lists, as Ibn Zimra said. Less clear is whether they concur in claiming that all four groups are Halakhah to Moses at Sinai (as Ibn Zimra also said they do), because the masoretic notes often do not attribute this information to any source. Even so, some writers associated all of the Masorah with Sinai, as is seen, for example, in the collection of sources cited in the introduction to Y. S. Norzi's *Minhat Shai* (translated in chapter 1). We now turn to the details of this talmudic passage.

Miqra' Soferim: *Miqra' Soferim* refers to the tradition associated with the Scribes (*soferim*) of vocalizing or "reading" (*miqra'*) certain words in a particular way. Although I. Yeivin has correctly observed that unequivocal explanation of the term is impossible,[12] some clarification can be attempted. The examples given by the Talmud (*'ereṣ, šamayim*, and *miṣrayim*) suggest that nouns of location are intended, but most interpreters assume that a broader type of observation is involved and that the three words do not exhaustively exemplify the range of possibilities. The most common explanation takes them to be pausal forms—*'ereṣ* > *'āreṣ, šamayim* > *šamāyim*, and *miṣrayim* > *miṣrāyim* (and many Talmud manuscripts actually contain the double phrases, even vocalization that suggests or supports these readings)—and that possibility casts doubt on the limitation to nouns of location, for verbs and other parts of speech also occur in pausal form.

Perhaps we should interpret the examples in relation to the locative forms *'arṣa, šamayma*, and *miṣrayma*. Numerous ancient witnesses demonstrate that postformative vowels were appended to place names (e.g., *Sodoma* in the Septuagint for Sodom, Gen. 13:10, 19:24, and 29:22), and a certain amount of interchange between forms such as *šm* and *šmh* was routine. The rabbis noted that often postformative *heh* was used in biblical texts in place of the preposition *'el*, "to" (BT Yev. 13b, PT Yev. 1:6, and Gen. Rab. 50, 3),[13] perhaps to limit the use of final *-a* to only these cases. PT Meg. 1:9, which claims that the men of Jerusalem used to write Jerusalem as *yrwšlymh* (note the similarity to the Greek form, *Hierosolyma*) and which is glossed by the Aramaic addition claiming this practice also applied to writing *tēman* as *tymnh* and *ṣafon* as *ṣpwnh*, may also be taken to suggest that the reading of other biblical texts also varied in this way. Compare Kutscher's data on *lhmh*, which often appears in the Dead Sea Scrolls in place of biblical *lhm*, and on similar phenomena.[14]

While it cannot be proved conclusively that all these examples reflect the same phenomenon, if they do, the last two suggest something much broader than the interchange of regular and locative forms, possibly the presence of a postformative vowel or partial vowel. In this context, midrashic expositions in the Babylonian Talmud that divide perfect verbs in the second-person masculine plural, such as *u-ḵeṯaḇetam* (Deut. 6:9), into two words, such as *keṯiḇa tamma* (Men. 34a, Shab. 103b, and Hul. 109b), take on great potential importance, because they may be additional evidence for the late preservation of a final vowel, particularly after final *mem* or *nun*, which is found in most of the examples listed earlier. Note also *wa-'aḇaḏetem*, interpreted as *'aḇoḏa tamma* (Yom. 24a); *u-leqaḥtem*, taken as *leqiḥa tamma* (Suk. 34b, 37a, Men. 27a, and *Tanhuma, Emor* no. 18); also *u-qešartam* (Men. 35b, PT Meg. 1:9 [71d]), and even *miḵtam*, divided into *makkaṯo tamma* (Sot. 10b). These must be contrasted with the absence of such expositions from the tannaitic midrashim and with two other examples that use the masculine form *tam*, such as *we-limmaḏtem* (Deut. 11:19), explained *še-yehe limmuḏeḵa tam* (Ber. 15b), and *we-samtem* (Deut.

11:18), taken as *sam tam* (Qid. 30b).[15] Seen in this context, *Miqra' Soferim* could be the attempt by the Scribes to establish the correct vocalization of the words in question without the final vowel and to retain it only in pausal forms and a few other isolated cases.

Iṭṭur Soferim: Several explanations of the term *Iṭṭur Soferim* are presented by Ibn Zimra in B.2 and B.3, the most popular today being "deletions of the Scribes." Nedarim lists five cases, four of which are readings *'aḥar/we-'aḥar*, in which the shorter form is preferred. Some masoretic lists specify the existence in the Bible of four or five such cases, but the Talmud contains no such stipulation.[16] Textual variants of prefixed *waw* are relatively common and, unless the phenomenon was originally linked to *'aḥar* or to these five cases, it is impossible to determine what its total range of incidence might be.

Qere We-La' Ketib and Ketib We-La' Qere: *Qere We-La' Ketib*, "read but not written," and *Ketib We-La' Qere*, "written but not read," are two limited groups of variants. The latter refers to words written in the Bible but not vocalized by the masoretes and omitted during a public reading; the former, to words not found in the written text but read aloud, now from marginal masoretic notes.[17] The Talmud here lists seven examples of *Qere We-La' Ketib* and five of *Ketib We-La' Qere*. The addition of "these are written but not read" at the end of the list may suggest that, at least for the Babylonian Talmud, these five are the limits of this phenomenon, but various masoretic sources differ widely in their lists.

Some writers saw these differences as evidence that the Talmud contains a mere sample of the places in which the phenomenon occurs, while others, including Ibn Zimra (end of paragraph 2), understood the lists to be exhaustive from each writer's perspective but not identical. Such inconsistency undermines the authority of this masoretic teaching, but, as he did with other debated points of law identified as Halakhah to Moses from Sinai, Ibn Zimra was quick to point out that these differences in detail do not alter their claim to that status.[18]

Ibn Zimra quoted the passage from Nedarim extensively, primarily to prove that all these terms actually describe phenomena classified as Halakhah to Moses from Sinai even when they occur in post-Mosaic books. He also insisted that the Masorah and the Talmud, though not agreeing on all the details in the lists, nonetheless do agree on their antiquity and authority. He continued by explaining that, even though these phenomena are associated with the *soferim*, one should not err by thinking that these pretannaitic Jewish leaders invented them. After some detailed discussion of specific examples, he concludes this section by observing that even examples of these phenomena found in post-Mosaic books such as Ruth and Psalms are also Halakhah to Moses from Sinai.

The observation that there are differences of opinion in matters classified as Halakhah to Moses from Sinai is significant, for it rejects Maimonides' claim that laws of this type are not disputed (Introduction to *Seder Zera'im*).[19] Perhaps Ibn Zimra was trying to uphold this position by minimizing the significance of the differences—other rabbis had disagreed with Maimonides on this point long before—but any intersections of Maimonidean thinking and this responsum that I have examined highlight Ibn Zimra's independence from the teachings of his Egyptian predecessor. Ibn Zimra's involvement with Maimonides' halakhic rulings, found in many comments throughout his writings, even in formal collections of glosses to parts of the *Mishneh Torah*, highlights the presence of Maimonides in his thinking, but their overall outlooks on the world were remarkably different.[20]

Ibn Zimra continues:

> [3] And if you ask, why, if they are all Halakhah to Moses from Sinai, do we call them *Miqra' Soferim*, or *Tiqqun Soferim*, or *Iṭṭur Soferim* [attributing them, as it were, to the Scribes, I would answer that] it is not correct to say that these [phenomena] were associated with the Scribes [merely] because they received them by uninterrupted transmission; for, in all cases of Halakhah to Moses from Sinai, the Scribes, who are the sages, similarly received by uninterrupted tradition that the matter is Halakhah to Moses from Sinai. Rather, the correct explanation is that all of these cases are Halakhah to Moses from Sinai, but the Scribes showed through careful analysis that it would be proper for us to read or to correct Scripture in this manner, even if it were not Halakhah to Moses from Sinai.

The precise definition of *halaḵa le-moše mi-sinai* has been a matter of extensive discussion and debate among rabbinic writers since talmudic times, and no consensus has emerged on whether the term means that the laws literally were received by Moses at Sinai (the most popular view) or that they are merely very old, as if given to him there, or that some other quality should be ascribed to them. Also unresolved is the theoretical relationship between these laws and the Bible, that is, whether they are or are not derived from its text, hinted at in it, associated with it, or totally independent of it. The relationship between this category of traditional laws and others also remains in dispute, particularly since its very name suggests that others were not Sinaitic or at least differ in some formal respect.

For the moment, Ibn Zimra was occupied with a different dimension of the problem, explaining the inherent contradiction between the relatively late dating of the phenomenon suggested by their being attributed to the Scribes and the early dating seemingly implied by the talmudic statement that he and others took to mean they were really given to Moses. For this purpose, it was expedient to equate the Scribes with the somewhat later sages and to group these and other laws together; *diḇrē soferim*, "words of the Scribes," is, after all, a common rabbinic designation for rabbinic laws. From Ibn Zimra's historical and halakhic vantage point, both groups were postbiblical and therefore of approximately similar halakhic weight.

Most rabbinic sources differentiate between two periods of history, texts, and classes of halakhic authority—biblical and rabbinic—but many acknowledge the contribution of an intermediate period, that of the Scribes. Ibn Zimra has accepted the two-part division, associating the Scribes with the rabbinic period. He could have responded differently, but this passage and the conclusion of B.4 reflect his very conservative bent and resemble Ben Adret's explanation of *Tiqqunē Soferim*:

> . . . but rather they [the Scribes] analyzed and found, according to the context of each of these verses, that the primary intention was not as appears from what is written in the book but rather is a different intention, and it [the text] should not have written this but rather the other. And they called these [words] *Tiqqune Soferim*, "corrections of the Scribes," only because they [the Scribes] analyzed and explained that they are euphemisms (*kinnuyim*).[21]

Tiqqune Soferim: With the introduction of *Tiqqune Soferim*, Ibn Zimra has gone beyond the lists of terms mentioned in the paraphrase of the question and in the Talmud (see B.8 for another example). *Tiqqune Soferim* refers to a specific group of biblical passages (the number ranging from seven to eighteen in different lists), designated by some midrashic and masoretic sources as "Corrections of the Scribes." Various explanations focused on the precise definition of "corrections" and "scribes" and attributed these "corrections" to the authors of the biblical books, to Ezra, to the postbiblical but prerabbinic Scribes, and to the rabbis themselves. Some writers felt this term to be a midrashic conceit, not evidence for altering the text; others disagreed. Regardless of any medieval or modern consensus, the term easily lent itself to the claim that the postbiblical sages tampered with the Bible, and it served as a major piece of evidence in anti-Jewish criticism of its unfaithful transmission, discussed later.[22]

In addition, the term *tiqqunē soferim* sometimes is used to describe other minor scribal conventions, such as replacing regular letters with larger or smaller forms, placing dots over specific letters, and beginning six predetermined columns with the six letters *b-y-h š-m-w*.[23] It also includes the poetic layout of words and lines in Exodus 15 and Deuteronomy 32 and the proper placement of open and closed paragraph divisions.[24] This usage is not reflected in the documents discussed here, but the fact that both groups of phenomena were generally considered Halakhah to Moses from Sinai is perhaps noteworthy. Notions associated with one group possibly were transferred to the other because of the shared ambiguity of their labels, or the label may have been applied to a broader range of phenomena because all of them were believed to be equally ancient.

In the context of the attacks just referred to, one can readily understand Ibn Zimra's addition of *Tiqqune Soferim* to the list of terms and its association with *Iṭṭurei Soferim*, which could similarly be taken as evidence of inaccurate textual transmission. *Miqra' Soferim* is less essential to his argument, since it refers to minor changes in vocalization, not in spelling. But the use of *Soferim* in all three terms is the uniting factor, and the presence of *Miqra' Soferim* in the prooftext from Nedarim required its retention here, even if the accusations of tampering with the text had been directed primarily at the other two devices.

By way of contrast, in *Sefer HaZikkaron* to Gen. 18:22, Abraham Baqrat argued that the absence of *Tiqqune Soferim* from Ned. 37b substantiates the assumption that this masoretic phenomenon is not a tradition handed down from Sinai to correct the text. It is, rather, an internal biblical matter, presumably always written this way in the Torah but thought by the Scribes to contain important nuances that avoided disrespectful statements about God. This is similar to the notion of *kinna ha-katub*, used by other texts to describe some of these phenomena.[25]

Solomon Ben Adret, in his commentary on the talmudic narratives, and Joseph Albo, fifteenth-century author of *Sefer HaIqqarim*, also challenged the Christian interpretation of the *Tiqqune Soferim* as early forgeries. They reasoned that no one falsifies a text and then publicizes what he has done.[26] In this vein, Ibn Zimra continues:

> [4] So, from now on, wherever you find *Miqra' Soferim* or *Tiqqun Soferim*, or *Iṭṭur Soferim*, let it not occur to you, heaven forbid, that the thing was lacking and they

> corrected it; for if you do not explain [it] this [way, as I have,] there is room for our adversaries to say [about every single matter], "Here the Scribes changed the text," as they accuse us daily. But the basic principle is that everything is Halakhah to Moses from Sinai, that this is how it is. But the Scribes determined that one [word] should be this way and another that way, even if not said [by rabbinic teaching] to be Halakhah to Moses from Sinai.

The allegations that the Jews had failed to transmit the Bible text correctly and had intentionally tampered with it were widespread and well developed centuries before the time of Ibn Zimra. Particularly noteworthy in this respect are the Qur'an itself, Ibn Hazam (died ca. 1064), the former Christian Ali at-Tabari (died 1085), and the former Jew Samau'al ibn Yahya al-Maghribi (twelfth century), but many others contributed to the effort.[27] Al-Maghribi claimed that the original Torah had been lost and replaced by one composed by Ezra, a notion similar to Qirqisani's idea, referred to earlier.[28] Thus far it has been impossible to identify Ibn Zimra's specific adversaries, but his living in Egypt suggests that Muslims were intended, and it is likely that their arguments were based on some of these earlier ones.

Despite their sharing a proclivity for intensive preaching, harsh public debate, composition of anti-Jewish polemical tractates, and general derision of many aspects of Jewish life, major differences existed between the responses of Muslims and Christians to the Hebrew Bible. Muslim criticisms of the rabbis' failure to preserve the scriptural text with maximum accuracy challenged the integrity of all Jews, as well as that of the Bible itself, and contrasted sharply with their own (unjustifiable) claims for a letter-perfect Qur'an text. But the Jews were neither a military nor a political threat to the Muslims, and while the Qur'an and later traditions sometimes disapproved of Jewish scriptures and contradicted them, in many periods Muslims tolerated the Jews and even extensively studied their Bible and related traditions.[29] On the other hand, because Christians had a much greater investment in the Bible, they were ultimately more respectful of it, but their own version of its text, accompanied by specifically Christian interpretations and applications, led to attacks of a very different nature. Moreover, the rabbinic sources that seemed to attribute these changes to the Scribes complemented New Testament criticisms of this same group. Together these factors were a recipe for non-Jewish criticism and Jewish defensiveness.[30]

Ibn Zimra next turns to Rashi's comment on the passage in Nedarim:

> [5] And now what Rashi, of blessed memory, wrote is understood [namely,] "and their reasons are not explained." In all cases of Halakhah to Moses from Sinai, is the reason not explained? Rather, he meant that the reason by which the Scribes showed through careful analysis that this is how it should be [even without regard to the notion of Halakhah to Moses from Sinai] is not specified.

In the comment in question, after a series of brief notes on some of the verses listed in the talmudic examples of *Miqra' Soferim*, *Iṭṭur Soferim*, *Qere We-La' Ketib*, and *Ketib We-La' Qere*, Rashi added "and their reason is not explained." This might be taken as a comment on the last example(s) or term(s), or on the four specific items mentioned in the Gemara, but Ibn Zimra preferred to see it as a note on the entire list, referring to the overall category of Halakhah to Moses at Sinai. Unless one were to postulate the presence of the term *Tiqqune Soferim* in this talmudic passage (for which I have found no evidence), Rashi's statement cannot apply to it, yet Ibn Zimra has included it anyway. He continued by claiming that expressions including the term *soferim* should not be attributed to them. These things are all old traditions merely associated with the Scribes and validated but not created by them. To claim otherwise would play into the hands of the enemies of the Jewish people, who constantly accuse them of textual improprieties.

> [6] Now, I have carefully checked all of these cases of *Ketib We-La' Qere* and *Qere We-La' Ketib* that the Talmud cites; not one of them is found in the Torah, [they occur] only in the Prophets and Hagiographa. And even though some texts read *zo't de-ha-miṣwa* [in B.2E2], which seems to be in *Parashat VaEthanan*, this is not so, for our texts (*sefarim*) do not read that way; but the correct wording is *w't* [not *z't*] *de-ha-miṣwa*, and it is in Jeremiah.

This passage contains important details about textual transmission. Specifically, Ibn Zimra noted that none of the instances where the text contains a written word that, according to the talmudic tradition, is not read, or where a word is read in the text but not written, appears in the Torah. To be sure, a long-standing problem, already noted, hampers the identification of one example. Ibn Zimra's statement is clear enough: the Talmud's reference to a word in relation to *ha-miṣwa* is in Jeremiah, not in Deuteronomy. Unfortunately, the printed text reads *z't de-ha-miṣwa* twice and therefore does not contain the correct citation. While this phrase can refer to Deut. 6:1 (*we-zo't ha-miṣwa*), it cannot refer to any verse in Jeremiah. Many writers have suggested that the correct reference is *w't*, not the similarly looking *z't*, which occurs in some texts with *ha-miṣwa* in Jer. 32:11 (cf. Norzi, ad loc.).

Though he never actually said so (probably to avoid the appearance of conceding ground in the argument), Ibn Zimra's goal in this paragraph seems to be to establish a second line of defense. Even if one could prove that the *Ketib We-La' Qere* and *Qere We-La' Ketib* traditions were evidence of a textual problem, at least the Torah, the holiest portion of the Bible, would be spared the taint of inaccuracy, because it contains no examples of either phenomenon. He then goes on to provide a rationale for such *Qere- u-Ketib* variations.

> [7] But even so, we need a reason, for we say that the text is written *yšglnh*, but is read *yiškabena* [e.g., Deut. 28:30], and is written *wb'pwlym*, but is read *[u]-ba-tehorim* [Deut. 28:27]. If the written text is primary, then he [i.e., the Torah reader] reads a word from memory [which is prohibited], but if the [oral] reading is primary, the Torah scroll is missing a word and is invalid for ritual use. Moreover, there are several cases of *Qere u-Ketib* in the Torah, like *n'r/n'rh* [Deut. 22:33, etc.], *skt/swkwt* [sic] [Lev. 23:42–43],[31] and many like these. In all cases, you must say that it is Halakhah to Moses from Sinai that they are written one way and read another.

This is an expansion of the question posed to Ben Adret, toward which Ibn Zimra is moving (cf. B.10, end). Let us examine the details.

b'pwlym/ba-tehorim: The reading *ba-tehorim*, "hemorrhoids," is substituted for *b'pwlym* in Deut. 28:27, 1 Sam. 5:6, 5:9, 5:12, and 6:4–5, and *yiškabena*, "will be raped," is substituted for *yšglnh* in Deut. 28:30, Is. 13:16, Jer. 3:2, and Zech. 14:2; cf. BT Meg. 24a. Apparently both groups of substitutions were motivated by the desire to eliminate offensive synonyms.

n'r/n'rh: The word *n'r* refers to females some eighteen times in the Torah (in Genesis 24 and 34 and in Deuteronomy 22); *n'rh*, Deut. 22:19, is the one exception. Normally the word is written *n'r* but vocalized *na'ara*. About two dozen cases of the consonantal spelling *n'rh* are found, mostly in Judges, Kings, Ruth, and Esther; note, however, the discussion in *Minhat Shai* to Deut. 22:19. A well-documented rabbinic tradition distinguishes between the ages of the females designated by *n'r* versus *n'rh*.[32]

Turning back to the argument, we see that, at first glance, Ibn Zimra's inclusion of *Ketib Haki u-Qere Haki*, "written this way, but read that way," seems to be a conscious attempt to slip this—the largest single group of official changes in the Bible text—into the passage in Nedarim, despite the absence of any textual evidence to support its presence there. Actually the situation is more complex. Although all *Qere u-Ketib* variants are treated alike by the halakhah (the text contains the *Ketib* while the *Qere* is substituted during a public reading), the masoretic literature often categorized them according to more specific orthographic details. Thus, for example, *Okhlah VeOkhlah* listed changes of one letter as *Ketib We-La' Qere* or *Qere We-La' Ketib*: five cases of *mem* read at the end of a word but not written (no. 143), fifty-six cases of *yod* read in the middle of a word but not written (no. 112), twelve cases of Aleph written at the end of a word but not read (no. 87), and so on. *Okhlah VeOkhlah* used the term *Ketib Haki u-Qere Haki* for interchanges, not additions or deletions—for example, two words read as one (no. 83), final *aleph* read as *waw* (no. 88), *heth* read as *heh* (no. 107). Soferim 9:8 also described *b'pwlym* (Deut. 28:27), read as *batehorim*, and *tšglnh* (Is. 13:16), read as *tiškabena*, and other cases, as *'ēlu debarim ketubim we-lo' niqra'im*, "words written but not read."[33]

Perhaps the person who asked the question used this terminology in the standard way, but Ibn Zimra, who based his response on the Babylonian Talmud, was forced to use the more limited definitions of *Ketib We-La' Qere* and *Qere We-La' Ketib* that appear in Nedarim. Nevertheless, since the masoretic usage includes much of what is commonly called *Qere u-Ketib*, it might seem justifiable to assume that Nedarim intended to include the entire *Qere u-Ketib* system and that only one type of example was actually listed, the addition or deletion of full words, but not the substitution of one full word for another. Indeed, this assumption is the justification for many of the efforts to impute to Nedarim the view that all of these types of masoretic notations are Sinaitic, though this seems not to be its intention.

Despite his belief that the tradition always contained these double texts, Ibn Zimra still wanted to defend their legal rationale. In short, they must be from Sinai, or anyone who would alter the reading to accommodate them would be in violation of the prescription to read it as given. This approach to determining early historical fact by reliance on what laws, sometimes even significantly later laws, do or do not permit, appears in many talmudic passages, including BT Shab. 104a, San. 21b, and Meg. 2b.

Moderns may assume that the lists in talmudic units B–F (B–E appear earlier in paragraph 2) were really a gloss to Rabbi Isaac's statement, but Ibn Zimra did not, as evidenced by his attributing them to Rabbi Isaac himself (paragraph 8). Even so, and even if we apply *Okhlah VeOkhlah*'s broader operative definition, the talmudic statement still fails to include the more limited masoretic category of *Ketib Haki u-Qere Haki*, used in the sense of interchanges that require no addition or deletion (reading two words as one, final *aleph* as *waw*, *het* as *heh*, etc.). At least that much has been read into Rabbi Isaac's statement and probably much more. But the assumption that Nedarim intended to include all of this material did not originate with Ibn Zimra. A similar grouping appears in H. Strack's edition of Aaron Ben Asher's *Diqduqei HaTeʿamim*, and many other medieval texts associate much if not all of the masoretic tradition with Sinai.[34]

> [8] And if you ask why Rabbi Isaac nevertheless included only those [examples] that are not in the Torah, one must reply that he included here only complete words that are read but not written or written but not read, while *ʿpwlym* and *yšglnh* are a substitution of one word for another to eliminate improper language. And now how the Torah could write *yšglnh* or *ʿpwlym*, which are improper expressions, is also resolved. Since a halakhah was given to Moses from Sinai to change the words when [the text is] read, it does not matter.[35]

Ibn Zimra's point is that only whole words seemingly added to the text or removed from it were listed. Ultimately there is no difference in authority between occurrences of *Qere u-Ketib̲* that appear in the Torah and those in the rest of the Bible or between this class of readings and the others. Rabbi Isaac listed only full words that were omitted from the text and read publicly or that were written in the text but omitted during public reading, not words to be omitted for which others are substituted. Aside from those listed and the *Qere Perpetuum* of the Tetragramaton, the only other examples of *Qere u-Ketib̲* in the Torah that are complete words are *ʿpwlym*, read *teḥorim*, and *yšglnh*, read *yiškab̲ena*.[36]

Having defined the terms and dealt with a few particularly thorny issues, Ibn Zimra next considers the counterclaims put forth by various unnamed writers whose allegations seem to lie behind the question. Before doing so, he cites (or paraphrases) an early rabbinic statement attributing all post-Mosaic discoveries (of meanings and applications of the Bible) to Sinai. This presentation appears to conflate two talmudic statements. The rabbis often suggested that much of the rabbinic tradition—including the Mishnah, the Tosefta, the Midrashim, and other texts—was received by Moses from God. In this vein, various Palestinian texts (e.g., PT Peah 2:6, Meg. 4:1, Hag. 1:8 and Lev. Rab. 22, 1, on Lev. 17:3) suggest that "even that which a pious and learned student (*talmid̲ wat̲iq*) would teach in the presence of his teacher was already said to Moses at Sinai." In contrast, BT Meg. 19b formulated the idea as "The Holy One, Blessed Be He, showed Moses the details of the Torah and the details of the Scribes (*diqduqē tora we-diqduqē soferim*), and what the Scribes would innovate (*ʿat̲id̲in le-ḥaddēš*)," namely the reading of the scroll of Esther on Purim. Ibn Zimra then turns to the historical question that derives from this claim.

> [9] And should you ask, how can something be Halakhah to Moses from Sinai if found in Ruth, or in the other scrolls, or in Psalms—recited by (*š'mrw*) David—etc., it would be correct to answer that we believe that everything was given on Sinai, even an analysis (*diqduq*) of a law that a learned and pious student (*talmid̲ wat̲iq*) would discover [many centuries later]; everything was said to Moses on Sinai.

Ibn Zimra's emphasis in this paragraph appears to be on the dating of the phenomena: they seem to be post-Mosaic but really are not. A few paragraphs later he alludes to the introduction to Abarbanel's commentary on Jeremiah, which contains an attempt to find some link between individual authors and the frequency of *Qere u-Ketib̲* in specific books.

Though almost a side comment, B.9 contains an important claim about the authorship of the nonpentateuchal biblical books. While *š'mrw dwd wkw-* can be read *še-ameru dawid̲ we-k̲ule*, "that David, etc., recited," the Hebrew seems better taken as *še-amaro dawid̲*, "recited by David," with the "etc." extending the entire clause, not just this last phrase. If so, and if we can assume that *'mr* here refers to composition (elsewhere talmudic passages also use it to mean "translate," not only "speak"), this thinking attributes all of the Psalms to David and thus fails to acknowledge the book's multiple authorship; in fact, it groups several books normally attributed to post-Mosaic authors with the Torah as Sinaitic. In the process, it tacitly rejects the statement in BT B.B. 14b–15a, which teaches that David wrote (*kat̲ab̲*) Psalms with the help of ten elders (one of whom presumably wrote the postexilic Psalm 137, which speaks of sitting by the rivers of Babylon) and therefore assumes at least a partially posthumous editorial role for him. The talmudic notion of multiple authorship of Psalms was adopted by many medieval writers, including Moshe Ibn Chiquitilla (Gikatilla) (eleventh century), Abraham Ibn Ezra (twelfth century), the Tosafists (twelfth to thirteenth century), and David Kimhi (thirteenth century). Extensive medieval discussions of the authorship of the five *megillot̲* also included the generally accepted talmudic attribution to various post-Sinaitic figures, and Rashbam (twelfth century) even allowed for the work of an editorial hand at the beginning and end of Ecclesiastes. Similar observations were made by other medieval writers about most of the books in the Bible, even parts of the Torah.[37]

In the context of his presentation, it matters not at all if the Talmud meant that Psalms was the work of David or of David and ten other people, including at least one postexilic writer; for Ibn Zimra, all of it is Sinaitic—and the claim was not totally new. The rabbinic interpretation of Ex. 24:12 in BT Ber. 5a may teach that the entire Bible was given on Sinai (if *miqra'* is not understood as only the Prophets);[38] PT Meg. 1:5 states that Esther was given on Sinai. Various rabbinic sources assume the Davidic authorship of the entire book of Psalms and, following the statement of Rabbi Meir in BT Pes. 117a, Saadiah attributed the entire book to a revelation to David.[39] Some works that repeated this attribution (e.g., Song of Songs Rabbah 4, 1) recognized the inherent inaccuracy in the statement and therefore offered a justification: David was the best musician, and so the entire book of Psalms was attributed to him. Belief in the Sinaitic origin of the Song of Songs—which seems to preclude Solomonic authorship—was also popular in some circles,[40] but not with all its medieval interpreters. Ibn Zimra's preference to disregard much of the rational discussion in favor of a less historical position reflects his mystical bent. What else, if anything, may have been intended by use of *'amar* in place of the talmudic *kat̲ab̲* remains to be clarified. That the latter term, *kat̲ab̲*, or its plural form, *kat̲eb̲u*, carries a range of usages within that talmudic passage seems certain. Bryna Brodt, one of my graduate students, suggested that a translation of *kat̲ab̲* or *kat̲eb̲u* as "published," rather than "wrote," might fit all of the passages contextually, would avoid some of the difficulties, and could allow for the publishing of some books even before they were completed.

The designation of post-Mosaic books (or their parts) as Sinaitic is possible because, in theory, legal, theological, or philosophical information originating at Sinai could have been transmitted in oral or written form for centuries and recorded in these books. Lacking the intermediate documentation, many readers perceive an unbridgeable gap between the proposed source and production of the final record, but as unlikely as that idea may seem to a contemporary historian, it is an essential part of the rabbinic belief in the antiquity and divine authority of the oral law, and one cannot categorically dismiss its application to the contents of all post-Mosaic scriptural passages. But the issue here is the spelling of the text, not its contents. How, for example, could a *Qere u-Ketib* tradition requiring a change in pronunciation during the public reading of words in postexilic books date from Sinai, if the texts themselves did not? One is thus forced to conclude that the texts, too, originated at Sinai, which is Ibn Zimra's claim, or that the *Qere u-Ketib* system—indeed, the entire category of laws called Halakhah to Moses from Sinai—is not completely Sinaitic, which was the position of the writers he criticized.

Ibn Zimra's argument has been enhanced by an interpretation of the word *diqduq* in the passage paraphrased in B.9. Originally *diqduq* referred to legal analysis; here it is taken as linguistic details, thus allowing him to claim that textual details were Sinaitic. A similar situation applies to the word as it occurs in the list of those who have no share in the world to come "even one who said the entire Torah is from heaven except for this *diqduq*, this *qal wa-ḥomer*, this *gezera šawa* . . . this is an example of '. . . because he has desecrated the word of God' [Num. 15:31]" [BT San. 99a]. Rashi says of the word *diqduq*, "*ḥaserot wi-yeterot*," "defective and plene spellings." According to A. Berliner and A. Harkavy, the word *diqduq* was used for grammatical matters in early Karaite literature and in early medieval Spanish grammatical works;[41] it cannot mean this in the talmudic passage. In fact, despite the existence in the Talmud and Midrashim of scattered observations demonstrating incipient grammatical stirrings, that branch of learning known since medieval times as Hebrew grammar did not yet exist in the talmudic age (although the development of Greek and Latin grammar definitely was long underway by then). But technically the matters under consideration here are halakhic, and if all halakhot were given on Sinai—which is what the Talmud is taken to mean—the extension of *diqduq* is legally consistent, if historically troubling, and not without some measure of irony when examined in the light of some later rabbinic hostility to grammatical knowledge.

The next paragraphs contain citations from several other early rabbinic texts, from a few of Ibn Zimra's medieval predecessors who discussed them, and from interpretations to which Ibn Zimra objected. They include Rashi; Rabbi Nathan of Rome, author of the *Arukh*, an important medieval dictionary of rabbinic Hebrew and Aramaic; and a series of unnamed but well-known exegetes and philosophers. Differences between the spellings attested in the writings of the rabbis and the masoretes are classified as *maḥloqet*, "disagreement," analogous to disagreements found in many other areas of rabbinic law. The next section continues with an attack on those Ibn Zimra believed were undermining the faith.

> [10] The summary of the matter is that you should not believe the words of those who say that confusion (*bilbul*) and errors (*šibbuš*) occurred in the scrolls (*sefarim*),

but rather that all [of these things] were said as Halakhah to Moses from Sinai, as they are written before us today. Do not believe the words of those who say that Ezra the Scribe and the subsequent Scribes corrected the corruption [of the text], heaven forbid, because there was no corruption. Nor [should you believe] the words of those who say that these matters are unclear and the *Qere* is the explanation the sages gave. Do not pay attention to all of these conjectures, but "Be sincere with the Lord your God" [Deut. 18:13] and believe what the rabbis of blessed memory said, that everything is Halakhah to Moses from Sinai. And *Qere u-Ketib̲*, and *Ketib̲ We-La' Qere* [sic], and plene and defective spellings, and *Miqra' Soferim*, and *Tiqqun Soferim*, and *Iṭṭur Soferim*, and *Qere We-La' Ketib̲*, and *Ketib̲ We-La' Qere*—all of them are Halakhah to Moses from Sinai.

And similarly they asked the Rashba, of blessed memory, "How can *b'pwlym* [Deut. 28:27] be read *ba-teḥorim*, or how can *yšglnh* [Deut. 28:30] be read *yiškab̲ena*?" And he answered, "[They are] Halakhah to Moses from Sinai."

Having established his case that there were no variants in the Bible text and having deflected the criticisms of various non-Jews, Ibn Zimra proceeds to go on the offensive against three well-known Jewish writers whose opinions on textual matters did not meet with his approval. The first of these unidentified targets was none other than the famous Bible commentator Rabbi David Kimhi (ca. 1160–ca. 1235). At the end of the Introduction to his Commentary on Joshua,[42] in what appears almost as an afterthought, Kimhi wrote:

As well, I will write the meaning of the *Ketib̲* and the *Qere*, and the *Ketib̲ We-La' Qere*, and the *Qere We-La' Ketib̲*, when I am able to explain them, each in its place. It seems that these words are found this way because, during the first exile, the scrolls were lost or carried off, and the sages who knew the Torah died; and the Men of the Great Assembly, who restored the Torah to its glory of old, found disagreement[s] among the scrolls and followed the majority, according to their opinions [of what was best to do]. In any place where they were not able to decide definitively, they wrote one [version of the text] but did not vocalize it [i.e., created cases of *Ketib̲ We-La' Qere*], or they wrote it in the margin but not inside the text [i.e., created cases of *Qere We-La' Ketib̲*], or wrote one way in the text and another in the margin [i.e., created cases of *Qere u-Ketib̲*].[43]

The precise relationship between Ibn Zimra's statement and Kimhi's is less than perfectly clear. Kimhi's key words for what happened are, "the scrolls were *lost* or *carried off*" (*'ab̲ed̲u ha-sefarim we-niṭṭalṭelu*) and "the Men of the Great Assembly . . . found disagreement (*maḥloqet̲*) among the scrolls." Ibn Zimra used the terms "confusion" and "errors" (*bilbul* and *šibbuš*), which do not occur here in Kimhi but which resemble the terms "loss" (*hefsed̲*) and "confusion" (*bilbul*) used by the authors of the comments next criticized. Kimhi's position was radical enough, but Ibn Zimra seems to have exaggerated it in order to discredit it, perhaps without even reading it in context. As will soon become clear, these three criticized positions seem to have been discussed on the basis of their joint appearance in another work where the word *bilbul* is used quite frequently, and therefore the identification with Kimhi is confirmed, while this minor change is explained easily.

A second writer who discussed the nature and origin of these variants was Profiat Duran (Efodi), who died in the early fifteenth century:

During those seventy years of the Babylonian exile, loss (*hefṣeḏ*) and confusion (*bil-bul*) began to overtake them [i.e., the holy books], so that the people forsook them. And, because the chief of the Scribes, Ezra the Priest, the Scribe, realized this, he armed himself and mustered all his strength to correct the errors (*ha-meʿuwaṯ*); and all the Scribes who followed him did likewise. They corrected those scrolls as well as possible, this being the reason for their remaining complete in the number of *parašiyyoṯ*, and of verses, and of words, and of letters, and of plene and defective spelling, and of irregular and regular usage, etc.

And for this reason, they were called Scribes; and they wrote books containing this [information]—the books of the Masorah. And in those places where loss and confusion encroached [upon the text], they left [variant: they made] the *Qere* and the *Keṯiḇ* for it to record the doubt about what was found.[44]

Ibn Zimra rejected Duran's position with equal force.

A third important figure who discussed this issue was Isaac Abarbanel (fifteenth to sixteenth century). The introduction to his Commentary on Jeremiah[45] contains a lengthy and strongly worded response to the explanations of *Qere u-Keṯiḇ* proposed by both Kimhi and Duran, as well as an original explanation of the phenomenon. As an alternative to their proposals, Abarbanel suggested that the *Keṯiḇ* is strange or obscure, or that it masks various secrets, and that the *Qere* is either an explanation thereof (this applies, in particular, to significant changes like ʿ*pwlym*, explained as *teḥorim*) or a correction of the sanctified error of a prophetic speaker. The latter notion apparently was ignored by Ibn Zimra or included in his earlier criticism, which seems to refer more to Kimhi.

Ibn Zimra's disapproval is clear and is topped off with a verse from the Torah. The choice of this verse, which prescribes faith in God in a context that prohibits following the misleading advice of pagan oracles, sends a clear message that is more general than its talmudic interpretation (BT Pes. 113b). Perhaps he was emphasizing the need to have faith in the tradition, while hinting at the importance of rejecting both Jewish and non-Jewish attacks against it.

The talmudic statement in Nedarim contains four terms: *Miqraʾ Soferim, Iṭṭur Soferim, Qere We-Laʾ Keṯiḇ*, and *Keṯiḇ We-Laʾ Qere*. Subsequent arguments were presented to include *Keṯiḇ Haki u-Qere Haki*—even examples of these categories from post-Mosaic books—and *Tiqqune Soferim*, though no evidence was presented that this principle was "stated by the rabbis, of blessed memory." The list in B.10 adds another category, plene and defective spellings, to be discussed here later. Moreover, the beginning of the list contains an apparent error, since *Keṯiḇ We-Laʾ Qere* appears twice, a second time together with *Qere We-Laʾ Keṯiḇ*; the customary designation for what we call *Qere u-Keṯiḇ* was *Keṯiḇ Haki u-Qere Haki*.

As he did hundreds of other times in his responsa, Ibn Zimra then cites a responsum of Ben Adret to support his answer. Ibn Zimra's wording is very close to that of a question posed to Ben Adret and his answer.[46]

[Question to Ben Adret:] You have asked: Since it is forbidden to read even one letter of the Torah not written in the text, how does the public reader read *yiškaḇena* when it is written *yšglnh*, and, similarly, regarding every word that is a *Qere u-Keṯiḇ*, for all are written in the Torah according to the written tradition (*ha-masoreṯ*) but not the reading tradition (*ha-miqraʾ*).

> Answer [of Ben Adret]: It is Halakhah to Moses from Sinai, as they said in Nedarim, [in] the chapter [entitled] "There is No Difference Between One Who Vows" [BT Ned. 37b]: *Miqra' Soferim*, and *Iṭṭur Soferim*, *Qere We-La' Ketib* and *Ketib We-La' Qere* are Halakhah to Moses from Sinai.

According to Ibn Zimra, the question posed to Ben Adret focused on the change of *bʿpwlym* to *ba-teḥorim* and of *wyšglnh* to *we-yiškabena*. The paraphrase in B.7 also contains both items. The printed text of Ben Adret's responsum offers only the second example, but the principle is the same; in any case, the matter is reported correctly. Ben Adret also added the passage cited above from Ned. 37b.[47] A similar question posed to Abraham Maimon was answered, "These are things that were transmitted to us in a tradition; and their secrets are sealed from us, and we do not know their true reasons."[48]

The discussion now returns to one particular *Tiqqun Soferim* and why it is impossible for *Iṭṭur Soferim* to reflect a uniform change of the text by all ancient communities.

> [11] And, similarly, as we say [in regard to the verse] "And Abraham was standing [before God" [Gen. 18:22], that it should say that God was standing before Abraham], but the verse paraphrased [its intention] out of respect for God.

This is one of the Tiqqune Soferim referred to earlier (B.3–4). Either a line of the responsum is missing or the reader is expected to understand the reference. The translation has been expanded accordingly.

Of all the *Tiqqune Soferim*, including the three in the Torah, this is the most famous and the most interesting, probably because, unlike the others, it appears in a well-known narrative and is not limited to some relatively minor pronominal element. In order to understand the logic behind the suggestion, one must examine the beginning of the chapter and many of the subsequent verses. Gen. 18:1 states that God appeared to Abraham, who immediately looked up and saw three men approaching. The first difficulty centers on the precise relationship between these four characters; was God one of the three, symbolized by all three, or a fourth visitor? The answer to this question will affect how one understands the use of singular and plural verbs and pronouns throughout the chapter. Thus in verses 3–4, *'im na' maṣa'ti ḥen be-ʿēneka, 'al na' taʿabor me-ʿal ʿabdeka*, "If I have found favor in your [sing.] sight, do not pass [sing.] your [sing.] servant by," which is addressed to one individual, differs from the plural usages in the subsequent *yuqqaḥ na' meʿaṭ mayim we-raḥaṣu raglēkem*, "let some water be brought and wash [pl.] your [pl.] feet." Also, one must establish the relationship between God's appearance in verse 1, the anonymous comment in verse 10, God's speaking in verse 13, and the ambiguous use of *'dny*, traditionally vocalized as a divine name but equally readable as a reference to the three guests, even in some masoretic traditions.[49] These concerns run through Genesis 18 and 19, and their resolution has a profound impact on how one interprets the entire narrative, even on how parts of it are vocalized.

One lesson learned from these inconsistencies suggests that "receiving guests is more important than receiving the divine presence (Midrash Psalms, chap. 18; Rashi, Commentary to Genesis, ad loc., etc.), which presumes that Abraham was confronted by four visitors, not three, and that he asked God to wait while he served his other guests. Aside from what this means about the importance of hospitality, it also suggests that God stayed around, possibly waiting for Abraham to finish with his responsibilities as host. In other words, God was still standing where left by Abraham and did not depart until the end of the story, in 18:33.

Under the circumstances, one can see why some interpreters might have continued this line of reasoning and suggested that 18:22 should have said that God was standing before Abraham. And since it did not say that, some early rabbis saw here the possible presence of a *Tiqqun Soferim*. This would have meant either that the text once said that God was still standing before Abraham and that it was changed out of respect for the deity, or that it never said this but euphemistically avoided the offensive description by saying that Abraham was still standing before God, even though the text mentioned no such standing for which this was the continuation. The former explanation follows the rationale behind calling this wording a *Tiqqun Soferim* and assumes that the Scribes introduced the change; the latter one is better described as *kinna ha-katub̲*, the term used by Ibn Zimra, as well as by *Midrash Tanhuma*, a number of masoretic sources, and Ben Adret.[50] The discussion now moves to another term that, like the previous one, seems to be associated with the Scribes.

> [12] And the author of the Arukh wrote, *s.v.*, ʿ-*ṭ-r* (and this is his language):[51]
>
> And it seems that in the beginning the villagers were not careful about the Bible text and read *we-saʿad̲u libbek̲em we-ʾaḥar taʿab̲oru*, "eat *and* afterwards travel on" [Gen. 18:5]; *qiddemu šarim we-ʾaḥar nog̲enim*, "The singers came first, *and* afterwards the players" [Ps. 68:26]; *ṣid̲eqat̲ek̲a ke-harerē ʾēl u-mišpaṭek̲a tehom rabba*, "Your goodness is like the high mountains, *and* your justice is like the great deep" [Ps. 36:7].
>
> They erred in these words at that time and thought that they were correct, because this way makes sense. And the scribes came along and removed these *waws* and read *ʾaḥar taʿab̲oru*, *ʾaḥar nog̲enim*, etc. [deleting the *waw*, meaning "*and*," in each case]. When they saw that the scribes removed these *waws*, they called these words *Iṭṭur Soferim*, and Rabbi Isaac came along and taught that they are Halakhah to Moses from Sinai. And, until recent times, they used to err and read *we-loʾ yiššamaʿ ʿal pik̲a*, "*and* it should not be heard in your mouth" [Ex. 23:13], but the scribes taught not to read the *waw* (thus far his language).
>
> I do not agree with this reasoning either, since he [merely] follows his opinion that ʿ*ṭwr* means "removal," as is written, "only they did not remove the high places," and we translate [it] *lʾ* ʿ*ṭrw* [2 Kings 12:4, etc.].[52]

Ibn Zimra has argued that the cases covered by *Iṭṭur Soferim* are restorations, not emendations. Though neither he nor the author of the *Arukh* makes the comparison, this line of reasoning resembles that proposed in the Talmud for a series of other textual changes that the rabbis discussed and wanted to reject but on which they ultimately compromised by suggesting that the accepted change was actually a restoration. Thus they said that the five final letters (*kaf*, *mem*, *nun*, *pe*, and *ṣadi*) suggested to be the contribution of "the seers" (a word play that read the five letters as the words *min ṣofek̲a*) were originally in the Torah but were changed to the common forms, as in Paleo-Hebrew (*ket̲ab̲ ʿib̲ri*), and later were changed back to what is now used (BT

Shab. 104a, Meg. 3a). Conflicting claims that the traditional Aramaic Torah translation was given on Sinai and also by Ezra were resolved with the statement that Moses received it, after which it was forgotten and later restored by Ezra (BT Meg. 3a). The term for this process, which appears six times in the Babylonian Talmud and never in the Palestinian, is *šaḵeḥum we-ḥazeru wi-yissedum*.[53] Continuing the explanation of *Iṭṭur Soferim*, Ibn Zimra applies this logic to a new situation.

> [13] But according to those who say that it [the designation *Iṭṭur Soferim*] is "for the beauty of the reading," like Rashi, of blessed memory, what is there to say? And, in addition, what could the rabbi, of blessed memory, say about *Miqra' Soferim* and *Tiqqun Soferim*? Moreover, since you allow the adversary to say that the texts became corrupt and it was necessary to remove the *waws*, he may also say that they added and deleted [elsewhere] at will, as they do say.
>
> And, moreover, should we assume that all people in the villages in which the Jews were scattered agreed to add these *waws*, but no others? And, just as they agreed to add these *waws*, why did they not agree to remove some extra *waws*, since the commentators are forced [for lack of a better explanation] to designate them "Extra *waw*, like the spirantized *feh* [*Fa al-ʿAṭf*] in Arabic"?

Another of Ibn Zimra's responsa focuses on the reason why the Bible was written without vowels and punctuation. There too he criticized those who underestimated the accuracy of the holy text:

> You should believe that there is not even one small word that does not contain secrets and combinations of divine names that we cannot fathom. And in the Torah, there is not even one letter that is unnecessary, or which is for "beautification of the reading," or like "spirantized *feh*" in Arabic, as many thought. [III, no. 1065 (543)]

Arabic *fa* is a weak, more or less untranslatable conjunction, and various commentators, including Saadiah, Yonah ibn Janah, and particularly Abraham Ibn Ezra, explained many seemingly superfluous *waws* in the Bible by analogy to it.[54] By relating the problem of *Iṭṭur Soferim* to this entire group of *waws*, Ibn Zimra has attempted to discredit both the analogy to Arabic *fa* and the parallel interpretation of *Iṭṭur Soferim*. He also managed a shot at Ibn Ezra (or at least at an interpretation frequently associated with him) and thereby grouped him with Kimhi, Duran (Efodi), and Abarbanel, who were criticized above.[55]

In doing so, Ibn Zimra has taken "beautification of the reading" (*tif'ereṯ ha-qeri'a*) to be an aesthetic rather than a functional quality and rejected it as a reason for the presence of letters in the Torah. It is interesting that he chose not to interpret *tif'ereṯ* here in its kabbalistic sense and to apply it to the talmudic concept of *tif'ereṯ ha-qeri'a*. Compare, for example, his statement in *Magen David*, "Know, my friend, that the *waw* hints at *tif'ereṯ* in several ways."[56]

In fact, it is puzzling that Ibn Zimra used the seemingly inappropriate term *tif'ereṯ ha-qeri'a* in his outburst against the suggestion that one consider some letters in the Torah as essentially unnecessary (as *Iṭṭur Soferim* or analogous to Arabic *fa*). *Tif'ereṯ ha-qeri'a* and analogous terms were used frequently by medieval grammarians (a group for which Ibn Zimra seems to have had little use) to describe otherwise inexplicable elements of vocalization. For example, David Kimhi frequently employed it to describe a dagesh that seemed unnecessary but improved the sound of the language, a "euphonic dagesh" (e.g., Jud. 20:32, Is. 58:3, and Ezek. 13:20), even in a *resh* (1 Sam. 28:10); an unexplained mappiq in a *heh* (Is. 28:4); and qameṣ ḥatuf (Ezek. 17:23 and 20:5). He also used it in explaining 1 Sam. 1:6; Is. 63:19; Jer. 9:4; Ezek. 21:15, 22:24, 27:19, and elsewhere.[57] The term is used by Rabbi Joseph di Trani in a discussion of whether the correct Hebrew spelling of *Qushtantine* should be with a *tet* or a *dalet*.[58] As far as I can tell, the term was not regularly employed to describe the use or suggested nonuse of letters in the text, the situation to which Ibn Zimra was reacting.

Moreover, Ibn Zimra's statement to the contrary notwithstanding, it seems that Rashi never used the term, and Rabbenu Nissim did not employ it here either. The latter's explanation (ad loc.) is built on the term *tif'ereṯ ha-lašon*, which he used three times in close proximity, not *tif'ereṯ ha-qeri'a*. Perhaps the association between *Iṭṭur Soferim* and the parallels drawn with *fa al-ʿaṭf* in Arabic lay merely in the notion of something being superfluous, but Kimhi's use of *tif'ereṯ ha-qeri'a* does not claim that such occurrences were gratuitous; rather he (and his predecessors, who used other terms)[59] suggested that these minor adjustments in vocalization were instituted to improve the pronunciation of the words. This aside, Ibn Zimra's very cogent argument refutes the interpretation offered in the *Arukh*, cited in B.12.[60]

Ibn Zimra now begins to conclude his presentation. Adopting a procedure frequently used by Ibn Ezra, whose merciless puns on his opponents' names and positions are legendary, Ibn Zimra turns the claim back on these writers, charging they, and not the Bible text, are the source of the confusion.

> [14] Accordingly, also in this opinion I see confusion, as in the others; therefore I advise you not to seek regarding this query more than what I have written to you. It is our tradition that everything is Halakhah to Moses from Sinai, and no change, nor error, nor any confusion, nor [loss through] forgetfulness ever occurred in the texts of our holy Torah (*be-sifrē toraṯenu ha-qeḏoša*) or in the texts of (*sifrē*) the Prophets or Hagiographa. And everything that was said [was said] with divine inspiration, except what they changed for King Ptolemy in the Torah they translated for him in his own language. But all other Torah scrolls remained correct, as they were received from Mount Sinai by direct transmission. However, there arose disagreements between the sages of the Talmud (*baʿalē ha-talmuḏ*) and the masoretes (*ḥaḵmē ha-masoreṯ*) in many places—like *pylgšym* [Gen. 25:6] [about which they said], "It is spelled *pylgšm*," and similarly *klwt mšh* [Num. 7:1] [about which they said], "It is spelled *klt*"; and many cases like these—just as disagreements arose in capital or civil laws.

The somewhat unusual directive to prevent the questioner from studying the matter more fully—which seems to have had more than its due share of influence in modern times—may have been motivated by the full text of the question, by Ibn Zimra's personal knowledge of his correspondent and his spiritual needs, or by a fear that further research would uncover additional problems. Whatever the reason, his position was clear; there were no corruptions in the texts. To be sure, changes had been introduced into the ancient Greek translation executed for Ptolemy, but these were for specific reasons and carefully controlled.

The latter observation refers to rabbinic tradition that various changes were introduced when the Torah was translated for Ptolemy. The lists of these changes vary,[61] but the basic principle behind them does not. Most early writers saw the passages in these lists as conscious changes made in the Greek translation to avoid problems in interpretation; some moderns prefer to see here a reference to a variant Hebrew version. It is clear from the phrase "in his language" that Ibn Zimra followed the former position.

The relevance of Ibn Zimra's comment is less obvious, particularly since it deals with the Greek text, and the preserved form of the query makes no mention of it. Inclusion may reflect an awareness of medieval disputes over the accuracy of the Bible text. In contrast to some Christian disputants, Ibn Zimra denied the relevance of the Septuagint for discussing the Hebrew text. In other words, while changes alleged to have been made in the Torah were in reality not changes at all, those in the Septuagint had been introduced intentionally by the sages. Beyond that, Ibn Zimra specifically noted that they were not revealed by the Holy Spirit, meaning that they lack the sanctity of the Bible, another frequently maintained Christian position. This notion is reinforced by various rabbinic texts that take a negative view of the enterprise, including *Megillat Ta'anit Batra'*, which notes, borrowing an image from the ninth Egyptian plague brought by Moses against Pharaoh, that "on the eighth day of [the month of] Tevet, the Torah was translated into Greek in the days of King Ptolemy, and darkness came into the world for three days."[62]

On the other hand, the frequently told rabbinic story of the translation of the Septuagint (e.g., Sof. 1:7, BT Meg. 9a, and PT Meg. 1:9 [71d]) did attribute the differences between the Hebrew and Greek to divine guidance. Perhaps this input was seen by the Septuagint's detractors as evidence of divine assistance in avoiding problems but by supporters as a sanctioning of the Greek text. Ibn Zimra has used somewhat different language and denied that the changes resulted from divine inspiration. His casual reference to the talmudic passage in question may result from its relative unimportance in the responsum, the fact that there are several variations among the scattered lists, or even the knowledge that there were many more than the dozen or so official variants listed in the Talmud—a fact sure to have been mentioned by Christian antagonists—but other secondary sources also may have influenced its inclusion (see chapter 7).

Still, differences did arise between the teachings of the masoretes and the talmudic rabbis about certain details in the Bible text. By emphasizing that all biblical books share the same textual accuracy, Ibn Zimra tried to avoid claims like those voiced in later centuries that defended the textual integrity of the Torah but not that of some of the postpentateuchal books. In fact, copies of the masoretic text of the Torah are more consistent both in spelling and in wording and less subject to variation than are copies of the rest of the Bible (see Norzi's statement, translated in chapter 1), but Ibn Zimra gives no hint of this fact.

The linking of disagreements over textual differences with disagreements in other areas of Jewish law serves to keep such problems within the framework of halakhic discourse and effectively removes them from what appears to have been a strictly scribal domain, wherein the prime concern is accurate reproduction of early copies, not legal theory. This factor places all discussion in the hands of the halakhic authorities, who were not necessarily scribes but could change scribal conventions through their decisions.

While such a position is undoubtedly sound as a matter of halakhah, the situations are not quite comparable. Laws are subject to interpretation, manipulation, and reorientation. But in the original text (which, according to the rabbinic tradition, undoubtedly existed), words were spelled either one way or another. Compromise seems virtually impossible in matters of orthography that are studied with reference to scribal precision, though they are an important part of the halakhic resolution of spelling problems and of such matters as differences in recording the inverted *nuns* (Num. 10:35–36), the problematic *waw* of *šlwm* (Num. 25:6), and the notion of suspending doubtful letters.[63]

Ibn Zimra assumed that the correct spelling could be determined through recourse to specific textual witnesses and analytical processes, and interestingly, he favored the testimony of Torah scrolls in this debate. They were correct; the problems arose because of disagreements between the rabbis and the masoretes. Yet in Responsum C, treated in the next chapter, he argued on halakhic grounds for changing scrolls—all of them, if necessary—to follow the Babylonian Talmud.

It is noteworthy that Maimonides' statement that, in some matters related to the writing of a Torah scroll, he relied on Ben Asher's masoretic codex (*Hilkhot Sefer Torah* 8:4) has had no impact on this discussion. According to a tradition of the Aleppo community, the famed Ben Asher codex was sent from Egypt to Aleppo during Ibn Zimra's lifetime, but this notion has been challenged for a number of reasons. Some modern writers have dated the transfer to the end of the fourteenth century, a rather likely suggestion, especially since Ibn Zimra seems to exhibit no knowledge of it, but similar texts did remain in Egypt.[64]

Having expressed his own opinion, Ibn Zimra next bolsters his position by reference to the writings of his famous Spanish predecessor, Rabbi Solomon Ben Adret, whom he cited earlier in a different connection and in Responsum A. As will be discussed in detail in chapter 6, the citation varies from that in the earlier text; indeed, in one sense it says just the opposite.

> [15] And if you say that we do not know on whom to rely, the Rashba, of blessed memory, was already asked about this, and he answered that:
>
>> In every case of plene or defective spelling with which some law has been associated—like *bswkwt/bskt* [Lev. 22:42–43], [and] *qrnwt/qrnt* [Lev. 4:7, etc.]—we rely on the sages of the Talmud (*baʿalē ha-talmuḏ*), who already analyzed the matter carefully. But if no law is derived from it [i.e., from the spelling], we rely on the masoretes (*baʿalē ha-masoreṯ*), who counted the defective and plene spellings, and about which [or: following which] books [or: scrolls] have been written (*we-niḵteḇu bah sefarim*). And if there are disagreements among the scrolls (*sefarim*), we correct the scrolls according to the majority, as is written "follow the majority" [Ex. 23:2].

Unlike the citation from Ben Adret found in Responsum A, which opens and closes with reference to its being "his words," this one can be taken as a paraphrase, but the precise intention remains unclear. Undoubtedly the position is strongly pro-Masorah, but whether Ibn Zimra was stressing the extent of the masoretes' efforts or their impact on the Torah text is uncertain. He then adds:

> [16] And it seems to me that, if they are [divided] half and half, we should rely on the Masorah and correct the scrolls; and, in this case, we do not say "allow the scroll to stand on its presumption of correctness"[65] since, whichever way you decide, one of them is invalid for ritual use; and it is improper for the Torah scrolls to differ. But it is very improbable that [all] the scrolls would be divided equally, and therefore the Rashba, of blessed memory, omitted this distinction.[66]

As was explained earlier, many medieval writers, particularly in Ashkenaz, were prepared to compromise on the issue of total textual uniformity. Though Ibn Zimra neither cited nor refuted them, he was not.

One of the most interesting aspects of this responsum is the reference to the earlier Responsum A in the following and final paragraph. At this juncture, in an attempt to support the value and authority of the Masorah, Ibn Zimra goes on to affirm that, when faced with changes introduced into several Torah scrolls on the basis of the spellings suggested by the Zohar, he rejected the changes and restored the earlier corrections on the basis of the Masorah. It will be recalled, however, that in the version of the story found in Responsum A, on Ben Adret's authority, he adopted the opposite stand!

> [17] And I have corrected scrolls (*sefarim*) that they changed to plene *waw*, following the Midrash [that reads] *ʾl tyrʾ ʾwtw*, "do not fear him" [Num. 21:34], and *ʿd drš ʾḥyk ʾwtw*, "until your brother seeks it" [Deut. 22:2], as in the expression *ʾwt bryt* and from the word *ʾwt* [meaning] "sign." I corrected it to be defective [i.e., *ʾwtw* to *ʾtw*] according to the Masorah,[67] and I have already written about this in another responsum. And I have written according to my humble opinion.

In conclusion, this responsum, which is concerned with defending a lengthy series of biblical and talmudic texts—indeed, the entire institution of rabbinic Bible transmission—against non-Jewish attacks, differs greatly in tone from the previous one, which required defending the Bible text against Midrash-based textual incursions. It is understandable that the earlier one, which required addressing challenges to the integrity of the Torah text from Jewish religious documents, called forth a positive claim about the Bible text and dismissed the midrashic attestations of spelling unless they were found in the Talmud and were of halakhic significance. It is also understandable that the polemical position to which the present responsum is addressed, reflecting a much more hostile attitude that sought to undermine the credibility of both the Bible and the rabbinic teachings about its transmission, required a different and consistently positive reaction to both text and tradition. What remains puzzling is how Ben Adret has now been made to support diametrically opposed positions and how Ibn Zimra himself, obviously remembering his previous presentation, has now given a totally different one. These matters will be discussed at length later, but first we must examine two other related responsa, one of which contains yet a third presentation of Ben Adret's position.

Ibn Zimra's Responsum C: The Talmud, the Torah Scrolls, and Fixing the Torah Text

And [regarding] what you asked, "Why [is *hw'*] found in the Torah [vocalized, apparently indiscriminately] *hu'* [or] *hi'*, [or why is "the girl" written apparently indiscriminately] *hn'r* [or] *hn'rh*"?

This matter was transmitted to the men of the tradition (*'anšē haqabbalah*) (and I am not one of her men), until the righteous one will come and teach [it].

Rabbi Solomon ben Shimon Duran (1400–1467)
She'eilot uTeshuvot HaRashbash (Livorno: 1742), no. 36

Introduction to Ibn Zimra's Responsum C

Like Responsum A, Responsum C deals with a very practical question which, though much more specific, is no less significant for the production of Torah scrolls. The questioner (whom Ibn Zimra calls *yeḏiḏi*, "my friend," a designation he uses in well over one hundred of his responsa) wanted to know if it was necessary to form the *waw* in the word *šalom*, "peace," of Num. 25:12 in a "cut" manner, especially since most scrolls seem not to have been written that way. The question derives from the conflict between the scribal practice of forming this letter like all others and the talmudic passage that suggests it should be different. To paraphrase the issue in language we saw earlier, the Talmud suggests that the *waw* should be written in a special way, but most scrolls differ. Is the correct practice determined by the Talmud or by the majority of scrolls?

The Query: How Should One Form the *Waw* of *šlwm* in Numbers 25:12?

Question:[1]

[1] You asked me, my friend, to tell you my opinion about the *waw* [of the word

> *šlwm*, "peace"] of *hinneni notēn lo 'et beriti šalom*, "Behold, I give him my covenant of peace" [Num. 25:12], which is found [written] in most scrolls in its normal manner, like other *waws*; but we require that it be [written] cut, as [is stipulated] at the conclusion of the [talmudic] chapter [entitled] "One Who Says," in Qiddushin [66b].

It is impossible to identify the author of the question or to determine whether he was aware of other references to the issue, but earlier writers discussed and described this *waw* in different ways. Among others, *Midrash Otiot Qetanot VeTa'ameihem* and Rabbi Bahya ben Asher (thirteenth century) followed the masoretic designation of the letter as *waw ze'ira*, "an undersized *waw*";[2] many writers preferred the language of the Babylonian Talmud, *waw qeṭu'a* or *waw qeṭi'a*, "a cut *waw*."

In principle, it should be fairly easy to demonstrate that the two terms actually refer to the same scribal presentation of the letter, and this seems to be the thinking of Rabbenu Tam in the passage translated earlier in chapter 1 and of Bahya in his Torah commentary (ad loc.). Even so, Menahem Di Lonzono (fifteenth to sixteenth century), *Or Torah* (ad loc.), disagreed, and much of the secondary literature seems to side with him. Rabbi Akiva Eiger Guens (1761–1837) devoted an unusually lengthy responsum to this question. In it, he differentiated between forming the letter cut and forming it undersized, and he expressed great displeasure at the latter designation, which suggests that the top of the letter should be smaller than that of a regular *waw*. He also discussed where it should be cut and whether the cut piece should remain or be removed. In other words, he defined the problem as whether the root *q-ṭ-'*, translated above as "cut," should actually be understood as "cut off" or "cut through." Ibn Zimra worked through many of the same considerations, but with somewhat less precision and in far less detail.[3]

This question asked only whether it is obligatory to write the *waw* as described in the Talmud, but since Ibn Zimra answered affirmatively, he also explained exactly how to do so. The process of analysis is important, because it demonstrates the manner in which a halakhic authority dealt with a scribal problem for which he had no ready solution.

The Reply: It Should Be Formed "Cut"

> [2] [One] must correct the scrolls and form the *waw* cut, because the Rashba, of blessed memory, wrote in a responsum that:
>
> > [In] every [case of] plene or defective spelling of legal import, like *qrnwt/qrnt*, "horns" [Lev. 4:7, etc.], [and] *swkt/swkwt*, "booths" [Lev. 23:42–43], one must correct the Torah scroll according to the Talmud, because they [i.e., the rabbis in the Talmud] examined the matter carefully, even if this is against the Masorah. But [in] a matter that is not of legal import, like *plgšym/plgšm*, "concubines" [Gen. 25:6] [and] *klwt/klt*, "finished" [Num. 7:1], we correct the Torah scroll according to the Masoret or following the majority of scrolls (*rob sefarim*).
>
> And I already dealt with this at length in another responsum.

As in Responsa A and B, Ibn Zimra has cited or referred to a responsum of Solomon Ben Adret. And because he understood this passage to be of legal import—

halakhic rules are associated with the shape of this *waw*—he relied on and defended Ben Adret's position that the text should be changed to conform to the shape suggested by the Talmud. It is uncertain if his reference to his own earlier discussion points to Responsum A or B; for reasons that will be clarified in chapter 7, A is somewhat more likely.

Once again, Ben Adret's statement appears in a new formulation. As in the other cases, he holds that the spellings of words presented the Talmud's halakhic discussions are definitive, but the text then adds that when the question occurs in a context that is not of legal significance, one should correct Torah scrolls to follow the Masoret or the majority of scrolls. Since the word *šalom* is treated in a halakhic context, the talmudic observation has the force of law, even though the majority of local texts, the *rob̲ sefarim*, seem to know nothing of this special *waw*. We shall return to this version of Ben Adret's ruling in chapter 7. In light of the Talmud's statement and in the absence of a positive local tradition about it, the major question here turns to exactly how to form this *waw*.

At first blush, it may seem significant that this unusual letter is not discussed in the Sifrei, the halakhic Midrash to the Book of Numbers. Since many halakhically relevant passages were treated in it, one might be tempted to interpret this silence as evidence of a textual tradition that wrote this *waw* in the regular way, but such a conclusion is totally irrelevant for Ben Adret and Ibn Zimra, who voiced concern only for the spelling changes suggested by the Talmud's halakhic discussions, not those of the Midrashim, and surely not for those omitted from the Midrashim.

Ibn Zimra continues:

> [3] And this case, too, is of legal import, for we learn from it that a blemished priest is unfit to officiate at a sacrifice, and if he did officiate, his offering is invalid, as we learn in Qiddushin, in the chapter [entitled] "One Who Says" [66b]:
>
> How do we know that the offering of a blemished priest is invalid?
>
> Said Rav Judah, said Samuel: Scripture says, "Behold I give him my covenant of peace" [Num. 25:12], [meaning] when he is complete (*šalem*) [i.e., physically whole], but not when he is defective.
>
> And [or: but], lo, it is written *šlwm* [plene].
>
> Said Rav Nahman: The *waw* of *šlwm* is cut.
>
> Thus, because of a cut *waw*, we learn that he [i.e., the priest who officiates in all future Temple services] must be [physically] complete, as it says afterwards, "And it should be for him and his descendants after him as an everlasting priestly covenant" [Num. 25:13].

This statement from the Talmud is ambiguous. The word *šalom*, "peace," can be read *šalem*, "complete," only when spelled defective; so the initial force of the comment suggests that the spelling was *šlm* and that this defective spelling (which is routine in the Torah) is, ironically, a sign of completeness. This *waw* is described in the Talmud as *qeṭuʿa*, "cut." In keeping with the way they interpreted the use of this root in other contexts, some writers suggested that *q-ṭ-ʿ* meant "absent" or "missing," or at least "silent," which would require *qeṭuʿa* to mean something like "cut out" and seems to prefer the spelling *šlm*, but I have found no evidence for a defective spelling of the word.[4]

An extra *waw* or *yod*, on the other hand, is often taken midrashically as a sign of fullness or completeness, while its absence is frequently understood to hint at something defective or incomplete. This interpretation allows *šlwm* to be taken as a sign of fullness without reference to the similarity of *šlm* and *šlwm*, and thus the plene spelling by itself may be a sign of fullness.

Rav Nahman's comment that the *waw* is cut can be taken to mean that *šlwm* looks like *šlym* and can be read *šalēm*, or that *šlwm* is not really fully plene; but it seems more in line with the first interpretation offered.[5] It cannot be taken as a rebuttal of the general principle that a blemished priest should not officiate, since this would violate the simple meaning of Lev. 21:17–18, 21, and 23.

> [4] And, regarding this, the Ritva, of blessed memory, wrote that (this is his language):
>
> > This matters for [the way we write] a Torah scroll; and one should change all our scrolls [in which the *waw* is] written in the normal way (thus far [his language]).

The actual statement of the Ritva (Rabbi Yom Tov ben Abraham Al-Ishbili, ca. 1250–1330), as preserved in his commentary to BT Qid. 66b, is slightly longer than Ibn Zimra's quotation; part of the beginning of his statement is discussed later in C.7:

> "The *waw* of *šlwm* is cut" [quotation of the words of Rav Nahman]: It seems that this means that it is cut in the middle for, if not, he should have said it is undersized. This matters for [the way we write] a Torah scroll; and one should change all our texts [in which the *waw* is] written in the normal way.[6]

Ibn Zimra continued to discuss the precise shape of this "cut *waw*." Various halakhic and masoretic sources refer to it as cut or as an undersized *waw*, which could mean shorter than a usual *waw*, almost in the shape of a *yod*, but he rejected this one in favor of a *waw* cut diagonally through the vertical.

> [5] And, [regarding] the shape of a cut *waw*, the Ritva, of blessed memory, wrote, "cut in two." And I checked in a copy (*sefer*) that came from Fez, which is as precise as possible, and it is cut, but it is cut on the diagonal like a thin thread—like a strand of hair—that divides it. And its form is just like a *waw*, but it is cut on the diagonal.

It is interesting that in this case Ibn Zimra consulted several reputable texts to see what they would offer (in C.5 and C.7). Obviously he was aware of several possible ways to interpret the talmudic passage and to form the *waw* in question, and his discussion leaves the impression that he seriously considered them. In other words, this was a problem that required a halakhic decision based on the evidence taken from the Talmud and supported by scribal practices. It was not to be resolved merely by recourse to one detached talmudic teaching, to one or another expert scribe, or to the majority of available local texts.

The next section of the answer may appear somewhat trivial, but it must be recalled that several of Ibn Zimra's other responsa are devoted to invalidating scrolls whose letters *heh* and *qof* were formed of contiguous quill strokes. In those discussions, he argued forcefully that *heh* and *qof*—and only *heh* and *qof*—consisted of two unconnected pieces. Having just supported the use of a *waw* that also contains two unconnected pieces, he felt duty bound to explain why that anomaly does not stand in violation of this other principle.[7] His answer, namely that the two pieces should be connected by a small thin line, ensured that this *waw* would remain one piece and is consistent with the position articulated in the other responsa, but it is not a convincing explanation of the simple meaning of the talmudic passage in question, which ultimately was his primary source. He could have used the principle of avoiding other two-part letters to argue for the removal of the bottom part of the *waw*, but as is explained further on, other options seemed preferable.

> [6] But, you may ask, regardless of whether it is cut on the diagonal or is actually divided, in either case it is really two letters, like two *yods*; and this is not the [correct] form of a *waw*, because it is divided. Indeed, we maintain that there are no letters with two [separate] parts except *heh* and *qof*, and [therefore] since it is divided [into two parts, we should say] it is invalid.
>
> Yet one may respond that the halakhah has been taught that this *waw* should be cut and different from [all] other *waws*. But it makes sense to me that it should [merely] appear to be cut, but not actually be cut. Rather, one should connect the two pieces of the *waw* with a thin thread [of ink] like a strand of hair, so that they are [really] connected and [so that they form] one [whole] letter but they look like two.
>
> Because it is so, it looks like there is no *waw* there, and we say regarding it "*šlm*, but not when he is defective."[8] And one may conclude similarly from the statement of the Ramah [Rabbi Meir Abulafia], of blessed memory, who wrote "*as if* they cut it into two pieces" (thus far [his language]), and he did not write "they cut it into two pieces," [implying that] it [merely] looks like it was cut into two pieces.

We have already seen that Rabbenu Tam and Rabbenu Bahya referred to this letter as undersized, thereby precluding its being cut in some other way and obviating all discussion of whether or not the cut piece should be connected to the rest of the letter. By way of comparison, in *Masoret Seyag LaTorah*, s.v. *šlm* (p. 72a), Rabbi Meir Abulafia wrote:

> . . . and one of them [i.e., references to *šlwm*, regularly spelled *šlm*] is cut. Its referent is "my covenant of peace" [Num. 25:12]; the *waw* of *šlwm* is cut, as if they cut it in parts (*be-falgaya*).
>
> And we learn from it in Qiddushin [66b] that the sacrifice of a blemished person [i.e., a priest] who officiates [at a Temple sacrifice], even unknowingly, is invalid, and therefore it [i.e., the *waw* of *šlwm*] is written cut, in order that it be as if no *waw* were written, meaning I [i.e., God] have not given him the covenant of priesthood to slaughter nonsacrificial animals, except if he is [physically] whole, not lacking anything.

Although Ibn Zimra cited Abulafia in over fifty responsa, this is the only one that refers to *Masoret Seyag LaTorah*. The four-word quotation is actually a paraphrase of three words in Abulafia's published text, and while the difference between them is insignificant, one can only wonder if the citation represents not a development of Ibn Zimra's interest in the Masorah but a borrowing from a secondary source. Had Ibn Zimra had access to *Masoret Seyag LaTorah* when he wrote Responsum A, it is hard to imagine why he would have ignored it completely, unless he disagreed with its emphasis on solving problems in accord with the Masorah; and had he had a copy when he wrote Responsum B, he could have used it then. It is easier to imagine that it came into his hands later, but even if so, it plays no serious role in the presentation. In a responsum that seems to have accumulated rather than having been composed in one sitting—a far from unique situation for Ibn Zimra—Abulafia's contribution is extremely brief (far less than that of Ritva, a younger Spanish commentator by several generations) and almost insignificant.

Ibn Zimra continues:

> [7] Later I saw that the *waw* in a Torah (*tora*) that Rabbenu Shem Tov Gaon,[9] of blessed memory, the author of *Migdal Oz*, wrote was actually divided into two. And in a copy (*sefer*) written by Rabbi Israel,[10] it is written in its normal manner; but he removed from it a thread of ink, as if to cut it, from which we may conclude that he was bothered by the same difficulty that I mentioned above—that [actually cutting it] would make the *waw* like two letters.
>
> And I think that the preferred form is that it should be divided [into two parts] with a thin thread [of ink] joining them, as I wrote above. And it is impossible to form it undersized for, if so, it [i.e., the Gemara] should have said "the *waw* of *šlwm* is undersized"; but, since it says "it is cut," one may conclude that it is normal [in size and shape] but that it is [merely] cut. And thus wrote Rabbi Yom Tov ben Abraham, of blessed memory.
>
> And even though the masoretes (*baʿalē ha-masora*) said that it is an undersized *waw*, our Talmud disagrees and lists the *waw* of [*wnpšw* in the phrase] *wnpšw lʾ hyh* [Ps. 22:30] in the alphabetic list of undersized letters. And this is how it [i.e., the *waw* of *šlwm*] is written in the Masoret of Rav Shem Tov Gaon, of blessed memory, in the Torah that he wrote. But it is possible that they do not disagree and [that] the designation "undersized *waw*" refers only to the upper piece.

Ibn Zimra's statement associates with the Babylonian Talmud the notion of writing *wnpšw* in an unusual way, but no such opinion is found there. This idea should probably be seen as another example of the phenomenon discussed earlier at the end of chapter 2, where traditions preserved elsewhere are cited as talmudic. Many writers assume the *waw* of Num. 28:13 to be unique, but some sources suggest otherwise. C. D. Ginsburg's lists of irregular *waws* do not include any reference to Ps. 22:30, but six texts he cited mention an undersized *waw* in *wnpšw ʾwth*, Job 23:13, and three of them also list the *waw* of Num. 25:12. Perhaps there were alternative traditions regarding the word, since six texts concur by listing only one of the two.[11]

Ibn Zimra refers here to "the Masoret of Rav Shem Tov Gaon, of blessed memory, in the Torah that he wrote." As was noted in chapter 1, the term *masoreṯ* may refer to the consonantal text of the Torah or to a Torah scroll, though either seems unlikely in this context. It may also connote a Bible codex containing masoretic notes. Any of them would provide the necessary evidence, but the third alternative seems to be the intended one.

Once again Ibn Zimra has found himself dealing with a conflict between the masoretic traditions and the Talmud, and again he has followed the Talmud. In Responsum B he explained how it can be that "our Talmud disagrees with the Masorah" by insisting that, even though they disagree, both were Halakhah to Moses from Sinai. He attempted to minimize the significance of differences between the Masorah and the rabbis in A.2 and A.14 as well. Here he concludes:

> [8] It is also possible to form it another way, namely lacking the bottom point, which, on other *waws*, is like the point of a needle. [In that case,] it is as if the point

is cut off, as if it had a [flat] base; and it is a complete *waw*, but the point is lacking, as if it were cut. This is how I thought to explain the matter at first, but it remained problematic for me, because it occurred to me that it would be a complete *waw*. Its point would be unnecessary, nor would its absence invalidate it; thus *šlwm* would really be plene, so how would we learn from it "when he is physically whole, but not when he is defective"?[12]

Therefore, the truth is what the commentators, of blessed memory, wrote, that "it is cut into two pieces." Also, the form written in the text of Rabbi Israel is not correct, for, if so, it is not a cut *waw*, but a limping [i.e., clipped] one, one over which the quill was passed. Therefore, the correct form, by which one can avoid all doubts, is: He should form it cut into two and join the two pieces with a thin thread of ink, and it will thus be severed and joined [at the same time].

And I have written what appears [correct] according to my humble opinion.

While Ibn Zimra's halakhic position on the letter in question is clear, some other aspects of his presentation are not. Far from resolving the anomalies that emerged from our reading of Ibn Zimra's first two responsa, the reasoning in Responsum C further confounds things. In keeping with what we saw earlier, Ibn Zimra preferred to solve the present problem through recourse to the Talmud, and he relied on Ben Adret's teaching to confirm that, because of the laws associated with the spelling, the talmudic presentation was binding. Yet in this case the text was somewhat ambiguous in that it failed to explain whether the cut *waw* was to suffer removal of a portion of the letter or mere separation of its parts. As a result, Ibn Zimra demonstrated a serious interest in the scribal treatment of the problem and sought out what must be presumed to be the best and most trustworthy models he could find, those produced by several highly acclaimed scribes. The evidence was such that it carried the confidence of the Jewish community that originated in Spain or that identified with its traditions.

Given that the local scrolls seem not to have followed the talmudic prescription, there was no need for Ibn Zimra to consult them. His statement from I, no. 363, "and even if the ancient scrolls are written that way, should the halakhah be abandoned for the sake of ignorant scribes?" could apply here as well. This comment, the problems he had with the tefillin produced in his community, and the questionable behavior of their scribe (VIII, no. 6) suggest that some local scribes were not worthy of his trust, but that point may be irrelevant here, where he looked to renowned scribes, and he did not introduce it.

Finally, Ibn Zimra has presented us with a third version of Ben Adret's responsum. This one seems to equate the Masorah with the testimony of the majority of the scrolls; it will be treated fully later.

The Cut Waw *Since Ibn Zimra's Time*

And what has actually become of this special *waw*? Many scribal manuals ignore the *waw* of *šlwm* in presenting the proper way(s) to write a *waw*, because they are primarily guides for the writing of Mezuzot and Tefillin, where the word does not appear, or because they require no variation from the way the letter is normally formed.[13] Many fragments of scribal guides have been reprinted in *Yalqut Tzurat HaOtiot*, which also contains a facsimile of the word *šlwm* from the Torah scroll of

Rabbi A. A. from Karamarna.[14] A diagonal split from high on the right to lower on the left is clearly visible—reflecting the notion found in *Or Torah* and elsewhere that the top portion is identical in form to a *yod*—but the lower leg of the *waw* seems to be slightly further to the right than the same part of the other *waws* in the picture, which suggests that the regular amount of space is covered by the letter's ink, but that the thin space between the parts of the *waw*'s leg required that the lower part be moved slightly to the right.[15]

The general thrust of the discussions in these manuals is that it is not necessary to correct the *waw* in question if it is written in the regular fashion, despite the talmudic statement and the preferences of Rabbi Yom Tov ben Abraham and Ibn Zimra. Note the presentation of Rabbi Solomon Eiger, author of *Gilyon Maharsha, Yoreh De'ah*, no. 275, paragraph 6:

> Regarding the matter of "the *waw* of *šlwm* is cut," [the author of] *Battei Kehunah* (Vol. 1, no. 21) mentioned that if it is complete like other *waws*, it must be fixed. And if they already removed the Torah from the Ark, one reads it. And regarding its form, he agreed that it should be undersized or scraped off at the bottom, not cut in the middle.

The fact that many medieval scrolls contained a regular *waw* in *šlwm* precludes using this phenomenon to draw conclusions about the relationships among scrolls; see Amarillio's report of the 800 scrolls examined to determine the actual majority practice in his city.[16] It is perhaps noteworthy that the Torah scrolls produced according to the Yemenite tradition, as well as those preserved by the Jews of Kaifeng, reportedly concur in having a regular *waw* here.[17]

Ibn Zimra's Responsum D: Logic and Vocalizing the Torah Text

In regard to an error in the word *ha-hi'* that is written with a *yod* in place of the *waw* [i.e., which should be spelled *hhw'* but is spelled *hhy'* and modifies a feminine noun], not one person in the world who has a brain in his head would agree to take out another [scroll] because of an error of this sort.

Rabbi Joel Sirkes (1561–1640)
She'eilot uTeshuvot HaBah HaHadashot, no. 42

Introduction to Ibn Zimra's Responsum D

Like Responsa A and C, Responsum D deals with a very specific and limited question, the correct vocalization of the word *hw'* in Lev. 25:33. The text reads: *wa-'ašer yig̱'al min ha-lewiyyim we-yaṣṣa mimkar bayiṯ we-'ir 'aḥuzzaṯo ba-yoḇel, ki ḇattē 'arē ha-lewiyyim hw' (hi') 'aḥuzzaṯam be-ṯoḵ benē yiśra'el.* In the New Jewish Publication Society translation, it is rendered as, "Such property as may be redeemed from the Levites—houses sold in a city they hold—shall be released through the jubilee; for the houses in the cities of the Levites are their holding among the Israelites."[1] In this case, the now anonymous questioner has asked whether the traditional vocalization of the word *hw'*, "it," as *hi'* should be changed to *hu'* on the authority of Rabbi Hizqiah ben Manoah, a well-known thirteenth-century Torah commentator from northern France.[2]

Two arguments might support the proposed change. The first is a perceived grammatical inconsistency regarding the antecedent of the pronoun *hw'*, which looks to be either the masculine plural, *battim* (in construct, *ḇattē*) or the feminine singular, *'aḥuzza*. The potential ambiguity of the gender of *hw'* is compounded by the fact that in most pentateuchal passages the independent feminine pronoun is actually spelled *hw'* but pronounced *hi'*, an issue noted earlier in connection with some of the texts described in the story from Soferim 6:4 (chapter 1). The second argument is the fact that the very next verse appears to contain the construction suggested here. Of particular theoretical importance is what appears as a respected medieval commentator's assumed freedom to deviate from the traditional vocalization, which suggests a certain independence from the reading traditions recorded in the Masorah and possibly the right to propose alternative vocalizations elsewhere.

Unlike the responsa treated in the preceding chapters, this one is not concerned with the consonantal text, with spelling, or with validating the text of a Torah scroll; discussion of whether the correct vocalization is *hi*ʾ or *hu*ʾ presumes agreement over a consonantal text of *hw*ʾ. Nor does it cite or even allude to the teaching of Ben Adret that played such a significant role in the other responsa. The responsum is included here because in it Ibn Zimra relies on the Masorah to prove his point.

The Query: Should One Pronounce *hw*ʾ in Leviticus 25:33 as *hu*ʾ or as *hi*ʾ?

> Question:[3]
> [1] You have asked me to tell you my opinion about what Hizquni wrote in *Parashat BeHar Sinai*, [namely] that [one] should read *hw*ʾ ʾ*ḥwztm*, "it is their portion" [Lev. 25:33] with a shuruq [i.e., as *hu*ʾ] and not with a ḥiriq [i.e., as *hi*ʾ]. And it is difficult for him [i.e., for you?] to nullify the reading [tradition] of your fathers. Yet some of the sages made the public reader who read it *hi*ʾ ʾ*aḥuzzaṯam* go back [and reread it *hu*ʾ], in accord with Hizquni's thinking. And they said [that], since the entire section (*paraša*) is written in the masculine gender, this too should be masculine.

As it appears in his Torah commentary, Hizquni's comment states, "*Hu*ʾ *aḥuzzaṯam* [Lev. 25:35]—Masculine, [vocalized] with a shuruq; and *aḥuzzaṯ* ʿ*olam hu*ʾ *lahem*, 'it is their perpetual claim' [Lev. 25:34], is the same." The notion attributed to the local sages by the questioner missed the point of the passage in Leviticus. While a grammatical inconsistency does occur in verse 31, it plays no role in the rest of the passage, and the six verses of the parashah, Lev. 25:29–34, are not consistently masculine. In Lev. 25:34, *hw*ʾ refers to *śaḏe migraš* ʿ*arēhem*, not to ʾ*aḥuzza*; any attempt to read ʾ*ḥuzza* as masculine is unconvincing and, as far as I have found, unsupported by other exegetes; Norzi rejected it flatly. Moreover, in his notes to Lev. 25:33, Kennicott recorded about a dozen witnesses to consonantal *hy*ʾ instead of the expected *hw*ʾ,[4] which, if nothing else, confirms the traditional vocalization as *hi*ʾ.

The Reply: It Should Be Pronounced *hi*ʾ

As might be expected, Ibn Zimra's response rejected Hizquni's suggestion and defended the traditional reading. More surprising, perhaps, is his citation of the related masoretic rubric.

> [2] Those who made the public reader go back [and read the word as *hu*ʾ] have not acted properly, for we should not abandon the reading tradition of our fathers and rabbis and all the codices (*sefarim*) in our possession—"[written] during the past 1,000 years, until today," all of them vocalized with a ḥiriq—[solely] because of Hizquni's reasoning and decision. For in several places we have found masculine [words] in place of feminine [ones] and feminine [words] in place of masculine [ones], and the earlier writers explained the reason [as] "any inanimate object can be either masculine or feminine." This is also the consensus of the grammarians, and thus have I seen [cited] in the name of Rabbenu Tam, of blessed memory.

The meaning of the phrase *me-ʾelef šanim ʿad ha-yom*, rendered as "[written] during the past 1,000 years, until today," remains uncertain. It is unlikely that the year 1000 of the Christian calendar is intended, and a reference to 1,000 years after the creation (according to biblical chronology, around the time of the birth of Noah) makes no sense. The phrase does not appear to mean "for the past 1,000 years" but if that were the intention, the period would begin in the sixth century, close to the time of the crystalization of many masoretic traditions. A date of 1000 according to *minyan šeṭarot* (beginning in 312 B.C.E.) would also fall into the prime period of masoretic activity, though it is somewhat doubtful that Ibn Zimra would have used that reference here, inasmuch as he contributed to the cessation of its use in legal documents.[5] Perhaps it should be understood as "from time immemorial" rather than as a specific historical designation.

Two types of evidence are cited in support of the decision. First, all *sefarim* (in this case, definitely Masorah codices) produced during the previous millennium agree on the vocalization. We cannot tell how Ibn Zimra knew this; perhaps he generalized from those available locally. Second, gender inconsistency is far from unknown in the Bible, and many medieval writers, including, it seems, Rabbenu Tam, agreed that inanimate objects can be either masculine or feminine.

Ibn Zimra provided no examples. Perhaps he was referring to cases like *maḥane*, "camp," which is used as both masculine and feminine in Gen. 32:9, and to words such as *šemeš* and *dereḵ*, which are modified by words in both genders. Because his interest was limited to inanimate objects, there is no reason to consider grammatically inconsistent constructions like *ki yiheye naʿara beṯula*, "if there be a virgin woman," Deut. 22:23.[6]

The linguistic principle to which Ibn Zimra referred, "any inanimate object can be either masculine or feminine," is well known, and extensive histories of its use have been reconstructed by M. Wilensky and by N. Allony. Scholarly attempts to identify its author have proved frustrating; the popular attribution to Abraham Ibn Ezra cannot be substantiated, and links with Rabbenu Tam are equally unconvincing.[7] Ibn Zimra continues:

> [3] Moreover, who told them that *ʾaḥuza* is masculine, not feminine? And if you say [it is masculine] because afterwards is written, "But the open field of their cities should not be sold (*u-śadē migraš ʿarēhem loʾ yimmaḵer*), for it (*hwʾ*) is a permanent possession (*ʾaḥuzzaṯ ʿolam*) for them" [Lev. 25:34],[8] perhaps it [i.e., *hwʾ*] refers to "the open fields of their cities." But truly there is no consistency regarding this, for this is the [normal] manner of the Bible regarding inanimate objects.

Ibn Zimra's simple dismissal here of grammatical irregularities as normal stands in curious contrast to his insistence elsewhere on the deep significance of seemingly irregular spellings and the absolute impropriety of attributing apparently superfluous, conjunctive *waws* to merely aesthetic considerations (III, no. 1068 [643]; see chapter 3). It suggests that, despite his willingness to cite "the consensus of the grammarians" when it suited him to do so, he failed to appreciate the very positive contributions to the study of biblical Hebrew that had been written in Hebrew and in Arabic by Jewish philologists between the tenth and the fourteenth centuries.

> [4] And Rashi, of blessed memory, suggested the forced explanation in *Parashat Negaʿim*, "because they are on a person who is animate, and because the diseases

themselves are possessed of life"; but there is no consistency regarding inanimate objects.

Rashi's commentary to *Parashat Nega'im* (Leviticus 13) contains a number of observations on the use of *hw'* and *hy'* (verses 8, 15, 22, 55, and 57), but none fits precisely Ibn Zimra's description. My inability to locate any such reference in Rashi's other writings suggests that this reflects either an interpretation of a passage in Rashi that I have been unable to relate to Ibn Zimra's observations, or a variant reading not found in all Rashi texts, or an erroneous attribution.

Ibn Zimra continues by citing a masoretic rubric that records fifteen cases of *hw'* vocalized *hi'* between the end of Leviticus 18 and the end of the book:

> [5] And I saw in the Masorah, and this is its language:[9]
>
> And from the end of the section (*sidra*) of the prohibited sexual unions[10] until the end of the book, [one always finds] *hw'* [vocalized as *hu'*], except for fifteen [cases vocalized as] *hi'*; and their list is:
>
> 1. *we-hi' šifḥa*, "and she is a handmaiden" [Lev. 19:20];
> 2. *zimma hi'*,[11] "it is an abomination" [Lev. 20:14];
> 3. *we-hi' tir'e*, "and she sees" [Lev. 20:17];
> 4. *gilleta*, "she revealed" [Lev. 20:18];
> 5. *nidda*, "[she is] forbidden" [Lev. 20:21];
> 6. *mhlkt* [read: *meḥallelet*], "she violates" [Lev. 21:9];[12]
> 7. *hi' bi-terumat*, "she (may eat) from the heave offering" [Lev. 22:12];
> 8. *'aṣeret hi'*, "it is a solemn assembly" [Lev. 23:36];
> 9. *šabbat hi'*, "it is a Sabbath" [Lev. 23:3];
> 10. *we-ha'abadeti 'et ha-nefeš ha-hi'*, "and I will destroy that person" [Lev. 23:30];
> 11. *neqēba*, "female" [Lev. 27:4];
> 12. *'aḥuzzatam*, "their inheritance" [Lev. 25:33];
>
> 13–15. *yobel hi'*, "it is the jubilee," three times in the context [Lev. 25:10, 11, and 12], etc.
>
> The entire parashah is written with a *waw*, and fifteen of the cases are read *hi'*; one of them is *hy' 'hwztm* [Lev. 25:33].

I have been unable to determine the precise source from which Ibn Zimra copied this list, though the issue underlying it is quite well known. As presented, it is very close to that recorded in the *Masorah Finalis* of the 1524–1525 Rabbinic Bible, list *hy-*, which contains the identical introductory passage and the same fifteen biblical examples, though the wording of a number of them differs slightly.

Among the more noteworthy but still relatively minor differences between these two lists is the fact that examples 11, *neqēba* (Lev. 27:4), and 12, *'aḥuzzatam* (Lev. 25:33), are in biblical order in the Rabbinic Bible, while Ibn Zimra's text has them reversed. In fact, his 11 should follow 13–15, *yobel hi'* (Lev. 25:10, 11, and 12), but the special combined formulation of these three cases and particularly its length seem to have caused it to be placed last. Perhaps a more significant indication of a relationship between the two lists is the fact that example 8, *'aṣeret hi'* (Lev. 23:36), should follow 10, *we-ha'abadeti 'et ha-nefeš ha-hi'* (Lev. 23:30), and both Ibn Zimra and the 1524–1525 Rabbinic Bible have it in the same incorrect position.

The passage immediately following the quotation from the Masorah has no parallel there in the Rabbinic Bible. It appears to be Ibn Zimra's attempt at a paraphrase of the rubric, particularly its introduction, and a repetition of the evidence about *ʾaḥuzzaṯam*; actually it is otherwise. The introduction speaks of the fifteen cases "from the end of the section (*siḏra*) of the prohibited sexual unions until the end of the book," while the concluding summary comments on the parashah, presumably *Behar*, which contains Lev. 25:33, or *Behar-Beḥuqoṯai*. In fact, the fifteen cases cover four *parašiyyot*, *Qedoshim*, *Emor*, *Behar*, and *Beḥuqotai*.

According to all accounts, the words in sections 13–15 actually conclude the list, so presumably the "etc." refers to the continuation of the masoretic material. In fact, given the way in which the citation was introduced, one would have expected it to conclude with *ʿ[aḏ] k[aʾn]*, "close quote," rather than *w[e]-ḵ[ule]*, "etc."

Though he did not discuss Ibn Zimra's citation of the passage, C. D. Ginsburg claimed this list of fifteen verses to be composite. In fact, from Lev. 18:23 to 27:34 (the end of the book) there are thirty-one cases of *hwʾ*, twenty-one vocalized *huʾ* and ten vocalized *hiʾ*. The rubric thus combines an original group of ten consistent examples with five additions, nos. 1, 3, 4, 6, and 10 in Ibn Zimra's list. According to this reasoning, the original ten deal only with *hwʾ* read as *hiʾ*; 1 and 4 are about *whwʾ*, read as *we-hiʾ*, and 10 is about *hhwʾ* read as *ha-hiʾ*, of which there are actually three more examples in this section that should have been included (19:8, 20:16, and 22:3). Even more distant are nos. 5 and 6, which belong to a masoretic list that records the cases of the rare consonantal *hyʾ* used with feminine nouns in place of the common spelling *hwʾ*.[13]

The concluding line of the paragraph seems to repeat the introductory one, but it differs in that now all of these cases are related to the parashah. Lev. 25:33 is found in *BeHar*, which extends from 25:1 to 26:2 and contains eight cases of *hwʾ*, four vocalized *huʾ* and four vocalized *hiʾ*. *Beḥuqotai* (Lev. 26:3–27:34), which is often joined with it in the annual cycle of synagogue-based Torah readings, contains seven cases of *hwʾ*, six vocalized *huʾ*, and one vocalized *hiʾ*. Together they add up to fifteen.

Thus it seems that this second comment is incorrect. If intended as a repetition of the introduction to the list, it erred by attributing the fifteen cases to the parashah, not to the nine chapters from 19:20 to the end of the book. If intended as an independent masoretic tabulation, it should indicate that there are eight cases of *hwʾ* in the parashah, of which four (including *hwʾ ʾḥztm* of Lev. 25:33) are read *hiʾ*, or there are fifteen cases of *hwʾ* in the parashah (actually the double parashah, *BeHar-Beḥuqotai*), of which seven, including Lev. 25:33, are read *hiʾ*. Ibn Zimra concludes:

> [6] And it is simple that we should not abandon the teachings of our fathers, and all the codices, and the Masorah, because of Hizquni's opinion.[14] And I have written what seems proper according to my humble opinion.

The fact that Ibn Zimra defended the traditional vocalization and cited the Masorah as evidence does not in any way contradict his position, articulated so forcefully in Responsum A, on not using it to determine the spellings of questionable words. Here the issue is only the vocalization, and he fully supported the belief that the Masorah contained the correct tradition and should not be changed casually by Hizquni or others of his persuasion.

The Literary Background of Ibn Zimra's Responsa: Rabbi Solomon Ben Adret and the Medieval Sefardi Halakhic Literature

> If an error is found [in a Torah scroll] regarding missing or extra letters [in plene or defective spellings], where the opposite is indicated in the Masorah . . . do we say that, since it is explicitly explained in the Masorah, definitely it is an error and we therefore take out another [Torah scroll]? . . . The reason [for not taking out another scroll after finding an error in the first] is that even if there is a definite error in this word, it is nevertheless probable that in the other scroll that we would take out there would also be a mistake of defective spelling instead of plene spelling, or vice versa. Therefore, they permitted [one] to finish the reading in the scroll.
>
> Yehezkel Landau (1713–1793)
> *Noda' BiYehudah, Yoreh De'ah*, no. 178

Ben Adret's Correspondence

The efforts of Jacob ben Hayyim Ibn Adoniyah (ca. 1470–ca. 1538), Menahem di Lonzano (1550–before 1624), Yedidiah Solomon Norzi (1560–1616), and other writers who tried to establish or publish the exact text of the Bible must be evaluated in the context of the Renaissance interest in restoring ancient literary works; but it is the extent of their activity, not its novelty, that is most noteworthy.[1] The many ancient and medieval sources that relate to this complex issue amply testify to a long and distinguished history of discussion, and they demonstrate that fixing the text of the Bible, especially the *matres lectionis*, was an ongoing process that had been debated since talmudic times, if not the Second Temple era, and that continued almost without interruption.[2] Despite the inability to solve every textual problem to universal satisfaction, the contributions of these Renaissance figures to the masoretic effort was vast, significant, and long-lasting. Ibn Zimra's input, by comparison, was far less extensive and primarily halakhic, not masoretic; but, in order to appreciate it, we must examine passages from both the halakhic and masoretic literatures, especially the writings of Solomon ben Abraham Ben Adret, prolific author and unchallenged rabbinic leader of Spanish Jewry up to his death in 1310, whom Ibn Zimra cited several times, as we have already seen. Accordingly, the analysis begins with an anonymous question posed to Ben Adret and moves from there to his response, and then, in the next chapter, to Ibn Zimra's use of it, all the while considering numerous parallel texts and discussions.

Ben Adret's Responsum as Preserved in His Responsa Collection

The following text, contained in a volume of responsa that some writers actually attributed to Nahmanides, Ben Adret's teacher,[3] is a learned question from a familiar correspondent regarding differences in plene and defective spellings of words in the Torah, as presented in the Talmud, the Midrashim, and various masoretic works. Approximately two-thirds of the answer was examined in chapter 2; the entire text is presented here, but only significant new information is discussed. The translation takes into account both the published text and Paris Manuscript 411, which, according to Professor Z. Dimitrovsky, who is editing the Ben Adret responsa, is generally very accurate (personal communication). While most of the improvements in this passage are of a linguistic nature and do not affect the contents, a few variants are designated "P" and are included in braces.

The Question Posed to Ben Adret This detailed and informed question, almost as long as the answer, challenged beliefs about a host of classical texts and issues and offered tentative suggestions. To save space, many questions in responsa collections were condensed or rewritten; its inherent value ensured that this one, probably written by a well-known rabbinic contemporary, was retained in what appears to be close to its full, original form.

> Is a Torah scroll invalidated for ritual use by [having] defective or plene spellings contrary to the Masorah?
>
> For I say the books of the Masorah (*sifrē ha-masora*) are not more authoritative than the books of the Talmud (*sifrē ha-talmuḏ*),[4] which stated: *pilagšim*, "concubines" [Gen. 25:6], is spelled *plgšm*, and similarly *wa-'aśimēm*, "and I will place them" [Deut. 1:13], is spelled *w'śmm*, and similarly *kalloṯ*, "finished" [Num. 7:1], is spelled *klt*, and similarly *qarnoṯ*, "horns" [Lev. 4:7, etc.], is spelled *qrnt*. But in our scrolls (*sefarim*), [they are spelled] *plgšym* {P: *pylgšym*}, with a *yod*; *w'śymm*, with a *yod*; *klwt*, with a *waw*; [and] *qrnwt*, with a *waw*, the opposite of what the sages have said. And we do not defer to the books of the Talmud to correct the scrolls (*ha-sefarim*), to change them, as I have received a tradition from you; so why should we defer to the books of the Masorah, "new things that have arrived of late" [Deut. 32:17]?
>
> Moreover, I have support for this tradition (*qabbala*) from the first chapter of Qiddushin [30a], which states that, in the time of Rav Judah and Rav Joseph, they were not expert in defective and plene spellings. How much less are we!

And we must conclude that those who expounded [the defective spellings of] *plgšm*, *w'śmm*, and *klt* found [matters] this way in their scrolls, but we will not defer to them; and we will retain our scrolls as they are.

Nonetheless, I am not surprised at the verses expounded in aggadic homilies (*derašot*), as we have stated. But [in the matter of] *qrnt/qrnwt* [which is a halakhic exposition], I defer to them [i.e., these sages and their expositions], because the House of Shammai and the House of Hillel accept them and disagree only over the priority of the reading [i.e., the traditional vocalization (*miqra'*)] or the tradition[al spelling (*masoret*)]; both make legal decisions on the basis of defective and plene spellings. My opinion was to change them [i.e., these questionable spellings], but I fear to do so; and I will wait until your word arrives and instructs us [what to do].

And [regarding] *bskwt/bskt*, "booths," we have found it in our scrolls as stipulated by the sages.[5] Tell me your opinion regarding this.

The questioner was aware of variations in the spellings of five specific words, *pilagšim*, *wa-'aśimēm*, *kallot*, *qarnot*, and *ba-sukkot*. He assumed the ancients' scrolls also differed in similar ways, but, apparently, that they all should theoretically conform to one standard, and he asked Ben Adret to establish the hierarchy of textual witnesses that would define it. He believed that Ben Adret's known position was not to change Torah scrolls to follow any unusual spellings that appeared to underlie Bible interpretations found in the Talmud, from which he concluded that changes would be even less proper if done on the basis of post-talmudic masoretic notes. But since related halakhic considerations perhaps gave *qrnt/qrnwt* greater significance than the other examples, he sought Ben Adret's advice. The case of [*b*-]*skt*, where the questioner's scrolls agreed with the ancient rabbis' spelling but not with other known scrolls, provided an additional source of concern.

In fact, the question combined four related queries:

1. In cases of disagreement, is the authority of the Masorah great enough to change the spelling of a word in a Torah text?
2. If so, why; for is not the Masorah less authoritative than the Talmud, on whose authority one generally does not change Torah scrolls?
3. Given that one generally is not allowed to change Torah scrolls on the authority of the Talmud, should one nevertheless change scrolls, even a majority of them, to conform to the Talmud's suggested spelling in halakhic discussions, the area of its greatest authority?
4. If the scrolls already agree with the Talmud [presumably against a majority of Torah scrolls], should they be changed?

The questioner also indicated his own positions on a number of issues, in some cases attributing them directly to Ben Adret:

1. Talmudic statements about the spellings of words are more authoritative than those of the Masorah [though the examples given to support this claim were taken from Midrashim, not from the Talmud].
2. Since talmudic teachings that reflect deviant spellings are insufficient to change Torah scrolls, surely masoretic teachings are no better.
3. Like the rabbis in the time of the Talmud, we are not expert in plene and defective spellings.

4. Torah scrolls in our possession have a greater presumption of accuracy than spellings affirmed by expositions in various ancient rabbinic texts, but halakhic expositions have greater authority than others and may override the scrolls' presumption of accuracy.

Thus the writer pressed Ben Adret to articulate a preference for, on the one hand, the testimony of the Torah scrolls themselves or, on the other, for any of the talmudic, midrashic, or masoretic teachings that may have suggested a spelling different from that attested in them.

The questioner's motivation remains unclear. The letter contains a large theoretical component, but much of it seems to derive from differences between his Torah scrolls and what appeared to be the correct text, at least as defined by the Masorah. A reading of Rabbi Meir Abulafia's *Masoret Seyag LaTorah* (completed in 1227), which underscored the Masorah's importance in contributing to a definitive Torah text but did not suggest it should be the sole factor,[6] may also have contributed to the question. In fact, Abulafia's comments on three of the five words mentioned in the question imply that further analysis may be necessary, as the following passages from *Masoret Seyag LaTorah* demonstrate.

> *we-li-b̲enē ha-pilagšim 'ašer le-'ab̲raham*, "to the sons of Abraham's concubines" [Gen. 25:6]: It [*hpylgšym*] is spelled doubly plene, with two *yods*, in all precise texts that have come into our hands. And it has been noted regarding them in the Masorah, "It is a unique, plene spelling in the Torah." But, in a midrashic exposition, it is derived from here that Hagar was [identical to] Q̣eturah, because it is spelled *hpylgšm*, lacking the *yod* before the *mem*. And indirectly you learn from this that it is spelled without the second *yod*. (p. 55a)[7]

> *wa-yehi be-yom kallot̲ moše le-haqim 'et̲ ha-miškan*, "and on the day Moses finished erecting the tabernacle" [Num. 7:1]: The texts are divided [regarding the spelling of *klwt*]. And [as to] the Masoret, some versions contain "plene *waw*," and it is noted regarding them in the Masorah, "All are plene, except for one that is defective," [namely]: *whyh kklt hšṭrym*, "and when the officers finished" [Deut. 20:9], about which was noted in the Masorah, "It is uniquely defective." And there are versions that state [about] *bywm klt mšh*, "lacking the *waw*." And it is noted regarding them in two masorot and in two places, "Defective in two places throughout the language [of the Bible, i.e.,] *wyhy bywm klt mšh* [Num. 7:1] [and] *whyh kklt hšṭrym* [Deut. 20:9]." And a midrashic exposition supports this last version, which derives from the defective spelling used in [the text about] the building of the tabernacle, that the Israelites were like a bride entering a bridal canopy. And according to everyone, one is plene: *wa-yehi ke-k̲allot̲ moše li-k̲etob̲*, "and when Moses finished writing." (p. 34a)

> *wa-'aśimēm be-rašēk̲em*, "and I will place them at your head" [Deut. 1:13]: In all precise texts, it [*wa-'aśimēm*] is spelled plene *yod* [i.e., *w'symm*] but according to a midrashic exposition it is spelled without the *yod*. (p. 70a)

Abulafia also discussed *qrnt* (p. 63b) and *bskt* (p. 47a), but he failed to record any disagreement among their rabbinic and masoretic treatments. Other passages in his work contain additional disagreements between the Bible texts assumed to underlie rabbinic expositions and those transmitted in the Masorah (e.g., *ḥdšykm*, "your [new] moons," p. 20b, and *ty'śh*, "will be made," p. 53b; see further chapter 2), but they have not been cited in the question.

The spellings of these same three problematic words (and others) also receive attention in the Torah commentary of Rashi (died 1105).

> *ha-pilagšim*, "the concubines" [Gen. 25:6]: It is spelled defective, for there was only one concubine; she is both Hagar and Qeturah.
>
> *wa-yehi be-yom kallot moše*, "and on the day Moses finished" [Num. 7:1]: It is spelled *klt*. On the day of erecting the Tabernacle, Israel was like a bride entering the bridal chamber.
>
> *wa-'aśimēm*, and I will place them" [Deut. 1:13]: The *yod* is lacking [i.e., *w'śmm*]. This teaches that the sins of Israel depend on their judges, for they should correct and direct them to the straight path.

The questioner cited neither Rashi nor Abulafia, and he had access to additional information mentioned by neither. He doubted the Masorah's authority as the major determinant of the consonantal text to be copied in Torah scrolls. He even believed that the Talmud should not be used at all in this process and that Ben Adret concurred but, before taking action to that effect, he sought the advice of his generation's leading rabbinic authority.

Not only did the questioner believe the Masorah irrelevant to this exercise, he placed relatively little stock in it at all. In Deut. 32:17 Moses warned the Israelites not to follow pagan gods, described with the words *ḥadašim mi-qarob ba'u*, "new, that came recently" or "newly arrived from nearby." Even in context, this phrase carries a pejorative connotation, but in later rabbinic literature it serves as an idiom carrying a full range of negative sentiments. Someone or something described as *ḥadašim mi-qarob ba'u* was new, faddish, upstart, unsteeped in the tradition, and generally unreliable, especially when differing from things well known and in accord with traditional thinking or practice; often innovations described this way were strongly opposed by the rabbinic authorities. For example, in his commentary to Is. 2:6, David Kimhi (twelfth to thirteenth century) applied it to new pagan books. Abraham Maimon (twelfth to thirteenth century) used it to describe the recitation of a forbidden blessing. It was applied to faulty halakhic decision making by Rabbenu Tam (twelfth century), Rabbi Joseph Colon (fifteenth century), Ibn Zimra, and many other sixteenth-century writers. Rabbi Meir Katzenellenbogen (Maharam) of Padua used it for those engaged in aggressive business takeovers; Rabbi Samuel Medina, for Marranos. In a passage later cited by Rabbi Moses Isserles, Rabbi Solomon Luria applied it to misguided followers of certain kabbalistic practices.

To be sure, the phrase was also used in the neutral sense of "new" by Rabbi Elijah Mizrahi and for business travelers by Rabbi Betzalel Ashkenazi. In the wake of the many migrations in and following the seventeenth century, the term was often applied to newcomers in a community, often in contexts dealing with their innovative practices and challenges to established norms. But even the term "newcomers" is not totally free of hostility, particularly when the people in question wished to change local practices and to add their own strange or questionable customs to popular ones. Fully neutral usages are found in only a small minority of instances and primarily during and after the seventeenth century; other medieval references I have found are almost unanimously negative.[8]

In this light, the questioner's use of the term can be understood as more than a bombastic use of a biblical phrase meaning "new"; it may be a negative comment—in fact, a strongly negative one—about the Masorah. Note also that the subsequent sentence uses the word "tradition" (*qabbala*) to mean "tradition learned from you," giving Ben Adret's teaching a level of authority at least equal to these other supposedly ancient and binding ones.

On the other hand, Abulafia, who undoubtedly respected the Masorah but did not rank its testimonies over all other types of evidence, described it as *ḥaḏašim ba'u mi-qaroḇ*. This slightly modified version of the phrase may suggest some distance from its contextal meaning and negative connotations. It exploits biblical language to suggest newness, but, not being a quotation, it may intend to avoid most of the negative association. The questioner's use of this verse may derive from Abulafia's, but this is hardly certain.

The interpretation of the term here is complicated by the slightly different wording of Paris Manuscript 411, which reads, *le-sifrē ha-masora mi-qaroḇ ba'u*. This formulation, if assumed not to be missing the word *ḥaḏašim* and when taken in the light of Abulafia's paraphrase of the same verse, may suggest somewhat less negativity than the wording in the printed text, though it affirms the recent vintage or foreign origin of the masoretic literature. At the very least, it is critical of recent masoretic compositions, in contrast to older ones whose value was assumed to be greater. As will be seen, Menahem Meiri (died early fourteenth century) specifically mentioned the value of old masoretic works; and other writers, including Abulafia, often followed ancient texts that differed from later Masorah codices. In a field where the antiquity of the evidence is one of the only qualities that permits its use to challenge talmudic authority or majority testimony, this shortened phrase remains a characterization that implies skepticism of the Masorah, albeit without disrespect. Taken in relation to the questioner's general understanding of the issues as well as his tone, at least some negative sentiment seems certain; I am inclined to see here considerably more.

Ben Adret's Answer Ben Adret's response comes to us in several forms, including independent documentation and citations and paraphrases in other rabbinic works. In order to facilatate textual comparison, the units have been labeled X, Y, and Z and occasionally subdivided. The published text of the responsum reads:

> [X] [1] It is my opinion that this is the truth, [namely] that one should neither add nor delete [letters] in any place in scrolls (*sefarim*) according to the Masoret or according to aggadic Midrashim, because, on the authority of their sages—who were expert in defective and plene spellings—they disagreed in [various] places, in [different] lands.
>
> [2] And it seems to me [that this is so] even regarding the pronunciation (*miqra'*) and regarding the tradition[al spelling (*masoreṯ*)], like the disagreement[s] between Ben Asher and Ben Naftali and similarly between the Westerners and the Easterners.
>
> [Y] And it seems to me that, on this matter [also] depends what they expounded regarding,

"... because he is stronger than we *(mmnw)*" [Num. 13:31], do not read *mimmenu*, "than we," but *mimmennu*, "than he" [BT Sot. 25a],

even though, in all the codices (*sefarim*) written in our region, there is no difference in the word *mmnw*, whether it refers to a plural [antecedent] or to a singular [one], even though in all [other] places, the pronominal element *-nw* is undotted in the plural and is dotted in the singular.[9] But I think there was a disagreement between the Easterners and Westerners regarding *mmnw*, [namely] that one [group] was accustomed [to vocalize] it like the other pronominal elements—without a *dagesh* when it referred to a plural [antecedent]—and one [group] was accustomed, like the custom of our place, to place a dagesh in all forms. And I think I found in the books of the Masorah that there is such a disagreement between the Easterners and Westerners.[10]

[Z] [1] And, in any case, anything cited in the Gemara in a matter of principle of law, like *qrnwt/qrnt*, "horns" [Lev. 4:7, etc.], and like *bswkt*[*/bskt*], "in booths" [Lev. 22:42–43], *lṭwṭpt*/[*lṭṭpt*], "for frontlets" [Ex. 13:16, Deut. 6:3, 11:18], [and] *wbn 'yn lw*, "and he has no son" [Num. 27:8], with a *yod* [BT B.B. 115a], which we expound [for legal purposes], "check it," since it is not written without a *yod*, like *m'n bl'm*, "Bilaam refused" [Num. 22:14] [BT Qid. 4a], with which is associated the principle that an inheritance is transferrable. In this case, we certainly correct a minority.

[2] And similarly, in each and every place, even with regard to defective and plene spellings, we correct the minority according to the majority, because there is an explicit biblical statement "... follow the majority" [Ex. 23:2].

And we learn in Tractate Soferim:[11]

Said R[esh] L[aqish]: Three scrolls were located in the Temple court, *Sefer "M'wn," and Sefer "Z'ṭwṭy,"* and *Sefer* "*Hy'*" {P: *sefer z'ṭwṭym we-sefer katub hy'*}.

In one they found *m'wn 'lhy qdm*, "the dwelling place of the most high" [Deut. 33:27], and in two they found written *m'wnh* [...].

In one they found *[wyšlḥ 't] z'ṭwṭy bny yśr'l*, "and he sent the Israelite youths" [Ex. 24:5], and in two they found [*wyšlḥ 't*] *n'ry* [...].

In one they found "she" [spelled] *hy'* eleven times, and in two [they found it spelled] *hw'* eleven times.

[In each case] they established [the reading in the] two and invalidated [the reading in the] one.

Ben Adret's answer was not exactly what the questioner anticipated; in fact, it differed in several significant ways. The question (a) asked about invalidating a Torah scroll in public use because of plene or defective spellings contrary to the Masorah; (b) stated that the Masorah is no more authoritative than the Talmud; (c) listed the four cases of *pilagšim, wa-'aśimēm, kallot*, and *qarnot* as being spelled one way by the sages in the Talmud and another in the scrolls; (d) mentioned a tradition or teaching received from Ben Adret on this subject that seems to have suggested never relying on the Talmud to change the Torah text; (e) referred to the passage in BT Qid. 30a, in which Amoraim admitted not knowing how to spell some of the words in the Torah; (f) referred to the use of these spellings by the House of Hillel and the House of Shammai; and (g) suggested that the questioner's Torah scrolls spelled *sukkot* as stipulated by the Talmud, in opposition to what was considered the normal spelling in scrolls.

According to the extant text, Ben Adret never responded to the statement about the tradition allegedly received from him (d), nor did he discuss the expositions of spellings by the House of Hillel and the House of Shammai (f), or the talmudic admission of not knowing how to spell the words (e). He did refer to five specific cases in which the rabbis associated laws with the spellings, but only two of them are found in the question; and *pilagšim*, being of no halakhic concern, is not one of them. Ultimately he did answer all the other questions; his position may be summarized in the following way, which simplifies comparison with the position outlined earlier:

1. One never changes the spelling of a word in a Torah scroll to follow the Masorah.
2. One never changes the spelling of a word in a Torah scroll to follow aggadic Midrashim.
3. In cases where the Talmud associated legal principles with the *matres lectionis* in the Torah text, one certainly changes a minority of scrolls to follow the spelling affirmed by the Talmud.
4. A majority of Torah scrolls may be used as the model for correcting the minority.

In short, Ben Adret discounted the value of almost all external witnesses to the text. Variations assumed by the aggadic Midrashim, by the Masorah, and even by the Talmud were not sufficient evidence to warrant changing Torah scrolls, unless the Talmud associated a law with the questionable spelling, or a majority of the scrolls also suggested the change be made; in the latter case, however, the change would be made even without any testimony from other rabbinic documents. The principle behind this argument is biblical, or, to be more precise, the talmudic interpretation of Ex. 23:2,[12] which established majority rule in certain cases of doubt.

The printed text of Ben Adret's responsum states that, in such verses of legal significance, "we certainly correct *the minority* of scrolls" (*waddai meṯaqenin ha-mi'uṭ*). This reading has been corrected by J. Penkower and S. Leiman, both because it lacks logical consistency and because of the wording that appears in Ibn Zimra's version of the passage and in other citations.[13] These lack the word *ha-mi'uṭ* and thus allow Torah scrolls to be corrected according to the Talmud, even if the majority were to be changed. Other aspects of Ben Adret's answer remain essentially as presented, including his relatively low estimation of the potential contribution to the discussion from both the Masorah and the aggadic Midrashim:

> It is my opinion that this is the truth [namely] that one should neither add nor delete [letters] in any place in scrolls (*sefarim*) according to the Masoret or according to aggadic Midrashim.

This resistance to using the Masorah is attributable to its containing many disagreements, which prevent systematic resolution of conflicts. Similar skepticism about the potential contribution of the Midrashim to determining the Bible text is consistent with many medieval Sefaradi statements about their exegetical value.[14]

Though fairly negative about the Masorah's ability to provide a definitive consonantal text, Ben Adret's response did not rule out its value in other matters, such as the placing of large and small letters, the use of dots over words, open and closed paragraph spacings, and other scribal anomalies, and he referred to it in his discussion of *mmnw*. But even here, he introduced the reference with "I think I found in the books of the Masoret," which suggests some distance from it. Moreover, many of these masoretic features are not halakhic necessities; their absence from Torah scrolls often does not render them unfit for public use.

In this respect, Ben Adret's position may deviate from that of Maimonides. Beginning in the seventh chapter of *Hilkhot Sefer Torah*, Maimonides set forth the detailed rules for producing a Torah scroll (in addition to partial discussion included in the earlier chapters primarily about Tefillin and Mezuzot). For all the length and detail of his presentation, nowhere in it does he mention the source from which a scroll should be copied—perhaps on the assumption that all proper scrolls were identical and acceptable, perhaps to avoid the entire issue. Only in discussing the nonconsonantal details, some of which he did not consider binding, did he introduce the value of various scribal traditions (7:8–11); and only in discussing the open and closed paragraph spacings did he mention consulting the famed Ben Asher manuscript, believed to be the Aleppo Codex, and in this context he devoted quite a bit of space to recording its paragraph divisions (8:4). He said he relied on it "in these matters," which could mean in all matters, including spelling, discussed in Maimonides' previous chapter, but the immediately preceding and subsequent contexts suggest that he was referring only to the open and closed paragraph spacings.

In *Hilkhot Tefillin* 2:3 (which precedes *Hilkhot Sefer Torah*), Maimonides insisted that plene and defective spellings in tefillin be as found "in the checked Torah scroll" (*ba-sefer tora ha-baḏuq*), a statement that suggests either that other scrolls were inadequate for this purpose or that at least this one was available and verified. Some writers have suggested this to be the same codex (identified by Maimonides only six chapters later), presumably because both were described as *baḏuq*. But Maimonides referred to the Ben Asher text in 8:4 as a *sefer*, whereas here in 2:3 and at the end of 8:4 he spoke of a *sefer tora*. The latter may actually be the Torah scroll he himself wrote, rather than the Ben Asher codex. Whether he copied his Torah text from that codex remains uncertain, but there is no unequivocal evidence that he required that the spellings of tefillin be copied from it.[15]

Maimonides did not emphasize spelling when he described the writing of a Torah scroll, and he surely did not produce a list of definitive spellings, like those found in some later scribal handbooks, as he did for the paragraph divisions and for the texts included in tefillin. Perhaps both he and Ben Adret intended to limit use of these Masorah codices to correcting details other than the spelling; perhaps only Ben Adret espoused this position.

Another of Ben Adret's Responsa or a Revision of the Foregoing One?

A Comparison of Two Copies of a Short Responsum by Ben Adret The official, autonomous version of Ben Adret's responsum is complemented by another one cited in at least two sixteenth-century works.[16] The postexpulsion era of the sixteenth century saw the gathering of Spanish exiles with other Jews in many foreign lands, particularly those in and around Turkey. Among them was the Spanish text expert Abraham Hasan. Shortly after being assigned to examine and correct Salonika's Torah scrolls, which had been collected from many distant lands and which exhibited a number of differences in spelling and layout, Hasan was thwarted by the local rabbinic authorities, who found his rigorous and systematic revisions of their most sacred texts troubling. His correspondence with contemporary rabbinic leaders discusses the halakhic and scribal authority for what he wished to do and his feelings about the obstacles placed in his path. In his verbose and flowery but not, on that account, less compelling epistle sent to Rabbi Elijah Mizrahi (1450–1526), and in a parallel letter to Rabbi Joseph Taitatzak, now printed as an appendix to it, he presented and sharply criticized Ben Adret's position.

Rabbi Joseph Caro cited that same responsum by Ben Adret without the negative reaction, in his masterful *Beit Yosef*, in the course of commenting on the passages about Torah scrolls in Jacob ben Asher's *Arba'ah Turim, Yoreh De'ah* no. 275. The two citations of the responsum warrant close comparison:

HASAN'S VERSION OF BEN ADRET	CARO'S VERSION OF BEN ADRET
[Summary of the Question:] Moreover, you said that, in the scrolls (*sefarim*), *kklwt mšh,*	[Summary of the Question:] You asked [regarding the fact] that, in the scrolls (*sefarim*), *klwt mšh,*
"*when Moses finished,*" is found plene (*šalēm*), and our rabbis said "it is spelled *kklt*." [And you asked] if the scrolls in which *kklwt* is found plene are an error.	"[when] Moses finished," [Num. 7:1] is found plene (*malē'*), but our rabbis said (in Midrash Rabbah, *Parashat Naśo'*): "it is spelled *klt*."
[Answer:] Know that, just as Ben Asher and Ben Naftali [the text says "Aleph and Nun"]	Answer: Know that, just as Ben Asher and Ben Naftali
were of different opinions in several places, I found that the Westerners and the Easterners were divided over some disputed words.[17] For they said in the Gemara(!): "*wlbny hplgšym* [Gen. 25:6]	were of different opinions in several places, I found that the Westerners and the Easterners were divided over disputed words.[17] For they said in the Gemara(!): "It [*pylgšym*, 'concubines,' in Gen. 25:6]
is spelled *pylgšm*"; but in the scrolls (*sefarim*) it is spelled plene (*malē'*). [And similarly] in many places. Moreover, you should know that anywhere we find a disagreement among the scrolls, they say in Tractate Soferim that one should follow the majority. Thus far his words.	is spelled *pylgšm*"; but in our scrolls (*be-sifrēnu*) it is spelled plene (*malē'*). And similarly in many places. Moreover you should know that anywhere we find a disagreement among the scrolls, they said in Tractate Soferim that one should follow the majority. Thus far his words.

These are two different witnesses to the same text, but several points must be addressed before a single unified version can be restored and compared with the longer responsum.

A. Both citations begin with the word ʿ*od*, "moreover," but Hasan uses it to refer to a previous inquiry by the questioner, while Caro refers back to a previous responsum attributed to Ben Adret, this one being the second in a series of three. Caro began the series with "The Rashba wrote in a responsum," cited the text, continued "and he wrote further" (*we-katab ʿod*) to introduce the present text, and concluded "and he wrote further" (*we-katab ʿod*) to present the third one. Hasan, on the other hand, began his citation of the question preceding the responsum ʿ*od ʾamarta še-nimṣaʾ ba-sefarim "kklwt moše" malē*ʾ, "furthermore you said that in the scrolls (*ba-sefarim*) *kklwt moše* is written plene." This use of ʿ*od* suggests that the present question was one of a series, possibly one that could have contained other questions related to spelling.

B. Despite their seeming similarity, the subjects of the two questions are not identical. According to Hasan's version, the question was about the word *ke-kallot* in the phrase *kkl(w)t moše*, "when Moses finished," while Caro's version reads *klwt moše*, which is found in Num. 7:1, *wa-yehi be-yom kallot moše le-haqim ʾet ha-miškan*, "and on the day Moses finished erecting the tabernacle."

The spellings of the various forms of the word *kl(w)t* have been the subject of much discussion in masoretic works. The phrase *kklt mšh* appears in Deut. 31:34, *wa-yehi ke-kallot moše li-ketob ʾet dibrē ha-tora ha-zoʾt*. . . , where it is generally spelled *kklwt*. Normally, discussions of this word focus on whether it should be spelled *klt* or *klwt* in Num. 7:1, though Abulafia extended his presentation to the phrase *wa-yehi ke-kallot ha-šoṭerim* (Deut. 20:9), *Masoret Seyag LaTorah*, p. 34a (translated above). As presented here, the two verses seem to be confused. Dimitrovsky has emended Hasan's version of the question to refer to Num. 7:1, but in light of Abulafia's note, it is possible that one could ask about either, though questions about both are unlikely and probably would not result in identical answers. Note, also, that the spelling of *kkltw/kklwtw* is an issue in Ex. 31:18; cf. Rashi and Norzi (ad loc.).

Meanwhile, a significant amount of discussion about whether *klt* in Num. 7:1 should be spelled plene or defective is on record. The rabbis expounded the defective spelling, yet the plene one was reportedly found in many scrolls—the situation recorded in both versions here. Caro's reading is preferable.

C. The term for plene spelling in Hasan's version of the question is *šalēm*, while Caro's is *malē*ʾ; both versions of the answer use *malē*ʾ. It is difficult to choose between them, but some later citations also use *šalēm*, and, since *malē*ʾ was the more popular term later and texts were more likely to be corrected to it, *šalēm*, the *lectio difficilior*, may be preferable.

D. No source for the rabbinic teaching contradicting the spelling of the biblical word *kklwt* is found in Hasan's version; indeed, the likely error in citing the verse means there probably is none. On the other hand, it is likely that the publisher, not Caro and surely not Ben Adret, included the reference to Numbers Rabbah; hence its appearance in parentheses. Whatever its origin, it is correct.

E. The printed text of Hasan says that unnamed authorities were divided over *aleph* and *nun* (*neḥlequ be-ʾalef u-be-nun*), but this wording is impossible. No such disagreement is found among the available masoretic sources, and Caro's reading,

"Ben Asher and Ben Naftali," is obviously correct. Both phrases can be abbreviated *b-'. . . b-n*, and, while Hasan's editor seems to have missed this fact, other medieval references to this lack of uniformity concur with Caro's reading.[18]

It is somewhat ironic that Hasan's attack on the scribal imperfections he found in Torah scrolls was preserved in such an imperfect text, a fact to which he himself alluded when citing Ben Adret, but this is not the only passage in his very long essay that requires textual improvement. The minor differences between the two versions of the question leave a general sense that Caro's is preferable, but the answers are essentially the same. The larger issue is the nature of the relationship between the shorter version of Ben Adret's response found here and the longer one discussed above.

A Comparison of the Long and Short Versions of Ben Adret's Answers A comparison of the two versions of Ben Adret's teaching yields some important facts and helps settle several important textual doubts.

A. All but one of the principal elements in the short answer appear in the longer one: (1) the reference to the differences of opinion between Ben Asher and Ben Naftali, (2) the reference to differences of opinion between the Westerners and the Easterners, (3) the admission that similar problems are common, and (4) the derivation from Soferim 6:4 of the principle that, in cases of disagreement among Torah scrolls, one should follow the majority.

B. The only major point found in the short answer but not in the long one is the reference to the supposed preference of the Gemara for the defective spelling of *ha-pilagšim* in Gen. 25:6, despite the plene spelling in the scrolls. The reference does appear in the question preceding the long version of the responsum, but it is not mentioned specifically in the long answer, which focused on halakhically relevant spellings.

C. The long question and both versions of the short answer concur in attributing the rabbinic discussion of *pilagšim* to the Gemara, even though it is not found there. Assuming there was never a time when the Talmud contained this material, this common reference establishes a very close link between the two texts that may transcend their having a single author.

D. The long version, meanwhile, differs from the shorter one in several significant ways: (1) the clearly articulated position that one should not correct scrolls on the basis of the Masorah, (2) an equally clear statement to the effect that one should not correct scrolls on the basis of the aggadic Midrashim, (3) a lengthy digression about a possible difference between two ways of vocalizing the word *mmnw* when it means "than him" or "than us," (4) specific reference to five other biblical texts of questionable spelling (awareness of them may be inferred from the reference to "many others" at the end of the short version, but they are not identified), (5) full citation of Soferim 6:4, and (6) discussion of the Talmud's importance in determining the spellings of words with which specific legal conclusions had been linked. As well, in discussing the plene and defective spellings, both the long question and its answer use the Aramaic terms *ḥaser* and *yatir* (in singular or plural), in contrast to the short questions, which are divided over the use of the Hebrew terms *šalēm* or *malē'*, and the short answers, both of which use *male'*.

The short version may be an abridgement of the long one, but this interpretation is far from certain. It would account for all of its contents; the discussion of *pilagšim* would have been derived from the learned question, not the answer. Ibn Zimra's citation of the long responsum in Ibn Zimra omitted the middle third as being irrelevant (probably because no one cared any longer about nonexistent differences in the vocalization of *mmnw*), and the passage from Soferim, while complete in Ibn Zimra, had already been abridged in the "full" text of the long responsum. One could even theorize that Hasan's beginning with *ʿoḏ* suggests that this was merely part of a much longer question that had been radically shortened.

One flaw in this reasoning is that the short text, as presented, specifies problems only in nonhalakhic contexts, and the major interest of the long version is in halakhic ones. Moreover, the shorter version lacks the longer version's definitive rejection of the authority of both the aggadic Midrashim and the Masorah with respect to the consonantal text, a modification already encountered in chapters 3 and 4 (Responsa B and C), where Ibn Zimra also shortened the full responsum by omitting the opening comments. In fact, the short answer is essentially a paraphrase of the conclusions in paragraphs X and Y of the long one. Were it a summary of the full longer response, the epitomizer would hardly be likely to have done such violence to its intention, unless its teachings were no longer accepted and were thought to require a thorough overhaul. That possibility, of course, is very likely, for support for the Masorah did increase in certain circles; and in the brief preliminary discussion of his edition of Ben Adret's writings, Dimitrovsky has mentioned the existence of extreme abridgements of Ben Adret's responsa and the radical changes sometimes introduced in them.[19] But while the possibility must be considered, we do not have a definite context for the change. And if this is what happened, it must be dated quite early, for we shall soon see that both versions were known to rabbinic writers in the generation immediately after Ben Adret.

For now, it is probably safer to conclude that the short text is an independent responsum that shares much with the longer one. This is essentially what Dimitrovsky did by printing the short version separate from the long one (which has not yet appeared in his edition). Ben Adret did write some very short responsa, even to Masorah-related questions. One is preserved only six paragraphs away from this one: number 238 in the volume of responsa attributed to Nahmanides. Two more are found in Caro's *Beit Yosef*, the first and third in the series in which this one appears; see also Baqrat, *Sefer HaZikkaron* to Gen. 11:31–32.

Another, quite different, sixteenth-century report of Ben Adret's thinking about this question is preserved in *Sefer HaZikkaron*, Gen. 25:6, in one of Baqrat's frequent discussions of problems that arise from Rashi's treatment of a variant Torah text:

> And the Rashba, of blessed memory [i.e., Ben Adret], was already asked about this, and from his response, it emerges that:
>
> > One should correct [a Torah scroll] neither according to the Masoret nor according to the Aggadah, except the places cited in the Talmud in a matter of law, like *qrnwt/qrnt*, "horns" [Lev. 4:25, etc.], and like *bskt/bskt/bskwt*, "in booths" [Lev. 23:42, etc.], and the like. These we surely do correct [according to the Talmud], and [in these cases] we do not follow the majority of scrolls (*sefarim*), even though everywhere we are in doubt, we correct the minority ac-

> cording to the majority, for there is an explicit biblical verse, ". . . follow the majority" [Ex. 23:2].

This is an abridgement of his responsum.[20]

This text is a summary of Ben Adret's long responsum, its major themes condensed but intact. Whether produced by someone else or by Baqrat himself (he admitted being Ben Adret's epitomizer in Lev. 11:47 but did not comment here), it is a much more accurate precis of the long text than the short version previously discussed. By confirming its contents, this summary provides additional evidence that the long version, with the anti-Masorah position intact, was available among Sefaradi writers of the expulsion period.

The relative lack of detail in the short responsum preserved by Caro and Hasan leaves it looking almost inconsequential relative to the longer one, but even in this form it reinforces several of the longer version's points. By noting that the masoretes often disagreed on textual matters, it affirms that their statements in other disputed areas cannot be taken as definitive, and it also suggests that the operative principle in treating doubtful cases should be to follow a majority of scrolls. Essentially it ignores both the orthographic implications of talmudic expositions (no halakhically significant verses are mentioned) and the potential contributions to be gleaned from the masters of the Masorah and the aggadic Midrashim. It surely does not contradict the long version's challenge to the value of the Masorah and the aggadic Midrashim.

The Impact of Ben Adret's Responsa in Medieval Times

Since Ben Adret's teachings influenced the Iberian rabbinic world and from there the entire Jewish world, we can examine the trajectories of these two responsa in the writings of some of his followers.

Rabbi Moses (Maharam) ben Gaon Halava Maharam Halava was a student of Ben Adret and a close friend of his son Judah.[21] A curious writer had asked him about the proper way to space some of the passages from the book of Numbers on the lines of a Torah scroll, and Maharam referred to the format in scrolls available to him in Barcelona and to the attitude of Rabbenu Nissim, who followed a particular practice, apparently in opposition to the Masorah.[22] He then added:

> Conflicting ideas of the sages of the Torah have multiplied exceedingly regarding laws, commandments, and prohibited and permitted things, so that the Torah anticipated the understanding of the people[23] and ended the matter with two principles. One is "follow the majority" [Ex. 23:2], and the second is [based on the rabbinic interpretation of the verse that says, "These are the Lord's festivals,] that you should proclaim them" [Lev. 23:2–4], [understood to mean] "that you, yourselves, should proclaim them" [emphasizing the independent role of the courts in the decision], even if they act in accidental, innocent, or intentional error [BT R.H. 25a].
>
> Our rabbis, of blessed memory, also gave a limit to their words by saying, "Any point of halakhah that is uncertain to you, go out and see how the community behaves, and behave in this way" [PT M.S. 4:2]. And were it not for these fences, the legs of Israel would totter, because they disagree even regarding the text of the Torah (*gufah šel tora*) and its reading.[24]

The next four paragraphs contain a list of cases in which individual rabbis challenged laws declared by others to be Halakhah to Moses from Sinai.

> [1] They said in the first chapter of Qiddushin and in the chapter [entitled] "There Is No Difference Between One Who Has Vowed" [BT Qid. 30a and Ned. 38a]:
>
> > In the West, they divide this biblical text into three verses: "And the Lord Said to Moses: 'Behold I come to you in a cloud of smoke [in order that the people will hear when I speak with you. And they will believe in you forever.' And Moses told the people's words to the Lord]" [Ex. 19:9].
>
> And even though everything is Halakhah to Moses at Sinai, as they said there, "'and *śom śeḵel*' [Neh. 8:8] refers to verse divisions" [cf. BT Ned. 37a].[25]
>
> [2] And in the chapter [entitled] "[One May Read the Megillah] Standing or Sitting" they said:
>
> > "Any [verse] division that Moses did not make, we do not make, either; [and Samuel said, We do make such divisions]" [cf. BT Meg. 22a].[26]
>
> [3] And in the chapter [entitled] "One Who Sleeps [Under a Bed," i.e., in a sukkah], they said:
>
> > [The definition of] a joint [between two pieces of a sukkah] is Halakhah to Moses at Sinai; anything that is less than three [handbreadths] is considered joined. Rabbi Shimon ben Gamaliel disagrees and says, "four" [cf. BT Suk. 16b, 18a].
>
> [4] And in the chapter [entitled] "The Skin and the Gravy," Rabbi Yose does not accept that compressed impurity pushes through and upward, but it is Halakhah to Moses at Sinai [that it does] [cf. BT Hul. 125b].
>
> There are many similar cases, and everything is settled through [the principle] "follow the majority." Therefore one should not introduce any innovation on the authority of the Masoret, because inherent in the innovation is a doubt of [creating something] invalid. Rather one should follow the scrolls of the majority of scribes who are worthy of being relied upon and the general custom.
>
> Know that in the Gemara and in the Midrashim they said "*kalloṯ* [Num. 7:1] is spelled *klt*"; "*pilagšim* [Gen. 26:5] is spelled *plgšym* [read: *plgšm*(?)]"; [and] "*wa-'aśimēm* [Deut. 1:13] is spelled *w'śmm*," but in the Torah scrolls in our possession, all are plene, and it never occurred to [anyone] to change [them]. And the Masorah should not be more authoritative than the Gemara and the Midrash.
>
> And the sages already established their words regarding changing texts according to this law of the Torah to follow the majority. They said in Tractate Soferim [6:4]:
>
> > Said Rabbi Shimon ben Laqish: Three scrolls were located in the Temple court, *Sefer* "*M'wn*," and *Sefer* "*Z'ṭwṭy Bny Yśr'l*," and *Sefer* "*Hy'*."
> >
> > In one they found written *m'wn 'lhy qdm*, and in two they found written *m'wnh 'lhy qdm* [Deut. 33:27]; they established [the reading in the] two and invalidated [the reading in the] one.
>
> Therefore one should not change [the text].[27]
>
> > In one they found written *wyšlḥ 't z'ṭwṭy bny yśr'l*, and in two [they found] written [*wyšlḥ 't n'ry* . . . [Ex. 24:5]; they established the reading in the two and invalidated the reading in the one.
> >
> > In one they found "she" spelled *hy'* eleven times, and in two they found it spelled] *hw'* eleven times; they established [the reading in the] two and invalidated [the reading in the] one.

> Therefore, one should not change from the way of the majority of scrolls.

He then answered the question about spacing the words, but the details are too distant from our present concern for the passage to warrant translation.

Much of Maharam's erudite contribution to the discussion is devoted to a series of examples in which laws designated as Halakhah to Moses from Sinai are disputed; the same is true of some matters attributed to the Masorah. This text discusses the identical type of inconsistency in the spelling of pentateuchal words that we have found in other rabbinic works of the period, and it parallels Ben Adret's responsa in several significant ways. Though it admits no awareness of a written form of Ben Adret's ruling, it reflects essentially the same disinclination to rely on the practices suggested by the Masorah in questionable situations. This responsum comes from the same general area in Spain as Ben Adret's, but a generation or so later. Were Ben Adret known to have written or ruled favorably toward reliance on the Masorah, even at the end of his life, Maharam Halava should have known of it. What we have here is the same generally unsupportive attitude, which had survived Ben Adret and, as we shall see, which spread throughout the Spanish region under his influence.

A closer look at the text suggests that Maharam's statement is actually an expansion and development of Ben Adret's, most likely of the long responsum. His discussion of the talmudic principle of inspecting scrolls and relying on what the people do suggests support for the evidence of the scrolls, and the statement

> Therefore one should not introduce any innovation on the authority of the Masoret, because inherent in the innovation is a doubt of [creating something] invalid. Rather one should follow the scrolls of the majority of scribes who are worthy of being relied upon, and the general custom. . . .

leaves no doubt about his position, which bears more resemblance to the long version of Ben Adret's responsum than to the short one. The three verses chosen for discussion—*kallot̲* (Num. 7:1), *pilagšim* (Gen. 26:5), and *wa-ʾaśimēm* (Deut. 1:13)—are reminiscent of the list in the long question, not the long answer, though one appears in the short question and one in the short answer. Were he the author of the question, we might assume that he referred to the sources correctly as "Talmud and Midrash" and that this was shortened to "Talmud" in later copies of the long responsum, including that version from which the short one was adapted, assuming that relationship to have existed.

Maharam Halava also discussed the Masorah in his Responsum 145, but in a very different context. In *Hilkhot Sefer Torah*, Maimonides took a very dim view of the range of variations in open and closed paragraph divisions found in Torah scrolls and, in what became a major problem for many subsequent rabbis, ruled that any deviation from one model invalidated the scroll. These divisions were based on Ben Asher's famous codex, believed by many to be the apex of masoretic creativity, but Maharam, like Rabbi Abraham ben Maimon before him and Rabbi Judah Mintz (and others) after him, found room for some legitimate deviation from these norms.[28] Resolution of the spacing issue has no direct relationship to the determination of spelling, but it is indirectly related to establishing the authority of the Masorah.

Also noteworthy, particularly in the context of ranking witnesses to the text, is his statement that "one should follow the scrolls of the majority of scribes who are worthy of being relied upon and the general custom." This is what many writers did, regardless of what they claimed.

Rabbenu Nissim ben Reuben Another reference to Ben Adret's teachings appears in the Talmud commentary of Rabbenu Nissim ben Reuben (fl. 1340–1380).[29] In discussing the rabbinic association of laws with *qrnt, qrnt, qrnwt* (Lev. 4:7, etc.) in BT San. 4a, he observed:

> *qrnt, qrnt, qrnwt*, "horns" [Lev. 4:7, etc.]: It is patently clear from this that, according to the Gemara, *qrnwt* should be spelled with a *waw* in a Torah scroll, in the paragraph about an individual's sheep offering [cf. BT San. 4a and Zev. 37b]. And some of the commentators of blessed memory, who wrote in the name of Rabbi Solomon [the printed text has *hr- r- š/slmy*], of blessed memory, wrote that *qrnwt* [i.e., spelled plene] is not [found] either in the written text (*ba-miktab*) or in the Masorah, and if so, it requires [further] investigation.
>
> And there is a similar situation [regarding] *be-yom kallot moše*, "on the day Moses finished" [Num. 7:1], [which should be spelled] plene (*šalēm*); and our rabbis say *plgšm* [Gen. 25:6] is [spelled] defective.
>
> And the Rashba, of blessed memory, wrote that this is a disagreement between the Easterners and Westerners, like the disagreements of Ben Asher and Ben Naftali,[30] and that anywhere we find disagreements among the scrolls (*sefarim*), they said in Tractate Soferim that one should follow the majority.

This presentation can be divided into two sections. The first paragraph deals with the *qarnot* question in Sanhedrin and may be an independent construction of Rabbenu Nissim, though it seems to have been informed by several comments of Rashi and the Tosafot. The last two paragraphs are clearly a reflection of Ben Adret's teaching. They refer to *be-yom kallot moše* (Num. 7:1) and *pilagšim* (Gen. 25:6), and they use *šalēm* to indicate "plene spelling."

This reference, it would seem, is to the short responsum, not the long one, and therefore it is less specific about the Masorah than are some others, but it adopts the same general position. It notes that the masoretic authorities themselves contradict each other, and it suggests that solutions to textual inconsistencies be reached by following a majority, presumably of Torah scrolls, and not, as others would later suggest, of masoretic documents.

Rabbi Isaac bar Sheshet Perfet Rabbi Isaac Bar Sheshet Perfet (the Rivash) was a controversial and somewhat tragic figure. Born in Barcelona in 1326 and later a student of Rabbenu Nissim and Rabbenu Peretz, he was exiled to North Africa as a result of the riots of 1391, and he served there as a colleague of Rabbi Shimon ben Zemah Duran. Bar Sheshet's works include many important responsa, one of which strongly resembles part of Ben Adret's, though it does not cite him. The query centers around two talmudic stories (in BT A.Z. 29b and B.B. 21b) that suggested to the questioner that ancient Bible manuscripts did not contain any vocalization. The answer begins by challenging the premise that a difference in reading would suggest the absence of vocalization; instead, the difference might be just another example of the differences among texts.

> Even if their books were vocalized, it is not difficult [to explain], if Rabbi Akiva erred in the reading of that verse [i.e., *ki tobim dodeka mi-yayin*, "for your love is sweeter than wine" (Song of Songs 1:2)], for it is possible that there was a disagreement about this word in their texts (*be-sifrehem*), just as today there are [disagreements] regarding many words between the Westerners and Easterners and between Ben Asher and Ben Naftali. And there was disagreement in the texts (*ba-sefarim*) even about exchanges of words. And the sages were in doubt and were forced to go according to majority, as we have learned in Tractate Soferim:
>
> > Said R[esh] L[aqish]: Three scrolls were located in the Temple courtyard: *Sefer* "*M'wn*," and *Sefer* "*Z'ṭwṭy*," and *Sefer* "*Hy*"'. . . .[31]

The answer continues by arguing that in fact no assumption that vocalization is lacking is needed to explain the story.

Unlike some of the texts examined earlier, this one demonstrates no close textual affinity to Ben Adret's responsa; still, it shows an awareness of the same general line of thinking and an ability to apply it as needed. Whether or not the author knew of Ben Adret's teaching, this letter is further evidence of its wide acceptance.

Rabbi Shimon ben Zemah Duran A reference to Ben Adret's position is also found in the responsa collection entitled *Sefer Tashbetz* by Rabbi Shimon ben Zemah Duran, a refugee from Majorca who served as a rabbinic leader of Algiers during the first half of the fifteenth century. The question posed to him concerned spelling differences suggested by the Talmud and Midrashim, on the one hand, and by the Torah scrolls on the other. Specifically they concern *himmol yimmol*, "let be circumcised" (Gen. 17:13); *ha-pilagšim*, "concubines" (Gen. 25:6); and *be-yom kallot*, "on the day [Moses] finished" (Num. 7:1). His answer was that the first is no problem, and while the spellings of the other two are disputed in the Midrashim,

> . . . The Rashba, of blessed memory, already wrote in a responsum that one should not rely on these Midrashot to correct the scrolls, and one should leave them plene (*šelemim*), except in a matter from which a law is derived, like *bskt/bskt/bskwt*, or *qrnt/qrnt/qrnwt*, etc.[32]

This reference must be to the long responsum, since the short one deals with neither the question of words whose spelling is of halakhic import nor the two examples cited, *ba-sukkot* and *qarnot*. The evidence from this document appears equivocal, because it does not mention the Masorah, yet this cannot be seen as support for a softening of the position against its usage. The question did not require dealing with it, and its absence from an otherwise very brief response enables us to draw no other conclusions.

Abraham Hasan In the course of discussing the textual inconsistencies among Salonika's Torah scrolls, which he had been engaged to check, Hasan reacted to the Masorah-related comments in Menahem Meiri's *Qiryat Sefer*. Meiri had faced the same types of problems that confronted other rabbis, and he attempted to resolve them as best he could. Hasan, himself ardently pro-Masorah, observed, correctly if too aggressively, that Meiri was ignorant of *Masoret Seyag LaTorah*. He was at once quite critical of what Meiri had done, and he took a very tendentious position in describing Abulafia's commitment to the Masorah. At the same time he argued, without due consideration of Meiri's real thinking on the subject, that no one could possibly think that Meiri would have considered following a majority of scrolls in place of the Masorah.

Hasan cited Ben Adret's short responsum as well, but even though it does not discuss the Masorah at all, he tried to force this same pro-Masorah notion into it. He clearly saw the possibility of reading Ben Adret's stance as favoring the use of the majority of scrolls, but he was very strongly opposed to doing so. Perhaps Hasan knew of the longer version of Ben Adret's responsum but had access only to the shorter one, which he cited and simultaneously accused of inaccuracy. His outrage was so great that he saw this rejection of the Masorah's control of doubtful cases as proof that Ben Adret really did not know what he was talking about and as clear evidence either that he must have been unaware of Abulafia's *Masoret Seyag LaTorah* (which is possible and clearly true of Meiri), or that he must have lived before it was written (which is not).

> I am unable to endure [this] even if the greatest [rabbi] in Israel will say this, for not by any means is it possible, that what they [i.e., Meiri and Ben Adret] said [was] that [the principle] "one should follow the majority" means the majority of scrolls (*sefarim*). Rather [it means] the majority of *masoroṯ*, as the holy Rabbi Meir HaLevi [Abulafia], peace be upon him, decreed, as the author of *Qiryat Sefer* [i.e., Meiri] clearly acknowledged . . . [we follow] the scribes and not the scrolls.[33]

To say the least, Hasan overstepped the evidence.

The Search for the Identity of Ben Adret's Correspondent

The identity of the writer who posed the initial, lengthy question to Ben Adret is somewhat removed from our primary concern but has implications for both the history of the conflict over the establishment of *matres lectionis* and Ibn Zimra's use of the available literature. In fact, his question was not completely new; many of Ben Adret's predecessors and contemporaries dealt with the spellings of the words in question, and a few are worth considering.

Rabbi Bahya ben Asher

In his Torah commentary (dated to 1291), Bahya ben Asher (died 1340) noted the midrashic spellings of a number of words, including *plgšym* (Gen. 25:6), *wbn ʾyn lw* (Num. 27:8), *wʾśymm* (Deut. 1:13), and *mzzwt* (Deut. 6:9); in some cases he even discussed the discrepancies between the rabbinic and masoretic spellings:

> *wlbny hpylgšym*, "and to the sons of the concubines" [Gen. 25:6]: The sages, of blessed memory, expounded, "It is spelled *plgšm* [i.e., defective]."
>
> *wʾśymm brʾšykm*, "and I will place them at your head" [Deut. 1:13]: And our rabbis, of blessed memory, expounded, "*wʾśymm brʾšykm*, it is spelled *wʾśmm* [defective] . . . ," even though in our texts it is spelled with a *yod*.
>
> *wktbtm ʿl mzzwt*, "and write them on the doorposts" [Deut. 6:9]: Our rabbis, of blessed memory, expounded, "It is spelled *mzwzt*."[34]

On the surface, Bahya, one of Ben Adret's well-known students, qualifies as the correspondent. He could have been aware of his teacher's position and would have felt comfortable approaching him for a definitive answer, as he did on other matters.[35] But while he was aware of the discrepancies between rabbinic claims about the spellings of these words and their actually attested spellings, his comments do not approach the detail of Ben Adret's. Indeed, they resemble more the presentation in Rashi's Torah commentary, where all of them are mentioned. If Bahya was the correspondent, he did not incorporate Ben Adret's answer into his commentary.[36]

Rabbi Judah ben Eliezer

The Riva (Rabbi Judah ben Eliezer) wrote a Torah commentary that goes by several names, including *Minhat Yehudah*, and is traditionally dated to 1313.[37] His comment on Gen. 25:6, translated earlier at the beginning of chapter 2, cites a number of important passages from Rashi and other early Ashkenazi writers who noted conflicts between the Masorah, the Midrashim, and the Talmud, but nothing in his presentation suggests more than shared interest in the problem that bothered Ben Adret's correspondent.

This passage demonstrates no direct connection with those discussed earlier, but it confirms that one locus of this problem's discussion centered on Rashi's Torah commentary and its treatment in the tosafist glosses and supercommentaries. It strengthens the possibility that the question to Ben Adret was influenced by the writings of Rashi or of the Tosafists but leads us to assume that both Rabbi Judah ben Eliezer and the men he cited resolved to their own satisfaction whatever conflicts they noticed.

Rabbi Shem Tov ben Abraham Ben Gaon

Shem Tov ben Abraham was another of Ben Adret's many important students. Among his literary contributions are *Migdal Oz*, a commentary on Maimonides' *Mishneh Torah* (including *Hilkhot Sefer Torah*), and a number of mystical works, but he was also a famous scribe who produced a model Bible text and was highly interested in masoretic matters. Shem Tov's literary contributions have been summarized by H. Michael,[38] and his Masorah-related activities have been described more extensively by D. S. Levinger.[39] Ibn Zimra cited him in Responsum C, regarding the cut *waw* in Num. 25:12 (see chapter 4).

The colophon to Shem Tov's model text contains the statement:

> I found the texts of the ancients sometimes divided regarding defective and plene [spellings] . . . and I was forced to labor an indescribable amount, until recently God blessed me and *Sefer Taggi* came into my hands, received by direct transmission [back] to its being copied from the twelve stones in Gilgal and the Masoret of Ezra and his court.[40]

Shem Tov was the recipient of several of Ben Adret's letters to Tudela[41] and surely would have been interested in his teacher's ideas about spelling, but the above passage suggests that, in his own mature work, Shem Tov derived a great deal of information about plene and defective spellings from masoretic sources. A full review of his literary legacy, especially his earlier work, might suggest otherwise, but he seems to have valued the masoretic literature far more than seems possible for the person who posed the question. Shem Tov was probably not its author, because he would have disagreed with the principles underlying its formulation.

Rabbi Moses (Maharam) ben Gaon Halava

Another close parallel to the original question to Ben Adret is found in the previously cited responsum by Maharam Halava. Maharam was a member of Ben Adret's household and school and a close associate of his son. Various sources place him in contact with Ben Adret; one of Maharam's responsa suggests that he knew Ben Adret while still too young to appreciate him, but his precise age at the time of Ben Adret's death is unknown. Surely he was in a position to have studied and cited the master's teachings. Whether he heard them directly or indirectly, Maharam could have applied to himself the phrase *še-kak̲ 'ani mequbbal mimmek̲a*, "for I have a tradition from you."[42]

Maharam's attitude to the Masorah is quite negative and approximates that of the questioner, who said, "And therefore one should not introduce any innovation on the authority of the Masoret, because inherent in the innovation is a doubt of [creating something] invalid." But perhaps the strongest evidence is the similarity between the original statement of the questioner, "for I say that the books of the Masorah are not more authoritative than the books of the Talmud," and that of Maharam, "And the Masorah should not be more authoritative than the Gemara and the Midrash."

Direct or close to direct contact possibly colored Maharam's understanding of Ben Adret's position, and his own distinguished mastery of the rabbinic material could have suggested additional preference for the "vulgar" version of the Torah text, found in precise Spanish scrolls, over the masoretic one. Perhaps he also disagreed somewhat and preferred a stronger stand than Ben Adret's. The major problem with this suggestion is Maharam's youth. While the evidence is very thin, one is almost forced to assume that he was too young during the years he spent with Ben Adret to write in the forceful way the questioner did, presenting his own views as aggressively as they now appear. Of course, one might attribute this very boldness and verbosity to Maharam's youth itself, and one could even postulate the presence of a learned accomplice, but such arguments are too speculative to be fruitful. Suffice it to note that, in the absence of a better candidate or contrary historical evidence, Maharam could have penned the question.

Rabbi Menahem Meiri

Meiri's Comment on Qiddushin 30a Menahem Meiri discussed the spelling variations in his commentary to BT Qid. 30a.[43] After explaining the talmudic passage that locates the centers of various biblical texts, he continued:

> But afterwards, doubts about the matter arose, and we do not know if the *waw* of *gḥwn* [Lev. 11:42] [reputed to be the middle letter of the Torah, in a text with an odd

number of letters] is on this side or on that [i.e., whether it is the last letter of the first half of the Torah, or the first letter of the second half, in a text with an even number of letters]. And one cannot say, "Let us bring a Torah scroll [and count]," because "they were expert in defective and plene spellings, and we are not."

And that we find Tiqqunim in the possession of the scribes—on which [or: on whom] we rely in writing a Torah scroll—they are only what they found in the scrolls with a presumption of having been checked (*ba-sefarim ha-muḥezaqim ba-meḏuyyaqim*), not that the matter is so clear. And because of this, I tend to rule leniently in this matter, not to invalidate a Torah scroll on account of this, because this [law stipulating that one must invalidate a Torah scroll if it contains such problems] was said only for that about which we are certain. And one should not rely even on the books of the *masoroṯ* so much, nor on Midrashot.

And we have found a disagreement between the Midrashot and the *masoroṯ* regarding the word *hpylgšym*, "concubines" [Gen. 25:6], which they expounded, "it is spelled *pylgšm*" [Gen. Rab. 61, 4]; and similarly [regarding] *w'śymm br'šykm*, "and I will place them at your head" [Deut. 1:13], "it is spelled *w'śmm*" [Deut. Rab. 1, 10]; and similarly [regarding] *bywm klwt mšh*, "on the day Moses finished" [Num. 7:1], "it is spelled *klt*" [Num. Rab. 12, 8]. And in the books of the Masorah, the three of them are plene. And similarly, we have found in the Masorah *qrnwt/qrnt*, "horns," [spelled in a manner that is] the opposite of what the sages have expounded.[44]

But regarding this, the geonim have agreed that since [the spelling] like this appears in the Talmud in a principle of law, like this [and like] *lṭṭpt [/lṭṭpwt]*, "for frontlets," and like *bskt/bskt [/bskwt*, "in booths," BT San. 4a–b], and like *[wbn] 'yn lw*, "and he has no son" [Deut. 25:5], which they expounded in a legal context, "check it" [cf. BT B.B. 115a, etc.]—for these we rely on the Talmud; but those in the haggadah, but not in a principle of law—like *pylgšm*, *w'śymm*, and *klwt*—one should neither decide between them nor invalidate [a scroll] because of them.

You have learned that any [case of] defective or plene spelling that is uncertain, since we are not expert, one should not rule so strictly regarding them, thereby invalidating a Torah scroll for ritual use, even though the Masorah, or the Tiqqunim, or even the Midrashot testify regarding them, since there is a disagreement among them. And this seems to me to be the case regarding open and closed paragraph divisions [and] regarding everything about which we are not expert and find a disagreement.

Of these five writers, Meiri's discussion most closely approximates the range of issues presented by Ben Adret. In brief, the principles underlying his statement are:

1. One should not change the Torah text to conform to the spellings in the Masorah.
2. One should not change the Torah text to conform to the spellings suggested by the Midrashim.
3. In matters of legal importance, one should rely on spellings suggested by the Babylonian Talmud.
4. In cases of disagreement in nonlegal matters, one cannot decide among the various witnesses, because we are in doubt about what is correct.

Rashi and the Tosafot relied on the testimony of the Masorah to challenge talmudic statements about biblical spellings. Abulafia had found the Masorah texts, although inconsistent at times, more usable for creating a definitive orthography than the Torah scrolls, which were so inconsistent that he could not rely solely on them.

Ben Adret, on the other hand, who was a child when Abulafia died, gave the greatest priority to the evidence in the Torah scrolls. Meiri accepted Ben Adret's teaching but, following what may be considered the Ashkenazi position taught by Rabbenu Tam, added that in doubtful cases several spellings would be deemed acceptable. He did not defend changes based on the Masorah, and only in halakhic discussions would he attribute any significance to the Talmud's expositions.

Meiri's leniency in disputed matters (point 4) is noteworthy, and in many ways it constitutes a compromise between what crystalized as separate Ashkenazi and Sefaradi responses to the problem. He took the statement in Qiddushin 30a seriously and also anticipated a number of subsequent arguments, but many facts and attitudes are shared with Ben Adret's questioner. No authority is given to aggadic Midrashim, but halakhic discussions in the Talmud are respected; and the two lists of problematic biblical verses are almost identical.

A potentially important word here is *maṣa'nu*, "we have found a disagreement," in the third paragraph, which seems to indicate that Meiri was claiming to have discovered the very problem put forth by Ben Adret's questioner, thus suggesting their shared identity. But Meiri is known to have incorporated into his work many of the teachings of his predecessors and colleagues, and the word *maṣa'nu* may also convey the sense of "we find," which carries no suggestion of originality. In either case, he was hardly the first writer to notice the problem, as demonstrated, for example, by the series of earlier writers cited in chapter 2.

If this text is derived from Ben Adret's responsa, it would have to be from the long version. Meiri mentioned seven different biblical verses: *ha-pilagšim* (Gen. 25:6), *wa-'aśimēm be-rašēḵem* (Deut. 1:13), *be-yom kalloṯ moše* (Num. 7:1), *qrnwṯ* (Lev. 4:7, etc.), *le-ṭoṭafoṯ* (Ex. 13:16, Deut. 6:3, 11:18), *ba-sukkoṯ* (Lev. 23:42–43), and *[u-ḇen] 'ēn lo* (Deut. 25:5), all of the verses mentioned in the long question and answer. He discussed the issues that emerged from the conflicts among early halakhic, aggadic, and masoretic texts, and he discussed the reliability of Tiqqunim as well. Meiri's position on the Masorah is slightly more sympathetic than what we have seen of Ben Adret's, and other small differences are noticeable, but in general this text reads like an expansion of Ben Adret's statenent; the second and key paragraph is a virtual quotation.

Meiri and Ben Adret are known to have corresponded,[45] and the latter's responsa do not always reveal their addressees. It is possible that Meiri was the anonymous correspondent here, but this connection cannot be established conclusively; too many little differences that require hypothetical explanations make a positive identification tenuous. Significantly, however, Meiri's answer concurs in granting the Masorah's spellings no serious weight in this discussion. And to the extent that one can assume his statement to be a reflection of Ben Adret's, it also confirms the latter's preference to avoid relying on the Masorah in such matters.

Meiri's Qiryat Sefer A subsequent presentation of this material is found in *Qiryat Sefer*, Meiri's combination of halakhic and masoretic regulations related to the production and use of Torah scrolls. It contains summaries of these laws and renders decisions in doubtful cases, thereby providing the guidance necessary for proper fulfillment of the religious obligation to produce a Torah scroll. Written in the form and style for which Meiri is justly famous, the book is a comprehensive discussion of the related talmudic and medieval sources. In it, he informs the reader that he has received and used a copy of the Torah made by Abulafia, but it has been suggested that he did not have access to (or did not even know of) *Masoret Seyag LaTorah.*[46] At the end of the third section of part two of *Qiryat Sefer* he wrote:

> And now we must clarify, in the matter of defective and plene [spellings], how we decide regarding that about which we have found disagreements between the Midrashim of our rabbis, of blessed memory, and the *early* [emphasis added] books of the Masoret that the sages of the [Hebrew] language wrote and the precise scrolls (*sefarim*). Namely, that, in the Midrashim of our rabbis, we find [regarding] *wlbny hplgšym* [Gen. 25:6], "It is spelled *plgšm*"; but in the books of the Masoret it is plene. [And similarly regarding *w'śymm br'šykm* [Deut. 1:13], they said "it is spelled *w'śmm.*"][47] And similarly, *bywm klt mšh* [Num. 7:1], in the Midrash they said "[it is spelled] *klt mšh*"; but in the books of the Masoret it is plene. And similarly [regarding] *qrnwt* [Lev. chapt. 4], "it is spelled *qrnt.*" And, similarly [regarding] *'t bryty šlwm* [Num. 25:12], the rabbis, of blessed memory, said, "The *waw* of *šlwm* is cut," but in the books of the Masoret they did not list it among the small letters; and many [other cases] are like these.
>
> And, regarding this, I have seen [written] by the leaders of the generation (*gedolē ha-dor*) that:
>
> > Anything that appears in the Talmud in a matter of legal principle and from which we derive any legal decision, we rely on the words of our rabbis, like *qrnwt/qrnt*, *bskwt/bskt*, [and] *ṭwṭpwt/ṭṭpt*; we rely on the law of the Talmud. And anything that comes via [or: in the manner of (*be-dereḵ*)] a Midrash, we rely on the books of the Masorah (*s[ifrē] ha-masora*).
> >
> > And if we find a disagreement among the books of the Masorah (*sifrē ha-masora*), we rely on the majority. And it is like what we learn in Tractate Soferim:
> >
> > > Three Torah scrolls were in [the Temple] court. In one they found *m'wn 'lhy qdm*, and in two they found *m'wnh*, and they established the [reading in] the two, and eliminated [that in] the one.
> > >
> > > In one they found *wyšlḥ 't z'ṭwṭy*, and in two they found *n'ry*, and they established the [reading in] the two, and eliminated [that in] the one [. . .].[48]

Because *gedolē ha-dor* is Meiri's standard designation for Ben Adret, this passage seems to associate him closely with Ben Adret's responsum, though it does not suggest that he penned the question. But it also thereby raises a serious question about the exact contents of Ben Adret's answer. According to the question posed to Ben Adret, the long responsum, and the short one, the consonantal text of the Torah should be determined by a majority of scrolls, except where halakhic discussions in the Talmud have priority. This position effectively eliminated any serious role for either the aggadic Midrashim or the masoretic literature, a point Ben Adret made explicit at the beginning of his response. And according to Meiri's Qiddushin commentary, one should neither decide between the readings found in the Torah scrolls and those suggested by such Midrashim nor invalidate a scroll because of them; in other words, Midrashim play no role whatsoever in determining the spelling of words in a Torah scroll. But according to the second report by Meiri, in *Qiryat Sefer,*

Ben Adret favored the masoretic literature when it contradicted the Midrashim, again limiting the influence of the Midrashim but according a greater degree of authority to the Masorah.

The Inconsistencies in Meiri's Reports of Ben Adret's Position This inconsistency regarding the value of the Masorah may be approached in several ways, none of which leads to a definitive determination.

A. Perhaps Meiri did not really attribute the statement to Ben Adret. When identifying his sources, Meiri routinely used honorific titles in place of the rabbis' names.[49] In introducing this one in *Qiryat Sefer*, he identified the source as *geḏolē ha-dor*, "the leaders of the generation," his standard label for Ben Adret; but that phrase may be an error or a reference to someone else. In this light, it may be significant that the parallel passage in the Qiddushin commentary attributes the idea to the *ge'onim*, presumably the earlier leaders of Babylonian Jewry. Sofer's introductions to the many volumes of Meiri's Talmud commentary that he edited indicate that this term can refer to quite a range of medieval writers, not just the Babylonian leaders commonly identified by that term. The rare *geḏolē ha-ge'onim* also appears once in *Qiryat Sefer* (p. 50), and Hershler's note associates it with a number of Ashkenazi writers, a group known to favor the Masorah. In Hullin, for example, Sofer identified the designation *geḏolē ha-ge'onim* as Rabbenu Hananel. Were it correct here, it would eliminate the connection with Ben Adret; still there is no concrete reason to suggest this change, and the paragraph otherwise is a virtual quotation of Ben Adret's responsum.

B. Meiri's identification of this unnamed source appears before the citation, and one may question where the report of Ben Adret's position ends and Meiri's own begins. In this case, we must theorize that Ben Adret's true feelings were those found in the responsum and that Meiri substituted his own for part of them in *Qiryat Sefer*. Perhaps he intended to credit Ben Adret only with the teaching that, in halakhically related spellings, one relies on the Talmud but not with what followed.

Such an interpretation requires that Meiri himself favored the Masorah more than Ben Adret did. That is easy to demonstrate from a comparison of Ben Adret's responsum and Meiri's writings, particularly from *Qiryat Sefer*, but the position is not as firm as one might wish. Support for the Masorah is tempered by other statements, such as that in Meiri's commentary on Qiddushin:

> And one should not rely even on the books of the *masoroṯ* so much, nor on Midrashot. . . . You have learned that [any case of] defective or plene spelling that is uncertain, since we are not expert, one should not rule so strictly regarding them, thereby invalidating a Torah scroll for ritual use, even though the Masorah, or the Tiqqunim, or even the Midrashot testify regarding them, since there is a disagreement among them.

Nor does unequivocal support for the Masorah emerge even from a general reading of *Qiryat Sefer*, though the masoretic literature is cited there more consistently. Compare, for example, the following brief passage from the introduction, which parallels what is found in the commentary on Qiddushin:

> And similarly, there arose disagreements between the grammarians [or: precise text masters (*medaqdeqim*)], the masters of the Masorah, and the sages, the masters of

> the homiletical exposition . . . even as there arose disagreements among the interpreters regarding various matters of law, and even regarding plene and defective spellings. . . . And from this I tend to say that every defective or plene spelling that is unclear, for example, there is a disagreement between the books of Tiqqunim or between the Midrash and the Masorah; one should not invalidate a Torah scroll because of them. (p. 15)

Even so, many passages do utilize the Masorah, and Meiri also described it very positively in his commentary on the third chapter of Avot, s.v. *masoret seyag la-tora*. There he saw the Masorah as a system of mnemonics used to recall and to link by association similar textual or grammatical anomalies, and he included it with other traditional rabbinic teachings.[50]

C. One might conjecture that Ben Adret's true feelings were reported by Meiri and that the texts of both the long and the short responsa are corrupt. The style of the shorter responsum lacks authority, and the language of the longer one can be improved upon in a number of ways from the medieval parallels. In fact, it is not difficult to construct a synthetic version of the two responsa that would accommodate all of the material preserved and presented in Ben Adret's name and to localize the differences among them into one or two sentences or clauses that easily could have been changed or corrupted. But ultimately any such reconstruction would require choosing between two somewhat different positions regarding the Masorah, and until that can be done with confidence, it should not be attempted. Moreover the tradition associating these responsa and their specific contents with Ben Adret seems to have been widespread in contemporary Spain, and, without supporting evidence of a contrary nature, this argument must be taken as unduly skeptical.

D. A fourth possibility suggests that the question itself influenced Ben Adret's answer (either as he wrote it or afterwards). In this case, his predispositions may have been reinforced by the trustworthiness of his learned and familiar correspondent, but this is merely a different way of shifting the responsibility for the idea to someone else. The introduction of the word *ha-mi'uṭ*, omitted by Penkower and Leiman,[51] might suggest a context for this more radical change but not an identity for its author—and it may have been an accident.

E. If Ben Adret's thinking changed over time, both the two independent responsa and Meiri's two reports could be correct. I have been unable to find any helpful parallels to the discussion of plene and defective spelling in Ben Adret's other writings, but evidence of such movement does appear in Meiri's.

The statement in Meiri's Qiddushin commentary, which is relatively unsupportive of the Masorah's authority, would presumably reflect an earlier period in which he shared the position of Ben Adret's first statement. *Qiryat Sefer*, with its more positive attitude toward the Masorah, was written near the end of his life, perhaps as a means of addressing this obviously well-known problem, and may have been influenced by another still unknown or unpublished statement by Ben Adret that reacted to a challenge to his earlier answer and recorded his change of mind. Without appropriate documentation, however, one cannot pursue this argument and, again, knowledge of Ben Adret's (allegedly "early") position was widespread, even after his death.

F. One might speculate that the positive statement about the Masorah cited by

Meiri in *Qiryat Sefer* was not actually Ben Adret's but rather a later modification produced in the light of the emerging support for Abulafia's work. But given Meiri's closeness to Ben Adret and the relatively brief time between their deaths, this possibility is very unlikely.

G. Meiri's initial statement does not replicate the *Sitz im Leben* of the responsum, which leaves room for some differences between them. Ben Adret was asked if "a Torah scroll is invalidated for ritual use by defective or plene spellings that are contrary to the Masorah." In *Qiryat Sefer*, Meiri was discussing "how we decide regarding that about which we have found disagreements between the Midrashim of our rabbis, of blessed memory, and the early books of the Masoret that the sages of the [Hebrew] language wrote, and the precise scrolls (*sefarim*)." His goal was the production of a proper text for use in Torah scrolls, but his starting point differed somewhat from Ben Adret's, and his more systematic, thorough, and theoretical approach could have led him to a slightly different presentation of the material.

H. One could imagine that a homoioteleuton caused the deletion of a key line of text in Meiri's presentation of Ben Adret, which originally contained four parts, not the three into which I have divided it. The passage now reads:

> [1] Anything that appears in the Talmud in a matter of principle and from which we derive any legal decision, we rely on the words of our rabbis. . . .
> [2] And anything that comes via [or: in the manner of (*be-dereḵ*)] a Midrash, we rely on the *books of the Masorah*).
> [3] And if we find a disagreement among the *books of the Masorah*, we rely on the majority.

Paragraph [1] is fine as it is and summarizes very well the position that one follows the talmudic spellings when they are halakhah related. The subsequent line should explain what to do about nonhalakhic passages (in the Talmud and possibly the Midrashim), and it begins as anticipated, "[2] And anything that comes via [or: in the manner of (*be-dereḵ*)] a Midrash. . . ." The problem is that it should say that such Midrash-based textual observations lack the authority to change the Torah text. Instead, the text jumps ahead by suggesting that in such cases one should follow the Masorah and that in case of disputes among masoretic texts one should follow the majority. While it is reasonable to argue that Meiri intended to strengthen the hand of the Masorah, it is not clear that such a position accurately reflects Ben Adret's teaching. In a sense, the preserved text of Meiri's summary of Ben Adret contains a non sequitur, "[2] And anything that comes via [or: in the manner of (*be-dereḵ*)] a Midrash, we rely on the books of the Masorah." It therefore could seem reasonable to expand paragraph [2] into two parts, though obviously the suggested reconstruction could be represented in many other ways.

> [2] And anything that comes via [or: in the manner of (*be-dereḵ*)] a Midrash, [we do not change the scrolls to follow it.
> [3] And when we seek information about other phenomena—irregularly shaped letters, Qere u-Keṯiḇ, etc.] we rely on the books of the Masorah.
> [4] And if we find a disagreement among the books of the Masorah, we rely on the majority. And it is like what we learn in Tractate Soferim. . .:

Several factors, however, argue against any such attempt at reconstruction. First, all six manuscripts of *Qiryat Sefer* that I examined concur in offering the text printed before us. Moreover, Meiri's presentation—shortly before the passage under discussion here—sets up a series of conflicts between several different groups of early rabbinic authorities. In this context, it is perfectly logical for Meiri to have presented his resolution in terms of these different categories.

> And, similarly, there arose disagreements between the grammarians [or: precise text masters (*medaqdeqim*)], the masters of the Masorah, and the sages, the masters of the derash . . . even as there arose disagreements among the interpreters regarding various matters of law, and even regarding plene and defective spellings. (p. 15)

While the contents of the reconstruction fit what we know of Ben Adret's use of these materials, I have found no support for the reconstruction in any primary or secondary presentation of Ben Adret's thinking on the subject. The reconstruction has the benefit of providing a framework for consolidating the long and short versions of Ben Adret's responsa, but I have declined to attempt this without sufficient reason to do so.

I. Finally, it is also possible that a much more minor change in the text of Meiri's report of Ben Adret's statement has led to the confusion. Meiri attributed to him the three-part statement that:

> [1] Anything that appears in the Talmud in a matter of principle and from which we derive any legal decision, we rely on the words of our rabbis. . . .
> [2] And anything that comes via [or: in the manner of (*be-derek*)] a Midrash, we rely on the *books of the Masorah* (*s- ha-masora*).
> [3] And if we find a disagreement among the *books of the Masorah*, we rely on the majority.

While it is conceivable that this really meant to suggest only that one should not use the Midrashim, and not that the Masorah should be used in such cases, surely such a notion could have been expressed more clearly. But it is possible that, instead of "books of the Masorah," *s[ifrē] ha-masora*, which now appears in the text, Meiri actually wrote or intended to write *ha-masoret*, which can refer either to the masoretic literature or to the consonantal Bible text, a meaning it carries in the Talmud and in some medieval texts, including Meiri's own commentary to BT San. 4a, where the word is used this way in the Talmud. The term *sifrē ha-masora* refers only to the masoretic literature (unless it can be shown to mean something like Tiqqunim, which is highly unlikely, since Meiri used that term freely). This very slight emendation (both terms could be abbreviated identically) would suggest that Meiri actually taught that the traditional consonantal text, the *Masoret*, presumably as found in the scrolls (or perhaps in the Tiqqunim), determined the text, except in those cases where the Talmud's halakhic discussions took priority. This theory fits nicely with the statement found in Ben Adret's responsum and also accommodates the subsequent passage in *Qiryat Sefer*, both of which continue by quoting the passage from Soferim, so often used to justify correcting scrolls according to a majority of scrolls. Perhaps even minimal access to Abulafia's efforts changed Meiri's perspective on the Masorah and, in the process, his representation of Ben Adret and the halakhic ideal.

Whether or not Meiri was Ben Adret's questioner, it should be clear that the only early evidence that Ben Adret supported using the Masorah to determine the orthography of the Torah was the presentation in Meiri's *Qiryat Sefer*, and Meiri appears to have overstated it somewhat, perhaps because of Abulafia's position, which had only recently come to his attention.

Brief Comments on the Masorah in Medieval Europe

One remarkable point that has emerged from many of these documents is the existence of a substantial number of medieval Spanish rabbis who were disinclined to use the Masorah to solve textual problems related to the use of *matres lectionis*. This fact may appear somewhat surprising, because Abulafia, in establishing his Torah text, relied both on carefully selected scrolls and on masoretic works; but *Masoret Seyag LaTorah* seems not to have undergone wide circulation, and the fact that he used both types of evidence may have allayed criticism. *Masoret Seyag LaTorah* was famous enough that one could easily question, on its basis, the authenticity of the negative attitude toward using the Masorah for orthographic determinations expressed individually by Ben Adret's questioner, by Ben Adret himself, by Meiri's commentary on Qiddushin, or by Maharam Halava in his responsum. But the number of those attestations, together with the other medieval Spanish responsa cited in this chapter, precludes a serious challenge to their authenticity. Together, they represent a formidable collection of evidence challenging the Masorah's absolute authority in the area of orthography; even Abulafia, sometimes touted as the Masorah's prime advocate, used it cautiously and, as was demonstrated in chapter 2, sometimes emended it.

Spanish scribes were deservedly famous for the precision of both their Torah scrolls and their codices,[52] so the accuracy of the former does not explain fully their being preferred over the latter. It seems, rather, that we have here residual evidence for the process of formal challenge to, and then acceptance of, the Masorah. At first, its authority was less than universally acknowledged, especially in the area of orthography, but, as we shall see in chapter 7, eventually it gained total control of all aspects of the Bible text—in some cases even over the spelling of words that were discussed by the Babylonian Talmud in halakhic contexts.[53]

The Amoraic literature underwent a similar period of testing during geonic times, when various questions solicited definitive rulings on the authority of the Midrashim, the Targumim, and the Babylonian Talmud. In short, the geonim accepted the Talmud as binding and equivocated on the Midrashim and Targumim. Halakhic Midrashim were adopted and defended, especially in the face of Karaite challenges to the rabbinic legal tradition; aggadic Midrashim were accepted when they made sense. Except for the universally recognized translation associated with Onkelos, Aramaic Targumim were deemed worthy of study only when they were known to have been produced by authoritative rabbis or under their supervision; others generally were not.[54] The rabbinic texts of roughly talmudic times were adjudicated in the subsequent geonic era. The post-talmudic masoretic literature seems to have undergone a similar review later in medieval times.

As well, the production of Torah scrolls was a long-standing practice governed by a substantial body of scribal tradition and halakhic regulations and possessing its own strong presumption of consistency and accuracy, and the Babylonian Talmud had long been accepted as the definitive source for the determination of almost all aspects of halakhah. Ben Adret's questioner assumed that this authority should have given the scribal tradition in the scrolls complete control of all spelling questions, an approach that represents the older way of handling the matter—older than the Talmud and older than the Masorah—that was obviously respected well into medieval times. Ben Adret reaffirmed this position but initiated a compromise that relied on the scrolls in all disputed cases that were not covered by the Talmud's halakhic expositions and on the Talmud's spellings in all cases that were, ostensibly a handful of disputed words. This position also confirmed the relatively strong commitment to the halakhic parts of the Talmud relative to the nonhalakhic ones and nontalmudic Midrashim, and it effectively grouped the Masorah with the last group.

Notwithstanding the antiquity of some of its constituent parts (not to mention the Bible itself), the Masorah as a literature was relatively new in medieval times and was still evolving. When compared with the antiquity of the Talmud or of the Torah scrolls themselves, it could be described quite literally as *ḥad̲aš̌im mi-qarob̲ ba'u*, "new things that have arrived recently," as we have seen it often was. To the extent that it appeared to encroach on the authority and sanctity of these unassailable ancient documents, it was seen as a hostile newcomer to the scene. But just as the Targumim, the Midrashim, and the Talmud had been challenged only to be accepted later—even if in some cases gradually or only partially—so too was the Masorah. The fact that Masorah codices were used in public readings by the Karaites[55] seems to have played no role in the documents discussed here, though one cannot dismiss totally its potential contribution to the Masorah's public image, especially in some communities. Modern attempts to associate the Karaites with production of the Masorah[56] seem irrelevant; challenges to it dwelled on its inconsistencies, not on the identities or religious affiliations of its creators or editors.

Scribes, masoretes, and those who fully appreciated the Masorah's potential contribution to the Bible text had always respected it. But systematic (if slow and deliberate) integration of the Masorah's nonorthographic features into the fabric of codified halakhic literature appears, in significant measure, to have been Maimonides' contribution, while Abulafia played an analogous role with respect to its orthographic aspects. Though Rashi and the Tosafists surely examined and discussed many of the contradictions between the Masorah and early rabbinic texts, their efforts appear extensive but not systematic, and their practical impact has yet to be demonstrated. As might be expected, those who lacked access to the Masorah, or who were accustomed to older procedures that relied solely on Torah scrolls, or who were concerned by the Masorah's internal inconsistencies hesitated to use it against a majority of Torah scrolls. But eventually almost all halakhic authorities who were willing to take a stand on the proper way to write a Torah scroll accepted the authority of the Masorah's presentation, if one could determine what it actually was.

The popular pro-Masorah position that eventually came to dominate the halakhic literature obscures somewhat the fact that it took centuries for the Masorah to achieve this status, a process still incomplete even in the sixteenth century. Ibn

Zimra's first responsum reflects the negative attitude, as do the various objects of Abraham Hasan's criticism.[57] Perhaps even Elijah Mizrahi's delicately worded response to Hasan, which hesitantly admitted ignorance of many of the works to which Hasan referred, should be included. Note also the complaint of Jacob ben Hayyim Ibn Adoniyah in his introduction to the Rabbinic Bible of 1524–1525:

> . . . many of the people, and with them many of the groups of our sages who are with us today, in this generation, value in their hearts neither the Masorah nor one of the ways of the Masorah, in their saying, what benefit will accrue to them from it; and it is almost forgotten and lost.[58]

Whatever one may think of his accomplishments in publishing the first masoretic Bible, this statement should not be dismissed as rhetorical ballast. The situation he described here was the reality of the age, and his goals included rescuing the Masorah from oblivion and establishing its hegemony. Some would say he wished to reestablish it, but it remains to be demonstrated that, other than in fairly limited circles, until the sixteenth century the Masorah ever really totally controlled disputed spellings of all words in Torah scrolls the way it did conrol most peripheral, nonorthographic details.

The introduction to Levita's *Masoret HaMasoret* contains another (poetic) complaint:

> For the scribes have intentionally erred and were not careful with the Masorah, but their primary concern was to write nicely [or: to decorate their writing] and to make the lines straight, in order not to change their forms, so that all the pages should be the same. Moreover, they decorated them with sketches and pictures, with ornaments and bows, and with buds and flowers. Therefore, sometimes they were forced to reduce or to augment the spaces (*ḥomoṯ*) of the pictures with words stated elsewhere that are superfluous here and out of place. And sometimes they [i.e., these masoretic rubrics] were completely omitted from their proper place or are not mentioned at all for lack of space. They had to interrupt in the middle of the subject, and the edifice was left incomplete and with parts missing.[59]

Whether regarded as unnecessary, too unintelligible, too esoteric, too unreliable, too inconsistent, or simply too out of fashion by early sixteenth-century exegetical standards, the Masorah had not yet been printed and was not well known. Its use in micrographic representations in medieval codices reflected some theoretical importance but often served aesthetic considerations far more satisfactorily than textual ones and demonstrated how peripheral it really was.[60] For many, it had lost much of its stature as the embodiment of the Bible's sacred textual tradition; in a sense it resembled the cantillation marks on the books of Psalms, Job, and Proverbs, which are preserved and printed even though most modern readers have no idea what they signify. In some cases, the Masorah served primarily as unwelcome evidence of the tradition's textual flaws. The very high cost of a fine copy of the Masorah exacerbated this situation, and the halakhic authorities' repeated use against the masoretes of the latter's inability to resolve their own internal disputes—even though, by all standards, they were relatively minor—undoubtedly took its toll on the Masorah's prestige and authority. One of the most striking statements confirming this attitude is Rabbi Judah Mintz's fifteenth-century criticism of Maimonides' uncompromising invalidation of all Torah scrolls that contained paragraph spacings differing from what he approved on the basis of Ben Asher's manuscript, though similar (if more cautious) sentiments anticipating Mintz's had already been expressed by Abraham ben Maimon, Menahem Meiri, and Maharam Halava:

> [Question:] Regarding what . . . [you] asked about a Torah scroll whose open and closed paragraphs are not correct according to the presentation of the Rambam. . . :
>
> [Answer:] My beloved, do not be surprised at this matter, for "there is nothing new under the sun" [Ecc. 1:9]; and [indeed] there are many [i.e., scrolls or places in them] like it, that are not correct according to his presentation. Therefore, one should not invalidate them. . . . [He continued by quoting the relevant passage from Maimonides.]
>
> We see . . . that he [i.e., Maimonides] invalidates any Torah scroll that is not written according to his presentation. Even so, it seems correct to say that we do not rely on him alone to invalidate other Torah scrolls that are not according to his presentation, for why did he see fit to affirm the words of Ben Asher, who corrected the [codex containing the] Twenty-Four [books of the Bible] that was in Jerusalem, to correct [all] the scrolls from it?
>
> He [Ben Asher] checked it for years and checked it many times [as Maimonides said]. For perhaps, if he had checked it again, or if he would have had in his possession a Torah scroll [actually written by] the masoretes (*baʿalē ha-masoreṯ*),[61] he would have agreed to it [instead]. For defective and plene readings invalidate a Torah scroll, and the main authority in this matter is the [ancient, pre-Ben Asher] masoretes.
>
> [Mintz next ran through the often repeated list of cases where Rashi and the Tosafot point out textual inconsistencies regarding *plgšym* (Gen. 25:6), *bywm klwt* (Num. 7:1), *whnś*ʾ (Lev. 15:10), *mʿbyrym* (1 Sam. 2:24), and "And he judged Israel for forty years" (cf. Jud. 16:31), BT Nid. 33a, Tos., s.v. *whnś*ʾ.]
>
> We see that we should take the [ancient, pre-Ben Asher] masoretes as primary and write [Torah scrolls] according to their tradition and abandon [the teaching of] our Talmud and the Palestinian Talmud.
>
> And we conclude: If so, why should we invalidate Torah scrolls that are written according to their presentation and follow [only] the presentation of Ben Asher, even more so since we have found Ben [replacing: Benei] Naftali disagreeing with Ben Asher regarding some words and letters? . . . [He then discussed a well-known problem about the spacing of paragraphs and verse divisions and concluded:]
>
> Therefore, it seems proper not to invalidate any Torah scroll, if they deviated from the presentation of the Rambam. And I have written what appears to me simple and truthful. Signed: The overworked Judah Mintz.

This situation changed briefly through the text-related efforts of Jacob ben Hayyim, Menahem di Lonzano, Solomon Norzi, and even later writers; but, as almost any student of the Bible will readily admit, the contemporary situation is hardly different from that described by Norzi (translated in chapter 1).

Things did not change much through the nineteenth century. Note C. D. Ginsburg's candid but very revealing observation about the general lack of scholarly competence in masoretic matters:

> Now, although almost every Introduction to the Bible speaks about the Massorah, and although the *textus receptus* of the Hebrew Scriptures is technically called 'the

> MASSORETIC Text,' yet I venture to say, without intending to give offence, but without fear of contradiction, that with the exception of a few Jews and one or two Christians, all those who have edited the Hebrew text, or written upon its Massorah in their respective Introductions, could neither master nor describe the entire domain of this ancient critical apparatus.[62]

Did the Masorah fare differently among Ashkenazi and Sefaradi writers? Ashkenaz was a center of interest in Gematriah and other interpretative strategies that sought meaning in the text's orthographic details, and a number of commentaries on the Masorah itself were written there.[63] Rashi's commentaries are sprinkled with related observations, and many of the Bible commentaries produced by the Tosafists and Hasidei Ashkenaz reveal an extensive concern for such matters. Indeed, the search for meaning in the spellings of words was an almost universal Ashkenazi concern, and much of the spelling-related exegesis found in the introductory sections (the so-called *parparot̲*) of Jacob ben Asher's Torah commentary, *Baʿal HaTurim*, can be traced to Ashkenazi roots. Even so, the number of minor textual variants in the Torah that the Tosafists' writings reveal—usually cases of plene or defective *waw* or *yod*—is in many cases almost directly proportional to the size of their commentaries.

Ben Adret's position emphasized the binding quality of the spellings that emerged from the Talmud's associating halakhic ideas with the Torah text, but he strongly rejected any attempt to allow the Midrashim to control its orthography. This attitude complements what might be described as a somewhat limited Sefaradi commitment to midrashic Bible interpretation and to the potential for finding meaning in spelling patterns, be they regular or not. Somewhat earlier, Ibn Ezra had claimed that spelling variations were of no cognitive significance, an opinion that both reflected this local attitude and contributed to it.

Some Spanish rabbis accepted the position that parallel accounts of a single biblical event that were expressed in different words were, in fact, saying exactly the same thing. Ibn Ezra articulated this position while comparing the two versions of the Ten Commandments (Long Commentary to Ex. 20:1) and in *Yesod Mora'*,[64] but the appearance of a similar notion in Ben Adret's writings brings it closer to our present discussion.[65] Some Spanish exegetes also believed that parallel poetic lines said the same thing in different words, a phenomenon often designated *kefel ha-ʿinyan be-millim šonot̲*.[66] Since such unfettered reading of whole blocks of text, which denied a special role for repetitions, parallelistic duplications, slight changes in phraseology, and the like—things that played such a major role in midrashic Torah interpretation—was so popular in medieval Spain that it might be assumed that Spanish commentators were not interested in relatively insignificant variant spellings. One might also conclude that the adoption of a liberal or seemingly radical literary exegetical posture would accompany a reduced concern for spelling, but this is not exactly the case.

Paradoxically, when taken as a group, Ashkenazi authorities, who were very interested in explaining or finding meaning in the *matres lectionis*, generally admitted, much more quickly than some of their Sefaradi colleagues, the existence of minor flaws in the Torah text's transmission. The latter, who on the whole were less concerned with this type of interpretation and perhaps for that reason less sensitive to such textual details, and many of whom genuinely believed they possessed a letter-perfect text, argued for the constant removal of any variations that might suggest a flaw in spelling (possibly because they were more aware of and more sensitive to non-Jewish polemics that raised this particular point). Even Abulafia, despite his orthographic interests and efforts, admitted being largely unable to explain the plene and defective spellings he charted.[67] The desire to use the meanings of the text to help anchor the correct spellings was also a problem. Ibn Ezra feared that claims for understanding the inconsistent spellings in the Bible would encourage highly subjective writers to observe and chart essentially erroneous spelling patterns on which they would then base spelling changes in words that did not conform to their theories. His Ashkenazi contemporary, Rabbenu Tam, went even further in outlawing the speculative emendation of rabbinic texts.

Thus (what might appear as) radical textual suppositions and radical hermeneutics are not necessarily complementary positions. Rabbi Judah the Pious, who offered many interpretations of plene and defective letters, also articulated some of the most startling ideas about the Torah's textual history that have been preserved in medieval rabbinic writings.[68] Centuries later, Rabbi Moses Sofer wrote gematriah-filled notes on the spellings in the Torah and comments on the Masorah, despite his openness about the inability to produce a letter-perfect text.[69] He was followed by Rabbi Moses Schick, his student, who tried valiantly to reverse the position found in *Sha'agat Aryeh* and in Sofer's responsum (though in the end he too conceded the validity of the problem); but he also considered the possibility that Moses' contribution to the Torah ended at *Ha'azinu*![70] Even today, Rabbi Mordecai Breuer, an internationally recognized authority on Masorah and textual matters, applies some very controversial assumptions in his exegetical endeavors.[71]

Be all this as it may, it is incorrect to see the search for meaning in the individual letters of the Torah as an exclusively Ashkenazi interest. The Zohar (a thirteenth-century Spanish document), Bahya, and Jacob ben Asher, to take three prominent examples, shared greatly in this approach to the text, developed it much further than its Ashkenazi predecessors, and had an enormous impact. Nor should one forget the mystical devotions built around the individual letters of the Torah and their combinations, believed by Spanish kabbalists to be potent divine names.[72] Moreover, kabbalistic thinking had a profound impact on interest in the Masorah. Felix Pratensis' Latin dedication of the 1517 Rabbinic Bible to Pope Leo X used the Bible text's arcane qualities as a rationale for publishing it,[73] and J. Penkower has demonstrated the impact of kabbalistic thinking on Jacob ben Hayyim's handling of the Masorah.[74] Kabbalah's importance to Norzi can be sampled via a brief perusal of his introduction, which is nicely seasoned with quotations from the Zohar; some later works actually ranked the Zohar's spellings above Abulafia's.[75] The Masorah's long-term success in taking and keeping control of the spelling of words in the Torah owed much to kabbalistic interests and support. Even so, and despite commitments to the Kabbalah evidenced by Ben Adret and Ibn Zimra, in many important rabbinic circles, halakhic decisions on the spelling of the Torah text remained largely outside its control.

Finally, in addition to the above considerations, one must reiterate the way in which belief in a letter-perfect Hebrew text accompanied allegience to the Masorah and responded to challenges from Christians and Muslims. The former routinely accused the Jews of failing to preserve the text properly and often tried to prove their case from traditional Jewish materials; the latter added to these attacks their own claims to possess a letter-perfect Qur'an. These pressures complemented the midrashic exegetical tradition, the halakhic textual requirements, the mystical beliefs, and other internal Jewish commitments to bolster the image of the letter-perfect text and to strengthen popular belief in it.

This chapter concludes by returning to the responsa of Ben Adret and Ibn Zimra. Despite some confusion that we sense over the precise contents of Ben Adret's answer and the intellectual context to which it belongs, it is possible to begin the discussion of Ibn Zimra's first responsum with Ben Adret's ruling and with the various attestations of it by his students and contemporaries and by their followers. In their various forms, portions of his answer were incorporated into Talmud commentaries (e.g., by Meiri and Rabbenu Nissim), into responsa (e.g., by Maharam Halava and Shimon ben Zemah Duran), into Torah commentaries (e.g., by Baqrat), into at least one halakhic epistle (by Hasan), and into halakhic works (e.g., Meiri's *Qiryat Sefer* and Caro's *Beit Yosef*), and a full text was also preserved, though transmitted in a volume of responsa attributed for a time to Nahmanides, Ben Adret's teacher. It was also cited by Ibn Zimra, as will be explored more fully in the next chapter.

Ibn Zimra, Ben Adret, Ibn Adoniyah, the Masorah, and Fixing the Torah Text in the Sixteenth Century

> There are some learned Jews whose entire range of knowledge lies in knowing the words of the Masoret and their glorious rubrics and their valuable allusions . . . and it is good for the learned to understand some of their words but to pay attention to master the meanings of the books, because the words are like bodies and the meanings are like souls.
>
> If someone does not understand the meanings, all of his effort has no value; it is worthless and [like chasing the] wind. He is comparable to someone holding a medical book in his hand, but he troubles himself to count how many pages are in the book, and how many lines are on every page, and how many letters are on every line. From such efforts, he will not be able to cure anything. And an expert in the Masoret who has not mastered any other subject resembles a camel carrying a load of silk. He does nothing for the silk, and the silk does nothing for him.
>
> Abraham Ibn Ezra (1089–1164)
> *Yesod Mora'*, beginning

Ibn Zimra and Ben Adret

Introduction

As was seen in chapters 2, 3, and 4, Ibn Zimra cited or paraphrased Ben Adret's teaching about correcting Torah scrolls in three different responsa. We must now compare these three presentations with what we have learned of Ben Adret's position from the independent testimonies and the other medieval citations discussed in chapter 6.

More than two centuries separated Ben Adret's death in 1310 from Ibn Zimra's writing of Responsum A. His presentation there makes clear that someone had altered three Torah scrolls on the basis of the Midrash of Rabbi Shimon bar Yohai (the Zohar) by adding two *waw*'s, thus changing the spelling of *'tw*, "him," to *'wtw* in

Num. 21:34 and in Deut. 22:2. For Ben Adret, even the Talmud had lacked sufficient authority to justify tampering with the independent, scroll-based tradition of the Torah text, except in a few limited, halakhically significant cases. But the attribution of the Zohar to Rabbi Shimon bar Yohai made it appear older than the Talmud and hence possibly more authoritative, and the sanctity attributed to the Zohar in some sixteenth-century circles required that the problem confonting Ibn Zimra be taken very seriously. His reaction was based on Ben Adret's.

Ben Adret's Ruling According to Ibn Zimra's Responsum A

It will be recalled that Ben Adret's long response contained three sections and appeared in several versions. For ease of comparison, all versions are now printed again; where possible, they are subdivided; their sections are labeled X, Y, and Z. Annotations and discussions of some points can be found earlier in the original presentations.

Ben Adret's answer preserved among his responsa:

> [X] [1] It is my opinion that this is the truth, [namely] that one should neither add nor delete [letters] in any place in scrolls (*sefarim*) according to the Masoret or according to aggadic Midrashim because, on the authority of their sages—who were expert in defective and plene spellings—they disagreed in [various] places, in [different] lands.
>
> [2] And it seems to me [that this is so] even regarding the pronunciation (*miqra'*) and regarding the tradition[al spelling] (*masoreṯ*), like the disagreement[s] between Ben Asher and Ben Naftali and similarly between the Westerners and the Easterners.
>
> [Y] And it seems to me that on this matter [also] depends what they expounded regarding
>
> > ". . . because he is stronger than we (*mmnw*)," do not read *mimmenu*, "than we," but *mimmennu*, "than he,"
>
> even though in all the codices (*sefarim*) written in our region there is no difference in the word *mmnw*, whether it refers to a plural [antecedent] or to a singular [one], even though in all [other] places, the pronominal element *-nw* is undotted in the plural and is dotted in the singular. But I think there was a disagreement between the Easterners and Westerners regarding *mmnw*, [namely] that one was accustomed [to vocalize] it like the other pronominal elements—without a dagesh when it referred to a plural [antecedent]—and one was accustomed, like the custom of our place, to place a dagesh in all forms. And I think I found in the books of the Masorah that there is such a disagreement between the Easterners and Westerners.
>
> [Z] [1] And, in any case, anything cited in the Gemara in a matter of principle of law, like *qrnwt/qrnt*, and like *bswkt [/bskt]*, *lṭwṭpt/[lṭṭpt]*, [and] *wbn 'yn lw*, with a *yod*, which we expound [for legal purposes], "check it," since it is not written without a *yod*, like *m'n blʿm*, with which is associated the principle that an inheritance is transferrable. In this case, we certainly correct *a minority*.
>
> [2] And similarly, in each and every place, even with regard to defective and plene spellings, we correct the minority according to the majority, because there is an explicit biblical statement "follow the majority"; and we learn in Tractate Soferim . . . [full quotation].

Ibn Zimra began with several cases in which the Talmud and the Torah scrolls disagreed over the spelling of *pilagšim*, *wa-ʾaśimēm*, and *kallot*, three of the four initial examples in the query to Ben Adret, and noted that no one had suggested altering them to follow the Talmud. (In fact, this possibility was considered by virtually everyone but routinely rejected.) If midrashic references to other spellings were sufficiently important, he argued, surely the scrolls would have been corrected to follow them. Since this has not been done, he concluded that midrashic authority is insufficient for this purpose, and therefore the Midrash of Rabbi Shimon bar Yohai should not be used for it either. In Ibn Zimra's mind, the authority of the Zohar did not approach that of the Talmud. He continued by quoting Ben Adret:

Ben Adret's answer preserved in Ibn Zimra's Responsum A:

> [X] [1] It is my opinion that this is the truth, [namely] that one should never add or delete [letters] in any place in scrolls (*sefarim*) according to the Masorah or according to aggadic Midrashim, because on the authority of their sages—who were expert in defective and plene spelling—the sages in their respective places disagreed with each other.
>
> [2] And it seems to me [that this is so] even regarding the pronunciation and regarding the tradition[al spelling], like the disagreement[s] between Ben Asher and Ben Naftali, and similarly between the Westerners and the Easterners, etc. Check it.
>
> [Y] [lacking because irrelevant]
>
> [Z] [1] In any case, anything discussed in the Gemara in a matter of principle of law, like *qrnwt/qrnt*, *bswkt/bskt*, [and] *wbn ʾyn lw*, which we expound [for legal purposes], "check it," since it is not written without a *yod*, like *mʾn blʿm*, from which we learn that an inheritance is transferable [from one relative to another], in this case, we certainly correct [the text].
>
> [2] But in each and every place, even with regard to defective and plene spelling, we correct the minority according to the majority, because there is an explicit biblical statement "follow the majority."

This presentation, though shorter than the original as we have it, essentially confirms Ben Adret's text as it appears in his long responsum. In discussing the problem, Ibn Zimra articulated the following principles:

1. Any plene or defective spelling with which a talmudic law is associated is to be considered final, and Torah scrolls should be corrected to conform to spellings found in these talmudic passages.
2. Biblical spellings that lack legal significance should not be altered on the authority of a Midrash.
3. Biblical spellings that lack legal significance should not be altered on the authority of the Masorah.
4. Other doubtful cases should be corrected to follow the majority of Torah scrolls.

Rules 2–4 are virtually identical to those used by Ben Adret (cf. chapter 6); the first one, in which Ibn Zimra required corrections of spellings that had legal import if they did not conform to those suggested by the Talmud, differs. While this difference may reflect an increased reliance on the Talmud and esteem for it in the sixteenth century, a textual variant in Ben Adret's responsum may be responsible for it. The printed version of Ben Adret's responsum states that, in cases of legal significance, "we certainly correct *the minority*" (*waddai me̠taqqenin ha-miʿuṭ*). Ibn Zimra's version of this passage lacks the word *ha-miʿuṭ* and requires scrolls to be corrected according to the Talmud, even if the majority of scrolls were to be changed.[1] At most, this approach may have afforded the Talmud more authority in this matter than Ben Adret would have deemed appropriate, but on other matters the texts of Ben Adret and Ibn Zimra agreed: Torah scrolls may be corrected to follow a majority of scrolls, but never to follow an aggadic Midrash or the Masorah. This impression of Ben Adret's thinking also appears in other rabbinic and scribal documents introduced in chapter 6.

Ben Adret's Ruling According to Ibn Zimra's Responsa B and C

Ibn Zimra's Responsum A contained a reaction to the emendations of a "self-designated sage" acting for a group of like minded people, and it was concerned only with the consonantal text of the Torah; Responsum B deals with various official notes about the text, including some matters that affect the production of Torah scrolls and might indicate early stages of textual uncertainty or instability. As we have it in paraphrased form, the query eliciting Responsum B focused on four talmudic terms, all found in BT Nedarim 37b; the answer perceived them as part of a larger corpus of masoretic materials and discussed them, along with other aspects of this corpus, and the corpus itself. In the course of this presentation, Ibn Zimra again had occasion several times to compare the Talmud and the Masorah.

In Responsum A (section A.2), he argued that the contents of masoretic notations, even though not necessarily agreed upon by both the Talmud and the Masorah, are considered by both as Halakhah to Moses from Sinai; but he accepted Ben Adret's position that relied on talmudic spellings in halakhic contexts and a majority of Torah scrolls elsewhere. In B.14, by way of contrast, he treated the Talmud and the Masorah as if they had equal importance and declined to favor one over the other; thus the Masorah's stature had risen in his mind and now shared that of the Talmud. This position is even clearer from a second statement (B.14), where he noted that disagreements arose between the talmudists and the masoretes, again giving them equal stature. As in Responsum A, he referred to Ben Adret's teaching regarding these differences, but this time he did not identify it as a quotation. He omitted the very important Paragraph X as well as the essentially irrelevant Paragraph Y, and he changed the language of Paragraph Z.

Ben Adret's answer preserved in Ibn Zimra's Responsum B:

> [X and Y are lacking]
> [Z] [1] In every plene or defective spelling with which some law has been associated—like *bswkwt/bskt*, [and] *qrnwt/qrnt*—we rely on the sages of the Talmud, who already analyzed the matter carefully.
>
> [2] But if no law is derived from it [i.e., from the spelling], we rely on the masoretes, who counted the defective and plene spellings, and about which [or: following whom] scrolls [or: books] (*sefarim*) have been written.

[3] And if there are disagreements among the scrolls (*sefarim*), we correct the scrolls according to the majority, as is written "follow the majority."

As before, Ibn Zimra rules that where the Talmud associated legal significance with orthographic details, Torah scrolls should be corrected to follow it; but here he adds that otherwise "we rely on the masters of the Masoret." And he issues this ruling in the name of Ben Adret who, as quoted in Ibn Zimra's first responsum, gave no authority whatsoever to the Masorah, a position Ibn Zimra had accepted there.

This second presentation of Ben Adret's teachings bears a striking resemblance to both Meiri's personal position and his reporting of Ben Adret's in *Qiryat Sefer*. It is obvious that two versions of Ben Adret's teaching were in circulation by the early fourteenth century, presumably before Meiri's death several years after Ben Adret's; and it is also clear that no single approach to the data collected above accounts fully for this situation. Moreover, we must now explain the independent appearance of these contradictory presentations in Ibn Zimra's responsa. And if this situation were not confusing enough, a third version of Ben Adret's statement appears in Ibn Zimra's Responsum C:

Ben Adret's answer preserved in Ibn Zimra's Responsum C:

[X and Y are lacking]
[Z] [1] [In] every [case of] plene or defective spelling of legal import, like *qrnwt/qrnt* [and] *swkt/swkwt*, one must correct the Torah scroll according to the Talmud, because they [i.e., the rabbis in the Talmud] examined the matter carefully, even if this is against the Massorah.

[2] But [in] a matter that is not of legal import, like *plgšym/plgšm* [and] *klwt/klt*, we correct the Torah scroll according to the Masoret or following the majority of scrolls.

This version of Paragraph Z is close to that in B, in that it is somewhat supportive of the Masorah, but in a slightly different way. In Responsum A, Ibn Zimra cited Ben Adret as accepting the spellings of words with which the Talmud had associated a law, and the testimony of a majority of scrolls in other cases. In Responsum B, the second clause was changed to support for the Masoret and for the use of a majority of scrolls, perhaps in matters other than of spelling, but this point is uncertain. In Responsum C, the second clause has been changed once again to suggest that nonlegal passages should be corrected to follow the Masoret or a majority of scrolls.

To be even more precise: Paragraph X from Ben Adret's original long responsum, which states that one should neither add nor delete letters on the authority of the Masorah or the aggadic Midrashim, is essentially the same as is found in Ibn Zimra's citation in Responsum A. Significantly, this passage has been omitted from the paraphrases in Responsa B and C, an omission that laid the foundation for subsequent changes in Paragraph Z. Note, however, that the contents of Paragraph X2 appear in the short version of Ben Adret's responsum and were referred to by many medieval writers (see chapter 6). Paragraph Y, which deals with whether a dagesh is sometimes included in *mmnw*, appears in Ben Adret, was omitted from Responsum A by Ibn Zimra, and was not considered again in Responsa B and C.

In short, aside from the omission of Paragraph X, all of the creative manipulation occurs in Paragraph Z. Ibn Zimra's Responsum A, which claims to contain a quotation of Ben Adret's responsum, does exactly that; and because it contains some better readings than the actual text preserved among Ben Adret's responsa, it has been used by scholars to improve on the language of the original. Paragraphs Z in Responsa B and C are accompanied by no claim of their being quotations, and comparison demonstrates that they are quoted from neither the long version of Ben Adret's responsum nor the short one discussed in chapter 6.

Paragraph Z of Ben Adret is reported in three parts in Responsum B and in two parts in Responsum C. In Responsum B, Z2 begins with a logical inference drawn from the omitted Paragraph X. If talmudic control of spelling were limited to cases of halakhic import, what determined the spelling of doubtful words discussed in nonhalakhic contexts? As we have it, Ben Adret originally said:

> . . . in each and every place, even with regard to defective and plene spellings, we correct the minority [of scrolls] according to the majority, because there is an explicit biblical statement "follow the majority."

In Responsum A, Ibn Zimra repeated this. In Responsum B, he provided an alternative: "But if no law is derived from it [i.e., from the talmudic discussion of spelling], we rely on the masoretes (*baʿalē ha-masoreṯ*)" In saying this, he demonstrates the influence of those who stressed the importance of the Masorah.

Paragraph Z3 continues: "And if there are disagreements among the scrolls (*sefarim*), we correct the scrolls according to the majority, as is written 'follow the majority' [Ex. 23:2]." This begins with Ibn Zimra's wording and concludes with Ben Adret's.

Paragraph Z of Responsum C contains only two parts. The first resembles the versions already discussed. The second is a essentially a condensation of what we have as parts 2 and 3 of the version of Paragraph Z as preserved in Responsum B.

Thus two questions remain: (1) what to do in cases where the evidence from the Talmud's nonhalakhic discussions suggests that the spelling of a word in the Torah may differ from what is in the scrolls; and (2) what to do when nontalmudic texts suggest differences, whether in halakhic or nonhalakhic contexts.

Ben Adret answered the second question quite clearly; one never introduces changes on the basis of the aggadic Midrashim or the Masorah. He did not answer the first one as specifically; neither did Ibn Zimra's Responsum A. But from the presentation in both, it seems that the understanding was that in all cases other than those where the Talmud's halakhic discussions determined pentateuchal spellings, one corrects the minority of scrolls according to the majority. Aggadic Midrashim are referred to as Gemara or Talmud with such regularity that, at least for this issue, there seems to be no intention to differentiate between them and the Talmud's aggadic passages.

In contrast, Ibn Zimra's Responsum B said to rely in such cases on the "masters of the Masoret," while Responsum C said to follow the Masoret—which effectively means the same thing—or the majority of scrolls. Regardless of how it is said, a contradiction remains between, on the one hand, Ben Adret as presented in his own work as well as Ibn Zimra in Responsum A and, on the other, Ben Adret presented in Ibn Zimra's Responsa B and C, as does an analogous one between different statements by Ibn Zimra.

One possible way out of this quandary is to assume that the contexts of the citations may have affected their contents. Responsum A, which deals with emendations based on a spelling suggested in a Midrash (the Zohar) required that Ibn Zimra rank the value of the midrashic literature as a determinant of the spelling of a word in the Torah. He rejected Midrash and the Masorah with it, in favor of retaining the consonantal text as it is found in the scrolls. Responsum B, meanwhile, dealt with a general attack by non-Jews on the rabbinic transmission of the Bible. Forced to defend the traditional handling of the text, including some troublesome terms and notions found in the Talmud, in the Masorah, and in some related rabbinic writings, Ibn Zimra strongly supported the entire traditional literature on the subject, especially the Masorah. Responsum C dealt with, and upheld the value of, the Talmud's teachings when they contradict the other witnesses; the Masorah was essentially irrelevant.

One might posit that Ibn Zimra wrote the three responsa at widely different times or relied on different sources for Ben Adret's text, but these assumptions are challenged by a reference to the first of his responsa in the second and to either the first or the second in the third. Even if Ibn Zimra had been pressured by the immediate circumstances to present Ben Adret's teachings in different ways, he did not forget completely what had gone before; rather, it seems that he changed his mind and, in the process, altered the representation of Ben Adret's position and chose to reinterpret his own past actions. Why?

Jacob ben Hayyim Ibn Adoniyah's Masoretic Bible

The year 1524–1525 marked a turning point in the history of rabbinic Bible study, for that is when the *editio princeps* of the masoretic Bible appeared.[2] This milestone has been described in detail, primarily because it served as a model for many subsequent Bible editions and offered an original treatment of the accompanying masoretic notes, and it surely is worthy of the attention it has received. No less significant, though, is Jacob ben Hayyim Ibn Adoniyah's brief but information-packed editorial introduction to the project, which deals with various problems he faced in fixing the Bible text. Though it was reprinted in editions not prepared by him, it has been omitted from some of the latest rabbinic Pentateuchs and Bibles, presumably because of its controversial author and contents or because these editions no longer reflect his editorial work.[3] This brief essay likely contributed to Ibn Zimra's dramatically altered attitude toward the Masorah and served as the basis for Responsum B.

In addition to promoting the Masorah itself, which was one overall purpose of printing it with the Bible, Ibn Adoniyah described the goals of his Introduction as:

1. Refuting Jewish writers who claimed that *Q̱ere u-Keṯiḇ* variants resulted from textual inconsistencies and inaccuracies
2. Demonstrating that differences exist between the Masorah and the Talmud and that the former is to be preferred over the latter as a witness to the text
3. Refuting non-Jewish allegations that the Jews altered the Bible text
4. Explaining the organization of the masoretic apparatus in his Rabbinic Bible

Since it does not relate to the problem at hand, the fourth goal need not detain us. The first three are treated at some length by Ibn Zimra in Responsum B, but since his responsum is not organized as well as Ibn Adoniyah's essay (which is also far less clear), the latter will determine the order of the following comparison between the two texts.

Refutation of Jewish Writers Who Attributed the Qere u-Ketib̲ *Variants to Textual Problems*

By the sixteenth century, the nature of the *Qere u-Ketib̲* variants had long been a subject of discussion, and various writers had allowed for the possibility that they reflect or correct early corruptions or textual difficulties. In his Introduction, Ibn Adoniyah dealt specifically with the approaches of David Kimhi, Profiat Duran (Efodi), and Isaac Abarbanel, allowing Abarbanel to refute his two predecessors and discussing at length only Abarbanel's position.[4]

Kimhi, the earliest of the three, suggested that the *Qere u-Ketib̲* variants originated during the first exile (in the sixth pre-Christian century). The sages who were textual experts had died, and the leaders were forced to make decisions regarding the integrity of doubtful passages. Where they were unable to decide, they passed along two versions, the *Ketib̲ We-La' Qere* and the *Qere We-La' Ketib̲*.

Duran also attributed the textual variations to the ravages of exile. He stressed the successful preservation of the texts but admitted that in a few cases the loss of proper spellings was evident and that textual confusion had taken its toll. According to him, the *Qere u-Ketib̲* variants record some of the doubts that remained.

Abarbanel rejected both of their suggestions. In his opinion, the text in Ezra's possession was perfect, and the notes now identified as *Qere* were added for other reasons. They may denote essential interpretations or secret meanings of the text, or they are attempts to improve on obscurities of language or on sanctified errors present in it. Abarbanel even linked the frequency of *Qere u-Ketib̲* usage to individual authors and specific groups.[5]

Ibn Adoniyah responded to these rather critical-sounding statements by arguing that the three had proposed their ideas as logical deductions, but "we rely solely upon our Talmud, which we have accepted upon ourselves." He declined to apply this argument consistently in determining the proper Bible text, but it served adequately as the pious-sounding base of an attack on Abarbanel's seemingly radical position. His refutation of Abarbanel began with a citation of the passage in Nedarim 37b, from which he concluded that the four categories of variants listed in the Talmud—*Miqra' Soferim*, *'Iṭṭur Soferim*, *Qere We-La' Ketib̲*, and *Ketib̲ We-La' Qere*—are Halakhah to Moses at Sinai. He then discussed the talmudic principle of substituting polite language for improper sounding words in the text (e.g., *ba-teḥorim* for *b'pwlym*, see BT Meg. 25b) and argued that these words were neither obscure nor unintelligible, as Abarbanel had suggested, but were well understood. He totally rejected Abarbanel's attribution of a continuous series of errors to the prophetic authors.

In a brief attempt to spare him the embarrassment of being charged with totally misguided speculation, Ibn Adoniyah suggested that Abarbanel, following the often controversial approach of Maimonides, was seeking a nontraditional explanation in place of a known traditional one.

He then observed that examples of these four phenomena are more common in the Masorah than in the Talmud and questioned whether only those mentioned in the Talmud should have the status of Halakhah to Moses at Sinai. Moving on to Soferim 6:4, he observed that if, as Kimhi claimed, Ezra had seen the texts to be in conflict, he would have corrected them internally, according to the majority, without adding marginal notes (unless they were evenly divided). Besides, he added, following a responsum by Ben Adret, if the *Qere* lacked authority equal to that of the text itself, its recitation during a public Torah reading would be a violation of the prohibition against reading a word not in the text.[6] Therefore, in effect, all such changes, even those not mentioned specifically in the Talmud, must enjoy a status equal to that of the Torah text itself.

> We learn from all these and similar teachings that all words that are *Qere We-La' Ketib* [or] *Ketib We-La' Qere*, and all the ways of the Masorah (*darkē ha-masora*) are Halakhah to Moses at Sinai, not as was written by these above-mentioned sages, as we have deduced from the Gemara, Nedarim. . . [37b].

It therefore seems that at first Ibn Adoniyah was willing to consider an idea similar to the first tradition associated with Ben Adret and Ibn Zimra in Responsum A, namely that changes in reading—but not necessarily orthography—with which the Talmud associated halakhic teachings are acceptable, but those supported only by the Masorah should not be so credited. After further consideration, he arrived at a different position, which regarded all masoretic notations as authoritative and Halakhah to Moses at Sinai, an idea supported by generalizing from the four terms so classified in Nedarim and from other considerations.

To be sure, one may argue that this talmudic passage should not be understood as limited to the four categories mentioned in it,[7] but it does omit much, if not all, of the extremely important and largest group of variants, *Ketib Haki u-Qere Haki*, also known as *Qere u-Ketib* discussed in other talmudic passages. Ibn Adoniyah followed a brief responsum by Ben Adret, in which the latter upheld the prohibition against reading words not in the text and yet defended doing exactly that with *Qere u-Ketib*. A ritual Torah reading that included such alterations could be valid only if the deviations possessed age, authority, and sanctity equal to those of the text. This argument compelled Ibn Adoniyah to broaden the definition and to consider as Sinaitic all masoretic changes, even those not in Nedarim.

Differences Between the Masorah and the Talmud

Continuing the discussion of disagreements among authoritative sources, Ibn Adoniyah analyzed a series of biblical words whose spellings were recorded in the Talmud. In his analysis of the comments on these passages by Rashi and the Tosafists, he claimed that these medieval writers, especially some of the latter, freely cited the testimony of the Masorah against that of the Talmud and even emended the Talmud on the strength of data recorded in the masoretic lists. Oddly enough, the evidence marshaled by Ibn Adoniyah shows that Rashi disagreed with the Masorah in troublesome cases more often than he followed it; yet Ibn Adoniyah continued to use the minority of cases to support his contention. Perhaps he felt justified in his claim because of even one such example in Rashi and the more strongly pro-Masorah position of the Tosafists.

He further noted discrepancies between various midrashic and talmudic statements on the one hand, and masoretic comments on the other, with respect to the spelling of words and the usage of *Qere u-Ketib*, and he pointed to otherwise unknown citations of *Qere u-Ketib* by Rashi and Saadia. In short, he found it normal for the Talmud and the Masorah to disagree, an observation made or alluded to by the Tosafists many dozens of times in their commentaries on the Talmud and hundreds more in those on the Torah.

In attempting to resolve this conflicting evidence about the state of the text, Ibn Adoniyah initially proposed that all plene and defective spellings follow the Talmud against the Masorah, because talmudic authority governs all other religious behaviors and the ancient rabbis must have known exactly what to do. But he went on to reject this notion, because Rashi (occasionally) and the Tosafot (more frequently) relied on the Masorah against the Talmud, and he concluded that all scrolls should be corrected according to the Masorah. This position is much more radical than those offered by the earlier writers, who were primarily talmudists and halakhists and anxious to afford the Talmud and parallel halakhic literature as much authority as seemed reasonable. By way of summation, I note the principles he has used:

1. All changes in the Bible text that are suggested by the Masorah at large are Halakhah to Moses at Sinai, a notion supported by the statement in Nedarim 37b and by the law that prohibits the reading of words not in the text but allows the changes indicated by the Masorah.
2. When differences between the Talmud and the Masorah exist, scrolls should be corrected to follow the Masorah, because Rashi and the Tosafot frequently relied upon it in preference to the Talmud's testimony, even though, in general, the Talmud is binding. (This was to be done, apparently, even in halakhic contexts, which usually were conceded to the Talmud.)

One can only wonder why Ibn Adoniyah allowed the argument to rest here. He seems totally innocent of Abulafia's potential contribution, and, though he cited Ben Adret, it was for another purpose altogether. Ibn Adoniyah could have enriched his discussion by considering and refuting Ben Adret's long responsum or could have supported his conclusion through reference to Meiri's *Qiryat Sefer* and the version of Ben Adret's teaching found there. Since he hailed from Tunisia, it is hardly likely that his presentation reflected an Ashkenazi bias that would give priority to the teachings of the Tosafists, but maybe he was self-conscious of his Sefaradi background and anxious to broaden it. Perhaps he was unaware of these relevant Sefaradi documents; perhaps he knew of Ben Adret's anti-Masorah position but was anxious to avoid challenging him; or perhaps he was more impressed by the information available from the rabbis of northern France and Germany or convinced that those rabbis would be more respected by the people for whom the Bible edition was being prepared. At least they provided the kind of support he needed to make the Masorah the definitive determinant of the Bible text. One could also argue that this was just another way to create the impression that his work was new and that the failure of Felix Pratensis to do to what was needed in his Bible edition of 1517 left him, Ibn Adoniyah, the only available candidate who could complete the task properly. But all this theorizing may be unduly critical. If we can assume that the introduction was written after the printing effort began and added after the first volume's layout was set, perhaps we can best understand the limits of Ibn Adoniyah's discussion to have been imposed by the amount of space he had allowed himself at the beginning of the 1524–1525 Rabbinic Bible, in which the essay appeared. He filled up four folios with small print and, after allowing room for his fourth concern, explaining how he had treated the Masorah, the amount of space left at the end amounts to less than twenty lines, or 250 words.

Refutation of Non-Jewish Allegations that the Jews Altered the Bible Text

Individuals referred to in Jewish literature as *minim*, best understood in this context as Christians or apostasized Jews, often claimed that the Jews and the rabbis of old had willfully changed various Bible texts. They derived some support for this claim from the differences between the Hebrew text and the Septuagint, but they assembled more damning evidence from within the traditional literature itself, including rabbinic statements about *Iṭṭure Soferim*, *Tiqqune Soferim*, and the changes introduced by those who translated the Torah for Ptolemy. Ibn Adoniyah discussed each of these issues and concluded that the criticism was groundless because, as Solomon Ben Adret and Joseph Albo had already argued, no one who intends to forge a document preserves the record of the forgeries for all to see. Even if the rabbis had made the changes, listing them undermined any effect they might have had; in fact, it assured preservation of the original texts, the exact opposite of their alleged intention.

In the course of the discussion, Ibn Adoniyah cited at length the statement on *ʿ-ṭ-r* found in the *Arukh* and he referred briefly to the talmudic passages that list the differences introduced into the Greek translation. Before going on to describe his own contribution, he marshaled further evidence for the value, accuracy, and contribution of the Masorah to the proper determination of the Bible text. He also made brief mention of two other Ashkenazi writers, Rabbi Meir Rothenberg, who lived in the thirteenth century, and the martyred Rabbi Mordecai ben Hillel, who, like Ben Adret, died in 1310, and their attempts to find meaning in or to associate talmudic halakhot with various masoretic rubrics.

From Ibn Adoniyah's report, it seems that he first came to believe in the Masorah's potential value for his project and then presented his case to the wealthy Venetian printer Daniel Bomberg, who invested heavily in order to acquire the necessary manuscripts. It was only when Ibn Adoniyah began to examine them that he discovered the extent of the complex, confusing, and contradictory situation in the various masoretic manuscripts and compositions. His argument in support of the Masorah, it seems, was based on principle, on its value to the medieval Ashkenazi rabbis, and on its ability to provide better guidance than any other type of evidence. At no point does he seem to have considered using Torah scrolls, even for the pentateuchal section of his project. I assume this is so partly because the scrolls lacked the masoretic information (including the vocalization and cantillation marks) he wanted to include, partly because they were too numerous and too scattered (not to mention too unwieldly) to consult with any degree of consistency, partly because using them on the Torah portion would have created an imbalance relative to many other parts of the Bible, and partly because by this time the medieval presumption of their containing a letter-perfect consonantal text could no longer be sustained, especially in Ashkenazi circles. If the correct text could be recovered, it had to be from the Masorah.

Despite Ibn Adoniyah's successes, the pressures from Christian critics and polemicists did not abate, as can be seen from a somewhat later comment by Aryeh de Modena (1571–1648). Editor of the Venetian Rabbinic Bible published in 1617–1619, he was well acquainted with the textual problems associated with such efforts and took credit for hundreds of improvements over previous editions, mostly in the texts of the commentaries. A questioner claimed, on the basis of earlier sources (probably Ashkenazi rabbis, who expressed similar notions quite frequently), that a public Torah reading need not be stopped to exchange a Torah scroll lacking an entire verse for a correct scroll. Modena rejected the idea and added:

> Aside from the fact that, according to the law, there is an answer, the entire respect of our nation is to respond to those who insult us by claiming that we forged [or: corrupted] the texts (*sefarim*). To the contrary, we have been extremely precise according to the Masorah, even regarding plene and defective spellings.[8]

Referring to Nahmanides' equation of the entire text of the Torah with a name of God and the fact that even one minor difference in the tip of a *yod* invalidated the scroll, he too defended the need for a letter-perfect text in order to avoid non-Jewish criticisms.

Ibn Zimra and Ibn Adoniyah

Comparison of Ibn Adoniyah's Introduction with Ibn Zimra's Responsum B reveals that almost all of the several dozen talmudic, targumic, and medieval sources cited by Ibn Zimra appear in Ibn Adoniyah's essay and that they are used the same way. Both discuss Nedarim 37b at length and the positions of Kimhi, Duran, and Abarbanel on *Qere u-Keṯiḇ*. The passage from the *Arukh* (some nine lines), including the reference to the targum of *saru* as *ʿaṭru*, is cited fully in both texts. Both men dealt with the conflict between the Talmud and the Masorah, even though this was not called for by the question to Ibn Zimra as we now have it. Both discussed the *Qere u-Keṯiḇ* problem in relation to Nedarim 37b, where it is not mentioned; both discussed the talmudic reference to "*z*ʾ*t* mentioned in connection with *ha-miṣwa*" and located it in Jeremiah rather than in Deuteronomy. Both discussed the examples from BT Meg. 25b about euphemistic changes introduced in the reading of the Bible for the sake of propriety. Both referred to, but did not quote, the discussion about changes in the Bible written for Ptolemy; both discussed the possibility of the texts' being divided equally on some points of spelling. Both cited the same short responsum by Ben Adret.

Ibn Adoniyah's essay is much longer than Ibn Zimra's responsum and includes many additional masoretic and rabbinic sources. Ibn Zimra, meanwhile, referred to several passages not mentioned by Ibn Adoniyah. These include primarily references to Rashi's commentary on the Talmud, Ben Adret's notion about correcting texts according to the Masorah, and Ibn Zimra's own earlier responsum.

Most of Ibn Adoniyah's additional sources relate to the Masorah, a field in which he had unquestioned expertise, but one that might be considered somewhat esoteric for a talmudic-halakhic authority like Ibn Zimra, especially if at first he believed the Masorah to be inferior to other sources of evidence about the text. Ibn Adoniyah cited a few of the references by name (e.g., Kimhi, Duran, Abarbanel, and one responsum of Ben Adret), whereas Ibn Zimra did not; moreover, several of the passages that appear in both texts are integral to Ibn Adoniyah's essay but not to Ibn Zimra's, and the issue of having an even split between the witnesses also seems to have originated with Ibn Adoniyah, though Meiri may deserve the credit for this point, and even Abulafia was confronted by it. Ibn Adoniyah's quotation from the *Arukh* actually contains a small piece lacking in Ibn Zimra's. All of this suggests that Ibn Zimra's responsum drew on Ibn Adoniyah's essay rather than the reverse. Of course, the wording of the question originally posed to Ibn Zimra might suggest the relevance of this extra material, but its loss precludes benefiting from such guidance.

We must conclude that Ibn Adoniyah's essay preceded Ibn Zimra's and that the collection of most of Ibn Zimra's sources and some of his conclusions in a very real sense depended on Ibn Adoniyah's prior efforts. Indeed, the questioner may have asked about Ibn Adoniyah's essay or based his query on it. But Ibn Zimra did not respond to each issue exactly as his predecessor did, as a comparison of his positions with the corresponding sections of Ibn Adoniyah's essay demonstrates.

Ibn Adoniyah's first concern was the attribution of *Qere u-Ketib* problems to ancient textual variants, and both writers agreed that all such notations are Halakhah to Moses from Sinai. Both offered this position as a counter to the same three medieval writers, and both utilized many of the same rabbinic sources, though Ibn Zimra's presentation is far shorter and less detailed.

The two writers' analyses of the disagreements between the Talmud and the Masorah on various points do not follow this pattern. Whereas Ibn Adoniyah voiced great respect for talmudic authority, he ultimately decided in favor of the Masorah. By way of contrast, in Responsum A, Ibn Zimra followed Ben Adret and rejected masoretic statements as having no authority, an attitude which, according to Ibn Adoniyah and others, was generally accepted in his day. In Responsum B, Ibn Zimra modified this position, allowing the masoretes full authority in all cases except those where the Talmud had associated a law with a particular spelling. This change in attitude represented a major, though incomplete, concession to Ibn Adoniyah's arguments. Ibn Zimra would not reject all talmudic claims, so he compromised by retaining them in words of legal importance, as Ben Adret had done earlier, and by giving the Masorah full reign everywhere else, undoubtedly in the vast majority of questions.[9] It is ironic that in many cases Ibn Adoniyah's argument in favor of the Masorah, which relied on what he perceived as the tendency of Rashi and the Tosafists to favor the Masorah over the spellings suggested in the Talmud, involved references to legal contexts. They may have convinced Ibn Zimra of the Masorah's value; yet in those very cases, he retained a commitment to the spelling suggested by the Babylonian Talmud. Ultimately Ibn Adoniyah was a masorete and favored the masoretic literature; Ibn Zimra was a halakhist and preferred the Talmud.

Ibn Zimra's qualified preference for the Masorah also resembles the second version of Ben Adret's teaching, preserved in Meiri's *Qiryat Sefer*. Differences in wording preclude its having been quoted in full from there, but it is possible that *Qiryat Sefer* played a role in Ibn Zimra's rethinking of the issue and reformulating his understanding of Ben Adret. Ibn Zimra frequently cited Meiri's Talmud commentary in his responsa, but he never referred to *Qiryat Sefer*. Had he seen it, he might have remembered the general idea; if a copy were in his personal library, one would expect greater influence on his other discussions.

Given this clearly documented change of position by Ibn Zimra, it is likely that this passage attributed to Ben Adret is largely Ibn Zimra's paraphrase. But one might suggest as well that Ben Adret too changed his mind at some point—conceivably, halakhists, who are groomed on Talmud and its related literature, find it easy to open up to competing authoritative texts only in later life—or that the printed texts of his responsum are corrupt. Since such conjectures remain exactly that, it seems equally possible that Ibn Zimra's attribution of this idea to Ben Adret reflects such strong commitment to Ibn Adoniyah's argument that he took it for granted Ben Adret also had agreed and did not bother to check again.

In theory, this position should eliminate all use of the principle of majority rule of readings in Torah scrolls in favor of the teachings of the masoretic works, unless they too are divided, in which case the spelling should be determined by a majority of masoretic works. Alternatively, it may suggest that the Masorah actually contains the text of the majority of scrolls, which should have been the textual reality, at least in theory. This process also fits the more widespread reliance on the principle of majority testimony used to resolve other halakhic questions.

Ibn Zimra's commitment to majority rule is still upheld and mentioned as part of the paraphrase of Ben Adret, though now it has become an argument of secondary importance, because plene and defective spellings of legal significance are to be controlled by the Talmud and all others by the Masorah. Other variations in spelling, it would seem, are to be determined by a majority of scrolls. If, in such cases, the scrolls are equally divided, the correct reading is to be determined by the Masorah. Thus the responsibility for resolving all textual problems, except for a few words discussed in the Talmud, rests ultimately with the Masorah.

This position was adopted with such conviction that the last observation in Ibn Zimra's responsum (B.17), the final element in his acceptance of the authority of the Masorah, is a reference to the restorations he made some time before, in the Torah scrolls that had been emended to follow the Zohar. Referring to his earlier responsum (A.2–4), in which, in Ben Adret's name, Ibn Zimra had totally rejected the authority of the Masorah, in responsum B he actually claimed that when confronted by that earlier problem, he had corrected these scrolls to follow the readings suggested by the Masorah! Of course in this case the readings in the scrolls and the Masorah would have been identical, but the earlier report did not suggest that any weight was given to this fact.

Ibn Adoniyah's third concern, responding to those who attacked the Jews for changing the Bible text, not only engaged Ibn Zimra but apparently was the raison d'être of the responsum. This appears to have been the stimulus for his questioner (though such a conclusion may reflect Ibn Zimra's reformulation), and it pervades his answer. Accusations of tampering with the Bible text had long been leveled at the Jews by Christians, Muslims, and apostasized Jews, and they derived support from, among other things, the differences between the Christian and Jewish versions of the Bible—something that was quite evident from even a casual comparison but that had been developed into a serious subject of study by Origen over a millennium earlier. Differences between approved Christian translations or authoritative Muslim versions of certain passages and the Bible itself constantly put the Jews on the defense; non-Jews eagerly searched for evidence of such tampering in the traditional literature itself.

However one understood the original intent of the statements about *Tiqqune Soferim*, *Iṭṭure Soferim*, *Qere u-Ketib̲*, and the origin of the already noted orthographic differences, a response was needed. It required refuting all attacks and supporting the traditional claims and practices, which was necessitated even more by the advent of printing, by the sixteenth-century interest in textual variants, and by the polemical nature of these accusations. In this respect, both Ibn Adoniyah and Ibn Zimra walked in the same path—a combination of redefined terms and logical argumentation; but here too there is a difference between them. Both men claimed that all of these masoretic notes are Halakhah to Moses from Sinai, giving them equal authority with the Bible; but Ibn Adoniyah also discussed the possibility that the rabbis may have altered the Bible text. Echoing Ben Adret and Albo, he rejected this notion as improbable, because no one alters a text and then lists the changes for all to see. Ibn Zimra never discussed the point, even heuristically.

Ibn Adoniyah, who wrote his introduction for a Bible being produced in a Christian publishing house, maintained positive relations with his employer. Work in that context, especially when interpreted in light of his later conversion to Christianity, might suggest that his refutation of the non-Jews' criticisms was somewhat less important to him than the other issues,[10] but one also might understand his position as a clever and sincere response to them. Knowing that his Christian colleagues would not accept the argument that everything was given to Moses at Sinai, he acknowledged as a straw man that the rabbis might have tampered with the text, but then he adduced objective evidence—the trail they left—as proof that they did not. Ibn Zimra had no such affiliations or possibly conflicting loyalties. He undoubtedly considered the interfaith polemic crucial, and his explanations are colored by his concern for how they would be perceived by the "adversaries"—as if they would read his responsum!:

> . . . for, if you do not explain [it] this way, there is room for our adversaries to say [about every single matter], "Here the Scribes changed the text," as they accuse us daily. (B.4)

> "Be sincere with the Lord your God" [Deut. 18:13] and believe what the rabbis, of blessed memory, said. . . . (B.10)

> Moreover, since you allow the adversary to say that the texts became incorrect and it was necessary to remove the *waws* [a reference to Iṭṭure Soferim], he may also say that they added and deleted [elsewhere] at will, as they do say. (B.13)

The identity of Ibn Zimra's adversaries is unclear. Ben Adret was involved in public disputations with both Muslims and Christians but, in the relevant passages in his own work, Ibn Adoniyah referred to his opponents as *minim*, which most likely excluded the former. Ibn Zimra did not use this term, and he was probably concerned primarily with criticisms lodged from the Muslim world. Comparison with the similar claim made in A.6 and the specific mention of "when we are among this nation who say that we have changed the Torah" seems to confirm this observation, since, in all likelihood, Ibn Zimra was living in Egypt when he wrote Responsa A and B, and at no point in his adult life did he live in a Christian country.[11]

Even so, one can rightly question whether Ibn Zimra may have borrowed some of his targets, as well as the ammunition with which to attack them, from Ibn Adoniyah's cultural context. The issue of a letter-perfect text would have been meaningful to Muslims, who attributed such accuracy to the Qur'an, but the information about the Septuagint would probably have been of more moment in Europe than in Egypt, even if it was the ancient home of Ptolemy, for whom the translation was prepared. Until precise local Muslim candidates for these criticisms of the Jews' handling of the Bible text emerge, I can only speculate. Suffice it to note that some earlier Muslim critics were aware of the Greek Bible and its differences from the Hebrew one.[12]

Dating Ibn Zimra's Responsa

The differences among Ibn Zimra's four responsa and the various factors that contributed to them have helped elucidate an important dimension in the changing halakhic attitudes toward the Masorah's potential contribution to fixing the Torah text. Rashi and the Tosafists (Ashkenazim) obviously valued the Masorah for determining the Torah's consonantal text, as is demonstrated by Bahya, Riva, Ibn Adoniyah, and others. Even though Abulafia had used it systematically in his *Masoret Seyag La-Torah*, Ben Adret (a Sefaradi), at least initially or at least according to many witnesses, saw it as inconclusive and less authoritative. He preferred the testimony of the scrolls themselves, or that of the Talmud when it contradicted the scrolls in orthographic situations deemed by the Talmud to be of legal consequence, although he did rely on the Masorah for other text-related traditions. Ibn Zimra seems to have maintained this position until he was convinced by Ibn Adoniyah's essay that, as a witness to the Torah's correct orthography, the Talmud was—and had always been perceived by Rashi and the Tosafot to be—inferior to the Masorah, which should be the determining testimony in most cases. He then linked this approach with another tradition of Ben Adret's thinking and actually changed the report of what he had done in Responsum A to fit his new position.

This reconstruction of events is quite rough, but a few dates are certain and allow a somewhat fuller picture of the chronology. Ibn Zimra lived in Egypt approximately from 1513 to 1553, after which he returned to the Land of Israel. Ibn Adoniyah's essay appeared in the Rabbinic Bible published in Venice in 1524–1525. We should therefore date Responsum B between 1524 and 1573, the year of Ibn Zimra's death, and Responsum A to the period between 1513 and 1524, perhaps after the conquest of Egypt by the Turks in 1517, which preceded Ibn Zimra's becoming the leader of the Jews of that country.

These limits are quite broad, but the *terminus ad quem* for Responsum B may be raised substantially. In 1537–1538 Elijah Levita spoke of Ibn Adoniyah as having apostasized and died.[13] We do not know whether this information reached Ibn Zimra, but if it did, Ibn Zimra is unlikely to have cited him by name, if at all (though the proliferation of converts who worked in the Venice printing establishments precluded avoiding all contact with their work). Accordingly, since there is no direct or indirect reference to Ibn Adoniyah, one might feel justified in assigning Responsum B to a date after 1538. But this dating is far from certain, since it is also possible that Ibn Zimra omitted his name in order to avoid attracting attention to a work on which he had relied so heavily, or, as appears from the omission of the names of Kimhi, Abarbanel, and others whose opinions he rejected within the responsum itself, because he did not routinely identify all his sources, particularly if he disapproved of what they had said.

This is also the case in III, no. 1068 (643) (partially translated in chapter 3), where Ibn Zimra rejects the view of Ibn Ezra and Ibn Janah on the analogy between certain usages of conjunctive *waw* and Arabic *fa* without reference to either writer. It is even more obvious in III, no. 967 (532), where, in defending the use of *Qedushot*, medieval liturgical poems added to the blessings of the *Amidah* prayer on Yom Kippur, he listed many authorities who accepted the practice and merely acknowledged the existence of dissenters. Elsewhere, however, Ibn Zimra named and criticized the writers to whose anonymous positions he objected here. This practice is particularly apparent from his treatment of the contributions of earlier Bible commentators and thinkers, which, though not major concerns of his responsa, are discussed in scattered reactions to some of their comments. As might be expected, he is very positive about Rashi, quoting and explaining his work in numerous places. His admiration for Nahmanides is also quite apparent, as is his willingness to be frankly critical of Elijah Mizrahi, as in III, no. 549, and VI, no. 2006.

The teachings of Abraham Ibn Ezra, David Kimhi, and Isaac Abarbanel, though discussed when needed, were also likely to be criticized or corrected. Such rejections of Ibn Ezra are found, for example, in I, no. 284, and II, no. 813, which refute his ideas about Mordecai's refusal to bow to Haman and about the plagues, although in III, no. 967 (532), in defending the use of *Qedushot*, he labeled Ibn Ezra, together with Solomon Ibn Gabirol and Judah HaLevi, *'anašim gedolim be-ḥokma*, "men great in wisdom" (not *be-tora*, "in Torah"). This list was expanded to include Saadiah, Rav Hai Gaon, and Maimonides in VIII, no. 191, where he fiercely defended the value of studying *ḥokma*, which in this context is perhaps best understood as philosophy or secular wisdom, though he admitted discouraging his students from doing so. He also liked what Ibn Ezra had to say about rain in Egypt and devoted a lot of space to it in VIII, nos. 140–141.

David Kimhi received worse treatment, as in II, no. 693, in III, no. 1066 (641)—where particularly harsh language was used in response to his claim that some Midrashim are "far from reasonable"—and in V, nos. 67 and 253, although he was received more positively in VII, no. 33. Ibn Zimra also criticized Abarbanel's handling of the story of Solomon and the two prostitutes in III, no. 634, but accepted his *Rosh Amanah* in I, no. 344, and V, no. 40.

These arguments about references to other writers are therefore inconclusive, but this same work by Levita provides another suggestion. Levita's *Masoret HaMasoret*, published in Venice in 1537–1538, includes several sharp criticisms of some previously accepted ideas about various aspects of the Masorah. One of these passages contains a strong attack against those who claimed all examples of *Qere u-Ketib* to be Halakhah to Moses from Sinai.[14] While this might be just another of the places where Levita criticized Ibn Adoniyah,[15] the comment seems more closely directed at Ibn Zimra. While Ibn Adoniyah suggested that all masoretic statements found in the Talmud were Halakhah to Moses from Sinai, Ibn Zimra carried the argument to a further extreme, despite the obvious problem that derives from the post-Mosaic dating of some texts in which these supposedly Mosaic notes appear:

> And if you ask, how can something be Halakhah to Moses from Sinai if found in Ruth, or the other scrolls, or Psalms—recited by David—etc., it would be correct to answer that we believe that everything was given on Sinai, even an analysis of a law that a learned and pious student would discover [many centuries later]; everything was given to Moses on Sinai. (B.9)

Compare this to Levita's:

> Would that anyone might provide someone who would listen to me and explain how it is possible to say about them [the cases of *Qere We-La' Ketib, Ketib We-La' Qere*, etc., found in post-Mosaic books] that they are a Halakhah to Moses from Sinai when, of all of the examples cited [in BT Ned. 37b], not one is in the Torah. . . . And this trouble was not enough for us, until some later writers wrote that every *Qere u-Ketib* in the entire Bible is a Law of Moses at Sinai.[16]

If the association of these two passages is correct, we may assign Ibn Zimra's second responsum to the period between 1524 and 1538, possibly to the period before Ibn Adoniyah's conversion.

It is theoretically possible for Ibn Zimra to have written in response to a question about Levita's book, but this scenario seems highly unlikely from what can be gleaned from the question and the answer; it would require a dating of Responsum B after 1538, which would allow at least thirteen years between the writing of the two responsa, time for Ibn Zimra's recollection of the events surrounding Responsum A to have faded. But having access to the book and not just a question about its contents would also necessitate the assumption that he knew of Levita's statement about Ibn Adoniyah's conversion and would force the improbable conclusion that he changed his attitude on this critical question on the basis of an apostate's essay. Also, if Ibn Zimra knew Levita's work when he wrote Responsum B, one would expect him to have used the opportunity to attack some of the other controversial ideas developed in it.

The sequencing of Responsa C and D is less certain. Responsum C refers to Ibn Zimra's having treated the discrepancies between sources regarding plene and defective spellings in an earlier responsum, but the reference could be to either Responsum A or B. His position in Responsum C, which calls for correcting nonhalakhic spellings "according to the Masoret or following the majority of scrolls," is not as strong as the pro-Masorah position taken in B and, if earlier than B, would perhaps indicate an initial move toward that stand, taken independently of Ibn Adoniyah's essay. Also, the reference to having discussed the issue in a prior responsum is better taken as a reference to only one, which would be A, supporting a sequence of A, C, B.

Even so, the pro-Masorah position in Responsum C suggests that it is later than Responsum B, which relied on Ibn Adoniyah's essay and shows strong evidence of its influence, and therefore that C is a slight softening of the position in B that gives a more balanced role to both masoretic and nonmasoretic sources. If I am correct in reading the last line of Responsum A as a veiled wish to be able to follow the Zohar's spelling, in effect an expression of less than total support for the Masorah's control of the Bible text's orthography, it is more likely that C postdates B, but this sequence is far from certain. The presentation in paragraph Z2 of Responsum C reads like a condensation of Z2-3 in Responsum B, but the examples cited, *pilagšim* and *kallot̲*, are not found in the paraphrase in that Responsum; they do appear in Responsum A, strengthening the relationship between it and Responsum C.

Responsum D concludes, "And it is obvious that we should not disregard the teachings of our fathers, and all the texts, and the Masorah because of Hizquni's opinion." Its casual support of the Masorah against what Ibn Zimra perceived to be a medieval emendation in the vocalization of a word from the Torah proves nothing about its relative date, and the rest of the text has little in common with the other issues developed here. If one could demonstrate that Ibn Zimra cited the masoretic rubric from Ibn Adoniyah's Rabbinic Bible, then D would have to be dated after 1524–1525, but that is impossible. They can be linked only through several unusual details and the minor error they share, but the only way to prove a connection would be to demonstrate that the rubric's formulation was Ibn Adoniyah's own contribution. That seems unlikely, for Ginsburg reported its being in a number of manuscipts.

Responsum D does not share the zealous commitment to the Masorah found in Responsum B, and it may reflect Ibn Zimra's attitude toward it before Ibn Adoniyah's influence took hold. If so, it should be dated before 1524. The absence of any concluding reference to his other discussions of the matter (in Responsum A, B, or C) offers slight support for this assumption. Indeed, Responsum D could be the earliest of the four.

I have attempted no dating of the various volumes of responsa in the hope of establishing a sequence for the individual texts in this way. Responsum A appears in Volume IV, while Responsum B, which undoubtedly postdates it, is in Volume III. Many of Ibn Zimra's responsa contain cross-references to earlier attempts to deal with the same or related matters. A thorough study of such occurrences might help us divide the eight volumes into their original notebooks and date them relatively, if not absolutely.

Fixing God's Torah Since the Sixteenth Century

> . . . In any case, nowadays I am able to exempt [everyone] from the commandment of writing a Torah scroll because of another law, namely that, even in the days of the Amoraim, they were not expert in defective and plene spelling, as Rav Joseph said to Abaye in the first chapter of Qiddushin (30a), "They are expert in defective and plene spelling; we are not expert." And a Torah scroll that lacks or adds even one letter is invalid for ritual use, so it is beyond our ability to fulfill this commandment.
>
> Rabbi Aryeh Leib Gunzberg (1695–1785)
> *Sha'agat Aryeh, Hilkhot Sefer Torah*, no. 36

Introduction

On a practical level, the primary purpose of the laws and customs surrounding the production of Torah scrolls was to counter any possible introduction of scribal errors and textual corruptions and to ensure the quality and accuracy of the text—in short, to prevent changes. Ibn Zimra's responsa contributed to this goal, but not as slavishly as one might assume. In various contexts, he defended the accuracy of Torah scrolls and the Masorah, and he argued against emending the Torah texts on the basis of alternative midrashic or zoharic spelling suggestions that deviated from established norms. On the other hand, he applied the talmudic discussion of the cut *waw* in Num. 25:12 in a way that would require changing all extant copies—a posture he assumed also when discussing the proper forms of the letters *heh* and *qof*. Wholesale changes were avoided, but halakhah controlled the text, which could and should be altered to conform to halakhic requirements, as he understood them.

Scribal halakhah demands that Torah scrolls be copied from other texts and not be produced from memory or in scriptoria, where many scribes took dictation from one reader; that texts found to contain errors be corrected quickly, so that they can neither be used ritually nor allowed to influence other texts; that they be graphically clean and neat and minimize the presence of letters or words outside the regular linear and columnar framework, which have produced so many dittographies and misplaced insertions in other books; that every letter be formed in a distinctive manner with absolutely no form of ligature and be recognizable to a nine-year-old child; that no foreign elements—scribal, calligraphic, artistic, masoretic, or exegetical—be included in the scroll; and that no one consciously change anything in its text. This type of strict control is evident from Maimonides' formulation:

> You will therefore have learned that there are twenty things, any one of which invalidates a Torah Scroll. If one [of these things] is done to it, it is considered like a Humash among the Humashim that one uses to teach children, and the sanctity of a Torah scroll does not apply to it, one should not read from it in public; and these are:
>
> (1) if it was written on the skin of a ritually impure animal [i.e., a ritually impure species]; (2) if it was written on the unprocessed skin of a ritually pure animal; (3)] if it [i.e., the skin] was processed for some purpose other than [using it to write] a Torah scroll; (4) if it was written other than on the side designated for writing: with respect to the unsplit hide of an animal (*gewil*), if on the side closest to the animal's flesh; with respect to a split hide, on the outer layer (*qelaf*), if written on the side closest to the animal's hair; (5) if some of it was written on unsplit hide and some of it on split hide; (6) if it was written on the inner layer of a split hide; (7) if it was written without the ruling of lines; (8) if it was written not in permanent black ink; (9) if it was written in other languages [i.e., not Hebrew]; (10) if a non-Jew or a similarly inpppropriate person wrote it; (11) if [the scribe] wrote the references to the Divine Name without [specific] intent; (12) if he deleted even one letter; (13) if he added even one letter; (14) if a letter touches another; (15) if the shape of one letter was worn down so that it cannot be read at all, or so that it is similar to another letter, whether the [problem] is in the writing itself or due to a perforation, a tear, or a blurring; (16) if he increased or decreased the space between one letter and another such that the word looks like two words, or two words appear to be one word; (17) if he changed the form of the paragraphs; (18) if he changed the form of the "songs" [e.g., Exodus, chapter 15]; (19) if he changed the rest of the text to be like a "song"; (20) if he sewed the parchment sections without the sinews of a ritually pure animal.
>
> All other things are a requirement but do not prevent [the Torah Scroll from being valid.][1]

Complementing these regulations was an extensive masoretic literature that registered regular, irregular, and anomalous phenomena, and even extensive quasi-masoretic charts, lists, and poetry that tabulated all sorts of other things, including the number of times each letter was used in the entire Bible. These practices have succeeded in a remarkable way. For the past two millennia—the rabbinic era, during which these practices were developed, codified, and sustained—the Torah has been preserved in an extremely accurate manner, far more so than might be claimed for other books, rabbinic or nonrabbinic, that were copied during even part of this time.

But the definition of textual accuracy is in many ways relative, not absolute. We live in an age of photographic reproduction and expect that a copy of an original will resemble it in virtually every way, but this is really not the premise of the laws about producing Torah scrolls. The ability to imitate an excellently executed original obviated the copyist's production of his own detailed layout, and this is one of the primary reasons for using a Tiqqun; but in theory, scribal regulations did not control the size of the letters, the number of letters on a line, the layout of most columns of text, the size of the columns, and the number of lines in each. Eventually most of these phenomena were standardized, but only as matters of custom, and in some cases adherence to them created other problems that stimulated strong objections by various halakhic authorities. Such was the case, for example, with regard to stretching letters in order to fill available spaces and to beginning every column of the Torah with a *waw*, except those six whose first letters spell out *b-y-h š-m-w*.[2]

But even in medieval times, some textual phenomena—such as details regarding the shapes of the letters themselves, unusually large or small letters, crowns on some letters, irregularly shaped letters, and the shapes of the "inverted *nuns*"—suffered such extensive variation that many authorities virtually abandoned the attempt to control them and accepted a range of possibilities as correct. One popular rationalization of the doubts about how to form the cut *waw* in Num. 25:12 was to write it like all others, which would be acceptable to everyone, at least after the fact; the very minor differences in the other suggested forms of the letter would have left the Torah ritually invalid according to some individuals or groups that rejected one or more of these variations. Thus the compromise that evolved in some circles entailed ignoring both the talmudic note that the *waw* should be formed in a cut manner and the medieval rulings like Ibn Zimra's, which invalidated all scrolls whose letter *waw* was formed otherwise.[3] Despite the best efforts of Maimonides and others, this same degree of variation prevailed in many of the open and closed paragraph divisions. It was also evident in the lack of orthographic consistency.

Spelling can carry a range of cultural implications. In some contexts, slight variations carry significant messages; in others, great variations are of no consequence. An American writer of English who consistently uses the British (originally French) spellings "colour," "honour," and "centre" is sending a very different message from one who sprinkles "hi-lite," "stic," and "nite-time" throughout his work. Biblical spellings are far from consistent, but the reasons are poorly understood, and we can only speculate about motives for the Bible's irregular spelling patterns that would have been meaningful in ancient times. To be sure, some pentateuchal words—*'oṯo* and *moše*, for example—are always spelled defective (*'tw* and *mšh*), so a rare plene spelling would indicate something unusual or amiss, but many other words vary extensively—in fact, orthographic inconsistency is the primary rule—and only the most flexible and creative interpreters can rationalize the phenomena as they appear. It is impossible to formulate simple rules that accommodate the entire text, and few explanations of even localized patterns are fully convincing.[4]

Overall, most variations of this type have no impact on the text's primary meaning and usually are of little or no significance other than for the spelling itself. Almost all of the cases discussed above fall under this heading, but they prove that letter-perfect accuracy is beyond reach unless achieved through a dynamic legal process that defines letter-perfection. To do this, the process must identify either a preferred text or every preferred reading. In either case, it must rely on legal reasoning, the proper ranking of textual witnesses, and the conscious exclusion of many sources of information, rather than on simple textual tradition. That is the importance of the rabbinic description of the competing spellings as *maḥhloqeṯ*, "disagreement," rather than as "corruptions" or "inconsistencies," and of incorporating this entire process into the halakhic system.

Over the millennia, as the evidence continued to grow and change, so did the process by which the text was fixed. Whatever its ultimate outcome will be, and however conservatively it will be practiced, this process has not yet run its course. Moreover, despite the assurance that many previously questionable spellings have been settled to the satisfaction of the halakhic system, the historical fact that numerous conflicting readings existed—and that many still exist—cannot be made to disappear, even through legal decisions. In other words, the history of the Bible text preserved by ancient, medieval, and modern rabbis and the Bible-related literature written by them contain eloquent testimony to both the care and the precision with which the text was preserved and also to an extensive list of minor textual variations. Even if all of them could be eliminated, the history of the discussion and the accompanying doubts cannot be. Halakhah may decide on an acceptable text or even a definitive one; the questions about witnesses to alternative spellings will remain forever.

Though most of the variants that are discussed in postmedieval rabbinic literature are relatively minor—the major ones were settled long ago—their incidence far exceeds the dozen or so examples whose existence is sometimes acknowledged, however hesitantly. Some of these passages are now presented, not to explore ancient doubts about the text but to demonstrate that many are well known and discussed in relatively recent rabbinic compositions. In fact, some of these historical questions about the text—to be treated separately from halakhic ones, when necessary—are still with us, and study of them can yield benefit from the learning and insights of rabbinic writers. Rabbi Akiva Eiger's list of twenty-one such cases in his *Gilyon HaShas* to BT Shab. 55b is one well-known example. Also new discoveries sometimes clarify issues of textual doubt that are preserved within the tradition but regularly escape popular detection or proper elucidation. Perhaps the best example with which to begin derives from the treatment of Deut. 6:20 in a passage from the Passover Haggadah.

Some Sample Problems

The Textual Problem with Deut. 6:20—Did the Lord Command "Us" or "You"?

The Passover Haggadah expounds four scattered pentateuchal descriptions of a father's reacting to his son's questions or teaching him; it takes them as references to four different children. Basing its analysis on earlier midrashic presentations or acting parallel to them, it describes these children as wise, wicked, simple, and unable to ask a question.

The question traditionally attributed to the wicked son is, "What is this service to you?" (Ex. 12:26); that of the wise son reads "What are the testimonies, and laws, and regulations that the Lord, Our God, has commanded you?" (Deut. 6:20). The Haggadah further observes that the wicked son, in the way he has formulated his question, has excluded himself from the community, and for centuries interpreters have been hard pressed to clarify the real difference between his question and that of his more scholarly brother. Why, in fact, did the wise son's question merit a more positive response than the wicked son's, when both excluded themselves in similar manner?

Many have responded to this quandary by explaining that the latter's reference to different types of laws shows some deeper appreciation of Judaism, and the reference to "our God" indicates that he meant to include himself; alternatively, the phrase "commanded you" was taken as an indication that the wise son recognized his legally exempt status as a minor. Were this the end of the discussion—as it is in many circles—few would remain dissatisfied with the exposition. If the wicked son were also envisioned as a minor, additional exposition of the potential offense in his tone might be required, but many premodern artistic renderings actually portrayed both sons as having come of age.[5]

All this give and take notwithstanding, careful examination of the ways in which the wise son's prooftext is cited demonstrates conclusively that, in antiquity, it existed in at least two forms, both well known and extensively preserved in rabbinic literature. The phrase as found in the masoretic text, "that the Lord, Our God, has commanded you" (Deut. 6:20), appears in many Yemenite Haggadot as "that the Lord, Our God, has commanded us," and a number of manuscripts of the Midrashim and the Palestinian Talmud concur in citing the verse this way in their formulations of the Midrash. This reading also underlies the translation preserved in the Septuagint and is confirmed by the Vulgate.[6]

Some writers have tried to cast doubts on the validity of this reading by pointing to other, similar interchanges, particularly to the similarity between the appearance of "you" and "us" in Greek,[7] but the range of sources that contain the variant precludes a common erroneous source, interference of one text in all the others, or widespread analogous error. Clearly some rabbinic circles, including the one that produced this passage from the Haggadah, possessed a different reading of this pentateuchal word. Eventually "you" became the accepted biblical reading, and rabbinic texts that preserved the alternative "us" were made to conform to it, thus generating the inconsistency and the rather involved interpretation of the Haggadah passage that emerged. Even so, the evidence of this other text was preserved in both Hellenistic and rabbinic texts and remains a constant focus of many who read the Haggadah every Passover.

The Spelling of Deut. 10:12 in Norzi's Minhat Shai

A second and very different type of case deals with the number of letters in Deut. 10:12, "And now Israel, what does the Lord, your God, ask of you except to fear the Lord your God, to walk in all His ways, and to love Him, and to serve the Lord your God with all your heart and with all your soul?" In most printed Bibles, this verse is spelled as follows:

> *w-ʿth yśrʾl mh y-h-w-h ʾlhyk šʾl m-ʿmk ky ʾm l-yrʾh ʾt y-h-w-h ʾlhyk l-lkt b-kl drkyw w-l-ʾhbh ʾtw w-l-ʿbd ʾt y-h-w-h ʾlhyk b-kl lbbk w-b-kl npšk.*

In his textual commentary, *Minhat Shai*, Norzi collected some of his predecessors' observations on the letter count:

[1] The *Ba'al HaTurim* wrote that the verse contains one hundred letters, corresponding to the one hundred blessings [to be recited daily].
[2] similarly the *Arukh*, s.v. *m'h*.[8]
[3] Also Rabbi [Abraham ben Nathan] Ibn Yarhi wrote in *Sefer HaManhig*,[9] in the name of Rabbi Jacob, may he rest in glory,[10] that he found in the Masoret on this verse [that] "it totals one hundred letters and that *šo'ēl* is spelled plene [i.e., *šw'l*]."[11]
[4] And thus the Ramban wrote in his commentary on *Sefer Yetzirah*, p. 23,[12] that thus wrote the mystic, Rabbi Yom Tov, in his book *Ketem Paz*,[13] in the name of the mystic, Rabbi Elijah, "that the word *šo'ēl* is plene, and the total of one hundred is reached in this verse."
[5] But in our texts it is defective [i.e., *š'l*], and thus wrote R[abbi] M[eir] H[aLevi Abulafia]:
š'l m'mk is defective, and similar to it is *wš'l 'wb wyd'ny* [Deut. 18:11].[14]
[6] And thus wrote Rabbenu Bahya in *Kad HaQemah*, *Bet*, s.v. *berakhah*:
Moreover, you will find ninety-nine letters in the verse, and with the addition of one, which the rabbis of blessed memory added, "Do not read *mh*, 'what,' but *m'h*, 'one hundred,'" they reach one hundred.[15]
[7] In addition, I saw [the book of] someone who wanted to add a *waw* to *la-leket* [reading *we-la-leket*] in order to complete the number [to one hundred], and he wrote that it is this way in the book of Rabbi Joseph Tov Elem;[16] but one should not rely on this at all.

In medieval times, did this verse contain 99 or 100 letters?

The earliest association of Deut. 10:12 with the recitation of 100 daily blessings is BT Men. 43b, where, for purposes of this midrashic teaching, not as an emendation, the Talmud reportedly altered the word *mh*, "what," in that verse to *m'h*, "hundred," by adding an *aleph*. This change relied on a number of factors, including the relatively similar pronunciations of both and the midrashic practice of suggesting similar and usually minor phonetic changes, known as *'al tiqrē* x *'ela'* y, "do not read *x*, but rather *y*," some 100 instances of which are found in the Babylonian Talmud. Additional stimuli may arise from the well-documented practice of using *aleph* as a vowel letter and from the spelling of the Aramaic interrogative pronouns *m'*, *m'n*, and *m'y*.[17] The Vilna text of Menahot contains the link between the verse and the recitation of one hundred blessings, but not the *'al tiqrē* treatment. Some witnesses seem to attest to it, because they have introduced it as a quotation from the Talmud; others are best not taken this way.[18]

Of the many medieval testimonies adduced in support of the verse's containing 100 letters, that of Rabbi Jacob ben Asher, the *Ba'al HaTurim* (ca. 1270–1340), is perhaps the most interesting. It offered several ways to associate this verse with the rabbinic custom of reciting 100 blessings each day:

A. In the Atbash alphabet *mh*, *mem heh*, equates to *yod* (10) + *tzadi* (90), which add up to 100; and
B. there are 100 letters in the verse.

Some editions of the *Ba'al HaTurim* contain a third statement:

C. the numerical value of *mmk*, "of you," is 100 (40 + 40 + 20).

The first proof builds on the validity of the Atbash alphabetic exchanges, a well-known midrashic procedure that switches *aleph* and *tav*, *bet* and *shin*, and so on. The second is based on counting the letters; this obviously was of interest to Norzi and the writers of his sources. Some counted 99, others 100; and some used the extra *aleph* to reach 100 (to be discussed shortly).

The third statement, paragraph C, not found in all editions of the *Ba'al Ha-Turim*, is based on the word *mmk* (*mimmeka*), "from you," but Deut. 10:12 contains the synonym, *m'mk* (*me-'immak*), not *mmk*. Jacob Reines points to similar associations of the daily recitation of 100 blessings with Micah 6:8, *u-ma ha-šem doreš mimmeka*, "and what does the Lord require of you," cited by a series of medieval authors, including Abudarham and Rokeah.[19]

It is uncertain if the text should contain this third statement in this form, but assuming that it should, it is unlikely that its author confused the two prooftexts (as suggested by his critics, noted but not identified by Reines), and it is even less likely that the reference to *mmk* is evidence for a variant reading here. Jacob ben Asher's phrase, *we-ken mmk 'ole mē'a*, should probably be understood merely as a reference to a parallel interpretation of the similar word in Micah, not a third support for the association here.

This third explanation, paragraph C, is found, for example, in the edition of *Ba'al HaTurim* published with *Or HaHayyim, Nahal Qedumim, and Nahal Eshqol*; in Reines' edition; and in the often reprinted Humash found in the hybrid edition of the *Miqra'ot Gedolot* that combines Torah and Nakh volumes from originally unrelated editions. It is not found in the *Ba'al HaTurim* printed with *Heikhal HaBerakhah*. *Torah Or*, a Humash printed with commentaries, contains the following, including the words in parentheses:

> "What the Lord your God asks of you": *mh* in Atbash is *yod* [+] *tzadi*, for He asks of you [to recite] 100 blessings every day. And there are 100 letters in the verse (if we count *šo'ēl* plene). And, similarly, *mmk* is 100.[20]

In the above discussion, Norzi cited or referred to approximately one dozen comments on the verse; many additional medieval references are available:

1. The Torah commentary entitled *Rabbotenu Ba'alei HaTosafot* discusses the first two proofs of the *Ba'al HaTurim*, together with others based on other verses.[21]
2. Rabbi Hayyim Paltiel's commentary on the Torah mentions the change of *mh* to *m'h* but states specifically that the verse contains 100 letters, presumably without the Aleph. It also refers to the Atbash association of *mh* and 100.[22]
3. Rabbi Eleazar of Worms mentioned the notion in his commentary.[23] He attributed the play on *mh* and *m'h* to Menahot and included a number of other interesting associations and proofs. He also offered two interpretations, depending on whether one follows a plene or defective spelling of *šo'ēl*.
4. One of the clearest syntheses of the two presentations is to be found in Joseph Bekhor Shor's Torah commentary, in which he explains that the

verse actually contains 99 letters which, when augmented by the extra *aleph* added by the rabbinic play on *mh*, reaches 100:

And from this verse our rabbis found support for the notion of (*ramezu*) [reciting] 100 blessings every day, as it is written, "What does the Lord, your God, ask of you . . . ?" "Do not read *mh*, but *m'h*." And 100 letters are found in this verse [which begins] "And now," if you read *m'h* with an *aleph*, for with *m'h* [spelled this way], there are 100 letters, because in the verse are one less than 100, and with the *aleph* they are a full 100. And now there are two [explanations], one that you read [*mh* as] *m'h*, and another that there are now 100.[24]

5. Israel ben Joseph HaYisra'eli arrived at the number 100 by counting the added *aleph* of *mh* > *m'h*, and he mentions an association with 2 Sam. 23:1.[25]
6. Note also the formulation of Rabbi Isaac ben Moses of Vienna in *Or Zarua'*:

And how much are you required to praise [God] every day? *Kaf* blessings, which is 100 blessings [the letter *kaf*, normally the numerical equivalent of 20, when spelled out as *k* + *p*, = 20 + 80], which one is required to recite every day. And this is what Scripture said in *Parashat 'Eqeḇ*, "And now Israel, what does the Lord your God ask of you, but to fear. . . ." And we say in [the talmudic] chapter [entitled] *HaTekhelet*:

> Rabbi Meir used to say: One is required to recite 100 blessings every day, as is said, "And now Israel, what [does the Lord your God ask of you]."

And Rashi, of blessed memory, explained, "Do not read *mh* but *m'h*." But Rabbenu Tam, of blessed memory, wrote in his *Tiqqun Torah*, "*šw'l* is plene, and that verse contains 100 letters." And some explain that *mh* adds up to 100 in Atbash.[26]

Most witnesses seem to support a count of 99 letters in Deut. 10:12, but support for 100 also is widespread. The orthographic data collected by Kennicott (ad loc.) contain eight instances of the plene reading, *šw'l*, and one or two examples of several other variants, including *we-la-leḵeṯ* for *la-leḵeṯ*, a reading Norzi associated with Joseph Tov Elem and discounted.

In Men. 43b the Tosafot claimed that *šo'ēl* is plene, as did some of the other medieval Ashkenazic commentators. *Paneah Raza'* by Rabbi Isaac ben Yehudah HaLevi contains a further witness to the link with 100 blessings but relates it to three verses, one each from the Torah, Prophets, and Hagiographa. He never offers a count of the letters in this verse, but the citation contains a plene spelling of *šo'ēl*, that is, *šw'l*.[27] Rabbi Natan Spira agreed that *šo'ēl* is plene and that the verse therefore contains 100 letters.[28] The plene spelling is also recognized, if only after the fact, by *Heikhal HaBerakhah*: "*š'l*: lacking the *waw* and, if it is found plene, it is acceptable (*kašer*) to read it [when one is] under great duress, if there is no other [Torah scroll]."[29]

No such legitimation appears in the seriatim listings of problematic passages in Rabbi Hayyim Palaggi's *Sefer Hayyim*,[30] or in Rabbi E. Z. Margaliot, *Sha'arei Efrayim*.[31] Uri Feivel HaLevi, the author of *Gidulei Heqdesh*,[32] recorded *š'l* as the correct spelling, as did Rabbi Solomon Ganzfried.[33]

Rabbi Barukh HaLevi Epstein discussed this matter in a number of places. In *Tosefet Berakhah* he listed five examples of rabbinic derashot that add an *aleph*, and he provided an additional list of examples of biblical language that omit *aleph* where it is anticipated. In *Torah Temimah* he offered a series of examples in which biblical numbers are rounded off by one digit—49 to 50, 69 to 70, and so on—which also might validate a claim that a verse of 99 letters actually contained 100.[34]

Rabbi Akiva Eiger's Gilyon HaShas, *Shabbat 55b*

Rabbi Akiva ben Moses Eiger Guenz (1761–1837) wrote several sets of glosses on the Babylonian Talmud. The first printing appeared in the Prague Talmud (1830–1835), and it has been included in most subsequent editions. *Gilyon HaShas*, the name these notes carry in the Vilna edition of the Talmud, has been the subject of ongoing interest, and several new editions and commentaries on it have appeared, particularly on Tractate Shabbat. The passage treated here picks up on the discussion in BT Shab. 55b and the Tosafot, s.v. *mʿbyrm*, and offers a list of approximately twenty additional places (no. 2 contains two examples) in which, one way or another, the rabbinic traditions about the Bible text conflicted with the Bible texts themselves.

The general impression gleaned from many contemporary books written about Eiger and *Gilyon HaShas*, except for the explications of Rabbi C. D. Chavel, which, published in 1959, perhaps preceded this trend, is that the subject of this passage is to be discussed as little as possible. Despite what must be errors in the printed text of *Gilyon HaShas*, most of the new editions offer no serious improvement over it; the notes by Moshe Berger, which claim to be based on an examination of Eiger's original handwritten marginalia, add very little to a straightforward reading of this passage.[35]

I have avoided the temptation to present a detailed exposition of the problems outlined here, which could be culled from the many Midrashim on these verses, from the classical commentaries on them and on the passages that contradict their spellings, from the vast scholarly literature that has explored most if not all of these passages, and from various Bible manuscripts and editions. These are in addition to the many secondary sources Eiger actually cited, which typify but do not exhaust the relevant considerations of commentators on both the Bible and the Talmud. Many of these works were mentioned in the notes to the previous chapters, where Eiger's examples 1, 4, and 18 were discussed at some length; *we-ʾiddak̲ zil gemar*. In the following translation, bracketed citations are mine and are often explanatory; those in parentheses are in the *Gilyon HaShas* found in the Vilna edition of the Talmud.

> [1] And similarly we have found in Niddah 33a, Tosafot, s.v. *whnwś*', that they wrote that [regarding the spelling of *whnwś*' in Lev. 15:10] our Masoret disagrees with the Talmud.
>
> [2] And in Megillah 22a, Tosafot wrote that *wa-yeḥal* [Ex. 32:11] is two verses from the preceding paragraph division, and similarly *we-hiqrab̲tem* [Num. 28:19]. But in our Torah scrolls, *wa-yeḥal* is four verses from the paragraph division, and *we-hiqrab̲tem* is three verses; and it is as Maharsha [Rabbi Solomon Edels] wrote there.
>
> [3] And in Pesahim 117a, in the Tosafot, s.v. *še-ʿomedim*, they wrote that it is impossible for a psalm to contain [only] two verses; but in our books, Psalm 117 is [indeed] two verses; see Maharsha, ad loc., side a.
>
> [4] And in Sanhedrin 4a, Rashi explained there that, regarding an individual's

sheep, *qarnot* [Lev. 4:34] is spelled *qrnwt*, plene; but in our Torah scrolls it is spelled defective.

[5] And [ibid.] on page 4a [read: 4b], Rashi wrote that, in the section [beginning] *we-hayah ki yebi'aka* [Ex. 13:16], [the word] *lṭṭpt* is spelled defective, and in the section [beginning] *we-hayah 'im šamoa'* [Deut. 11:18], it is spelled plene; but in our Torah scrolls it is spelled plene in *we-hayah ki yebi'aka* also.

[6] And [ibid.] on page 20a [the Talmud suggests that a word in 2 Sam. 3:35] should be written *lhkryt* and be read *lhbrwt*; but in our texts (*sefarim*) the written form is also *lhbrwt*.

[7] Also ibid., p. 103a, [the Talmud suggests that] "*wyhtr lw* [2 Chron. 33:13] should be *wy'tr lw*"; but our texts [actually] have *wy'tr*.

[8] And in Baba Batra 9a, [the Talmud suggests] that *prws* [Is. 58:7] should be [spelled with] a *shin*; but in our texts it is written [i.e., diacritically marked] with a *sin*. And see Maharsha's commentary to the *Aggadot*, ad loc.

[9] And in Qiddushin 30a, [the Talmud says] *whtglḥ* [Lev. 13:33] is the middle of the verses [in the Torah]; but in the model texts (Tiqqunim), in *Parashat Ṣaw*, in the verse *wa-ye'epod lo bo* [Lev. 8:7], it is marked that this is the middle verse of the Torah.

[10] And in the Palestinian Talmud, which Tosafot cited in Ketubot 7b, [it says] that *bmqhlt brkw 'lhym* [Ps. 68:27] is defective, but in our texts it is plene.

[11] And in Rashi['s commentary] on the Humash, *Parashat Terumah*, [it says] that [the initial *waw* of] *we-'et kol 'ašer 'aṣawe* [Ex. 25:22] is an extra *waw*; but we have *'et* written without a *waw*; see [the commentary of] Rabbi Elijah Mizrahi, ad. loc.

[12] And in Midrash Rabbah, Shir HaShirim, on the verse *'ḥzw lnw šw'lym š'lym* [Song of Songs 2:15]: "Said R. Berachiah, 'the first is plene, the second is defective.'" But in the Masorah it is not so; rather both are defective.

[13] And in Berachot 7b, it [i.e., the word "to destroy it"] is written *lklwtw*; but in our texts of 1 Chron. 1:17 it says *lblwtw*.

[14] And in Pesahim 3a, [the Talmud mentions the] *waw* of *ṭhwr* [Deut. 23:11]; but in our texts the word is spelled *ṭhr*, without the *waw*.) [Chavel explained that the parentheses were added because the text is actually plene.]

[15] And in Nedarim 37b, [the Talmud says] *'t* of *hwgd hwgd* [Ruth 2:11] is read but not written (*Qere We-La' Ketib*); but in our texts it is [both] written and read, as the Ran wrote, ad loc.

[16] And regarding the verse, "I [read: *'anoki* for *ani*] am the Lord your God who took you out (*hwṣ'tyk*) [from Egypt]" [Ex. 20:2], it says in the Palestinian Talmud, Sukkah, chapter 5: [read: 4:3] that it [*hwṣ'tyk*] is [spelled] without the *yod*; but in our texts it is plene.

[17] And in Midrash Leviticus Rabbah, chapter 9 [regarding] *wsm drk* [Ps. 50:23], "R. Yanai said: It is written *wšm*"; but in our texts it is written with a *sin*.

[18] And in Rashi's commentary in the Humash, Gen. 24 [read: 25(:6)], [it says] *hpylgšm* is spelled defective; but in all texts (*sefarim*) it is plene.

[19] And in Midrash Genesis Rabbah, chapter 77 [read: 73], "Resh Laqish said: *ha-notarot* [Gen. 30:36] is spelled *hntrt*; but in all our texts (*sefarim*) it is spelled *hnwtrt*.

[20] And in Eruvin 32a, in Tosafot, s.v. *'ašer*, [it says] that Rashi wrote that *'šr lw' ḥwmh* is written in Lev. 25:[30]; and they wrote that the *Ketib* is *'šr lw*, while the *Qere* is *l'*. But, in our texts, the *Ketib* is *l'*, with an *aleph*, and the *Qere* is *lw* [with a *waw*], as [the author of] *Tosafot Yom Tov* wrote, ad. loc. [9:6].

In sum, this list of twenty-one rabbinic variants contains nine differences in plene and defective spelling (1, 4, 5, 10, 12, 16, 18, 19, and the problematic 14); eight of a consonantal nature, including switches of *sin* and *shin* and variations in reports of *Qere u-Keṯiḇ* (6, 7, 8, 11, 13, 15, 17, and 20); and four in the division of the text into paragraphs (*parašiyyot*) or verses (2A, 2B, 3, and 9). Twelve of them, including seven of the nine recorded differences in plene and defective spelling (1, 2A, 2B, 4, 5, 9, 11, 14, 16, 18, 19, and 20), appear in the Torah. Again, this is far from an exhaustive list of such cases; many more can be culled from the extensive data collected by Norzi, Berlin, Rosenfeld, Aptowitzer, and others.[36]

Almost all of these examples derive from sources composed before medieval times, and they demonstrate quite clearly the nature (but not the full extent) of the ancient variations in Bible texts that remain in our editions of standard rabbinic works. They are the kind of evidence routinely presented to prove the less than letter-perfect state of the text, but some scholars define the masoretic text as a product of the efforts of the medieval masoretes.[37] In essence, this means that at least from the destruction of the Temple to about the time of Aaron Ben Asher (the most famous member of the group) there was no absolute uniformity among Bible texts, and that these masoretes, however they mangaged it, fixed—that is, set—the official text. Everyone assumes they copied the letters from one or more older texts (obviously originating in scrolls), but technically all previously existing texts would then be "premasoretic."

According to this reasoning, eventually Ben Asher's text became the official one, and all others should have been made to conform to it; but as has been seen, this never really happened fully. Commitment to different but no less authoritative scribal practices, conflicting masoretic traditions, scribal inaccuracies, rabbinic teachings, and simple disagreement, as well as other factors, all conspired to prevent this ideal from becoming a reality.

This manner of reconstruction has the benefit of making the perfect masoretic text an ontological reality, and it helps explain the scholarly excitement and debates over the Aleppo Codex and Leningrad B19, both well known Ben Asher manuscripts; but it does not take into account the reality of tens of thousands of Torah scrolls that existed before, during, and after Ben Asher's lifetime. Nor does it give any consideration to the many shreds of textual evidence—however marginal or potentially erroneous—that have been culled from other "pre-masoretic" witnesses, particularly the Talmud and Midrashim. That is what the questions asked of Ben Adret, Ibn Zimra, and other medieval rabbis were all about, and that problem will remain high on the agenda for those who seek to understand the details of the actual state of the Bible text in late antiquity.

Despite these historical questions, Torah scrolls remain prized and frequently used ritual objects, and scribes have continually worked as carefully as possible to copy them, always holding dear the belief that they were producing as accurate and correct a text as they could. Unfortunately even this commitment and care could not guarantee a letter-perfect text, as the next example demonstrates.

Corrections in a Modern Scribal Manual

In order to assist scribes with the preparation of Torah scrolls, handbooks that contain lists of plene and defective spellings have been developed and printed. Presumably these books provide a textual standard that can be relied upon, and therefore one should be able to assume that they have had a serious impact on scribal activity and on standardizing the text.

One interesting, recent example of an effort to confront the minor orthographic variants in the Torah is found in *Da'at Qedoshim*, a collection of halakhic materials on scribal matters, originally published in Lvov (1896) and reprinted several decades ago.[38] It contains a manual that lists, in order, every problematic spelling in the Torah. Culled from Abulafia's *Masoret Seyag LaTorah*, Lonzano's *Or Torah*, and other masoretic and scribal guides, it purports to give the correct spellings of all questionable words, in twenty-five large, double-columned pages. What is so fascinating—and so revealing—is the presence of the many dozens of handwritten interlinear and marginal corrections that have been added to the reprinted text through the process of photomechanical reproduction. Someone altered many of the supposedly accurate directions found in this guide, which, if taken seriously, directed or misdirected modern scribes for over a century. Perhaps they still do lead some people astray, but a new edition of *Da'at Qedoshim* omits the problematic lists, thereby eliminating any potential source of scribal confusion and its inherent evidence of textual uncertainty.[39]

Decoding the Torah's Secrets from an Imperfect Text

For thousands of years, readers have found the contents of the Torah meaningful and, as we have seen repeatedly, for much of that time those best acquainted with its textual details acknowledged that various copies contain minor spelling inconsistencies. Despite the vast number of real and imagined ambiguities discovered and created by industrious interpreters over the centuries, for the most part the Bible text makes sense as it is. Therefore it should be read and understood (and applied, if one so chooses) in as straightforward a manner as possible. Modern readers may disagree about how to do this, about to what extent rabbinic teachings should control the effort, or even about whether they should do it at all, but the student of any text must avoid certain pitfalls of interpretation, one of which would be totally reformatting that text into new words in order to scour it for highly anachronistic references. Yet this very procedure is being carried out by computer-aided mathematicians and other interested parties who assume the Bible text is letter-perfect and able to provide limitless information on both past and future events. Such thinking is not unprecedented and conforms to certain assumptions about the Bible popularized both in the early midrashic literature and in later exegetical imitations of it. This approach to the text may be entertaining, even inspiring, but it cannot be sustained in the face of reasoned challenges, particularly our understanding of the state of the Bible text. Why, then, has this decoding craze captured the attention and imagination of so many unsuspecting modern readers, including many for whom the Bible is not a holy or binding text?

Every generation of readers has left its own unique imprint on the Bible; some have created highly innovative interpretative strategies. Often these resulted from applying their era's best thinking to the Bible and producing what, at the time, seemed like the most advanced understanding possible. Thus some writers combined the Bible with essential elements of Greek thought, Aristotelian, Platonic, or neo-Platonic; others added from the sciences of their ages, and still others from what we might call the humanities. Each generation has helped clarify the Bible, but anyone schooled in the history of its interpretation can easily identify the intellectual context in which almost any extensive sample of interpretation was produced. Like art, music, and literature, interpretation has styles that reflect clearly and distinctly the cultures and contexts of individual interpreters, the schools they represent, and the creative worlds in which they worked, including their cutting-edge ideas, interpretative tools, fads, and erroneous beliefs.

Some interpretative efforts are based on permanently valued modes of analysis, but even they sometimes lead to inappropriate results; indeed, academic preferences often change very quickly. While the rabbinic world is less capricious, there too changes confront many of the rabbis' followers with an interesting dilemma. What should be done with interpretations produced by millennia of learned, pious thinkers that are no longer popular or even defensible? Scholars often examine them as part of the history of Bible interpretation—intellectual history mirrored against the sacred text—without placing a value on them. Many moderns would prefer consigning them to the bibliographic scrap heap, which is the fate of much contemporary scholarship, but a similar reaction cannot serve rabbinic interests.

To be sure, many rabbinic writings have little or no long-term impact or value. Still they remain theoretically available to potential readers, as do the erroneous ideas they and other more popular works contain. Once such ideas have been worked into the fiber of rabbinic thought, many rabbis are reluctant to consider their rejection. But, to take one poignant example of many, some writers are happy to expunge the scientific parts of premodern Bible commentaries—because old science is seen as bad science, and its presence is seen somehow to discredit a commentary's timeless appeal to readers from another age—yet they retain other, equally dated ideas of no less questionable value. Often they also prefer to censor critical-sounding notions out of rabbinic works, either by carefully avoiding any discussion of them or by actually removing them from specific editions or translations, because critical thinking is unfashionable in some of the communities to which these texts and translations are directed or in which they are marketed. Only marginally better is a strategy that allegorizes no-longer-acceptable notions in order to avoid challenging or rejecting what appears as the literal intentions of authoritative writers.

Another response accepts the legitimacy of all these teachings and merely assigns them complementary positions in a poorly defined hierarchy of interpretation. This approach may appear respectful of the interpreters but actually casts aspersions on the texts they all labored to explain, because the defense of dozens of outdated or inferior interpretations does the primary text no credit and complicates any serious effort to understand it. Adding to this notion the belief that the Torah is divine often produces an even stranger result, for the belief in God's omniscience is often taken to suggest that all these interpretations offered by centuries of pious interpreters must, of necessity, have been intended by God to be associated with the text.

To be sure, many rabbis argued endlessly to defend or to defeat particular interpretations, and they often rejected outright those with which they disagreed; but this spirit of challenge, debate, and resolution is often lost on latter-day students of these texts. Moreover, though it is self-evident that texts can carry far more than one meaning (so disagreeing parties may really be able to find or to create support for their conflicting interpretations), this acknowledgement may have been carried too far. As we saw in chapter 1, at least since the sixteenth century, mystics have spoken of not two or seven or seventy theoretical interpretations of the Torah, as did the ancient or medieval rabbis, but 600,000—in some cases 2,400,000. In fact, variants in the mishnaic teaching associated with the name of Ben Bag Bag suggest this idea may be substantially older. The radical postmodern notion that a text is only what the reader finds in it seemingly complements this earlier rabbinic one and helps legitimate limitless numbers of poorly conceived and relatively useless explanations or homiletical applications. These virtually infinite numbers of interpretations, all deemed to be of divine origin, allow anything to be said in the name of the text, and only the stouthearted dare disagree.

Over the years, astronomy, mathematics, biology, philosophy, medicine, linguistics, and physics all have had an impact on Bible study, but so have astrology, alchemy, chiromancy, and numerology. Because the last four are based in part on outdated and discredited science, often they have been edited out of commentaries or their translations in order to make them more accessible to some contemporary sensibilities. In other cases, however, such materials have found a hallowed place in some classical interpretations, where they remain and continue to influence popular thinking. It is in this context that one must consider the recent rush of books and articles devoted to decoding the Bible.

Decoding requires reconfiguring all words in a text in grids of varying sizes, thereby juxtaposing letters originally located at extensive intervals. This reconfiguration creates new combinations of letters that look like words when they are read frontward, backward, or diagonally and that seemingly reveal allusions to events that took place long after the texts were actually written. Dedicated decoders of the Hebrew Bible claim to find allusions to historical, religious, or political matters that are meaningful to Jews. Christians find references to christological matters; Muslims are doing likewise with the Qur'an and revealing notions more suited to their interests.

Some who reconfigure sacred texts this way claim the procedure actually allows people to predict the future. "Yitzhak Rabin" was decoded together with a reference to murder, a device that led some bibliomancers to predict his assassination; "Benjamin Netanyahu" was decoded in close proximity to "chosen," supposedly anticipating his election as prime minister of Israel, despite polls to the contrary. Predictions of mass destruction have been decoded for 1996, 2000, and 2006, but the uneventful passing of the first two dates has forced decoders to consider that their predictions may be only possibilities, not certainties.

Decoding generates almost an infinite number of letter combinations, but that fact is far from a convincing demonstration that these wordlike groupings possess independent meaning. For that to be so, detailed knowledge of the future must have been encoded in the text when it was formed, which means that some higher intelligence knew the future and intended what is perceived as encoded information. It also necessitates that the decoded combinations of letters be convincing representations of the people, dates, and events with which the decoders link them. Despite the simplicity and clarity attributed to the decoding process, interpreting many of the decoded messages is largely intuitive and subjective. The decoded information claimed to predict Rabin's assassination, for example, could also be interpretated to mean that he was a murderer.

Most important in our context, decoding also assumes that transmission of the Torah text has been so accurate that these messages are still intact. The many doubts about the text that have been discussed by the rabbis cited and analyzed in this book demonstrate how far the extant text is from this ideal, even if textual perfection itself has defenders within traditional Jewish thinking and would be a most welcome fact, were it possible.

Modern claims to have discovered in the Bible hints of future events, especially mass destructions, share much with what motivated pseudonymous writers of apocalyptic books, who, in late antiquity, attributed to early Bible characters detailed knowledge of the future. It seems that God's forewarning Abraham, Moses, or Joseph about the Babylonian exile or the destructions of the Temple tempered the horrors of these events as perceived by subsequent generations and strengthened their faith in divine omniscience and omnipotence. So too with the present search for encoded messages about the Holocaust, Rabin's assassination, or a modern Armageddon.

Some mathematicians say the probability that the decoded messages are accidents is virtually nil; others disagree.[40] But despite disputed claims that these decoded messages can be validated statistically, contemporary readers are expected to set aside any philosophical or theological or textual-philological objections to them. Even if this entire process is mathematically justifiable, does that give it priority over every other form of human knowledge? Bible scholars, for example, have no use for this entire endeavor, which shares none of their assumptions and conclusions. The decoders may have overstepped the limits of what they can actually demonstrate, regardless of the rationality of the mathematical arguments they have advanced.

As we have seen, the halakhic literature does not support the assumptions underlying the decoding processes either, because it cannot sustain a rational argument in favor of the existence of an identifiable, letter-perfect text. Despite the halakhic preference that all Torah scrolls be identical, the simple fact is that they are not, and the rabbis often admit this fact. The scrolls are very much alike, but the past 2,000 years have witnessed numerous rabbinic debates about the spellings of hundreds of words in the Torah and thousands in the Bible.

The Bible, particularly the Torah, may be the most accurate text transmitted by hand since antiquity, but major theoretical differences exist between high-level accuracy, with one copy of the text declared letter-perfect by fiat, and with letter-perfect unanimity among thousands of extant handmade copies and printed editions. Rabbinic discussions of variant spellings usually impact on meaning no more than spelling "colour" with or without the "u," but such deviations are of great consequence for claims about a letter-perfect text and the search for encoded messages based on letter counts. A difference of one letter changes everything; doubts about many letters still exist.

Rashi mentioned a few inconsistencies in his Torah commentary (see chapter 1); others are discussed by Rabbi Meir Abulafia, Rabbi Solomon ben Adret, Rabbenu Tam, Rabbi Menahem Meiri, Rabbi Moses Isserles, Rabbi Moses Sofer, and others (chapters 2 through 6). Twenty-one are listed in Rabbi Akiba Eiger's *Gilyon HaShas* (translated earlier in this chapter). Many more are discussed in Norzi's *Minhat Shai*. In fact, the Talmud, the Midrashim, and the Tosafists often interpreted spellings that differ from those in our Bibles. Some medieval Sefaradim (e.g., Ibn Ezra) mocked attempts to relate spelling and meaning; some Ashkenazim who disagreed (e.g., Rabbi Eliezer of Worms, author of *Sefer HaRokeah*) interpreted words two ways in order to accommodate spelling variations!

In attempts to fix the text, rabbinic responsa weigh the evidence of Torah scrolls and Masorah codices; talmudic and midrashic discussions; writings of grammarians, halakhists, scribes, and experts on scribal matters; Tiqqunim; oral traditions among practicing scribes; and even printed books. These sources agree about most things, but often they disagree about some textual details. Further refinement may lead to halakhically valid determinations, but not necessarily to the original text; nor can legal decisions erase the documented data on inconsistencies, regardless of what they suggest as logical solutions to the perplexities associated with writing Torah scrolls.

Though some medieval writers defended the notion that all Torah scrolls should be and could be identical and letter-perfect, Rabbi Moses Isserles ruled that, during a public reading, one does not replace a Torah scroll containing a mistake in plene or defective spelling (i.e., the presence or absence of a *waw* or *yod* that is used as a vowel letter), because "our Torah scrolls are not so accurate." In so doing, he relied on the teachings of Rabbenu Tam and successive generations of like-minded Ashkenazi rabbis. Rabbi Yehezkel Landau refused to replace such a faulty Torah, because the replacement could be assumed to contain other similar errors. Rabbi Moses Sofer taught that scribes do not recite a blessing before commencing to write a Torah, because no one knows how to spell all the words. Some halakhic authorities said this situation renders it impossible to produce a proper Torah scroll (chapters 1 and 2)!

Because many of these variants are documented in ancient rabbinic works, some writers date the production of the definitive Torah text to the Middle Ages. Such dating requires abandoning any association between the decoded messages and Mosaic spelling and relocating the claim for the text's accuracy in medieval, not biblical times. Even reliance on one preselected model is difficult; the earliest possible choices are medieval, and their use cannot lead to textual certainty. Despite Maimonides' seeming acceptance of the so-called Aleppo Codex, that manuscript lacks almost the entire Torah and cannot provide the model we seek unless it is reconstructed from secondary witnesses; even its own authority was challenged in medieval times (see end of chapter 6). Other codices are less authoritative; other forms of textual determination are highly subjective and prone to error.

Belief in the presence of encoded messages often leads to a circular argument, particular on a popular level. The text is letter-perfect, so the decoding is valid; and the messages are meaningful, so the text must be accurate. But if the letter-perfect text cannot be validated independently—and it cannot be—one totally uniform text does not exist. Therefore belief in encoded messages can be sustained only if one posits that the encoder anticipated all future spelling doubts and validated all of the resultant variations.

As preposterous as this notion may seem, it is not entirely new. It was espoused by kabbalists who recognized the existence of textual variations and also believed the Torah contained extensive esoteric teachings; but even they taught it as a general principle and did not apply it systematically, as the decoders do (chapter 2). If different texts all can be valid, and decoded messages are to be used for prognosticating, the existence of variant texts suggests another possibility. A particular Ashkenazi scroll may hold the most authoritative predictions about sporting events or American presidents, while Sefaradi scrolls or codices may be most useful for predictions related to disease or the weather. Yemenite texts may be best for the stock market or Israeli politics; the (reconstructed) Aleppo Codex may be most accurate at anticipating the outcomes of military engagements.

Alternatively, one may ask why the absurdities inherent in all this should even concern modern readers—and this group is not limited to rabbis, Orthodox Jews, Jews in general, or faithful Christians—or even tempt them to dismiss all other rational considerations, which it clearly does. The simple answer is that, for vastly different reasons, many people are unable to take seriously the surface messages of the Bible: required faith in God, divine interference in history, troubling stories, sacred and immutable commandments, values and regulations that challenge freedom of action and modern attitudes, and the like. Rather, many people are focused on contemporary history and politics, on Israel and the Holocaust, on the rapidly deteriorating state of the social order, and, quite like earlier generations, on the fear of global destruction. Despite their avowed skepticism, agnosticism, or atheism, they remain intrigued by the Bible, and they are seriously moved by the same mystical-magical considerations that influenced many earlier generations of readers, whose confrontations with the text serve as both stimulus and model for the present one.

This may explain some of the interest of the non-Orthodox in the decoding efforts, but Orthodox Jews approach this matter in a very different way. Over the centuries, devotion to the authority of the Torah and to its rabbinic interpretations and applications has been supported through associations with a great many details of spelling. And questions about these details, while not new, are both unsettling and difficult to deal with on a popular level, because they seem to undermine commitment to both the Torah and rabbinic authority, to some details of religious law, and therefore, in some minds, to the entire system of Jewish religious life. Moreover, extensive influence of midrashic interpretation or of preaching from the Bible may have seemingly elevated projecting their own ideas into the text over extracting the original, articulated ideas from the text. The former, after all, minimizes the need to focus on knowing the simple meaning of the Bible for its own sake.

Impressed by modern technologies capable of doing exhaustive manipulations that imitate the isolated ones of earlier times, contemporary enthusiasts are finding comfort in a system of reading that reinforces their personal needs, accommodates their concerns, and restores some of the Bible's mystique in a seemingly scientific way that sounds pious, avoids the text's real issues, and enables them to co-opt it for purposes largely different from the Bible's original ones. Christians are actively pursuing this approach because it allows them to affirm that the New Testament is foretold in Jewish Scriptures, an attitude with long and deep roots in the history of Christian theology and Bible interpretation.

In point of fact, the discovery of esoteric meanings in mechanically generated letter combinations shares much with ancient and medieval textual manipulations that originated as pious play and with now-discredited notions once sustained through studying the movements of the stars and the shapes of human skulls. Because it was associated with some scientifically accurate information and cast in scientific language, such thinking was often confused with science, but eventually more sophisticated study helped debunk it.

Time, money, and energy should not be wasted in attempts to reconfirm the past or to predict the future and in casuistic rationalizations of why that future did not unfold as predicted in stars, in tea leaves, in palm lines, or in reconfigured Bible texts. We should discourage the search for allegedly encoded esoteric messages and support discussion of the exoteric ones, which, despite their visibility, are in danger of being lost. Their recovery and examination is a far more pressing need for our time, however the believing and nonbelieving communities choose to react to them.

A Final Word

Scribes continue to copy Torah scrolls, and learned readers of them continue to challenge some of these efforts. But there are only two ways to have a perfect text: either because it is an ontological reality or because it has been created by some prescriptive dialectic process. Barring some unexpected and truly earthshaking discovery, one far more significant than the Aleppo Codex and the Dead Sea Scrolls, the opportunity to exercise the first option—declaring a newly discovered copy of the Torah to be the true Torah text—is not anticipated. I cannot imagine how one would garner a consensus on the identity and value of any candidate for this status, should it be discovered, but no one anticipates such a discovery. Indeed, the recovery of the Aleppo Codex and the history of debates about it are a good example of the scholarly tumult that can be raised around the availability of a newly disclosed text and the distance that remains from the ideal model I have in mind. Even so, one can hardly avoid fantasizing about the challenges such a discovery would present.

This fascinating question was discussed briefly in part of a letter by Z. A. Yehudah,[41] in which he recounted the Hazon Ish's answer to it. Were such a text to be found and to differ from that presently in use, he claimed, it—not the extant masoretic text—even if it had belonged to Rabbi Akiva or to Moses, would be subject to revision. The text we have is the halakhically correct one, even if it evolved; the discovered one would be "inconsequential for halakhah."

In a compelling response,[42] Professor Sid Leiman challenged Yehudah's report and asserted that he had actually substituted for the position of the Hazon Ish much of his own thinking, which was confused and unacceptable. In fact, said Leiman, were Moses' Torah to be found, it would be "most consequential for halakhah," though he did not explain how.

I have nothing to add to the question of whether Yehudah has misrepresented the Hazon Ish by substituting his own ideas for his teacher's; Leiman's case is well argued. But in practice, one could respond to such a hypothetical discovery in one of two ways (other than ignoring or rejecting it fully). Either accept it lock, stock, and barrel as the halakhically correct Torah text, or collate its readings with extant models that have been used and debated until now. In the former case, this new copy would be the Torah, to the exclusion of all other versions and, if it differed from those copies now in existence—which, for the sake of the discussion, everyone (Leiman more carefully than Yehudah) concedes—it and all that accompanies it would replace what we now have and what everyone else may seem to have had for the last few thousand years.

In the latter case, this newly discovered text would be examined letter by letter and carefully integrated into the fabric of masoretic and scribal-halakhic debate. If so, its impact would vary from passage to passage—indeed, from letter to letter—and, unlike what was envisioned in the first scenario, it would be far from pervasive; in reality, it would be almost inconsequential. Given the traditionally conservative rabbinic response to change, particularly to changes this radical, I cannot imagine how it would be possible to realize the first option; but the second one, as I fathom it, does not fit Leiman's suggestion that the text would be "most consequential for halakhah," though if even one letter were changed because of it, that might qualify.

However one responds to the second option, the theoretical and practical problems of unifying the readings in all extant scrolls will be with us for a long time. Even if a collation of all Torah scrolls could be produced (which, given anticipated international capabilities for scanning, transmission, and computerized analysis, seems within the realm of the possible), and even if it were then used to construct a text, a serious question would remain about the extent to which these results would be ideal. Other models could be selected, but the theoretical questions would be largely the same.

Perhaps most curious, though, is Yehudah's description of how Moses' Torah might appear: written in paleo-Hebrew script, as some rabbinic sources and all archaeological ones suggest it would have been; incomplete, in keeping with the talmudic opinion that Joshua finished the Torah after Moses' death; and differing in plene and defective spelling, in *Qere* and *Keṯiḇ* (which must mean that sometimes the *Qere* is the written text rather than a traditional reading variation of it), and in the forms of letters. Any of these would be enough to invalidate the text halakhically, though Leiman is surely correct in asserting that, while Masorah codices are equally invalid for ritual purposes, their contents are still very important and influential. Were this newly discovered text a Masorah codex, particularly one very much like other highly respected codices, or (since codices had not yet been invented) even such a scroll, then its variants could be integrated into the system with relative ease, because most of it would already be agreed upon and there would be so few potential problems.

Everyone, it seems, traditionalist or critic, agrees that the Torah was produced before the invention of the codex, so the possibility of finding Moses' copy in codex form seems extremely remote. As a scroll in the very unconventional form described by Yehudah, it would challenge the tradition at every turn. I doubt if such a text would carry much if any halakhic weight, and as I understand the thinking of several generations of Soloveitchiks about the possibility of restoring anything related to rabbinic traditions from scientific discoveries—much less the possibility of restoring the Torah text in this way—in their opinion such considerations would be impossible (see chapter 1).

As an indication of this assumption, I offer the following brief example of a situation that developed in Jerusalem a few years ago.[43] A pious, apparently well-intentioned individual decided to publish a model Tiqqun for scribes interested in preparing handwritten scrolls of biblical books other than the Torah.[44] The reputation of the Aleppo Codex led him to choose it as his model, and he prepared the text accordingly. This act outraged many members of the Haredi rabbinate, who issued all sorts of bans on his work and criticisms of it. In short, dozens of rabbinic authorities took exception to his use of this reportedly early and authoritative Ben Asher manuscript, which differed in some of the paragraph divisions from the layout they preferred, one that descended from a model attributed to the Gaon of Vilna.

The innovator challenged the ban, which led to the case being taken before the Haredi courts of Jerusalem. During the evaluation of the innovator and his product, as well as the criticisms of him and the other related issues, the courts were put in the rather unusual position of having to consider the authority of the Aleppo Codex, how to relate to its presentation of the Bible text, and whether to follow its deviations from other textual information in their possession. In turn, this debate led to other discussions of the production of scroll copies of the biblical books in question and other related scribal matters.

I cannot tell if this issue has run its course, but clearly it became a matter of great concern to the many rabbis who issued statements, most of whom seem to have been concerned, above all else, with avoiding change of any sort. These Haredi rabbis were willing to debate the issue in public—for which they deserve our interest and gratitude—but above all else they favored tradition as they had it, not as it had been discovered. I believe that, if confronted by an ancient scroll that claimed to be from Moses or any other authority from early biblical times but differed from those in use today, the vast majority of Orthodox rabbis would adopt a similarly restrained posture. In short, conservatism dominates discussions of biblical texts by most halakhic Jews and, as far as I can tell, it will continue to do so for the foreseeable future.

I suspect that, in contemporary terms, the most one could hope for this hypothetical, newly discovered old text would be the formal recognition that accompanies teaching it in some appropriate contexts together with the traditional one, which, however its details are controlled, would be retained for all ritual and halakhic purposes. Such a compromise would acknowledge the discovery's importance while retaining formal commitment to the traditional text, and to some extent this is actually happening today. When teaching Psalm 145, an alphabetic acrostic that lacks a line beginning with the letter *nun*, some people mention the nun-line preserved in the Septuagint and discovered in the Dead Sea Psalm Scroll.[45] They would never consider reciting the line thrice daily as part of the *Ashrei* prayer, but they have found an educational niche for it nonetheless. The same is true for other ancient texts: the Nash papyrus; the silver amulets from the seventh pre-Christian century that contain the priestly blessing; and even Dead Sea Scrolls fragments of Exodus, Samuel, Jeremiah, Daniel, and other books, which offer alternative, interesting, and sometimes very attractive (but not for these reasons necessarily preferable) versions of Bible texts that differ from masoretic ones.

Yehudah may not have presented the Hazon Ish accurately, but in the name of halakhic process and, much more significantly, at the cost of admitting that in many ways the Torah text has evolved, he did offer a good approximation of the reasons many people—including some respected halakhic authorities of the past several centuries—would use to avoid taking this new discovery seriously. Would that we had the opportunity to find out. In the meantime, whether the process of fixing God's Torah requires confirming the contents of the immutable text or offering corrections, it will continue for the foreseeable future, as it has in the recoverable past.

Notes

One. Fixing God's Torah

1. See, for example, the collection of studies in *Qumran and the History of the Biblical Text*, ed. Frank Moore Cross and Shemaryahu Talmon (Cambridge: Harvard University Press, 1975); Emanuel Tov, *Textual Criticism of the Hebrew Bible* (Minneapolis: Fortress Press, 1992), a revised and enlarged translation of *Biqoret Nusah HaMiqra'* (Jerusalem: Mossad Bialik, 1989); and Eugene Ulrich, *The Dead Sea Scrolls and the Origins of the Bible* (Leiden: E. J. Brill, 1999).

2. The search for scientifically valid information about the spelling of ancient Hebrew is usually based on epigraphic materials. For many years the standard work was Frank Moore Cross and David Noel Freedman, *Early Hebrew Orthography: A Study of the Epigraphic Evidence* (New Haven, Conn.: American Oriental Society, 1952), subsequently complemented by David Noel Freedman, "The Massoretic Text and the Qumran Scrolls: A Study in Orthography," *Textus* 2 (1962): 87–102. Later it was supplemented by L. A. Bange, *A Study of the Use of Vowel-Letters in Alphabetic Consonantal Writing* (Munich: Uni-Druck, 1971), and by Ziony Zevit, *Matres Lectionis in Ancient Hebrew Epigraphs* (Cambridge, Mass.: Harvard University Press, 1980); note also Werner Weinberg, *The History of Hebrew Plene Spelling* (Cincinnati: Hebrew Union College Press, 1985), and *Essays on Hebrew by Werner Weinberg*, ed. Paul Citrin (Atlanta: Scholars Press, 1993.

Recent treatments that focus more on the Bible and try to unravel its enigmatic orthographic patterns include: Menahem Cohen, "*HaKetiv Shel HaNusah HaShomroni*," *Beit Miqra'* 21 (1976): 54–70; idem, "*HaKetiv Shel HaNusah HaShomroni: Zikkato LeKetiv Nusah HaMasorah uMeqomo BeToldot HaKetiv*," ibid., 361–391; Francis I. Anderson and A. Dean Forbes, *Spelling in the Hebrew Bible* (Rome: Biblical Institute Press, 1986), reviewed by James Barr in *Journal of Semitic Studies* 33 (1988): 122–131; James Barr, *The Variable Spelling of the Hebrew Bible* (Oxford: Oxford University Press, 1989); and the much larger, cooperative effort, *Studies in Hebrew and Aramaic Orthography*, ed. David Noel Freedman, A. Dean Forbes, and Francis I. Anderson (Winona Lake, Ind.: Eisenbrauns, 1992).

These modern searches for patterns in the use of plene and defective spellings in different parts of the Bible were anticipated in at least one context by Rabbi Moses Aryeh Trestino, author of *Be'er Sheva'* (Vilna: Menahem ben Barukh, 1845), in a lengthy and very interesting comment on Est. 9:7 (pp. 30b–31b). The latter is mentioned briefly in Hanokh Zundel

Joseph's note on the early rabbinic dispute over whether the spelling of *m'byrm* (1 Sam. 2:24) should be *m'byrym*; see *Anaf Yosef*, a commentary on *'Ein Ya'aqov* (repr., New York: Pardes, 1955), Vol. 1, *Shabbat*, p. 25a.

3. In what manner and to what extent the various printings of the Bible differed from each other can be sampled in Christian David Ginsburg, *Introduction to the Massoretico-Critical Edition of the Hebrew Bible* (London: 1897; repr., New York: Ktav, 1966), pp. 779–976, and in Jordan Penkower's Hebrew University thesis, *Jacob ben Hayyim and The Rise of the Biblia Rabbinica* (1982).

For halakhic discussion of the impact of printing itself, see Yehezkel Landau, *Sh'eilot uTeshuvot Noda' BiYehudah* (repr., New York: Otzar HaSefarim, 1973), Vol. 2, *Hoshen Mishpat*, no. 43, and Moses Sofer, *She'eilot uTeshuvot HaHatam Sofer, Hoshen Mishpat* (repr., Jerusalem: Makor, 1970), no. 143. The secondary literature includes Abraham Berliner, "*Ueber den Einfluss des ersten hebraeischen Buch-drucks auf den Cultus und die Cultur der Juden*," *Jahres-Bericht des Rabbiner-Seminars zu Berlin* (Berlin: 1883–1884), trans. into Hebrew in his *Ketavim Nivharim* (Jerusalem: Mossad HaRav Kook, 1969), Vol. 2, pp. 111–143; Simhah Assaf, *BeOholei Yaaqov* (Jerusalem: Mossad HaRav Kook, 1943; repr., undated), chap. 1, "'*Am HaSefer' VeHaSefer*"; Abraham Yaari, *Mehqerei Sefer: Peraqim BeToldot HaSefer HaIvri* (Jerusalem: Mossad HaRav Kook, 1958), pp. 170–178, 245–255; Yitzhaq Zeev Kahana, *Mehqarim BeSifrut HaTeshuvot* (Jerusalem: Mossad HaRav Kook, 1973), pp. 272–306, "*HaDefus BaHalakhah*"; Malachi Beit-Arie, *The Makings of the Medieval Hebrew Book: Studies in Palaeography and Codicology* (Jerusalem: Magnes Press, 1993), pp. 251–273, "The Relationship Between Early Hebrew Printing and Handwritten Books: Attachment or Detachment"; and Israel Shabbetai Schepansky, *She'eirit Yisrael* (Brooklyn: I. Schepansky, 1999), pp. 1–23.

4. Examples include Mordecai Breuer's detailed treatment of the Aleppo Codex in *Keter Aram Tzovah VeHaNusah HaMequbbal Shel HaMiqra'* (Jerusalem: Mossad HaRav Kook, 1976); the notes to the third volume of his edition of the Bible, *Ketuvim* (Jerusalem: Mossad HaRav Kook, 1982), pp. 393–409; and his pamphlet "*Miqra'ot SheYesh Lahem Hekhrea'* (Jerusalem: Tevunot, 1990), which discusses two classic problems in the text of Est. 8:11 and 9:2 and the vocalization of *zkr* in Deut. 25:19. Also, Ginsburg, *Introduction*; the three-page list of variants printed at the end of the pocket-size Koren Bible (Jerusalem: Koren, 1962), unnumbered pages that were omitted from the folio edition prepared for use in synagogues; the introduction to *Miqra'ot Gedolot 'HaKeter': Yehoshua'*, ed. Menahem Cohen (Ramat Gan: Bar Ilan University Press, 1992); and Jordan Penkower, *Nusah HaTorah BeKeter Aram Tzovah* (Ramat Gan: Bar Ilan University Press, 1993). See also the lists found near the ends of the supplementary material in the volumes of Menahem M. Kasher's *Torah Shelemah* (Jerusalem: Makhon Torah Shelemahm 1927ff) that conclude individual books of the Torah. The material discussed throughout this book is quite different from the seemingly similar study by Bart D. Ehrman, *The Orthodox Corruption of Scripture: The Effect of Early Christological Controversies on the Text of the New Testament* (New York: Oxford University Press, 1993), which deals with the early stages of the production of the books of the New Testament. It is closer to David Weiss Halivni's *Revelation Restored: Divine Writ and Critical Responses* (Boulder, Col.: Westview Press, 1997), but his volume concerns rabbinic evidence about the state of the Bible in prerabbinic times and the possibility of integrating a critical understanding of the Torah's production with rabbinic traditions, themes that I do not address here.

5. See, for example, Tov's outstanding work, *Textual Criticism of the Hebrew Bible*, p. 24:

> When M [the Masoretic text] became the central text, at first of a central stream in Judaism and later of the whole Jewish people, no further changes were inserted into it and no additions or omissions were allowed . . . not even in small details such as the use of *matres lectionis*.

Despite this overstatement, Tov acknowledges the existence of the variations to which I am referring, though he does not see them as a part of the halakhic refinement of the text.

This position can be contrasted with that of Rabbi Moses Feinstein, who took a more extreme view of them. He interpreted Maimonides' statement identifying anyone who denies the divine origin of every word in the Torah as a heretic (*Mishneh Torah, Hilkhot Teshuvah* 3:8) to apply to every last letter of the text, *Iggerot Moshe, Orah Hayyim*, Vol. 4 (New York: Moses Feinstein, 1981), no. 24, pp. 39–42. For further discussion, see Louis Jacobs, *Principles of Judaism* (New York: Basic Books, 1964), chaps. 8–9, and the extensive documentation in Marc B. Shapiro, "The Last Word in Jewish Theology? Maimonides' Thirteen Principles," *The Torah U-Madda Journal* 4 (1993): 187–242, most of which is devoted to this concern. I thank Proffessor Jeffrey Tigay for providing me with a copy of Sid Z. Leiman, "Masorah and Halakhah: A Study in Conflict," in *Tehillah LeMoshe: Biblical and Judaic Studies in Honor of Moshe Greenberg*, ed. Mordechai Cogan, Barry L. Eichler, and Jeffrey H. Tigay (Winona Lake, Ind.: Eisenbrauns, 1997), pp. 291–306, which is closely related to my global concerns, as well as a typescript of his "The Bible 'Codes': A Textual Perspective," delivered at the Princeton University conference on the Bible codes, April 28, 1998.

6. Harry Orlinsky perhaps said it most clearly in the prolegomenon to the reprint of Ginsburg's *Introduction*, p. xviii: "There never was, and there never can be, a single fixed masoretic text of the Bible! It is utter futility and pursuit of a mirage to go seeking to recover what never was." This reflects Alexander Sperber's somewhat earlier observation, "*There never existed The Masoretic Text, and consequently never will be*" (his italics), *Grammar of Masoretic Hebrew* (Copenhagen: B. Munksgaard 1959), p. 51, cited by Moshe H. Goshen-Gottstein in "The Rise of the Tiberian Bible Text," in *Biblical and Other Studies*, ed. Alexander Altmann (Cambridge: Harvard University Press, 1963), p. 117, n. 122. Sperber's statement was described by Goshen-Gottstein as "grossly nihilistic" and "misleading" but containing a "kernel of truth."

7. The halakhic refusal to include the vocalization in Torah scrolls was discussed by Solomon ben Abraham Ben Adret, *She'eilot uTeshuvot HaRashba HaMeyuhasot LeHaRamban* (Warsaw: I. Goldman, 1883; repr., Israel, n.d.), no. 238, and by David Ibn Zimra, *She'eilot uTeshuvot HaRadbaz* (repr., New York: Goldman—Otzar HaSefarim, 1967), III, no. 643. Though collected for a different purpose, an interesting group of medieval discussions of the vowels and cantillation marks has been published by Nehemiah Allony in "*Sefer HaTorah VeHaMitzhaf BeQeri'at HaTorah BeTzibbur BeAdat HaRabbanim uVeAdat HaQara'im*," *Beit Miqra'* 24 (1979): 321–334; repr. in idem, *Meḥqerei Lashon VeSifrut*, Vol. 5 (Jerusalem: Reuben Mass, 1992), pp. 271–284. See also the discussion of Rabbi Barukh Kalai in *Meqor Barukh* (Izmir: Abraham Gabbai 1659), pp. 53a–55b (the second item numbered 36); he tried to differentiate in this respect between the vowels and the cantillation marks. For further analysis and documentation, see Moshe Idel, *Kabbalah: New Perspectives* (New Haven, Conn.: Yale University Press, 1988), pp. 213–218, and idem, "Infinities of Torah in Kabbalah," in *Midrash and Literature*, ed. Geoffrey H. Hartman and Sanford Budick (New Haven, Conn.: Yale University Press, 1986), pp. 141–157.

8. The early history of the written interpretations of the Masorah lies beyond my present interest, but an important talmudic reference to a book that contained such interpretations, an early written collection of midrashic material examined by Rabbi Joshua ben Levi (who opposed recording such things), is noteworthy. It associated the number of *parašiyyot* in the triennial cycle of Torah readings with the age of Abraham (175), the number of biblical Psalms with the age of Jacob (147)—our Hebrew Bibles contain 150 psalms!—and the number of times *halleluyah* is recited with the age of Aaron (133). Cf. further PT Shab. 16:1 (1bc) and, on the number of psalms, Nahum Sarna, *Songs of the Heart* (New York: Schocken, 1993), pp. 15–19.

9. Gershom Scholem, *On the Kabbalah and Its Symbolism* (New York: Schocken, 1965),

p. 65, based on Luria's *Sefer HaKavanot* (Venice: 1610), p. 53b. Vital's idea is developed in *Sha'ar HaGilgulim* (Jerusalem: Yeshivat Kol Yehuda Press, 1985), introduction, no. 17, p. 48. See further Moshe Idel, "Infinities of Torah in Kabbalah" and "Between Authority and Indeterminacy: Some Reflections on Kabbalistic Hermeneutics," in *Death, Ecstasy, and Other Worldly Journeys*, ed. John J. Collins and Michael Fishbane (Albany: State University of New York, 1995), pp. 249–268. Muhammad al-Ghazzali (1058–1111) noted that, according to some scholars, every verse of the Qur'an can be understood in 60,000 ways, but that even more interpretations remain uncounted. Others point to 77,200 kinds of knowledge, which when multiplied by four (the literal and inner meanings, as well as the starting and terminal points of understanding), suggest 308,800 potential interpretations. See further Helmut Gaetje, *The Qur'ān and Its Exegesis: Selected Texts With Classical and Modern Muslim Interpretations* (Oxford: Oneworld, 1996), p. 229.

10. The first and most popular reading appears with some variations in *Mishnah: Codex Paris*—Paris MS 328–329, introduced by Moshe Bar-Asher (Jerusalem: Makor, 1973), p. 653; *Mishnah Ketav Yad Parma C*—De Rossi MS 984 (Jerusalem: Makor, 1971), p. 513; Abraham Katsh, *Ginzei Mishnah* (Jerusalem: Mossad HaRav Kook, 1970), pp. 123, 125; *Mishnah Im Perush HaRambam—Naples:* 1492, introduced by A. M. Habermann (Jerusalem: Makor, 1970); and *Mishnah Im Peirush Rabbenu Moshe ben Maimon*, ed. Joseph Kafih (Jerusalem: Mossad HaRav Kook, 1970), p. 304.

The second version of the statement is found in W. H. Lowe, *The Mishnah on Which the Palestinian Talmud Rests* [Cambridge University Library Add. 470:1, dated to ca. 1400] (Cambridge: Cambridge University Press, 1883), p. 148a, and it is discussed by Charles Taylor in *Sayings of the Jewish Fathers Comprising Pirqe Aboth* . . . (Cambridge: Cambridge Unversity Press, 1897; repr., New York: Ktav, 1969), pp. 42, 96–97, 172–173. The third version appears in *Kaufmann Manuscript: Faksimile-Ausgabe des Mischnacodex Kaufmann* A50, ed. Georg Beer (repr., Jerusalem: Makor, 1968), Vol. 2, p. 346.

11. The citation from Bengel appears in Jaroslav Pelikan, *The Reformation of the Bible; The Bible of the Reformation* (New Haven, Conn.: Yale University Press, 1996), p. 23.

12. M. San. 10:1 or 11:1 and Avot 3:11 (the numbers vary somewhat with the edition), which contain two complementary lists of people with no share in the world to come, deal mostly with issues directly related to the interpretation and application of the Torah. (Reference to "embarrassing one's fellow" is exceptional, but since it is lacking from many manuscripts and medieval commentaries and may therefore be considered a late addition, it is irrelevant to the original purpose of the lists.) Taken in this way, these passages reflect a very restrictive attitude on the range and contents of interpretations the rabbis would permit, particularly when the verses and interpretations formed parts of ongoing sectarian debates. This position is potentially quite different from that attributed to Ben Bag Bag.

13. The Soferim text is found in *Masekhet Soferim*, ed. Michael Higger (New York: Ginsburg Linotyping, 1937), pp. 169–171, and by Joel Mueller (Leipzig: J. C. Hinrich'sche Buchhandlung, 1878), p. xii. Higger's text presents the last two clauses in the final paragraph in reverse order, as does the citation in Paris MS 411 of Ben Adret's Responsa, but other editions and citations are unanimous in retaining the order of the previous two paragraphs, and I have followed them here. This manuscript also contains several other small textual differences, but generally they do not affect the meaning of the passages in which they occur.

For modern discussion of this passage and its parallels, see Jacob Z. Lauterbach, "Three Books Found in the Temple of Jerusalem," *Jewish Quarterly Review* 8 (1917–1918): 385–423; M. H. Segal, "The Promulgation of the Authoritative Text of the Hebrew Bible," *Journal of Biblical Literature* 72 (1953): 41–45; Saul Lieberman, *Hellenism in Jewish Palestine: Studies in the Literary Transmission, Beliefs, and Manners of Palestine in the I Century* B.C.E.–*IV Century* C.E. (New York: Jewish Theological Seminary, 1962), pp. 21–27; Shemaryahu Talmon,

"The Three Scrolls of the Law that Were Found in the Temple Court," *Textus* 2 (1962): 14–27; and Solomon Zeitlin, "Were There Three Torah-Scrolls in the Azarah?" *Jewish Quarterly Review* 56 (1966): 269–272.

Early parallels include *Sifrei Al Sefer Devarim*, ed. Louis Finkelstein (Berlin: HaAggudah HaTarbutit HaYehudit BeGermaniah, 1939; repr., New York: Jewish Theological Seminary, 1969), p. 423, no. 356; PT Ta'an. 4:2 (68a); and *Avot DeRabbi Natan B*, ed. Solomon Schechter, 3rd ed. (New York: Feldheim, 1967), p. 129. The Sifre text, while perhaps the earliest, is incomplete, and in many circles Soferim was better known and carried more halakhic weight than the Palestinian Talmud and *Avot DeRabbi Natan*. This, plus the fact that its version of the story is the clearest, explains why it is the preferred source.

14. The spellings of *m'wn* and *m'wnh* are generally plene in the rabbinic texts; the Bible spells the latter defective.

Within rabbinic literature, references to "three *sefarim*" appear in several contexts: (1) the three scrolls of this passage; (2) midrashic references to Solomon's literary output (Proverbs, Song of Songs, and Ecclesiastes); (3) halakhic discussions of reading three different copies of the Torah on specific occasions, e.g., when the New Moon falls on the Sabbath during Hanukkah; (4) the claim that the book of Numbers was divided into three books; (5) three books in which God records the names of good, evil, and marginal people; and (6) rabbinic expositions of verses that suggest one scroll, but not two or three, is needed for an accused adulteress, a divorce, or a *mezuzah* (BT Sot. 18a, Git. 20b, etc.). While types 2–5 have no connection with the subject under discussion, type 6 may appear to. In fact, these last examples discuss the ritual use of these scrolls (as does similar treatment of the citron on Tabernacles) and have no bearing whatsoever on the question of determining the Torah text through a majority of three attested readings. See further Isaac Jacob Weiss, *She'eilot uTeshuvot Minhat Yitzhaq*, Vol. 1 (Jerusalem: Makhon Hatam Sofer, 1975), pp. 81–83, no. 35.

15. Possible etymologies of *za'aṭuṭē* are reviewed in S. Talmon, *The Three Scrolls*, pp. 25–26.

16. The eleven passages in question are listed in various places in the Masorah manuscripts and editions. Ginsburg has discussed them in *The Massorah* (London: 1880; repr., New York: Ktav, 1975), *Heh*, no. 113, Vol. 1, p. 305, and Vol. 4, pp. 294–295. For one later halakhist's evaluation of the severity of such a flaw, see the quotation preceding chapter 5 of this book.

17. Many editions and manuscripts of the various texts contain alternative names for the scrolls, but most other differences are relatively minor; see further the comments of the Vilna Gaon, ad loc. Some Sifrei texts list two places that included the erroneous *za'aṭuṭē*, Ex. 24:5 and 24:11; the texts of Soferim vary—some mention one verse and some the other—but the medieval citations generally contain only the former. See L. Finkelstein, ed., *Sifrei Al Sefer Devarim*, p. 423, for additional Sifrei variants, including the attribution of these textual decisions to the sages, "*ḥakamim*." PT Ta'an. 4:2 reports that one scroll had nine cases of *hi'* spelled *hy'*, while two had eleven cases. *Avot DeRabbi Natan* adds a passage in which Rabbi Yose attributed the name *Sefer "M'wn"* to its having come from Beit Ma'on.

Varied or truncated forms of the passage appear in *Midrash Tannaim*, ed. David Hoffmann (Berlin: Itzkovski, 1908), p. 222; *Midrash HaGadol*, ed. Solomon Fish, Vol. 5 (Jerusalem: Mossad HaRav Kook, 1975) p. 776; *Midrash HaHefetz*, ed. Meir Havatzelet (Jerusalem: Mossad HaRav Kook, 1990–1992), p. 479; and *Yalqut Shimoni: Devarim*, Vol. 2, ed. Isaac Shiloni (Jerusalem: Mossad HaRav Kook, 1991) p. 704. Note also the wording of the citation found in Solomon Ben Adret's responsum, translated in chapter 6 of this book.

18. The Torah speaks of writing on whitened stone (Deut. 27:2–8). Of some related interest is the Bilaam material on white plaster found at Deir Alla: J. Hoftijzer and G. van der Kooij, *Aramaic Texts from Deir 'Alla* (Leiden: E. J. Brill, 1976); Jo Ann Hackett, *The Balaam Text from Deir 'Alla* (Chico, Cal.: Scholars Press, 1980); and *The Balaam Text from Deir 'Alla*

Re-Evaluated (Leiden: E. J. Brill, 1991). Ancient metal texts include the silver amulets from the seventh century B.C.E. that contain the priestly blessing (G. Barkay, *Ketef Hinnom: A Treasure Facing Jerusalem's Walls* [Jerusalem: The Israel Museum, 1986]) and the Copper Scroll from Qumran; writing on humans is mentioned in M. Git. 2:8.

Ancient writing materials are discussed by G. R. Driver in *Semitic Writing from Pictograph to Alphabet*, 3rd ed. (London: Oxford University Press, 1976), pp. 3–17 and passim; Joseph Naveh, *Early History of the Alphabet: An Introduction to West Semitic Epigraphy and Paleography* (Jerusalem: Magnes, 1982), chapt. 1; and Meir Bar-Ilan in *Mikra: Text, Translation, Reading and Interpretation of the Hebrew Bible in Ancient Judaism and Early Christianity*, ed. Martin Jan Mulder (Minneapolis: Van Gorcum, 1990), pp. 24–28. Though it deals primarily with scripts, Albertine Gaur, A *History of Writing* (London: British Museum, 1984, 1992), is also helpful, especially pp. 88–99, as is Johannes Pedersen, *The Arabic Book*, trans. Geoffrey French, ed. Robert Hillenbrand (Princeton, N.J.: Princeton University Press, 1984).

19. In none of the three primary parallel texts does the context of the story or the preserved fragment relate to prescriptive matters of Torah production. Of course, this is a major consideration of Tractate Soferim, the latest of the four, but, as will be seen, its interpretations and potential applications are quite varied.

20. Song of Songs Rabbah 5, 1, commenting on Song of Songs 5:14. For images of Moses receiving a scroll from heaven, see the black and white reproductions from the Chludov Psalter and the Bible of Charles the Bald (both in the Biblioteque Nationale, Paris) in Irwin R. Goodenough, *Jewish Symbols in the Greco-Roman Period* (Princeton, N.J.: Princeton University Press, 1964), Vol. 11, plates 94 and 96; also folio 25b from the Moutiers-Grandval Bible in the British Library, reproduced in Janet Backhouse, *The Illuminated Manuscript* (Oxford: Phaidon, 1979), p. 15. Whether these presentations reflect the midrashic application of the scroll model to the tablets or the popular Jewish notion that the entire Torah was received by Moses at Sinai, Jewish sources seem to have influenced the artists, directly or indirectly.

21. The quotation is taken from Moshe H. Goshen-Gottstein, "The Rise of the Tiberian Bible Text," p. 86; see, in general, pp. 79–122; cf. also Reuben Margoliot, *HaMiqra' VeHaMasorah* (Jerusalem: Mossad HaRav Kook, 1964), pp. 13–16. For summaries and evaluations of these scholarly theories, see Moshe H. Goshen-Gottstein, "Hebrew Biblical Manuscripts: Their History and Their Place in the H[ebrew] U[niversity] B[ible] P[roject] Edition," *Biblica* 48 (1967): 243–290, and Shemaryahu Talmon, "The Old Testament Text," in *The Cambridge History of the Bible*, ed. P. R. Ackroyd and C. F. Evens (Cambridge: Cambridge University Press, 1970), pp. 159–199, repr. as the first chapter of Cross and Talmon, *Qumran and the History of the Biblical Text*.

See also Rabbi Isaac Judah Yehiel Safran's *Heikhal HaBerakhah* (Lemberg: 1869; repr., New York: Kelilath Yofi, n.d.), Vol. 1, Introduction, verso of title page; and Mordechai Breuer, *Keter Aram Tzovah VeHaNusah HaMequbbal Shel HaMiqra'*, pp. 91–94.

22. Such halakhic protests are found, for example, in *Quntres Masoret SeTaM: Berurei Halakhah VeDivrei Hesber Odot Masoret Hagahat SeTaM uVediqah Al Yedei Computer* (New York: Mishmeret Masoret SeTaM, 1992?). For a modern protest against the Aleppo Codex and its use see the discussion at the end of chapter 8.

23. One example of the kinds of problems to be encountered can be found in a Yemenite manuscript of Daniel, noted by Shelomo Morag in the introduction to his *Sefer Daniel: Ketav Yad Bavli-Temani* (Jerusalem: Qiryat Sefer, 1973), which includes a facsimile of the manuscript. These variants include both substantive changes in the text and alternative *matres lectionis* in the Aramaic portion of the book that Morag has compared with the changes in the full Isaiah text from Qumran ($1QIs^a$). See also Ginsburg's, *Introduction*, and *Studies in Hebrew and Aramaic Orthography*, ed. David Noel Freedman et al.

For further discussion of BT Qid. 30a and its implications, see, in addition to those Talmud commentaries not limited to halakhic interests, Abraham Jaffe, *Mishnat Avraham* (Zhitomer: A. Shadov, 1868; repr., Jerusalem, 1968), pp. 10–15; Jacob Bachrach, *Ishtadlut Im Shadal* (Warsaw: Shuldberg, 1896–1897) Vol. 1–2, chaps. 99, 102, etc.; Gerard E. Weil, "*Les Decomptes de versets, mots et lettres du Pentateuque selon le manuscrit B 19a de Leningrad,*" in *Melanges Dominique Barthelemy*, ed. P. Casetti, O. Keel, and A. Schenker (Freibourg: Editions Universitaires, 1981), pp. 652–703; and Francis I. Anderson and A. Dean Forbes in *Studies in Hebrew and Aramaic Orthography*, pp. 297–318.

24. So claimed Rabbi Yehiel Mikhal of Glogau in *Nezer HaQodesh*, his commentary to Genesis Rabbah 80, 5, p. 399b, which argued that scrolls should not be corrected following the principle of majority testimony at all, because this rule applied only to scrolls of the Temple (*sifrē ʿazara*), not to "the scrolls of our dispersion." Uri Feivel HaLevi, author of *Miqdash Meʿat*, printed in *Daʿat Qedoshim* (Lvov: 1896; repr., Jerusalem: n.p., 1964), p. 28a, n. 45, rejected this opinion on the basis of Ben Adret's responsum cited by Rabbi Joseph Caro (analyzed here in chapter 6). For discussion by several members of the Soloveitchik family, see later in this chapter.

25. Among others, Saadiah and Abraham Ibn Ezra did not believe that the entire Torah had been recorded on these stones; see Ibn Ezra to Deut. 27:2, Nahmanides' comments, ad loc., and discussion of these and other writers in Menahem M. Kasher, *Torah Shelemah*, Vol. 19 (New York: American Biblical Encyclopedia Society, 1959), pp. 354–355. On *Sefer Taggi(n)* see *Sefer Taghin*, introduced by J. J. L. Barges (Paris: 1866); the sixth chapter of Rabbi Shem Tov ben Abraham ben Gaon's *Badei HaAron uMigdal Hananel*, published there, and with a facsimile of the full manuscript in *Badei HaAron uMigdal Hananel LeRabbi Shem Tov ben Avraham ben Gaon*, ed. Samuel Loewinger (Jerusalem: Mizrah uMaʿarav, 1977); and Yehuda Ratzaby in *Torah Shelemah*, Vol. 34, ed. Menahem M. Kasher (Jerusalem: Beit Torah Shelemah, 1978), pp. 82–90.

26. The midrashic texts about the Torah of Rabbi Meir have been the subject of many studies, including Jonathan Paul Siegel, *The Severus Scroll and 1QIs[a]* (Missoula, Mont.: Scholars Press, 1975).

27. Saul Lieberman, *Hellenism*, pp. 20–27. This would seem to have no connection to the three text types described in several places by Frank Moore Cross, such as in *The Ancient Library of Qumran*, 3rd ed. (Minneapolis: Fortress, 1995), pp. 138–142. Emanuel Tov has criticized this presentation in *The Text-Critcal Use of the Septuagint in Biblical Research*, rev. ed. (Jerusalem: Simor, 1997), chap. 6.

28. Discussion of the thirteen Torah scrolls is found in *Pesiqta DeRav Kahana*, ed. Bernard Mandelbaum (New York: Jewish Theological Seminary, 1962), Vol. 2, pp. 441–442; *Midrash Tehillim*, ed. Solomon Buber (Vilna: Romm, 1891), p. 386, to Ps. 90:3; and Deut. Rab. 9,9. It was mentioned by Maimonides in the Introduction to his *Mishneh Torah*, and it was discussed by Menahem M. Kasher, *Torah Shelemah*, Vol. 19, p. 330. Rabbi Hayyim Herschenson, *Malki BaQodesh* (St. Louis: Moinester, 1919), Vol. 2, pp. 217, 234, suggested that, had the thirteen scrolls been available when the event in Soferim took place, the majority might have confirmed *mʿwn* or *zʿṭty*. See also, Saul Lieberman, *Hellenism*, p. 86, and Hava Lazarus-Yafeh, *Intertwined Worlds: Medieval Islam and Bible Criticism* (Princeton, N.J.: Princeton University Press, 1992), p. 44.

29. Abraham HaLevi, *Ginat Veradim*, ed. Pinhas Ovadiah (Jerusalem: Yeshivat Yismah Lev—Torat Moshe, 1991), Vol. 1, p. 95, col. b. The introduction lists the initial date of publication as 1716. The notion that these scrolls were merely three exceptional texts among the many correct ones in the Temple has been suggested by Rabbi Isaac Landau in his commentary on Soferim 6:3 (Suvalk: A. A. Marksohn, 1862).

30. Examples include the marginal notes to the Neophyti Targum: Gen. 22:1 and 11, 31:11, 46:2, *Targum Yerushalmi* (i.e., Fragmentary Targum) to Gen. 35:18, etc.; Pseudo-

Jonathan to Gen. 27:27, 28:22, 31:47, 32:3, 42:23, 45:12, to Num. 7:13, 19, 85, 86, and presumably to other intermediate verses lacking in the text because they are repeated so frequently, 28:7, and to Deut. 11:24, 23:19, and 25:7–8. See further B. Barry Levy, *The Language of Neophyti 1: A Descriptive and Comparative Grammar of the Palestinian Targum* (Ann Arbor, Mich.: University Microfilms, 1975), p. 255; idem, *Targum Neophyti 1: A Textual Study*, Vol. 1 (Lanham: University Press of America, 1986), p. 162; and Avigdor Shinan, *Targum VeAggadah Bo* (Jerusalem: Magnes Press, 1993), pp. 113–115.

31. Frederic W. Madden, *History of Jewish Coinage and of Money in the Old and New Testament* (1864; repr., New York: Ktav, 1967), pp. 443–446; Adolph Reifenberg, *Ancient Jewish Coins* 2nd edition, reprinted from *Journal of the Palestine Oriental Society* 19 (1941): 59–81, 286–313, and plates IV–VIII and XIII–XXII (Jerusalem: 1947), nos. 137–145; Shmuel Zev Reich, *Masoret HaSheqel* (Toronto: S. Z. Reich, 1986), pp. 85–86; Jacob Meshorer, *Otzar Matbe'ot Yisrael* (Jerusalem: Yad Ben Zvi, 1997), pp. 217–218. Note also what appears as the complementary evolution of the first part of the Greek name of Jerusalem, *hierosolyma*, from a simple transliteration of the Hebrew *yeru-* to Greek *yero-* to *hiero-*, "holy."

32. Josephus, *The Jewish War*, Vol. 1 (Cambridge: Harvard University Press, 1968), II, 427, pp. 490–491. Also M. Me'ilah 3:7, BT Shab. 116b, Git. 49a, Qid. 28b, PT San. 7:12 (25d), and many more. Num. Rab. 4:11 compares *šeqel ha-qodeš* and *šeqel heḏyoṭ*. See further Roger T. Beckwith's discussion of possibly related Greek terms from Jewish Hellenistic literature in *The Old Testament Canon of the New Testament Church* (Grand Rapids: Eerdmans, 1985), pp. 80–83, 105–109; Harry A. Wolfson, "On the Septuagint Use of *To Hagion* for the Temple," *Jewish Quarterly Review* 38 (1947): 109–110; and Naphtali Weider, "'Sanctuary' as a Metaphor for Scripture," *Journal of Jewish Studies* 8 (1957): pp. 165–175.

Ancient presentations of scrolls housed in a temple-like shrine have been reproduced many times. A series of sketches appears in Irwin Goodenough, *Jewish Symbols in the Greco-Roman Period* (Princeton, N.J.: Princeton University Press, 1953), Vol. 3, nos. 964–967, 973–974.

33. See Nahum Sarna, introduction to *Hamishah Humshei Torah: Ketav Yad Sefaradi Qadum* (Jerusalem: Makor, 1974); Meir Bar-Ilan, p. 24; *Le Livre Au Moyen Age*, ed. Jean Glenisson (Paris: Presses du Centre national des lettres, 1988), pp. 14–21, "Du rouleau au codex"; and Johannes Pedersen, *The Arabic Book*.

34. The Hebrew vocalization and the English transliteration of *msrh* and *msrt*, as well as the history of the words and their usages, are discussed in Eliezer Ben-Yehudah, *Milon HaLashon HaIvrit HaYeshanah VeHaHadashah* (Jerusalem: 1912; repr., New York: T. Yosseloff, 1959), Vol. 4, pp. 3140–3141; Wilhelm Bacher, "A Contribution to the History of the Term 'Masorah,'" *Jewish Quarterly Review, O.S.* 3 (1891): 785–790; Zev Ben Hayyim, "*Masorah uMasoret*," *Leshonenu* 21 (1957): 283–292; and Shraga Abramson, *Yesh Em LaMiqra'; LaMasoret*," *Leshonenu* 50 (1986): 31–36.

The Kaufmann manuscript of the Mishnah is vocalized, but the text of Avot 3:13 (there 3:16), Vol. 2, p. 341, lacks the word *msrt*. In its place, one finds *ma'aśeroṯ(!) seyaḡ la-tora*, a reading also discussed, ad loc., in *Tosafot Yom Tov*, the commentary by Rabbi Yom Tov Lipmann Heller (1579–1654). In Sheq. 6:1, the word is vocalized with a qameṣ, and no dagesh is placed in the *samekh*.

35. Yedidiah Solomon Norzi, *Minhat Shai*, repr. in *Miqra'ot Gedolot: Sefer Otzar Perushim Al HaTorah* (New York: Shulsinger Brothers, 1950), pp. 5–6. Four whole or partial copies of this introduction exist in manuscript, including Parma no. 895 (identified in the following discussion as P), Kaufmann, no. 43A (K), and British Museum, Add. 27,198. The last, described by G. Margoliouth, *Catalogue of The Hebrew and Samaritan Manuscripts in the British Museum* (London: British Museum, 1965), Part I, no. 231, is an autograph containing two versions of the introduction: what appears to be an early draft full of changes (here called

D[raft]) and a complete, relatively clean copy (B). The Kaufmann manuscript appears to be in the same hand, but a part near the end is missing. Parma is by far the easiest to read. The printed text has been checked against all four manuscripts; in most places cited here they are identical, but a few significant variants will be discussed.

The Introduction to *Minhat Shai* was first published by Adolf Jellinek, as *Jedidjah Salomo Norzi's Einleitung, Titelblatt und Schlusswort zu seinem masoretischen Bibelcommentar* (Wien: Brueder Winter, 1876; repr., Israel: ca. 1970), from which the 1950 reprint was copied. See now *Yedidiah Shelomo Refael Norzi: HaNosafot LeMinhat Shai*, ed. Zvi Betser (Jerusalem: World Union of Jewish Studies, 1997).

36. *Perush Rabbi Avraham Min HaHar*, ed. Moshe Yehuda Blau (New York: M. Blau, 1975), p. 27. Ben Asher's *Quntres HaMasoret*, cited in Aaron Dotan, *Ben Asher's Creed* (Missoula, Mont.: Scholars Press, 1977), pp. 21–23, used the terms *hktwb* and *hbṭwy* to refer to the written and oral traditions. Dotan correctly equated them with the talmudic terms *masoreṯ* and *miqra'*. For a survey of the treatment of the term *'em la-miqra'* in rabbinic literature, see Reuben Margaliot, *Margaliot HaYam* (Jerusalem: Mossad HaRav Kook, 1957), Sanhedrin, 4a, pp. 21–22. In *Yesh Em LaMiqra'; LaMasoret*," Abramson has demonstrated that some medieval writers used the terms *miqra'* and *masoreṯ* as the equivalent of *Qere* and *Keṯiḇ*.

37. Several examples of this usage can be seen in the colophons cited in Izhak Ben-Zvi's "The Codex of Ben Asher," *Textus* 1, e.g., pp. 4 and 13.

38. The commentary from Mahzor Vitry was discussed by I. Ta-Shema, "*Al Perush Avot SheBeMahzor Vitry*," *Qiryat Sepher* 42 (1967): 507–508. It and those of Rabbi Ovadiah Bertinora, the Vilna Gaon, and Rabbi Israel Lipshuetz, are found in *Mishnayot Tif'eret Yisrael* (repr., New York: Pardes, 1953). See also Shimon ben Tzemah Duran, *Magen Avot* (Leipzig: L. Schnauss, 1855), pp. 49a–b, and Barukh HaLevi Epstein, *Barukh SheAmar* (Tel Aviv: Am Olam, 1965), p. 119.

39. BT Meg. 3a and Ned. 37b.

40. *Yalqut MeAm Loez*, trans. Samuel Yerushalmi (Jerusalem: Or Hadash, 1972), pp. 137–138.

41. *Beit HaBehirah Al Masekhet Avot*, ed. Benjamin Zev Prague (Jerusalem: Makhon HaTalmud HaYisraeli HaShalem, 1964), pp. 50–51.

42. *Mishnah Berurah* (repr., New York: A. I. Friedman, 1964), Vol. 2, *Orah Hayyim* 141, 8, n. 47.

43. Letter of Aristeas, 32. Compare the translations and notes on this well-discussed passage by [H. T.] Andrews in *The Apocrypha and Pseudepigrapha of the Old Testament*, ed. R. H. Charles (Oxford: Oxford University Press, 1913), pp. 97–98; by Moses Hadas, *Aristeas to Philocrates* (Philadelphia: Dropsie, 1951), pp. 112–113; and by R. J. H. Shutt in *The Old Testament Pseudepigrapha*, ed. James H. Charlesworth (Garden City, N.Y.: Doubleday and Company, 1985), p. 15. Elias Bickermann preferred to see this description as pointing to flaws in the Hebrew text, "The Colophon of the Greek Book of Esther," *Journal of Biblical Literature* 63 (1944): 345, while Paul Kahle understood it to refer to previously existing Greek texts, *The Cairo Geniza*, 2nd ed. (Oxford: Basil Blackwell, 1959), p. 213. Both ideas are already found in Charles, p. 98. Note also M. H. Segal, "The Promulgation of the Authoritative Text of the Hebrew Bible."

In the scholia to Dionysius Thrax (himself, from the second century B.C.E.), we find a description of the collection and editing of Homer in a manner that resembles some of the presentations of the collecting, editing, and translating of the Bible culled from pre-Christian sources. Among the striking parallels is the claim that the gathered texts of Homer were reviewed by 72 *grammatikoi*, text experts. See further James I. Porter, "Hermeneutic Lines and Circles: Aristarchus and Crates on the Exegesis of Homer" in *Homer's Ancient Readers: The Hermeneutics of Greek Epic's Earliest Exegetes*, ed. Robert Lamberton and John J. Keaney

(Princeton, N.J.: Princeton University Press, 1992), esp. pp. 67–69. On *grammatikoi*, see John E. Sandys, *A History of Classical Scholarship* (London: Hafner, 1967), Vol. 1, pp. 6–11.

44. *Beit David, Hilkhot Sefer Torah* (Salonika: Betzalel Ashkenazi, 1734; repr., Jerusalem: Yeshivat Torah LiShemah, 1990), p. 88a, end of col. a; see Yitzchak Isaac Ben Jacob, *Otzar HaSefarim* (Vilna: Romm, 1880), p. 72, no. 300 for discussion of the publication date.

45. Hasan's documentation of this incident, *Iggeret HaSofer*, appeared in *HaSegulah*, a typed periodical produced in Jerusalem and distributed to one hundred subscribers 5 (1938), nos. 53–56. Where I have checked, it is similar to the more recent edition, *Iggeret HaSofer Rabbi Abraham Hasan MiSaloniqi*, ed. Meir Benayahu, *Sefunot* 11 (1971–1978), pp. 207–229. The text is discussed further later.

46. Hayyim Palaggi, *She'eilot uTeshuvot Lev Hayyim* (Salonika: 1874), Vol. 2, p. 121b, no. 176, also cited by Rabbi Ovadiah Yosef, *Yehaveh Da'at*, Vol. 6, no. 56, pp. 289–294. See further Palaggi's *Hiqeqei Lev* (Salonika: 1840) pp. 87a–89b, no. 48 and the sources cited there. On Palaggi himself, see Simon L. Eckstein's Yeshiva University dissertation, *Rabbi Palaggi, His Life, Works and Influence on the Jewish Community in Izmir (1970)*, now reworked as *Toldot HaChabif: The Work, Life and Influence of Rabbi Hayim Palaggi (1787–1868), Chief Rabbi of Izmer-Turkey* (Jerusalem: Haleviyim, 1999).

47. This procedure has been adopted by Mordechai Breuer in his study of the Aleppo Codex and its relationship to other model codices. Using it, admittedly after selecting those witnesses he finds most worthy, has yielded a surprisingly high level of agreement among the texts. See further his *Keter Aram Tzovah VeHaNusah HaMequbbal Shel HaMiqra'*.

48. Cited on the title page of Arnold B. Ehrlich, *Mikra Ki-Pheschuto* (repr., New York: Ktav, 1969).

49. On Abulafia in general, see Bernard Septimus, *Hispano-Jewish Culture in Transition: The Career and Controversies of Ramah* (Cambridge: Harvard University Press, 1982). I. Ta-Shema discussed the state of the text, manuscripts, and medieval reception of *Masoret Seyag LaTorah* in his "*Yetzirato HaSifrutit Shel Rabbi Meir HaLevi Abulafia*," *Qiryat Sefer* 43 (1968): 119–126; Mordechai Breuer has examined Abulafia's masoretic work in *Keter Aram Tzovah VeHaNusah HaMequbbal Shel HaMiqra'*.

50. Meir Abulafia, *Masoret Seyag LaTorah* (Florence: Isaac Da Paz, 1750; repr., Israel: Zion, 1969), Introduction. I have been unable to locate the edition of Florence, 1754, mentioned by Septimus, p. 137, n. 92; it was published again in Berlin in 1761.

51. Among the many positive responses to Abulafia's efforts are those of Abraham Hasan and Mordecai Breuer, as well as Y. S. Norzi, who praised him excessively. However, as will become clear later, Solomon ben Adret seems not to have relied on his work or even to have known about it and, while Meiri did use some of Abulafia's other material, he too seems to have been unaware of *Masoret Seyag LaTorah*.

52. *Megaleh Amuqot* (Lvov: 1795).

53. Abraham Ibn Ezra, in the standard version of the Introduction to his Torah Commentary, *HaDerekh HaHamishit*, published in *Torat Hayyim* (Jerusalem: Mossad HaRav Kook, 1986), p. 10, but not in the alternative version, pp. 299–306. In fact, Prov. 30:22 is the only place in the Bible where *yimlok̲* is spelled plene, a point mentioned in *Midrash Haserot ViYeterot*, in *Battei Midrashot*, ed. Solomon Wertheimer (Jerusalem: Ketav VeSefer, 1968) Vol. 2, p. 256, no. 49. Ibn Ezra's comment, which attributes the plene spelling to the copyist or the editor of Proverbs and not to divine or authorial sources, is theoretically irrelevant to questions of Torah spelling, but not to the orthography found in other biblical books. See, further, his Long Commentary to Ex. 20:1. Ibn Ezra's concerns about possible changes to the spellings of biblical words may contain a reaction to the *'al tiqrē* phenomenon. See, further, chapter 1 of his *Yesod Mora'*, ed. J. Baer (Frankfort am Main: 1840: repr. in *Kitvei R[abbi] Avraham Ibn Ezra*, Vol. 2, Jerusalem: Makor, 1970) and trans. H. Norman Strickman (North-

vale, N.J.: Jason Aronson, 1995), where he compares extensive study of masoretic details to doing numerological studies of a medical book instead of using its recipes to heal illness, and to a camel's carrying a load of silk that is useless to it; and *Safah Berurah*, ed. Gabriel Lippmann (Fuerth: D. J. Zuerndorffer, 1939), p. 76, where he calls such matters *ṭoḇim le-ḥasre leḇ*, "good for those lacking intelligence."

54. *Or Torah* was published as the first of ten "fingers" in *Shetei Yadot* and later reissued independently. For the history of publication, see Yitzchak Isaac Ben-Jacob, *Otzar HaSefarim*, p. 29, no. 565.

55. The term *Miqra'ot Gedolot* is relatively late and seems to have appeared more or less simultaneously with the now accepted reduction in size of the printed Rabbinic Bibles in the nineteenth century. The early, sixteenth-century editions of the Rabbinic Bibles often bore titles like *Esrim Ve-Arba'*. At that time the term that was used to describe them was *miqra' geḏola*, which contrasted with *miqra' qeṭanna*. The former was actually a translation of the Latin *Magna Biblia*, "big Bible," even its feminine form. In fact, *miqra' geḏola* referred to the folio size of the printed page and had nothing to do with whether the edition contained rabbinic commentaries. See further B. Barry Levy, "Rabbinic Bibles, *Mikra'ot Gedolot*, and Other Great Books," *Tradition* 25 (1991): 65–81.

56. Bomberg's Bibles have been discussed by Christian David Ginsburg in his *Introduction*, by Chaim Dov Friedberg in *Toldot HaDefus HaIvri BeItalia* (Tel Aviv: Bar-Juda, 1956), pp. 60–66, and in the various works devoted to early Venetian publishing; see chapter 6, n. 1 of this book.

57. The use of this verse creates a pun on *peṯaḥ*, "the doorway," and *paṯaḥ*, the simple a-vowel.

58. *Mikhlol Yofi* (Amsterdam: 1684; repr., Israel: n.d.). For an explanation of how he used Radak, see the conclusion, *Hatimat HaSefer*, pp. 219a–b.

59. Menahem Recanati, *Perush HaTorah* (repr., Jerusalem: S. Monson, 1961).

60. The passages translated can be found in the printed text on pp. 13–15.

61. Even in the 1950 edition of the *Miqra'ot Gedolot*, which combined the two reprints, the introduction accompanied only the commentary on the Torah and the Five Scrolls, because that six-volume publication did not include the Prophets and Hagiographa.

62. The source of my information is Jordan Penkower, *Jacob ben Hayyim and the Rise of the Biblia Rabbinica*, a very detailed discussion of the textual priorities and editorial methods of Felix Pratensis and Jacob ben Hayyim. A wonderful but far from unusual example of Norzi's range of sources appears in his comment on Deut. 10:12; see chapter 8 of this book.

63. Saraval was mentioned by Yehudah Aryeh MiModena in *Ziqnei Yehudah*, ed. Shlomo Simonsohn (Jerusalem: Mossad HaRav Kook, 1957), pp. 51–52, and by Ludwig Blau, *Kitvei Yehudah Aryeh MiModena* (Budapest: Kalai, 1906), no. 5, pp. 114–116.

64. I have been unable to verify any of these reports of his correspondents' replies from other sources. A passage in *Midrash Haserot ViYeterot* (Vol. 2, p. 249, no. 48) suggests that Aaron's name cannot be spelled plene if Moses' is always defective. Norzi's comment, ad loc., suggests an awareness of the problem but provides no additional support for the plene spelling. Relying on the Spanish manuscripts to which he had access, on Abulafia's comment in *Masoret Seyag LaTorah*, and on Lonzono's in *Or Torah*, he declared the defective spelling to be correct. Benjamim Kennicott mentioned about a dozen texts with the plene spelling in *Vetus Testamentum Hebraice cum Variis Lectionibus* (Oxford: 1776–1780); they include a text published in Venice in 1739.

65. Joseph ben Shneur HaKohen, *Minhat Kohen* (Kuru Tsheshme: 1598). Rabbi Eliah Arbara is discussed briefly in Solomon Abraham Rosanes, *Divrei Yemei Yisrael BeTogarmah*, Vol. 3 (Gusiatin: 1914), p. 57. Ishkofia, Skoplje, is known as Uskub in Turkish and as Skopje in Macedonian and was relatively unknown in the West until it became the subject of daily

media reports during the recent war in the Balkans. For a brief history and bibliography, see *Encyclopaedia Judaica*, Vol. 14, col. 1648–1649. A number of published responsa deal with problems there, including the legitimacy of a tax imposed on guests, the length of time certain property claims (*ḥazaqa*) were considered valid, and the correct way to spell the city's name.

66. I. Ta-Shema, "*Yetzirato HaSifrutit Shel Rabbi Meir HaLevi Abulafia*," pp. 125–126.

67. For another contemporary example of equivocating on a few spellings, see Penkower's discussion of Rabbi Samuel Vital, *Nusah HaTorah BeKeter Aram Tzovah*, pp. 81–90.

68. *Beit HaBehirah Al Masekhet Qiddushin*, 3rd ed. (Jerusalem: A. Schreiber, 1963), to Qid. 30a.

69. *Ginat Veradim*, Vol. 3, p. 96.

70. Moshe Goshen-Gottstein, "Bible Manuscripts in the United States," *Textus* 2 (1962): 38.

71. Pp. 30b–31b.

72. See, for example, the sources cited by Norzi in *Minhat Shai* to Deut. 10:12, translated in chapter 8; and the inconsistent references to spelling in Jacob Gellis, *Ba'alei HaTosafot HaShalem* (Jerusalem: Mifal Tosafot HaShalem, 1982–1995), passim.

73. For a list of rabbis who fulfilled this halakhic requirement, see Solomon Z. Havlin, "*Sefer Torah SheKatav LeAtzmo Rabbenu Nissim MiGirondi*," *Alei Sefer* 12 (1986): 11–12.

74. This problem was encountered in many different situations and is discussed in a wide range of halakhic works. The Talmud objected to reading anything other than a complete scroll, but necessity and the widespread Karaite practice of reading from a vocalized codex required that questions regarding the propriety of these other options be answered again and again; see N. Allony, "*Sefer HaTorah VeHaMitzhaf BeQeri'at HaTorah BeTzibbur BeAdat HaRabbanim uVeAdat HaQara'im*," and Ezra Fleischer, *Tefillah uMinhagei Tefillah Eretz-Yisraeliyim BeTequfat HaGenizah* (Jerusalem: Magnes Press, 1988), chap. 7.

As well, an entire literature surrounds the validity of Maimonides' ruling that one can recite a blessing upon reading an inaccurately written scroll; see the notes to *She'eilot uTeshuvot Rabbenu Moshe ben Maimon: Pe'er HaDor*, ed. David Yosef, 2nd ed. (Jerusalem: Makhon Or HaMizrah, 1984), pp. 29–33. Regardless of the decision, the discussions were often precipitated by situations in which no proper scroll was available. Many later authorities rationalized permission to read an obviously inaccurate scroll, because no other scroll could be had or because it could not be corrected on the Sabbath, when the error was discovered. The modern gathering of Torah scrolls from the many corners of the diaspora has rekindled the same debates in Israel, particularly among the Sefaradi communities. See, further, Shalom Isaac HaLevi, *She'eilot uTeshuvot Divrei Hakhamim: Yoreh De'ah* (*Bar Ilan University Judaic Library*) no. 27, and Ovadiah Yosef, *Yehaveh Da'at* (Jerusalem: Aleph Bet, 1976), Vol. 6, no. 56, discussed later.

75. Goshen-Gottstein, "Bible Manuscripts," p. 37, suggested that full Masorah texts constituted some 10 percent (or possibly less) of the total available medieval Bible manuscripts. While I am unable to offer a more accurate figure for his estimate, which was based on the number of Masorah codices or fragments in existence, I should think that fewer than 10 percent of the population regularly used one.

76. Paul Kahle's reports are found in *The Cairo Geniza*, chap. 2; see also Amnon Shamosh, *HaKeter* (Jerusalem: Makhon Ben Zvi, 1987).

77. On formal *ḥilufim*, see Ginsburg, *Introduction*, pp. 241–286; Yeivin, *Introduction*, pp. 141–143, nos. 155–156; and especially Eliezer Lipschuetz, "Mishael ben Uzziel's Treatise on the Differences between Ben Asher and Ben Naphtali," *Textus* 2 (1962): Heb. pp. 1–58, and idem, "*Kitab al-Ḥilaf*, the Book of the Hilufim", *Textus* 4 (1964): 1–29. On *Sevirin*, see Tov, *Textual Criticism*, p. 64, and the literature cited there. The theoretical and practical aspects of *maḥloqeṯ* as a factor in halakhic decision making have been explored extensively in the two-

volume collection of primary sources *Controversy and Dialogue in Halakhic Sources*, ed. Hanina Ben-Menahem et al. (Jerusalem: Israel Diaspora Institute, 1991–1993), and Moshe Halbertal, *People of the Book: Canon, Meaning and Authority* (Cambridge: Harvard University Press, 1997), chap. 2.

78. See, for example, the lengthy discussion of Rabbi Azariah of Fano, in which he said, speaking of Maimonides' reliance on the Ben Asher codex in Jerusalem for determining paragraph spacings, "And who would dare to disagree with its words which are based on an old tradition, without having in hand a clear proof from the masters of the Gemara to decide against it?" *She'eilot uTeshuvot Rabbi Azariah MiFano (Bar Ilan University Judaic Library)*, no. 106. For him, the Ben Asher text was authoritative; the Babylonian Talmud was more so.

This conflict was also noted by Rabbi Moses Sofer (1762–1839) in *She'eilot uTeshuvot Hatam Sofer* (Vienna: 1895; repr., Jerusalem: Makor, 1970), *Orah Hayyim* no. 52, trans. here in chapter 2. Formal lists of the differences between the Easterners and the Westerners record textual and vocalization differences; also prominent are different verse divisions discussed already in the Talmud and major differences in vocalization systems.

79. *Ginat Veradim*, Vol. 3, p. 95, no. 6.

80. *She'eilot uTeshuvot Da'at Kohen: Yoreh De'ah* (Bar Ilan University Judaic Library), no. 166.

81. *Fundamentals and Faith: Insights into the Rambam's Thirteen Principles*, ed. Mordechai Blumenfeld (Spring Valley, N.Y.: Feldheim, 1991), pp. 90–91. Note the remark of Rabbi Benjamin Lau in "*Sefer Torah Temani BeQehillah Ashkenazit*," *Tehumin* 15 (1995): 452: ". . . it is not in our power to determine with certainty what is the precise text that Moses brought down from Mount Sinai."

82. The important geonic responses to the question of why nonexistent verses are quoted in the Talmud does not alter this observation. For full documentation, see Yeshayahu Maori, *Midreshei Hazal KeEdut LeHilufei Nusah HaMiqra'*, in *Iyyunei Miqra' uFarshanut* 3 (1993): 270, n. 14. This article has appeared in English translation in *Modern Scholarship in the Study of Torah: Contributions and Limitations*, ed. Sholom Carmy (Northvale, N.J.: Jason Aronson, 1996), pp. 101–130.

83. Theoretically, some textual variations could have been attributed to differences among the thirteen Torah scrolls said to have been produced by Moses, especially since at least twelve of them were claimed to have been written on the day he died, but this notion seems to have been developed extensively only by non-Jewish critics; see the sources cited by the authors at the end of n. 28.

84. Ephraim E. Urbach, *Ba'alei HaTosafot*, 4th ed. (Jerusalem: Mossad Bialik, 1980), index, s.v. R. Jacob b[en] r[av] Meir.

85. On the citations and names, see *Kitvei Yad HaGenizah: Ginzei Yerushalayim*, ed. Samuel A. Wertheimer (Jerusalem: R. Mass, 1982), texts, pp. 50–55. It has been theorized that originally the work was a part of Rabbenu Tam's *Sefer HaYashar*, ibid.; the passage next quoted is found on p. 97.

86. The earliest source for the "cut *waw*" is BT Qid. 66b. It is discussed more fully in chapter 4, because it is the subject of one of Ibn Zimra's responsa.

87. Rabbenu Tam harbored no particular animosity toward the Masorah, as can be seen from his citing it in the discussion of Dunash's grammatical observations. Even so, he noted that it contains some late additions; *Sefer Teshuvot Dunash Ben Labrat Im Hakhra'ot Rabbenu Ya'aqov Tam*, ed. Zvi Philipovski (London: 1855) p. 11.

88. *Shulhan Arukh, Orah Hayyim* 143, 4. The impact of Rabbenu Tam's teaching on this point can be charted throughout the medieval Ashkenazi codes and halakhic essays that treat Torah scrolls, only a few of which will be explored here. The authority of Rabbi Moses Isserles reinforced it. For examples of the differences between Ashkenazi and Sefaradi Bible texts,

see H. J. Zimmels, *Ashkenazim and Sephardim: Their Relations, Differences, and Problems as Reflected in the Rabbinical Responsa*, 2nd ed. (London: Marla, 1976), pp. 140–142.

89. My translation of the text published in *Jacob Ben Chajim Ibn Adonijah's Introduction to the Rabbinic Bible*, ed. Christian David Ginsburg (London: 1867; repr., New York: Ktav, 1968), p. 78.

90. Norzi, Introduction, pp. 8–9. This passage is helpful in filiating the manuscripts, but it cannot be used in isolation. The alternate reading from the Zohar is not found in D, neither in the base text nor in any of the numerous and lengthy marginal notes that eventually found their way into the final copy. B has the passage in the margin. K includes it as placed here in the English translation, while the printed text incorrectly placed it immediately after "like a song." It is not found in P at all, though the passage it was intended to augment or to replace appears in parentheses, which suggests its existence was known to the scribe or to someone who used the manuscript later.

91. The printed text has here "the name of the King," as do D and B; P and K have "the holy Name," a phrase used in close proximity. In P, the source is designated as page 122 of the Zohar, probably because of the great similarity between *b-* and *d-* in the Italian style of Hebrew script.

92. P and D omit the phrase *sodoṯ u-remazim*, "symbolic meanings and allegories." Routinely overlooked by historians of Jewish Bible interpretation, this list of types of interpretations is too distant from the concern here to warrant extensive comment now. It is unusual in its length and clarity and is worthy of further discussion, particularly insofar as it relates to approaches seeking meaning in the individual letters of the text and it augments the popular medieval taxonomy, PaRDeS.

93. The previous paragraphs can be found in the printed text on pp. 9 and 6. Here *sifrē* cannot refer to Torah scrolls, with which it is listed, so it must be more general in meaning, i.e., "texts" or "books," or perhaps "codices."

94. The printed reference to the end of [PT] A.Z. is totally erroneous. All four manuscripts have "Soferim, chapter 6." Apparently *swp[rym] p[ereq] w-* was misread as *sof ʿ[aḇoḏa] z[ara]*. The association with the Palestinian Talmud is carried over from the previous reference, and the misreading was facilitated by the similarity of *waw* and *zayyin*.

95. For additional discussion, see Judah Moscato's commentary, *Qol Yehudah*, in Yehudah HaLevi, *HaKuzari* (Warsaw: I. Goldman; repr., Israel: Hadaran, 1959).

Norzi's version of the dialogue appears in the standard Hebrew translation of the *Kuzari* by Ibn Tibbon, with the commentaries *Qol Yehudah* and *Otzar Nehmad* (Warsaw: I Goldman, 1880; repr., Israel: Hadaran, 1959), but the text seems to be corrupt, since the roles of questioner and respondent, held by the Sage and the King, should be reversed. Judah Even-Shemuel's Hebrew translation (Jerusalem: Devir, 1977), p. 122, differs:

> (26) Said the Kuzari: So what is to be done, if a change is found in one of the manuscripts of the Torah, or in two, or more?
> (27) Said the sage: It is necessary to accept the reading of the majority of manuscripts—for the majority cannot be incorrect—and to reject the opinion of the minority. And so should one act regarding the *masoreṯ*; in a place where the minority disagrees, one should follow the majority.

The paragraphs preceding these two deal with the transmission of the rabbinic tradition, while the subsequent ones discuss possible corruptions in the Torah and what to do about them. The major question is the precise meaning of the Arabic phrase *fi al-naqlin* (David H. Baneth, *Kitab al-Radd wa-'l Dalil fi 'l-Din al-Dhalil* [Jerusalem: Magnes, 1977], p. 115). Ibn Tibbon has translated it as *ba-maʿaṭiqim*; C. Touati, as "*avec les transmetteurs*" (*Le Kuzari: Apologie de la Religion Meprise* [Paris: Peeters, 1994] p. 115). But Hirschfeld offered, "The same process applies to traditions" (*Judah Hallevi's Kitab al Khazari*, trans. from the Arabic by

Hartwig Hirschfeld [London: M. L. Cailingold, 1931], p. 145, par. 260), and Even-Shemuel's modern Hebrew rendition of the Arabic concurred, *we-kak yeš linhog gam be-nogēa' la-masoret*, "And so should one act regarding the *masoret*."

Whether *al-naqlin* here refers to tradition in general, to the rabbinic handling of that tradition (*masoret*), or to the masoretic literature (Masoret) is largely a function of how one understands the context into which these two paragraphs are set, but the associations between *al-naqlin*, *ma'aṭiqim*, and the concept of *masora* are well established. See further the important discussion of Z. Ankori in *Karaites in Byzantium* (New York: Columbia University press, 1957), pp. 224–239, and Moshe Zucker's articles, "*Qeta'im Mi-Kitab Tahsil al-Sharai' al-Sama'iyah LeRasag*," *Tarbits* 41 (1971–1972): 373–410, and "*Qeta'im MiPerush Rav Sa'adiah Gaon LaTorah MiKitvei Yad*," *Sura* 2 (1955), references for which I am pleased to thank Dr. Diana Lobel. Note also Moshe Zucker, "*LeVa'ayat HaMahloqet BaMasoret*," *Sefer HaYovel LiKhevod Shalom Baron* (Jerusalem: American Academy for Jewish Research, 1975), pp. 319–329, and the treatment of *tawatur*, "reliable transmission," by Hava Lazarus-Yafeh, in *Intertwined Worlds: Medieval Islam and Bible Criticism*, pp. 41–47.

Applying the notion of "transmission" to a written text obviously implies a great deal of conceptual overlap with "copying," and one example of such an interpretation problem is found in Prov. 25:1. Many have taken *'ašer he'eṭiqu 'anšē ḥizqiya* to mean "that the men of Hezekiah transmitted," though the Targum and some medievals explained it as *kaṯeḇu*, and the New JPS translation has "copied." Saadiah translated it *allati naqaluha qawm ḥizqiya* (*Oeuvres Completes de R. Saadia ben Iosef Al-Fayyoumi*, ed. Joseph Derenbourg, Vol. 6, *Les Proverbes* [Paris: Leroux, 1894] p. 142, and *Mishlei Im Targum uFeirush HaGaon Rabbenu Saadiah*, ed. Joseph Kafih [Jerusalem: Vaad LeHotza'at Sifrei Rasag, 1976]) ad loc. In the passage from the introduction to his Torah commentary translated above, Ibn Ezra attributed the spelling of *yimloḵ* to "*ma'aṭiq sefer mišlē*." Note also his frequent designation of the talmudic rabbis as *ma'aṭiqim* or *ma'aṭiqē ha-miṣwoṯ*, which emphasizes their roles as "transmitters" of the tradition, not as "recorders," though, again, both elements are present. In other medieval texts, *le-ha'aṭiq* can mean "to translate."

96. The previous paragraphs can be found in the printed text on p. 12.

97. The contents, the agenda, and the general phenomenon of the introductions to medieval Jewish Bible commentaries require extensive analysis, as do initial sections of many aggadic midrashim, which are themselves introductions of a related type.

98. J. Simha Cohen, *The 613th Mitzvah* (New York: Ktav, 1983).

99. Judah Loew, *Tif'eret Yisrael*, ed. Hayyim Pardes (Tel Aviv: Makhon Yad Mordecai, 1979), chap. 67, n. 2404.

100. Moshe Hayyim Haraz, *Otzar Hayyim* (Jerusalem: M. H. Haraz, 1983), pp. 24–25.

101. Byron L. Sherwin, *Mystical Theology and Social Dissent: The Life and Works of Judah Loew of Prague* (London: Associated University Presses, 1982), p. 42.

102. *Gilyon HaShas HaShalem* (Jerusalem: Samuel Hillel HaKohen, 1987). The text is translated in chapter 8 of this book.

103. *The Zohar*, trans. Harry Sperling and Maurice Simon (London: Soncino, 1931–1934).

104. Eliezer Katz, *HaHatam Sofer* (Jerusalem: Mossad HaRav Kook, 1960).

105. Moshe J. Burak, *The Hatam Sofer* (Toronto: Beth Jacob Congregation, 1967).

106. J. Nahshoni, *Rabbenu Moshe Sofer: HaHatam Sofer* (Jerusalem: 1981).

107. Shimon Hirschler, *Me'oran Shel Yisrael: Rabbenu Aqiva Eiger* (Brooklyn: Makhon Shem MiShemuel, 1990), Vol. 2, p. 201, no. 4.

108. Solomon Z. Schick, *Torah Shelemah* (Satmar: Z. Schwartz, 1909), *Bereishit*, p. 126a.

109. For this reason and to clarify the issues, I have translated many of the texts discussed instead of merely citing them.

110. Rabbi Leiner's summary of the Soloveitchik position is found in his *Sefer 'Ein HaTekhelet* (Warsaw: 1892; repr. with his earlier works, *Sefunei Temunei Hol* [1887], and *Petil Tekhelet* [1888] Jerusalem: 1983), p. 13.

111. For more recent discussion of the identity of the *hilazon*-shellfish, see *The Royal Purple and the Biblical Blue: The Study of Chief Rabbi Isaac Herzog and Recent Scientific Contributions*, ed. E. Spanier (Jerusalem: Keter, 1987).

112. This nineteenth-century rabbinic disagreement has been discussed in *MiBeit Midrasho Shel HaRav*, a collection of lecture notes attributed to Rabbi Joseph Dov Soloveitchik and published by an anonymous group of his students (Jerusalem: 1978) pp. 55–58, but several mistakes there must be corrected, e.g., p. 56, paragraph B, read *g- pesuqim* for *g- pe'amim*; p. 57, end, *'azlinan baṯar masoreṯ ma'aśe ha-halaḵa* seems to make no sense; p. 58, read *'anan la' beqi'inan be-ḥaser u-mạlē'*, not *be-ḥ-d-*. See also Joseph B. Soloveitchik, *Shi'urim LeZekher Abba Mari, Z[ikhrono] L[iVerakhah]* (Jerusalem: Y. D. Soloveitchik, 1984), pp. 220–239, esp. pp. 228–239, and the presentation by Zvi Schachter, *Nefesh HaRav* (Jerusalem: Reishit Yerushalayim, 1994), pp. 34–58, esp. pp. 53–58 and n. 26. (The application of this argument to the Talmud's recovery of the meanings of Hebrew words through recourse to seemingly non-Jewish users of cognate languages, discussed in Schechter's presentation, differs from the way many medieval philologists understood the early rabbis. See, for example, Yonah Ibn Janach, *Sefer HaRiqmah*, ed. Michael Wilensky [Berlin: 1929; repr., Jerusalem: HaAkademiah, 1964], Introduction, pp. 16–19). Related discussion is found in Meir Orlean, "*Birkhot HaTorah Shel Qeri'at HaTorah BeTzibbur,*" *Beit Yosef Sha'ul*, ed. Elchanan Asher Adler (New York: Rabbi Isaac Elchanan Theological Seminary, 1994), Vol. 4, pp. 199–214.

113. Upon arriving in Israel, Nahmanides learned of an ancient coin written in paleo-Hebrew script, and he promptly applied its weight to relevant treatment of weights in the Talmud. For further discussion of similar coins and the writing on them, see *She'eilot uTeshuvot Maharam Al-Ashqar* (Jerusalem: 1988), no. 64; Azariah De Rossi, *Me'or Einayyim* (Vilna: 1866; repr., Jeruslem: Makor, 1970), Vol. 2, pp. 450–452; Shmuel Zev Reich, *Masoret HaSheqel*; and B. Barry Levy, *Planets Potions and Parchments: Scientific Hebraica from the Dead Sea Scrolls to the Eighteenth Century* (Montreal: McGill-Queens University Press, 1990), pp. 62–63.

114. *She'eilot uTeshuvot Zivhei Tzedeq*, ed. J. Peretz, Vol. 3 (Jerusalem: Makhon Or HaMizrah, 1981), p. 16, no. 11.

115. See *She'eilot uTeshuvot Divrei Hakhamim: Yoreh De'ah* (*Bar Ilan University Judaic Library*), no. 27.

116. *Torat Hayyim*, Vol. 7, ed. Mordecai Leb Katzenellenbogen (Jerusalem: Mossad HaRav Kook, 1993), p. 447. Rabbi Benjamin Lau has discussed this matter in "*Sefer Torah Temani BeQehillah Ashkenazit*," *Tehumin* 15 (1995): 446–472, as did Uri Dasberg before him in "*Zihui Sefer Torah*," *Tehumin* 1 (1980): 511. He lists fourteen differences between Yemenite and Ashkenazi Torah scrolls, the nine listed above as well as (1) the unity of Poti-Phera in Gen. 41:45, which Ashkenazim have as two words; (2) the size of the *mem* of *moqda* in Lev. 6:2, which Ahkenazim have undersized; (3) a paragraph division that Ashkenazim lack in Lev. 7:22; (4) a paragraph division that Yemenites lack in Lev. 7:28; and (5) the shape of the *waw* in *šlwm* in Num. 25:12, which Yemenites write in the regular way while Ashkenazim have it "cut."

117. *Keter Torah* (Jerusalem: 1964).

118. *Shel'eilot uTeshuvot Yehaveh Da'at*, Vol. 6 (Jerusalem: O. Yosef), no. 56, pp. 289–294.

119. See also his *Yabia' Omer, Orah Hayyim* (Jerusalem: Porat Yosef, 1969), Vol. 5, p. 146, no. 47, sec. 5, and *Yalqut Yosef* (Jerusalem: O. Yosef, 1990), Vol. 2, pp. 139–166.

120. The data on spelling collected by Benjamin Kennicott and by Johann De Rossi in

Variae Lectiones Veteris Testamenti ... (Parma: 1784–1798) are very significant, if incomplete and too frequently inaccurate, but often they are ignored in favor of the more substantial textual divergences that have become evident since the eighteenth century and because their authors lost the support of modern scholars for having defended the theory of a single prototype from which all texts evolved. Their conclusions were summarized by Frederic Kenyon in *Our Bible and the Ancient Manuscripts*, 5th ed. (New York: Harper and Row, 1958), p. 71: "... the variants in the manuscripts were so negligible, and their conformity in peculiar forms and even of single letters was such, that all extant manuscripts had descended from a single archetype."

Note also Paul Kahle's typically disparaging tone in commenting on Kennicott's work in *The Cairo Geniza*, p. 5, followed by that of Moshe Goshen-Gottstein. Bleddyn J. Roberts was more to the point when, critiquing these eighteenth-century works, he observed: "Earlier Geniza manuscripts ... show a practical uniformity of consonantal transmission, but considerable variation of vocalization and of the use of *matres lectionis*," *The Old Testament Text and Versions* (Cardiff: University of Wales Press, 1951), p. 24.

121. The entire endeavor of textual restoration (emendation) has undergone profound changes throughout this century. Though many traditionalists will find Tov's *Textual Criticism of the Hebrew Bible* too radical for their tastes, it offers a highly responsible and relatively conservative approach to the subject, as does his *The Text-Critcal Use of the Septuagint in Biblical Research.*

122. Samuel David Luzzato is a good example of a traditionalist who was willing to emend nonpentateuchal texts; see Morris B. Margalies, *Samuel David Luzzatto: Traditionalist Scholar* (New York: Ktav, 1979), pp. 120–123. The follow-up to Marc Shapiro's article (mentioned earlier in note 5) in the *Torah U-Madda Journal* 5 (1994): 188, n. 6, effectively excommunicates Luzzatto, who, it seems, is now better left outside the canon of acceptable Orthodox writers, though it remains to be seen if this exclusion was necessitated more by the integrity of nineteenth-century Orthodox thinking or the expectations of its late twentieth-century followers.

123. See, for example, John Gray, *The Legacy of Canaan: The Ras Shamra Texts and Their Relevance to the Old Testament* (Leiden: E. J. Brill, 1965), and James Barr, *Comparative Philology and the Text of the Old Testament* (Oxford: Clarendon Press, 1968).

124. See M. Spiegleman, "The Truth of Torah: The Role of Textual Transmission," *Ten Da'at* 3, no. 2 (1989): 33–34, who wished to discuss these matters with high school students, and the responses by Sholom Carmy, "Teaching About Textual Transmission: How Important? How Necessary?" ibid. 3, no. 3 (1989): 44; Moshe Bernstein, "Textual Transmission, Continued," ibid. 4, no. 1 (1989): 35–36; and Sholom Carmy, "Textual Transmission: A Response," ibid., p. 37. While all of these writers admitted the legitimacy of the matter, the general thrust of the responses was to keep it quiet.

See further B. Barry Levy. "The State and Directions of Orthodox Bible Study," in *Modern Scholarship in the Study of Torah: Orthodox Forum IV*, ed. Shalom Carmy (Northvale, N.J.: Jason Aronson, 1996), pp. 67–68.

125. A classic presentation of this material is found in the first part of Moshe Soloveitchik and Zalman Rubasheff, *Toldot Biqoret HaMiqra'* (Berlin: Devir, 1925), reissued in Zalman Shazar (formerly Rubasheff), *MiPardes HaTanakh* (Jerusalem: Kiryat Sefer, 1979). See also Uriel Simon's, "Who was the Proponent of Lexical Substitution Whom Ibn Ezra Denounced as a Prater and a Madman?" in *Sefer Zikkaron LeEphraim Talmage*, ed. Barry Walfish (Haifa: Haifa University Press, 1993), pp. 217–232.

On the dating of the list of thirty-two hermeneutical principals, see Moshe Zucker, "*LePitron Ba'ayat Lammed Beit Middot uMishnat Rabbi Eliezer*," *Proceedings of the American Academy of Jewish Research*, Vol. 23 (1954), pp. 1–39; also Hermann L. Strack and

G. Stemberger, *Introduction to the Talmud and Midrash* (Minneapolis: Fortress, 1992), pp. 25–34.

126. See Emanuel Tov, *Textual Criticism of the Hebrew Bible*, and *The Text-Critical Use of the Septuagint in Biblical Research*, 2nd ed. (Jerusalem: Simor, 1997).

127. See Tov, *Textual Criticism of the Hebrew Bible*, pp. 55–57, and the literature cited there.

128. Anchor Bible commentaries on Psalms (Garden City N.Y.: Doubleday and Co., 1966–1970); Anton C. M. Blommerde, *Northwest Semitic Grammar and Job* (Rome: Pontifical Biblical Institute, 1969); K. J. Cathcart, *Nahum in the Light of Northwest Semitic* (Rome: Pontifical Biblical Institute, 1973); etc. Yitzchak Avishur has offered an evaluation of this approach and an extensive discussion of the relations between biblical and Canaanite psalms in *Studies in Hebrew and Ugaritic Psalms* (Jerusalem: Magnes Press, 1994).

129. Perhaps the most famous example of rabbinic withdrawal from an approved practice because of its use by non-Jews was the deletion of the Ten Commandments from the daily liturgy (BT Ber. 12a), but philosophy, comparative philology, and science, once considered indispensable adjuncts to Jewish thought, were jettisoned as they became too unwieldy or grew beyond the control of most rabbinic leaders. See further B. Barry Levy "On the Periphery," in *Students of the Covenant*, ed. David Sperling (Atlanta: Scholars Press, 1992), pp. 159–204, esp. pp. 164–172.

130. Mordechai Breuer may or may not qualify as a halakhic authority, but his claim that the author of *Shaʿagat Aryeh* was sensitive to certain redactional aspects of the composition of Chronicles had serious personal ramifications; "*Torat HaTeʿudot Shel Baʿal Shaʿagat Aryeh,*" *Megadim* 2 (1988): 9–22. On his contribution in general, see Meir Ekstein, "Rabbi Mordechai Breuer and Modern Orthodox Biblical Commentary," *Tradition* 33 (1999): 6–23.

131. In contrast to rabbinic conservatism in treating the Bible text, the traditional attitude toward emending rabbinic texts is much more open. Medieval and postmedieval authorities who studied from manuscripts were sensitive to the types of textual variations that appeared in different witnesses to mishnaic, midrashic, targumic, and talmudic teachings, and they routinely discussed them. In fact, the practice of emendation was so popular that some authorities banned it (see the statement by Rabbi Malakhi Cohen, *Yad Malakhi* (Berlin: E. Hertz, 1857; repr., Israel: Am Olam, 1964), Part I, p. 53a, and his sources).

Even so, the need to improve texts was quite apparent, as many writers from the past three centuries have continued to demonstrate. Note the textual changes routinely introduced into the Talmud by, for example, the Vilna Gaon, Rabbi Hayyim Bachrach, and Samuel Strashun, and the critical glosses of Raphael Rabbinovicz, *Diqduqei Soferim*, with letters of approbation from seven rabbis, including Solomon Kluger, Joseph Saul Nathanson, Jacob Ettlinger, and Isaac Elchanan (repr., New York: 1960); the systematic marginal notations in *Mishnayot Tifʾeret Yisrael* (repr., New York: Pardes, 1953), and the marginal notes in the Vilna edition of the Babylonian Talmud (Vilna: Romm, 1835–1854) and in the Zhitomir edition of the Palestinian Talmud (1860–1867). These were augmented by the brilliantly creative suggestions of Rabbi Barukh HaLevi Epstein, *Meqor Barukh* (New York: M. P. Press, 1954); by the important contributions of Rabbi Reuben Margoliot in his series of small books, many conveniently reprinted in recent years by Mossad HaRav Kook; by Israel Zvi Feintuch, *Mesorot VeNusehaʾot BaTalmud*, ed. Daniel Sperber (Ramat Gan: Bar Ilan University Press, 1985); and by many others.

On occasion, some rabbinic authorities have tried to invalidate the study of existing textual variants, e.g., *Qovetz Iggerot . . . Hazon Ish*, ed. S. Greeneman (Bene-Berak: S. Greeneman, 1956), Vol. 2, p. 37, no, 23—a text that has stimulated an extensive and far from uniformly positive response—but the vast effort by religious writers to restore and to publish proper editions of many early rabbinic texts, especially the new series of critical editions of the Mishnah and the Babylonian Talmud being prepared by Yad HaRav Herzog in Jerusalem, and the many volumes and journals that contain new or improved editions of classical texts, demonstrate how remote this attitude is from their thinking.

132. See further Doron Witztum, *HaMeimad HaNosaf* (Jerusalem: D. Witztum, 1989); Yitzchak Hirsch, *Yisrael, HaSod VeHaTakhlit* (Israel: I. Hirch, 1989); and *Discovery* (n.p.: Aish HaTorah, 1991). In *Remazim BaTorah BeShitat Dillug* (Herzliah: J. Furst, 1994), Joseph Furst has tried to demonstrate the antiquity of this approach to interpretation, including its extensive use by Rashi. Doron Witztum, Eliahu Rips, and Yoav Rosenberg have also offered an attempt at a serious mathematical validation of it, "Equidistant Letter Sequences in the Book of Genesis," *Statistical Science* 9, no. 3 (1994): 429–438.

More recently, Michael Drosnin's, *The Bible Code* (New York: Simon and Shuster, 1997), which contains a reprint of the article by Witztum et al., hit the *New York Times* best seller list and made the decoding craze a household term. Note also Robert M. Haralick and Matityahu Glazerson, *The Torah Codes and Israel Today* (Jerusalem: Lev Eliyahu, 1996). In *Yeshua* (Canada: Y. Rambsel, 1996), Yacov Rambsel has applied this same methodology to the search for Jesus and related christological teachings. An even newer presentation, Jeffrey Satinover's *Cracking the Bible Code* (New York: William Morrow, 1997), explores the decoding phenomenon within the context of modern cryptology.

Rabbi Norman Lamm has commented on the early presentations and the method in *Torah Umadda* (Northvale, N.J.: Jason Aronson, 1990), p. 47: "No amount of intellectual legerdemain or midrashic pyrotechnics—or even sophisticated but capricious computer analysis of sacred texts—can convince us that the Torah somehow possesses within itself the secrets of quantum mechanics, the synthesis of DNA, and the like." Note also Brendan McKay, Dror Bar-Natan, Maya Bar-Hillel, and Gil Kalai, "Solving the Puzzle," *Statistical Science* 14 (1999): 150–173, which contains a mathematical refutation of the codes procedures developed by Witztum et al., as well as an extensive bibliography.

133. As was already noted, one of the very few exceptions is Rabbi Yaakov Weinberg's *Fundamentals and Faith: Insights into the Rambam's Thirteen Principles*, cited earlier. Aryeh Kaplan's *Handbook of Jewish Thought* (New York: Maznaim [sic], 1979), an approximately 300-page listing of principles of Judaism, including several chapters (some 60 pages) on traditional attitudes about the Bible, is extremely cautious, despite its apparent openness.

I have dealt with the Orthodox reactions to the Bible's textual inconsistencies briefly in "On The Periphery: North American Orthodox Judaism and Contemporary Biblical Scholarship," pp. 169–170, and in an essay, "On Textual Integrity and Educational Integrity," to appear in a forthcoming book tentatively entitled *The Academy and the Hebrew Day School*, and I have taught and lectured about it for decades. But my impression of the discomfort with this issue felt by most members of this religious community, particularly the North American branch, has not changed much throughout this time. The request by *Orthodox Forum IV* for my article on "The State and Directions of Orthodox Bible Study," which advances this discussion; the publishing of a translation of Maori's important article in that same volume; and Marc Shapiro's extensively documented piece in the fourth volume of the *Torah U-Madda Journal*, as well as the supplementary treatment in the subsequent volume, alter this impression only slightly. (For this purpose, I omit Leiman's important survey, because it remains out of the Orthodox mainstream literature in a scholarly festschrift.)

It is too soon to know what if any lasting impact these efforts will have, but their very existence does suggest that at least some Orthodox publications are willing to sustain serious discussion of this once well-developed, subsequently suppressed, and therefore, for many people, still very troubling subject. Perhaps the most telling datum is the fact that hundreds of people attended sessions entitled "Orthodoxy and Biblical Criticism" and "Fixing God's Torah" at the Edah Convention in New York in 1999. Obviously many Orthodox Jews are starved for information about these subjects and seek it out when given the opportunity.

Two. Ibn Zimra's Responsum A

1. On the name, see H. J. Zimmels, *Rabbi David ibn abi Simra* (Breslau: 1932), p. 5, n. 2.

2. A list of published responsa and bibliography up to 1930 is found in Boaz Cohen, *Kuntras Ha-Teshubot* (Budapest: 1930; repr., Westmead: Gregg International, 1970), pp. 47 (no. 122), 67 (no. 491), 70 (no. 554), 135 (no. 1698), and index, *s.v. David b[en] r[av] Shelomo abi ibn [sic] Zimra'*. A later bibliography and detailed study of him and his work, especially the responsa, are found in Israel Goldman, *The Life and Times of Rabbi David Ibn Abi Zimra* (New York: Jewish Theological Seminary, 1970). Throughout his work, Goldman has identified the various communities with which Ibn Zimra corresponded.

A very extensive bibliography of Ottoman Jewry and related matters, as well as a survey of its history, can be found in Stanford J. Shaw, *The Jews of the Ottoman Empire and the Turkish Republic* (New York: New York University Press, 1991), but Shaw's treatment of rabbinic matters must be used very carefully. For example, on p. 101 he identifies Rabbi Elijah Mizrahi's mathematical work as *Sefer HaMisbat* (read: *HaMispar*) and reports that he wrote "a detailed commentary on Rashi's criticism of Maimonides, strongly defending the latter," which could be improved to "a detailed commentary on Rashi's Torah commentary, strongly defending it against the criticisms of Nahmanides."

3. About fifty of Ibn Zimra's Bible-related responsa have been republished in Adin Steinsaltz, *Perush HaMiqra' BeSifrut HaShe'eilot VeHaTeshuvot: Biblical Interpretation in the Responsa Literature, 8th–16th Centuries* (Jerusalem: Keter, 1978).

4. The responsa analyzed below are far from unknown to the scholarly world, but they have yet to receive the attention they deserve. In addition to their brief treatment by Goldman, the first is mentioned in *Yad Mal'akhi* (Berlin: Z. Hertz, 1857; repr., Israel: Am Olam, 1964), Part I, p. 42b, s.v., *ḥiluf*. The second has been discussed briefly by H. J. Zimmels in *Rabbi David ibn abi Simra*, p. 48, and by Louis Jacobs in *Theology in the Responsa Literature* (London: Routledge and Kegan Paul, 1975), pp. 119–120. The first, the second, and most of the fourth have been reprinted with punctuation, but without discussion, in Adin Steinsaltz, *Perush HaMiqra' BeSifrut HaShe'eilot VeHaTeshuvot.*

Jordan Penkower corrected a passage from Responsum B in "Maimonides and the Aleppo Codex," *Textus* 9 (1981): 40, n. 3, as did Sid Z. Leiman in *Tradition* 19 (1982): 303. Penkower also discussed a number of the responsa, including Responsum B, there and in *Jacob Ben Hayyim and the Rise of the Biblia Hebraica* (Hebrew University Dissertation, 1982). He has come closest to the proper elucidation of the material, but his focus on Ibn Adoniyah has kept him from fully analyzing Ibn Zimra's efforts. Other rabbinic discussions of these texts are cited later. The premodern work that explores the range of texts and issues closest to those with which I deal (and which I obtained only when my research was virtually complete) is *Devar Moshe: Yoreh De'ah, Hilkhot Sefer Torah* (Salonika: 1750), Vol. 3, no. 8, by Rabbi Hayyim Moses ben Solomon Amarillio (1695–1748).

5. Hebrew texts of Responsa A, B, and D can be found in *She'eilot uTeshuvot HaRaDBaZ*, Vols. 1–7 (repr., New York: Goldman—Otzar HaSefarim, 1967); responsum C is in a supplementary eighth volume, ed. Isaac Zvi Sofer (Bene-Berak: Et Sofer, 1975). Otherwise unidentified references to volumes and numbers of Ibn Zimra's responsa to be cited here are to these editions.

The translations have been subdivided and numbered for ease of reference. For example, A.3 refers to the third unit of Responsum A, translated in chapter 2; B.9, to the ninth unit of Responsum B, treated in chapter 3. Though these divisions reflect natural breaks in the flow of the text, they are not original with Ibn Zimra.

6. See the important collections of sources and analysis in David Rosenthal, "*Al Derekh Tippulam Shel Hazal BeHilufei Nusah BaMiqra'*," *Sefer Yitzhak Aryeh Zeligman*, ed. Yair

Zakovitz and Alexander Rofe (Jerusalem: E. Rubinstein, 1983), Vol. 2, pp. 395–417, and in Yeshayahu Maori's lengthy treatment of the later rabbinic rationales for this class of expositions, "*Midreshei Hazal KeEdut LeHilufei Nusah BaMiqra'*. . ." in *Iyyunei Miqra' uFarshanut*, Vol. 3 (1993) pp. 267–286, translated as "Rabbinic Midrash as Evidence for Textual Variants in the Hebrew Bible: History and Practice," in *Modern Scholarship in the Study of Torah: Contributions and Limitations*, ed. Shalom Carmy (Northvale, N.J.: Jason Aronson, 1996), pp. 101–130.

7. For example, Gen. 26:5; Ex. 2:5, 13:16, 14:2, 25:22, 25:31; Num. 7:11, 15:39; and Deut. 1:13, all cited and discussed by Abraham Baqrat in *Sefer HaZikkaron*. *Sefer HaZikkaron* was completed in 1507, published in Livorno in 1845, and reprinted in Jerusalem in 1968. It is also available in a well-annotated edition by Moshe Phillip (Petah Tiqvah: M. Phillip, 1985); see Phillip's introduction, pp. 28–29.

8. Samuel Abraham Poznanski, *Mavo Al Hakhmei Zarefat Mefarshei HaMiqra'* (Warsaw: 1913; repr., Jerusalem: 1965) p. civ; and Ephraim E. Urbach, *Ba'alei HaTosafot*, 4th ed. (Jerusalem: Mossad Bialik, 1980), index, s.v. Rabbi Judah ben Eliezer.

The passage has been translated from the vulgar edition, *Rabbotenu Ba'alei HaTosafot Al Hamishah Humshei Torah* (repr., Jerusalem: Lewin-Epstein, 1967), p. 23, and has been compared with the text published by Jacob Gellis in *Sefer Tosafot HaShalem*, Vol. 2 (Jerusalem: Hotza'at Mif'al Tosafot HaShalem, 1983), p. 289. According to Gellis, the material is found in a number of sources, but both his text and the vulgar one require some adjustment. The latter, for example, reads *baraita* where the former has the preferable *Bereshit Rabbah*; apparently the similarity of *b- r-* and *br-* led to the error; the former, on the other hand, has *qeṭoreṯ* where *Qeṭura* is to be expected.

9. The citation appears on p. 94 of *Hizquni: Perushei HaTorah LeRabbenu Hizqiah b[en] R[av] Manoah*, ed. Charles B. [Chaim Dov] Chavel (Jerusalem: Mossad HaRav Kook, 1982).

10. This is one of the other places in which Rashi discussed the plene or defective spelling of words. For published lists of over two dozen cases, see Saul Kleiman, *Yalqut Rashi* (Kansas City: Quality Printing and Publishing, 1942), pp. 408–417; actually there are many more.

The data provided by Gellis, ibid., n. 8, are reminiscent of the situation with *pilagšim*. Rashi texts that discuss spellings of *mezuzoṯ* as *mzzt*, *mzzwt*, *mzwzt*, and *mzwzwt* are available.

11. See Sid Z. Leiman, "Masorah and Halakhah: A Study in Conflict," in *Tehillah LeMoshe: Biblical and Judaic Studies in Honor of Moshe Greenberg*, ed. Mordechai Cogan, Barry L. Eichler, and Jeffrey H. Tigay (Winona Lake, Ind.: Eisenbrauns, 1997), pp. 291–306.

12. *Torah Shelemah* (Satmar: Z. Schwartz, 1909), Vol. 1, p. 126a, translated in chapter 1.

13. Zohar, III, 203b. The intention of this statement is somewhat obscure, but parallels to one or both of these terms can be found in the Zohar I, 4a, II, 96b, and III, 163a, and in *Zohar Hadash, Yitro* 36b. Another comparison of "upper" and "lower" academies appears in *Tiqqunei Zohar* 22, 63b. This recognition of differences between the heavenly and earthly Torahs should be compared with the Muslim treatment of the Qur'an, mentioned in chapter 1.

14. Daniel Parish, *Otzar HaZohar* (Jerusalem: Aleph Beit, 1977), 3: 585b–586a, lists some twenty passages from the Zohar that discuss plene or defective spellings. Variations between the masoretic text and that assumed by the Zohar have been discussed by Malakhi ben Ya'aqov HaKohen, *Yad Mal'akhi* (Berlin: E. Hertz, 1857; repr., Israel: Am Olam, 1964), Part I: *Kelalim*, pp. 42b–44a, and *Nitzutzei Orot* to Zohar III, 184a. See also *Re'ayah Mehemna*, Zohar III, 254a; and Abraham Jaffe, *Mishnat Avraham* (Jessnitz: 1868; repr., Jerusalem: 1968), p. 15.

15. Jacob Katz, *Halakhah VeKabbalah* (Jerusalem: Magnes, 1986); Louis Jacobs, *A Tree of Life: Diversity, Flexibility, and Creativity in Jewish Law* (Oxford: Oxford University Press, 1984), chap. 5. On Ibn Zimra and Kabbalah, see I. Goldman, *The Life and Times of Rabbi David Ibn Abi Zimra* (New York: Jewish Theological Seminary, 1970), pp. 70–74.

16. IV, no. 1172 (101).

17. The word *h-g-h* has a broad range of meanings in rabbinic literature, and even the more specific use here is sometimes equivocal. In some contexts I have been tempted to render it "emend," meaning willful and subjective changes in the text, but elsewhere it means "check" or "check and correct," i.e., "fix," something that was required, not to say much more positively received. In most places I have translated it "change."

18. Known also by many other names, but most commonly today as the Zohar; cf. Isaiah Tishby, *Mishnat HaZohar* (Jerusalem: Mossad Bialik, 1971), Vol. 1, pp. 37–38, "Names of The Zohar"; in the English translation by David Goldstein, *The Wisdom of the Zohar* (London: Oxford University Press, 1989), pp. 22–23.

19. The printed text of the responsum reads *'wtw*, but the context requires the defective spelling, *'tw*. The reference here is to Zohar, *Huqat*, III, 184a. The phrase "do not fear him" also appears in Deut. 3:2, in a review of the passage in Numbers, but it seems that the Zohar's discussion did not apply to it. Note the similar argument in Zohar, *Lekh Lekha*, I, 94a, applied to *'wtw* in 2 Sam. 15:25 (not in 1 Sam. 17, as cited by Barukh Halevi Epstein in *Torah Temimah* [New York: Goldman—Otzar HaSefarim, 1962] to Deut. 22:2, n. 14, a correction that escaped Jacob Moses Feldman, *Mesivat Nefesh* [Brooklyn: 1982]).

20. The independent phrase *'o<u>t</u> beri<u>t</u>*, "sign of the covenant," never occurs in the Bible, but *'o<u>t</u> ha-beri<u>t</u>* is found in Gen. 9:12 and 9:17, while *le-'o<u>t</u> beri<u>t</u>* is used in Gen. 9:13 and 17:11. Only the last refers to circumcision.

21. See Louis Ginzberg, *Legends of the Jews* (Philadelphia: Jewish Publication Society, 1938), index, s.v. "Og," for references, to which may be added the Neophyti Targum to Num. 21:34. An opinion cited by Bahya ben Asher at Num. 21:34 suggested that the Og of Moses' time was a descendent of Abraham's slave, also named Og.

22. Note also the story about how Rabbi Hayyim Ibn Attar frightened away an attacking lion; Louis Jacobs, *Holy Living: Saints and Saintliness in Judaism* (Northvale, N.J.: Jason Aronson, 1990), p. 109, and Jacob Milgram's discussion in *Anchor Bible: Leviticus* (New York: Doubleday, 1991), pp. 746–748.

23. The popular impact of the belief in circumcision's prophylactic properties may also be seen in the inclusion in the high holiday liturgy of the poem *Ki Hinei KaHomer BeYad HaYotzer*, which contains the refrain *la-beri<u>t</u> habbeṭ we-'al tefen la-yēṣer* (cf. Ps. 74:20 and BT R.H. 17b). Notwithstanding alternative explanations of this point by the appropriate commentaries or failure to discuss it at all, one must acknowledge the possible validity of a reading that sees this prayer as a supplication based on circumcision's being a sign of commitment to fight the inclination to sin through submission to one's sexual desires. Of course, this is far from the intention of the verse in Psalm 74, from which the refrain is derived and which most commentaries associate with the general patriarchal covenant(s), not specifically with circumcision. But a few writers do highlight the element of circumcision even here.

Daniel Goldschmidt's treatment of the poem is found in his *Mahzor LeYamim Nora'im*, Vol. 2 (Jerusalem: Qoren, 1970), p. 36; *Sefer Arugat HaBosem, Auctore R. Abraham b[en] R[av] Azriel*, ed. Ephraim E. Urbach, Vol. 3 (Jerusalem: Meqitze Nirdamim, 1962), pp. 493–494 and 552–553, does not discuss this interpretation. The kabbalistic commentary on Psalms by Rafael Immanuel Hai Ricchi (1688–1742), *Hoze Tziyyon* (Livorno: 1742), cited in Aaron Walden, *Miqdash Me'at* (Warsaw: 1890; repr., Israel: 1974), Vol. 1, p. 34, does. See also Elliot Wolfson, *Circle in the Square: Studies in the Use of Gender in Kabbalistic Symbolism* (Albany: State University of New York Press, 1995), chapter 2.

24. See, in addition to the standard grammatical handbooks, Cyrus H. Gordon, "The Substratum of Taqiyya in Iran," *Journal of the American Oriental Society* 97 (1977): 192, and Stefan C. Reif, *Shabbethai Sofer and his Prayer-Book* (Cambridge: Cambridge University Press, 1979), p. 24.

25. E.g., *Sefer HaKuzari* III, 24; *Teshuvot HaGeonim: Sha'arei Tzedeq* (Salonika: 1792), Vol. 4, no. 302; Rabbi Tzemah Duran's *She'eilot uTeshuvot Yakhin uVoaz* (Bar Ilan University Judaic Library) Vol. 1, no. 134; *She'eilot uTeshuvot Maharam Al-Ashqar* (Jerusalem: S. L. A. Publishers, 1988), no. 18, p. 62, col. b. The wording of the question accompanying the responsum of Rabbenu Nissim is typical: *we-'atta ba-'awonoṯenu 'aḥar še-niṯbaqšu ba-yešiḇa šel ma'ala, qamu ha-miṯḥakkemim we-raṣu le-hatiro. . . . She'eilot uTeshuvot HaRan*, ed. Aryeh L. Feldman (Jerusalem: Makhon Shalem, 1984), p. 38, no. 5; see the similar line in Rabbi David HaKohen's *She'eilot uTeshuvot HaRadakh* (Bar Ilan University Judaic Library), no. 17.

26. Jacob Al-Gazi, *Emet LeYa'aqov* (Livorno: 1774).

27. Meir Abulafia, *Masoret Seyag LaTorah* (Florence: Isaac Da Paz, 1750; repr., Israel: Zion, 1969), p. 8a; Menahem Meiri, *Qiryat Sefer*, ed. Moshe Herschler (Jerusalem: 1956; repr., Jerusalem: Makhon HaTalmud HaYisraeli HaShalem, 1965); Yedidyah Solomon Norzi, *Minhat Shai, Miqra'ot Gedolot: Sefer Otzar Perushim Al HaTorah* (repr., New York: Shulsinger, 1950), Num. 21:34.

28. *The Lisbon Bible of 1482* (Tel Aviv: Nahar-Miskal, 1988), p. 136a; Rabbinic Bible (Venice: Daniel Bomberg, 1524; repr., Jerusalem: Makor, 1972), 1: 358; Leningrad B19A (repr., Jerusalem: Makor, 1971), 1: 179; The Spanish Pentateuch of 1241, copied from Codex Hilleli (Jerusalem: Makor, 1974), Vol. 2, p. 370.

29. Johann De Rossi, *Variae Lectiones Veteris Testamenti . . .* (Parma: 1784–1798); Benjamin Kennicott, *Vetus Testamentum Hebraice cum Variis Lectionibus* (Oxford: 1776–1780); Solomon Ganzfried, *Kesset HaSofer* (Los Angeles: 1957); Samuel Rosenfeld, *Mishpahat Soferim* (Vilna: Romm, 1883) p. 63a.

30. Reproduced in Israel Yeivin, *Geniza Bible Fragments with Babylonian Massorah and Vocalization* (Jerusalem: Makor, 1973), Vol. 1, p. 135.

31. *The Massorah* (London: 1880; repr., New York: Ktav, 1975), Vol. 4, p. 162, no. 1432.

32. Jacob ben Asher, *Perush Ba'al HaTurim Al HaTorah LeRabbenu Ya'aqov bar Asher*, ed. Jacob Koppel Reinitz, 3rd ed., (Ben-Berak: J. Q. Reinitz, 1974) to Deut. 22:2. Baruch Halevi Epstein also suggests that *'tw* was spelled plene in some (Spanish?) medieval manuscripts; *Torah Temimah*, ad loc.

33. For example, in 4QEx^{f}, Ex. 40:9 and 13; David Noel Freedman and K. A. Mathews, *The Paleo-Hebrew Leviticus Scroll* (Winona Lake, Ind.: Eisenbrauns, 1985), p. 60.

34. Isaac Judah Yehiel Safran, *Heikhal HaBerakhah* (Lemberg: P. Balaban, 1869; repr., New York: Kelilat Yofi), Vol. 4, p. 149b.

35. At least in the Torah, the spelling of *'tw* is quite regular. In contrast, that of *'wtm*, "them," is not, and therefore it has been the subject of a fair amount of discussion. It was singled out for attention in the introduction to Nahmanides' Torah commentary, *Perush HaRamban Al HaTorah*, ed. Charles B. [Chaim Dov] Chavel (Jerusalem: Mossad HaRav Kook, 1962), p. 7. See also Solomon Frensdorff, *Massorah Gedolah* (Hanover: 1876; repr., New York: Ktav, 1968), p. 227; and Yedidyah Solomon Norzi, *Minhat Shai*, Gen. 15:19, Ex. 29:3, and Ezek. 20:21. Interesting as well are the midrashic treatments that read *'tm* (*'oṯam*) as *'attem*: Sifra, *Emor* no. 9; BT B.B. 21a; etc.

Note also the treatment of *'wtw* in the book of Judges by Menahem Cohen, *Miqra'ot Gedolot HaKeter* (Ramat Gan: Bar Ilan University Press, 1992), Introduction, pp. 13*–15*, and in "*Mahu Nusah HaMasorah uMah Heqef Ahizato BeToldot HaMesirah Shel Yemei HaBeinayim?*" *Iyyunei Miqra' uFarshanut* 2 (1986): 237–238; the more general discussion in Francis I. Anderson and A. Dean Forbes, *Spelling in the Hebrew Bible* (Rome: Biblical Institute Press, 1986), pp. 189–191; James Barr, *The Variable Spelling of the Hebrew Bible* (Oxford: Oxford University Press, 1989), pp. 158–161; and *Studies in Hebrew and Aramaic Orthography*, ed. David Noel Freedman, A. Dean Forbes, and Francis I. Anderson (Winona Lake, Ind.: Eisenbrauns, 1992), pp. 28–29.

36. I.e., note the spelling of *'yn*, perhaps punning on *'yn*. Rashi, ibid., end, associates this presentation, which suggests that *'yn* is a plene spelling of *'n*, with similar manipulations in BT Qid. 4a. See also *Tosafot Yom Tov*, M. Yev. 2:14; the sources cited in Alexander Kohut, *Aruch Completum* (Vienna: 1878–1892; repr., New York: Pardes, 1955), Vol. 6, p. 192, n. 2; and other commentaries to BT Qid. 4a and B.B. 115a, including Raphael Rabbinovicz, *Diqduqei Soferim* (repr., New York: Edison Lithographing, 1960), Baba Batra, p. 326, n. 40.

37. E.g., James Barr, *The Variable Spelling of the Hebrew Bible.*

38. On *ṣr*, see *Bereishit Rabbah* 61, 6, ed. Yehuda Theodor and Chanoch Albeck (Berlin: 1903; repr., Jerusalem: Wahrmann Books, 1965), Vol. 2, pp. 669–670; note the reference there to Abarbanel's commentary to Is. 23:7–8 and to Azariah De Rossi, *Me'or Einayim, Imrei Binah*, chap. 14, p. 200. On *tnynm*, see Gen. Rab. 6, 4 (Vol. 1, p. 52).

39. Samuel Jaffe Ashkenazi, *Yefei To'ar* (Fiorda: 1692; repr., Jerusalem: Wagshal, 1989), and Yehiel Mikhal of Glogau, *Nezer HaQadosh* (Jessnitz: 1719; repr., Israel: ca. 1991). General application is found in Abraham ben Meir Jacobs, *Haser uMale' BaTanakh* (Jerusalem: R. H. Cohen, 1977), and Mordecai S. Remland, *Leqet MiTanakh* (Brooklyn: J. Niselbaum, 1983). See also Jacob S. Weinfeld, *Mishnat Ya'aqov*; Elazar Bromer, *Mishpat Katuv*; and Yitzhaq ben Mordecai, *Em LaMiqra' VeLaMasoret*. These three small books interpret *Qere u-Ketib* and related matters (Jerusalem: Eshkol, 1978). An excellent sample of the different ways writers interpreted the words they observed to be spelled plene or defective can be culled from *Midrash Haserot ViYeterot*, ed. Solomon Wertheimer, *Battei Midrashot* (Jerusalem: Ketav VeSefer, 1968), pp. 203–232.

40. Gen. Rab., Vol. 1, p. 661; no geniza fragments of the passage were published by Moshe Sokoloff, *Qeta'ei Bereishit Rabbah Min HaGeniza* (Jerusalem: Israel Academy of Sciences and Humanities, 1982). Norzi, *Minhat Shai*, Gen. 25:6, provides a lengthy bibliography.

41. *Ariel: Rashi HaShalem* (Jerusalem: Makhon Harry Fischel, 1986), Vol. 1; Abraham Baqrat, *Sefer HaZikkaron*, ed. Moshe Phillip, pp. 135–136. Almost every late supercommentary on Rashi discussed *p(y)lgšyym*; in particular, see Solomon ben Judah of Hanau, in *Binyan Shelomo*, cited by Yitzchak Isaac Auerbach, *Be'er Rehovot* (Josefof: 1878), by Yehiel Michal of Glogau, *Nezer HaQodesh*, and by Chaim Dov [Charles B.] Chavel, *Perushei Rashi Al HaTorah*, ad loc. More recent is the discussion of Rabbi Shimon Schwab, *Ma'ayan Beit HaSho'eivah* (New York: Mesorah, 1994), p. 60.

42. Gellis, p. 289.

43. *Perush HaRoqeah Al HaTorah*, ed. Chaim Konyevsky, Vol. 1 (Bene-Berak: Yeshivat Ohel Yosef, 1978), p. 191.

44. BT San. 91a, Rashi; note the suggested emendation in Isaac ben Yehudah HaLevi's *Paneah Raza* (Israel: Makhon Torat HaRishonim, 1998), p. 120.

45. Cf. Gellis, no. 3, and Roqeah, the first citation noted as verse 6 (between verses 1 and 5); Isaiah Horowitz, *Shenei Luhot HaBerit* (repr., Jerusalem: 1968), p. 69b. On Samael, see Joseph Dan, "Samael and the Problem of Jewish Gnosticism," in *Perspectives on Jewish Thought and Mysticism*, ed. Alfred L. Ivry, Elliot R. Wolfson, and Allan Arkush (Amsterdam: Harwood, 1998), pp. 257–276.

46. *Humash HaRe'em*, ed. Moshe Phillip (Petah Tiqvah: 1994) ad loc. For an attempt at an explanation, see *Yefei To'ar*, ad loc.

47. Cf. Cyrus H. Gordon, *Ugaritic Textbook* (Rome: Pontifical Biblical Institute, 1967), pp. 103–104, and Mitchell Dahood, *The Anchor Bible: Psalms*, Vol. 3 (New York: Doubleday, 1970), pp. 382–383 and 408–409.

48. For further exploration of this interpretative approach, see the literature cited in n. 39.

49. This manuscript has been discussed by Christian David Ginsburg, *Introduction to the Massoretico-Critical Edition of the Hebrew Bible* (London: 1896; repr., New York: Ktav,

1966), pp. 569–573, and G. Margoliouth, *Catalogue of the Hebrew and Samaritan Manuscripts in the British Museum* (1899; repr., London: British Museum, 1965), pp. 52–53. Special thanks to Brad Sabin Hill for assisting me in examining the manuscript during my visit to the British Library.

50. The motif of treating Israel like a bride has a long and extensive history. One particularly interesting source is found in Todros ben Yosef HaLevi Abulafia's *Sha'ar HaRazim* (Bene-Berak: 1986) pp. 134–135, and Chajim Aryeh Erlanger's accompanying notes provide many medieval parallels; in the edition of M. Kushnir-Oron (Jerusalem: Mossad Bialik, 1989), p. 88. See also Elliot Wolfson, *Circle in the Square*, chap. 1.

51. Judah Calais, *Mesiah Ilmim* (Jerusalem: Horev, 1986). Cf. Joseph ben Issachar of Prague, *Yosef Da'at* (Prague: Gershom Katz, 1608) p. 130a, and especially Abraham Baqrat, *Sefer HaZikkaron*, ad loc.; also the comments of Zev Wolf Heidenheim, *Sefer Moda' LaBinah, Kollel Sefer Havanat HaMiqra'* (Vilna: 1927; repr., New York: Malkhut, 1969), p. 46b.

52. See further I, no. 446 and II, no. 596. Samples of this form of the letters, where both vertical parts of the *heh* touch the horizontal, are found in the ancient "Uzziah Inscription" in Solomon A. Birnbaum, *The Hebrew Scripts*, Vol. 2 (London: Paleographia, 1957), plate 88, and in later Hebrew manuscripts, passim; and in Hermann L. Strack, *The Hebrew Bible—Latter Prophets: The Babylonian Codex of Petrograd* (repr., New York: Ktav, 1971), passim. For further discussion of the rabbinic sources, see Menahem M. Kasher, *Torah Shelemah*, Vol. 22 (Jerusalem: American Biblical Encyclopedia Committee, 1967), pp. 163–166; *Mishnat Avraham*, chap. 23; Eliyahu Lichtenstein's introduction to Rabbenu Nissim's *Hidushei HaRan . . . Avodah Zarah* (Jerusalem: Mossad HaRav Kook, 1990), pp. 18–23; and Shraga Abramson, "*Al HaOt Het BaHalakhah*," *Mehqarim BeLashon* 5–6 (1992): 81–90.

53. See the similar comment by Rabbi Isaac bar Sheshet, *She'eilot uTeshuvot LeRabbi Yizhaq bar Sheshet*, ed. David Metzger (Jerusalem: Makhon Or HaMizrah, 1993), Vol. 1, pp. 150–152, no. 146.

Whether halakhah must conform to the Babylonian Talmud is an interesting, longstanding issue but beyond my present concern. In addition to the standard handbooks, see Zvi Hirsch Chajes, *Darkhei HaHora'ah*, in *Kol Sifrei HaMaharatz* (Jerusalem: Divrei Hakhamim, 1958), Vol. 1, and Louis Jacobs, *A Tree of Life*. It is clear from many sources that will be cited that, in the matter of the Bible's textual accuracy, the Babylonian Talmud was not the universally accepted final arbiter, though it did have some impact, and many post-talmudic rabbis who routinely drew upon it for other purposes took guidance from its scribal and textual information as well.

54. Hatam Sofer, *She'eilot uTeshuvot Hatam Sofer, Orah Hayyim* (repr., Jerusalem: Makor, 1970), Vol. 1, no. 52; see also *Liqutei He'arot Al Sefer Teshuvot Hatam Sofer* (Jerusalem: 1969), Vol. 1, *Orah Hayyim*, p. 82, which dates the responsum to early in 5575 (i.e., late 1814 or early 1815).

Additional support for this position is found among Sofer's followers in *She'eilot uTeshuvot Maraham Schick, Yoreh De'ah* (repr., New York: 1961), no. 254, and in Akiva Sofer's *She'eilot uTeshuvot Da'at Sofer* (Jerusalem: S. B and Y. L. Sofer, 1965), p. 13, no. 19.

55. *She'eilot uTeshuvot Hatam Sofer, Qovetz Teshuvot* (Jerusalem: Makhon Hatam Sofer, 1973), no. 55; *Liqutei Teshuvot Hatam Sofer . . . SheLo Nidpesu BeTokh Shishah Helqei Sifro HaGadol* (London: n.d.) p. 33, no. 35. Procedures for the recitation of a blessing by the purchaser or the writer of a Torah scroll are discussed by Shalom Joseph Klein in *Sefer Qol Soferim*, repr. in *Sefer Liqutei Sifrei Setam*, 6th ed. (Jerusalem: 1981) p. 41, par. 6. Following Rabbi Moses Schick, the writer suggested that a person faced with the opportunity to recite such a blessing do so over the Torah and a new garment or fruit to avoid any legal objection to reciting it only because of the Torah. *Sefer Liqutei Sifrei Setam* also contains a series of prayers and confessions recited by some scribes in conjunction with their work. Two un-

numbered pages near the end of the volume contain blessings to be recited by scribes. A typed, photomechanically reproduced note found at the bottom of one page attributes them to *Em LaMasoret*, written by the "the saintly" Aryeh Leb Harif, who presumably recited them, but warns the reader that, according to the operative halakhah, they should not be recited. For a summary of the various halakhic positions, see *Mishnat Avraham*, chap. 4, pp. 44–45.

56. BT B.M. 18b, 27a, and 28a.

57. Rav Hai Gaon, Commentary to Haggigah, in B. M. Lewin, *Otzar HaGeonim* (Jerusalem: Hebrew University, 1932), Haggigah, Commentaries, pp. 59–60.

58. Rav Sherira Gaon, *Megillat Setarim*, ibid., Haggigah, pp. 59–60; see also *Sefer HaEshkol*, ed. Chanoch Albeck (repr., Jerusalem: Wagshall, 1984), Book I, pp. 157–162 and notes. Hai's statement has been expanded and clarified in various medieval texts, which demonstrates its popularity; details are provided by Lewin and Albeck.

59. *Otzar HaGeonim*, Haggigah, Commentaries, pp. 59–60.

60. On the authority of Midrash, see Maimonides, *Guide for the Perplexed* III, 43; the essay attributed to Abraham ben HaRambam, printed in the beginning of *Ein Yaʿaqov* (repr., New York: Pardes, 1955) and in Reuben Margoliot, *Rabbenu Avraham ben HaRambam* (Jerusalem: Mossad HaRav Kook, 1953), pp. 79–98; Nahmanides' disputation with Pablo Christiani, ed. Chayim Dov [Charles B.] Chavel in *Kitvei HaRamban* (Jerusalem: Mossad HaRav Kook, 1973), Vol. 1, pp. 308–309; and Zvi Hirsch Chajes, *Darkhei HaHoraʾah* and *Mavo HaTalmud*, both printed in *Kol Kitvei HaMaHaRaTz*, Vol. 1, the latter translated as *The Student's Guide Through the Talmud*, 2nd ed. (New York: Feldheim, 1960), chaps. 17–32.

Also Saul Lieberman, *Shekiʿin* (Jerusalem: Wahrmann, 1970), pp. 81–83; Marc Saperstein, *Decoding the Rabbis: A Thirteenth-Century Commentary on the Aggadah* (Cambridge: Harvard University Press, 1980), chap. 1; Jeremy Cohen, *The Friars and the Jews: The Evolution of Medieval Anti-Judaism* (Ithaca, N.Y.: Cornell University Press, 1982); Marvin Fox, "Nahmanides on the Status of Aggadot: Perspectives on the Disputation at Barcelona, 1263," *Journal of Jewish Studies* 40 (1989): 95–109; and Robert Chazan, *Barcelona and Beyond: The Disputation of 1263 and Its Aftermath* (Berkeley: University of California Press, 1992), pp. 142–157.

61. The wording is somewhat clumsy, but almost identical to that in Ben Adret's published text, which states, ". . . *lefi še-neḥlequ ba-meqomoṯ ba-ʾaraṣoṯ ʿal pi ḥaḵamēhem*." The wording cited by Ibn Zimra is " . . . *lefi še-neḥlequ bi-meqomoṯēhem be-ʾarṣoṯam ʿal pi ḥaḵamēhem*." Note the similar construction, *we-ʿal ken neḥlequ be-ʾarṣoṯam li-meqomoṯam* . . . , in Ben Adret's response to a Christian in *Hidushei HaRashba* . . . *Perushei HaHaggadot*, ed. A. Feldman (Jerusalem: Mossad HaRav Kook, 1991) p. 148.

62. *Teshuvot HaRashba HaMeyuhasot LeHaRamban* (Warsaw: I. Goldman, 1883).

63. See Moshe Goshen-Gottstein, "The Rise of the Tiberian Bible Text," in *Biblical and Other Studies*, ed. Alexander Altmann (Cambridge: Harvard University Press, 1962), pp. 79–122; I. Yeivin, *Introduction to the Tiberian Masorah* (Missoula, Mont.: Scholars Press, 1980), pp. 141–145; Eliezer Lipshuetz, "Mishael ben Uzziel's Treatise on the Differences between Ben Asher and Ben Naphtali," and the introduction to the same, *Textus* 2 (1962): Heb. 1–58, and 4 (1964): 1–29.

64. Cf. Yeivin, *Introduction*, pp. 139–141.

65. Abraham Baqrat, *Sefer HaZikkaron*, ed. M. Phillip, p. 135, n. 5.

66. Hayyim Moses Amarillio, *Devar Moshe: Yoreh Deʿah, Hilkhot Sefer Torah*, Vol. 3, p. 23b, col. 1.

67. The printed text of Ben Adret reads, ". . . like *qrnwt/qrnt* and like *bskt, ltwtpt, wbn ʾyn lw*"; Paris Manuscript no. 411 of Ben Adret's responsa (p. 181) reads, "*kqrnt, qrnt, qrnwt*," as do various medieval discussions. Perhaps *lṭwṭpt* has been omitted by Ibn Zimra or a scribe, and the double or triple phrases are preferable: ". . . and like *bskt* [/ *bskwt*, and like *lṭwṭpwt*]/*lṭwṭpt*,

[and like] *wbn 'yn lw*." The printed text of the question to Ibn Zimra does not ask about *lṭṭpt*, but it is included in Meiri's list also (see chapter 6, where the texts are translated), and it was mentioned by several other writers. The phrase *wbn 'yn lw* also appears in Deut. 25:15, but the reference in Numbers is intended. These double texts could have been taken by scribes or printers as dittographies that required correction, as probably happened in the many places where the quotation *wbn 'yn lw*, usually the last item in a series, really should be introduced with a conjunction, *w-wbn*.

68. The interpretation of *me'ēn Bile'am* attempts to differentiate between *m'n* and *m'yn*. For further discussion, see Jacob ben Asher, *Perush Ba'al HaTurim Al HaTorah*, ed. J. Reinitz, Vol. 2, p. 328, nn. 12–13.

69. The text here says *mšmšt*, but the correct reading, found in Ibn Zimra's quotation, is *mmšmšt*.

70. The abbreviation *r- l-* is notorious for misleading copyists, printers, and interpreters, particularly since Resh Laqish and Rabbi Levi lived in approximately the same time and place. For another example, see B. Barry Levy, "Why Bar-naš Does Not Mean 'I'," in *Sefer Zikkaron LeEphraim Talmage*, ed. Barry Walfish (Haifa: Haifa University Press, 1993), p. 97, n. 12.

71. Note that here the text speaks of one of the "sages," *ḥakamim*, while the original reference in A.1 is to *eḥad min ha-mitḥakkemim*, "one of the self-designated sages." This reflects the perspective of those who emended the Torah scrolls, who took their leader—who is being paraphrased here—to be a sage, not the assumption that *ḥakam* and *mitḥakkem* are interchangeable or that Ibn Zimra slipped or had a change of heart.

72. Taken from BT Meg. 3a, where it appears as the statement of Jonathan ben Uzziel about his having translated the books of the Prophets.

73. This echoes a statement by Qirqisani (early tenth century), who attributed to the rabbis the belief that "the Torah which is in the hands of the people (of Israel) is not the one brought down by Moses, but is a new one composed by Ezra, for, according to them, the one brought down by Moses perished and was lost and forgotten." See further Leon Nemoy, "Al-Qirqisani's Account of the Jewish Sects and Christianity," *Hebrew Union College Annual*, Vol. 7 (1930), pp. 331–332, from which this translation is excerpted; Moshe Perlmann, "The Medieval Polemics between Judaism and Islam," in *Religion in a Religious Age*, ed. Solomon D. Goitein (Cambridge: Association for Jewish Studies, 1974), pp. 103–138; *Encyclopaedia Judaica*, Vol. 14, col. 658; Hava Lazarus-Yafe, *Intertwined Worlds: Medieval Islam and Bible Criticism* (Princeton, N.J.: Princeton University Press, 1992); and Camilla Adang, *Muslim Writers on Judaism and the Hebrew Bible: From Ibn Rabban to Ibn Hazm* (Leiden: E. J. Brill, 1995).

74. In BT Yoma 69b, the phrase is applied to the Scribes, to whom much of the early "masoretic" activity was often attributed.

75. Note the attitude in the letter addressed to Hai Gaon in B. M. Lewin, *Otzar HaGeonim, Hagigah*, Responsa, p. 17, preserved in *Commentar zum Sepher Jezira von R. Jehuda b. Barsilai*, ed. Solomon Zalman Hayyim Halberstam (Berlin: 1855; repr., Jerusalem: Makor, 1970) p. 104.

76. Jordan Penkower, *Textus* 9 (1981): 40–41; Sid Z. Leiman, *Tradition* 19 (1982): 303. This suggestion was also discussed at some length and rejected by Rabbi Hayyim Moses Amarillio, *Devar Moshe: Yoreh De'ah, Hilkhot Sefer Torah*, Vol. 3, pp. 23b–24a.

77. Ibid., p. 23a, col. 1.

78. Hasan in "*Iggeret HaSofer Rabbi Abraham Hasan MiSoloniqi*," *Sefunot* 11 (1971–1978): 213–221.

79. *Beit David*, p. 85a, col. b.

80. Israel Jacob Al-Gazi, *Sefer Emet LeYa'aqov: HaMishpat HaShelishi* (Livorno: 1774).

81. *Sifrei HaHida* (Jerusalem: Havatzelet, 1986), *LeDavid Emet*, chap. 11, pp. 18–19.

82. *Tur: Yoreh De'ah*, no. 275 (end); which is also responsum no. 14 in *Teshuvot HaRashba*, ed. Hayyim Zalman Dimitrovsky (Jerusalem: Mossad HaRav Kook, 1990), Vol. 1, part 1, p. 51, and in other texts cited and translated below.

83. Elijah ben Azriel of Vilna, author of *Me'orei Or*, cited by his student, Jonah Landsofer, in *Mikhtav MeEliyahu*, a commentary on Lonzono's *Or Torah* (Hamburg: 1738), p. 7a, Gen. 25:6.

84. E.g., those noted by Rabbi Akiva Eiger, *Gilyon HaShas*, BT Shab. 55b, translated in chapter 8.

85. Cf. C.7; BT Yom. 33a; Marcus Jastrow, *A Dictionary of the Targumim, The Talmud Babli and Yerushalmi, and the Midrashic Literature* (1903; repr., New York: Jastrow, 1967), *s.v. gmr'*; Eliezer Ben-Yehudah, *Milon HaLashon HaIvrit HaYeshanah VeHaHadashah* (Jerusalem: 1912; repr., New York: T. Yosseloff, 1959), *s.v. gmr'*; and Chanoch Albeck, *Mavo LaTalmud* (Tel Aviv: Devir, 1969), pp. 3–7.

86. *Migdal David: Sefer HaMitzvot*, ed. Moshe Herschler (Jerusalem: Makhon Shalem, 1982), p. 94.

87. *She'eilot uTeshuvot Maharam Halava*, ed. Moshe Herschler (Jerusalem: Makhon Shalem, 1987), p. 171.

88. Meiri's commentary on Qiddushin was edited by Abraham Sofer (Jerusalem: A. Schrieber, 1963).

89. *Sefer HaTashbetz* (Lemberg: 1891; repr., Tel Aviv: Offstat Yisrael Ameriqa, n.d.), Vol. 3, no. 160.

90. E.g., BT Men. 42a, cf. Rashi, ad loc.

91. *Tosafot HaShalem*, Vol. 2 (Jerusalem: Mif'al Tosafot HaShalem, 1983), p. 91.

92. See further the lengthy discussion of the text of Rashi in *Minhat Shai*, ad loc.

93. For additional examples of the Zohar's line of reasoning found in the classical exegetical literature, see Menahem M. Kasher, *Torah Shelemah*, Vol. 19 (New York: American Biblical Encyclopedia Society, 1959), pp. 369–373, and Abraham Joshua Heschel, *Torah Min HaShamayyim BaIspaqlariah Shel HaDorot* (London: Soncino, 1965), Vol. 2, pp. 123–145.

94. *LeDavid Emet*, p. 18.

95. This is directed largely at a responsum of Rabbi Judah Mintz, part of which is translated in chapter 6.

96. *Beit David*, p. 88a, col. a–b.

Three. Ibn Zimra's Responsum B

1. III, no. 594.

2. The text is a little rough at this point, and Ibn Zimra's Hebrew style is far from inspiring, but *kl mh š'th rw'h šhšnwyym* looks like an error. Perhaps *šhšynwym* should be changed to *še-hem šinnuyim* or *me-ha-šinnuyim*.

3. "Halakhah to Moses from Sinai" is here translated according to its literal meaning, but many other interpretations have been offered; see the summary in *Intziqlopedia Talmudit* (Jerusalem: *Hotza'at Intziqlopedia Talmudit*, 1959), Vol. 9, col. 365–387. Over the years, the position of Maimonides (1135–1204)—who claimed that such laws were not subject to dispute—and that of Rabbenu Asher ben Yehiel (ca. 1250–1327)—who interpreted the phrase as "a matter as clear as a law to Moses at Sinai" but obviously not really Sinaitic (*Hilkhot Miqva'ot*, chap. 1)—have stimulated lengthy and heated debates. For some continuation of the classical rabbinic discussion, see the presentations in Zechariah Frankel, *Darkhei HaMishnah* (Breslau: 1859; repr., Tel Aviv: Sinai, 1959), chap. 1; the sharp response by Samson Raphael Hirsch in *Jeschurun* (1860–1861), translated in *Samson Raphael Hirsch: The Collected Writings*, Vol. 5

(New York: Feldheim, 1988), pp. 229–239; Reuben Margaliot, *Yesod HaMishnah VeArikhatah*, 3rd ed. (Jerusalem: 1933; repr., Jerusalem: Mossad HaRav Kook, 1988?), pp. 40–43; Joseph B. Soloveitchik, *Shiurim LeZekher Abba Mari ZaL*, Vol. 1 (Jerusalem: Y. D. Soloveitchik, 1983), pp. 224–239; and David Weiss Halivni, "Reflections on Classical Jewish Hermeneutics," *Proceedings of the American Academy for Jewish Research*, Vol 62 (1996), reworked in *Revelation Restored: Divine Writ and Critical Responses* (Boulder, Col.: Westview Press, 1997), pp. 54–75. For treatment of the term by Nachman Krochmal, see Jay M. Harris, *Nachman Krochmal: Guiding the Perplexed of the Modern Age* (New York: New York University Press, 1991), pp. 246–247. For further discussion and bibliography, see Menahem Elon, *Jewish Law: History, Sources, Principles*, 2nd ed. (Jerusalem: Magnes, 1978), pp. 192–194.

4. The identity of this verse is uncertain. The most likely choice is Ruth 2:11, "And Boaz spoke up and said to her: 'It has been told to me of (='*et*) all that you did with your mother-in-law'," but the texts are divided. Rabbenu Nissim (BT Ned., ad loc.) noted that '*et* appears as a regular word; our texts lack it altogether. The Vilna Gaon deleted the entire phrase from the Gemara, but many manuscripts contain it. Cf. *Massekhet Nedarim Im Shinuyei Nusḥa'ot MiTokh Kitvei Yad. . .*, ed. Moshe Herschler, Vol. 1 (Jerusalem: Makhon HaTalmud HaYisraeli HaShalem, 1985), ad loc., and Alexander Sperber, *A Historical Grammar of the Hebrew Language* (Leiden: E. J. Brill, 1966), p. 494.

5. There is some textual confusion about '*ly* being *ly* here and in the next entry, but most witnesses support the former.

6. The identification of this reference has been hampered by a number of long-standing problems, including texts that read *z't* instead of *w't*; see Loewinger's discussion in his prolegomenon to the reprint of Victor Aptowitzer's *Das Schriftwort in der Rabbinischen Literatur* (New York: Ktav, 1970), pp. xix–xxii. A similar error has interfered with the text of B.6, where Ibn Zimra identified *z't* as a passage in Jeremiah; the printed text reads *z't* (presumably in Deut. 6:1), when it should have *w't*, referring to Jer. 32:11.

Read by itself, this verse seems to require *we-'et̲* before *ha-miṣwa*, parallel to the other uses of '*et̲* in the verse—'*et̲ sefer ha-miqna*, '*et̲ he-ḥat̲um*, and *we-'et̲ ha-galui* (cf. the reading in Jer. 32:14—'*et̲ sefer ha-miqna ha-ze, we-'et̲ he-ḥat̲um, we-'et̲ sefer ha-galui ha-ze*), but this assumes that *ha-miṣwa we-ha-ḥuqqim* continue the series. Christian David Ginsburg, in *Introduction to the Massoretico-Critical Edition of the Hebrew Bible* (London: 1896; repr., New York: Ktav, 1966), p. 316, noted that the Leningrad manuscript has *Ket̲ib̲—w't hmṣwh, Qere—we-ha-miṣwa*. A great deal of evidence from Talmud manuscripts supports a reading of *we-'et̲ ha-nefeš*; see Herschler, pp. 321–322. The phrase '*et̲ ha-miṣwa* also appears in Josh. 22:5 and 1 Kings 13:12, while *we-'et̲ ha-miṣwa* is found in 1 Kings 2:43.

7. Let the archer not draw his bow," Jer. 51:3 (reading '*l* rather than '*l*), where a presumed dittography *ydrwk/ydrwk* is corrected by omission of one word, usually the second.

8. See Herschler, p. 322, and Ginsburg, *Introduction*, p. 316.

9. Perhaps *l'*, "not," should be emended to '*l'*, "rather." If so, the subsequent words should be translated "adds or deletes."

10. Presumably, Ibn Zimra spoke only of the four categories of masoretic notes mentioned in Ned. 37b. In his prolegomenon, Loewinger has also compared the lists of the last two phenomena in the manuscripts of the Talmud and various masoretic works and has shown that both vary from text to text. He concluded that "the absence of a number of examples which appear in the Masoretic literature from the list in the Talmud is in part due to the differences between the Bible manuscripts used by the Amoraim and those used by the Palestinian Masoretes" (p. xxv). This may have been anticipated by Ibn Zimra, who referred to the Nedarim passage as being in "our Talmud," edited in Babylonia, in contrast to the masoretic lists, which are of Palestinian origin; but this is a common way of citing the Babylonian Talmud and the distinction may not have been intended.

11. Moshe Herschler, *Nedarim*, Vol. 1, pp. 318–322; the reader is encouraged to examine all of the variants, the parallels, and Herschler's other references. The supplementary volume, *Hagahot VeHashelamot MiKitvei Yad LeMasekhet Nedarim* (Jerusalem: Makhon HaTalmud HaYisraeli HaShalem, 1985), contains fewer important variants to this passage.

12. Israel Yeivin, *Introduction to the Tiberian Massorah* (Missoula, Mont.: Scholars Press, 1980), p. 52, no. 92.

13. Ed. Yehudah Theodor and Chanoch Albeck (Jerusalem: Wahrmann, 1965), p. 518.

14. See further Ginsburg, *Introduction*, p. 308; Yeivin, *Introduction*, para. 92; Eduard Yechezkel Kutscher, in *HaLashon VeHaReqa' HaLeshoni Shel Megillat Yesha'yahu HaSheleimah MiMegillot Yam HaMelah* (Jerusalem: Magnes, 1959), pp. 343–355.

15. Note also Ibn Janach's comment on *ha-ša'ar ha-taḥtona* (Ezek. 40:19), which suggests that the final *heh* is unnecessary; *Sefer HaRiqmah*, ed. Michael Wilensky (Berlin: 1929; repr., Jerusalem: HaAkademiah LaLashon HaIvrit, 1964), Vol. 1, p. 94.

16. On the limited value of such numerical designations, see Ginsburg, *The Massorah*, Vol. 4, *Waw*, 17h. In his *Introduction*, p. 309, Ginsburg listed a dozen additional verses where the evidence shows a problem with the *waw*, but it is unclear if any masoretic sources associated all of these other verses with the concept of Iṭṭur Soferim. The variants, plus or minus the *waw*, may merely reflect equally acceptable syntactic possibilities; and the fact that four of the five cases cited by the Talmud are related to a particular usage of the word *'aḥar/we-'aḥar* supports a claim for the limited range of the phenomenon. A summary of early discussions of Iṭṭur Soferim, including the precise identity of this reference, is found in *Minhat Shai* to Num. 12:14, where the phrase *we-'aḥar tē'asēf* appears.

17. In early Masorah manuscripts, *Qere u-Keṯiḇ* variants were often marked on the relevant page through the placing of a marker such as two dots (..) or such as a final *nun* in the margin opposite the appropriate place in the text; the actual *Qere* might be found, if at all, in a list added to the end of the manuscript. See further Yeivin, *Introduction*, pp. 52–53.

18. See also the references listed by Herschler, ad loc.

19. *Haqdamot HaRambam LaMishnah*, ed. I. Shailat (Jerusalem; Ma'aliyot, 1992), p. 38 (Arabic text, pp. 336–337). See the list of cases taken from *She'eilot uTeshuvot Maharam Halavah* translated here in chapter 6; also the discussion by Rabbi Yair Chaim Bachrach, *She'eilot uTeshuvot Havot Ya'ir* (Lemberg: 1896; repr., Jerusalem: 1986) no. 192 (between 191 and 193, but actually labeled 199).

20. Particular deference to Maimonides is seen in I, no. 229 and IV, no. 1176. The best systematic presentation of Ibn Zimra's thinking is I. Goldman, *The Life and Times of Rabbi David Ibn Abi Zimra* (New York: Jewish Theological Seminary, 1970).

21. *Hidushei HaRashba: Perushei HaHaggadot*, ed. A. Feldman (Jerusalem: Mossad HaRav Kook, 1991), p. 34.

22. See further, W. E. Barnes, "Ancient Corrections in the Text of the Old Testament," *Journal of Theological Studies* 1 (1900): 387–414, repr. in *The Canon and Masorah of the Hebrew Bible*, ed. Sid Z. Leiman (New York: Ktav, 1974); Saul Lieberman, *Hellenism in Jewish Palestine* (New York: Jewish Theological Seminary, 1950), pp. 28–37; Carmel McCarthy, *The Tiqqune Soferim and Other Theological Corrections in the Masoretic Text of the Old Testament* (Goettingen: Vandenhoeck and Ruprecht, 1981), the most extensive tabulation to date; Leon Nemoy, "Al-Qirqisani's Account of the Jewish Sects and Christianity," *Hebrew Union College Annual* 7 (1930): 60; and Jeremy Cohen, *The Friars and The Jews* (Ithaca, N.Y.: Cornell University Press, 1982), pp. 148–153; Menahem M. Kasher, *Torah Sheleimah*, Vol. 29, pp. 133–136; Abraham Joshua Heschel, *Torah Min HaShamayim BeIspaqlariah Shel HaDorot* (London: Soncino, 1965), Vol. 2, pp. 375–377, *še-kinna ha-kaṯuḇ*.

23. Copies of the Samaritan Pentateuch sometimes have the owner's name worked into the marginal letters of one column in order to create a permanent sign of ownership and thus

to prevent theft. Some Torah scrolls are written so that every column begins with *waw*, except six that spell out *b-y-h š-m-w* and thereby add a divine name. Gen 1:1, Gen. 49:8, Ex. 14:28, Ex. 34:11, and Num. 24:5 contain the first five exceptional letters. It is not clear how the sixth example can be differentiated from all the other columns that begin with *waw*—unless this was in Torah scrolls not laid out with a *waw* at the top of each colume—but it is sometimes listed as Deut. 31:28.

24. As, for example, in the appendices to Meir Abulafia, *Masoret Seyag LaTorah* (Florence: Isaac Da Paz, 1750; repr., Israel: Zion, 1969), beginning on page 84a.

25. *Sefer HaZikkaron* to Gen. 18:22, p. 123.

26. See *Sefer HaIqqarim* (repr., New York: Pardes, 1963), Book III, chap. 22, p. 247; critically edited and translated by I. Husik as *Sefer HaIkkarim* (Philadelphia: Jewish Publication Society, 1930), Vol. 3, p. 200.

27. See Salo W. Baron, *A Social and Religious History of the Jews* (Philadelphia: Jewish Publication Society, 1957), Vol. 5, chap. 24, "Socioreligious Controversies," esp. pp. 86–94 and notes; Yosef Hayim Yerushalmi, *From Spanish Court to Italian Ghetto* (New York: Columbia University Press, 1971), pp. 422–432; and W. Adler, "The Jews as Falsifiers: Charges of Tendentious Emendation in Anti-Jewish Christian Polemic," *Jewish Quarterly Review Supplement* (Philadelphia: Annenberg Research Institute, 1990), pp. 1–27. *Intertwined Worlds: Medieval Islam and Bible Criticism*, by Hava Lazarus-Yafeh (Princeton, N.J.: Princeton University Press, 1992), offers an excellent analysis of many dimensions of the ways in which Moslem writers criticized the Bible, including its transmission. Unfortunately, her presentation is limited to earlier medieval writers and provides no insight into these activities during the sixteenth century.

28. His *Ifham al-Yahud*, "Silencing the Jews," has been translated by Moshe Perlmann in *Proceedings of the American Academy of Jewish Research*, Vol. 32 (1964). See also D. S. Powers, "Reading/Misreading One Another's Scriptures: Ibn Hazm's Refutation of Ibn Nagrella al-Yahudi," in *Studies in Islamic and Judaic Traditions* (Atlanta: Scholars Press, 1986), pp. 109–121.

29. Interesting discussion of the interaction of Jews and Muslims over the Bible is found in Steven M. Wasserstrom, *Between Muslim and Jew: The Problem of Symbiosis Under Early Islam* (Princeton, N.J.: Princeton University Press, 1995), particularly pp. 136–156.

30. Even so, one cannot lose sight of the virtually constant though far from universal use of Jewish resources by Christian exegetes to help them understand the Bible. Note, for example, Herman Hailperin, *Rashi and the Christian Scholars* (Pittsburgh: University of Pittsburgh Press, 1963), esp. pp. 103–264; A. Grabois, "The Hebrew Text of the Old Testament and Christian Scholarship: A Chapter in XIIth Century Jewish–Christian Relations" (Heb.) in A. Gilboa et al., ed., *Studies in the History of the Jewish People and the Land of Israel in Memory of Zvi Avneri* (Haifa: University of Haifa Press, 1970), pp. 97–116, and the literature cited there; Sarah Kamin and Avrom Saltman, eds., *Secundum Salomonem: A Thirteenth Century Latin Commentary on the Song of Songs* (Ramat Gan; Bar Ilan University Press, 1989); and Sarah Kamin, *Jews and Christians Interpret the Bible* (Jerusalem: Magnes, 1991).

In Reformation times the interaction with Jewish Bible interpretations and other rabbinic works became even more extensive. The Christian involvement with the publishing of the early Rabbinic Bibles is a case in point, but some Christian interpreters explored this literature extensively. See, for example, Harris Francis Fletcher, "Milton and Rashi," *Journal of German and English Philology* 27 (1928): 300–317; idem, *Milton's Rabbinical Readings* (Urbana: University of Illinois Press, 1930); G. Hobbs, "Martin Bucer on Psalm 22: A Study in the Application of Rabbinic Exegesis by a Christian Hebraist," in *Histoire de l'exegese au XVIe siecle*, ed. O. Fatio and P. Fraenkel (Geneva: Librairei Droz, 1978), pp. 144–163; G. Lloyd Jones, *The Discovery of Hebrew in Tudor England: A Third Language*

(London: Manchester University Press, 1983); J. Friedman, *The Most Ancient Testimony: Sixteenth-Century Christian-Hebraica in the Age of Renaissance Nostalgia* (Athens: Ohio University Press, 1983); Aaron L. Katchen, *Christian Hebraists and Dutch Rabbis* (Cambridge: Harvard University Press, 1984); H. F. van Rooy, "Calvin's Genesis Commentary—Which Bible Text Did He Use?" *Our Reformational Tradition* (Solverton: Potchefstroom University for Christian Higher Education, 1984), pp. 203–215; William McKane, *Selected Christian Hebraists* (Cambridge: Cambridge University Press, 1989); P. T. Van Rooden, *Theology, Biblical Scholarship and Rabbinical Studies in the Seventeenth Century* (Leiden: E. J. Brill, 1989); M. Walton and P. Walton, "In Defense of the Church Militant: The Censorship of the Rashi Commentary in the Magna Biblia Rabbinica," *Sixteenth Century Journal* 21 (1990): 385–400; S. Burnett "The Christian Hebraism of Johann Buxtorf" *(1564–1629)* (dissertation, University of Wisconsin, 1990); *L'Hebreu au Temps de la Renaissance*, ed. I. Zinguer (Leiden: E. J. Brill, 1992); and Frank E. Manuel, *The Broken Staff* (Cambridge, Mass.: Harvard University Press, 1992).

31. Rabbinic *derashot* associated the laws regarding the minimum number of walls required for maintaining a ritually valid *sukkah* with the spellings of *skt/skwt*, e.g., BT Suk. 6b. Usually variations of the *skt/skwt* type, where a defective spelling is vocalized a particular way, are not classified as *Qere u-Keṯiḇ*. To do so reinforces the association with the terms *'em la-miqra'* and *'em la-masoreṯ*.

32. For references, see *Torah Shelemah* to Gen. 34:3, note 13; for use of this data as an argument against the *Qere u-Keṯiḇ* being evidence of errors, see, in particular, the introduction to Abarbanel's commentary on Jeremiah.

33. *Okhlah VeOkhlah*, ed. Fernando Diaz Esteban (Madrid: Consejo Superior de Investigaciones Científicas, 1975). Soferim, ed. Joel Mueller (Leipsig: J. C. Hinrichs'sche Buchhandlung, 1878), p. xvi, and by Michael Higger (New York: DeVei Rabbanan, 1937), pp. 204–205. The same examples are discussed in T Meg. chap. 3 and in BT Meg. 25b using Hebrew terminology that is close to the *Qere u-Keṯiḇ* idiom. Occasionally the Babylonian Talmud used similar language in cases not recorded as *Qere* and *Keṯiḇ* in our Bibles. Whether this suggests a different tradition or merely double use of the terms requires further attention.

34. *Diqduqe HaTe'amim*, ed. Hermann Strack, (Leipsig: 1879; repr., Jerusalem: Makor, 1970), p. 53, no. 6. Dotan intentionally omitted the passage from his edition, *The Diqduqe HaTe'amim of Aharon ben Moshe ben Asher* (Jerusalem: HaAkademiah LaLashon HaIvrit, 1967); it is found in the texts he has designated as T.19.13 and T43.

35. This is the standard explanation of these changes, as well as three other words so altered in a total of sixteen places; cf. Robert Gordis, *The Biblical Text in the Making: A Study of the Kethib-Qere* (Philadelphia: Dropsie, 1937), p. 86. Ibn Zimra's statement apparently rejected Maimonides' claim that Hebrew is called *lešon ha-qoḏeš* (understood here as "holy language"), because it has no words for such matters (*Guide for the Perplexed* III, 8). That this is not the literal meaning of the term *lešon ha-qoḏeš* is clear, not only from this passage, but also from the Aramaic, *lešan (baiṯ) quḏša*, used to describe the Hebrew word *hinneni*, "here I am"—which is, in fact, *lešon ha-qoḏeš* (better understood as "the language of the sanctuary," i.e., biblical Hebrew)—in a number of places in the marginal notes to the Neophyti Targum and the *Targum Yerushalmi*; see further chapter 1, n. 30.

The most extensive modern study of the *Qere u-Keṯiḇ* variants is Gordis's, augmented by a new prolegomenon found in the reprinted edition and also in his *The Word and the Book: Studies in Biblical Language and Literature* (New York: Ktav, 1976). See also Harry M. Orlinsky, "The Origin of the Kethib-Qere System: A New Approach," *Vetus Testamentum* 7 (1959): 184–192; Alexander Sperber, *A Historical Grammar of Biblical Hebrew*, pp. 493–506; James Barr, "A New Look at Kethib-Qere," *Oudtestamentischen Studien* 21 (1981): 19–37; Mordechai Breuer, *Leshonenu* 45 (1981), pp. 209–260, M. H. Segal, *Mavo HaMiqra'* (Jerusalem: Kiryat Sefer, 1978), pp. 859–877; Ginsburg, *Introduction*, pp. 183–186; and Yeivin, *Introduction*, pp. 52–61.

36. See, in addition to T Meg. 3:39–40 and BT Meg. 25b, Maimonides' *Hilkhot Sefer Torah* 7:11, and Abraham Geiger, *Urschrift und Uebersetzungen der Bibel in ihrer Abhaengigkeit von der innern Entwickelung des Judenthums* (Breslau: 1857, 1928) pp. 385–423, translated as *HaMiqra' VeTargumav BeZiqatam LeHitpathutah HaPenimit Shel HaYahadut* (Jerusalem: Mossad Bialik, 1972), pp. 248–271.

37. Brought to the attention of the scholarly world by Saul Lieberman through the comment of H. L. Ginsberg, *Studies in Koheleth* (New York: Jewish Theological Seminary, 1950), p. 1, commentary to Ecc. 1:2. The text was published by Adolf Jellinek in *Commentar zu Kohelet und dem Hohen Liede von R[abbi] Samuel ben Meir* (Leipzig: L. Schnauss, 1855; repr. Israel, n.d.), p. 1, and again with translation in *Perush Rabbi Shemuel ben Meir LeQohelet*, ed. Sarah Japhet and Robert B. Salters (Jerusalem: Magnes Press, 1985).

38. Michael Wilensky, *Mehqarim BeLashon uVeSifrut* (Jerusalem: HaAkademiah LaLashon HaIvrit, 1978), pp. 95–103, "*Kavanatah Shel HaMilah Miqra'*."

39. See further Uriel Simon, *Arba' Gishot LeSefer Tehillim* (Ramat Gan: Bar Ilan University Press, 1982), translated as *Four Approaches to the Book of Psalms* (Albany: State University of New York Press, 1991); Moshe Sokolow's annotated translation of Saadiah's introduction to Psalms in *Proceedings of the American Academy for Jewish Research*, Vol. 51 (1984), pp. 154–174; and James Kugel, "Topics in the History of the Spirituality of the Psalms," in *Jewish Spirituality*, ed. Arthur Green, Vol. 1 (New York: Crossroad, 1986), pp. 113–117.

40. See Saul Lieberman, "*Mishnat Shir HaShirim*," in Gershon Scholem, *Jewish Gnosticism, Merkabah Mysticism, and Talmudic Tradition* (New York: Jewish Theological Seminary, 1965), pp. 118–126.

41. Eliezer Ben-Yehudah, *Milon HaLashon HaIvrit HaYeshanah VeHaHadashah* (Jerusalem: 1912; repr., New York: T. Yosseloff, 1959), Vol. 2, pp. 984–986.

42. A fine new edition of the introduction to Kimhi's commentary on the Former Prophets can be found in Menahem Cohen, *Miqra'ot Gedolot: 'HaKeter,' Yehoshua'—Shoftim* (Ramat Gan: Bar Ilan University Press, 1992), Heb. 14. For some time this introduction was censored out of reprinted Rabbinic Bibles, though some newer reprints do contain it. Undoubtedly this omission was deemed necessary because of this passage about errors in the Bible text. Nathan Goldberg, *The Commentary of Rabbi David Kimhi on the Book of Joshua* (Columbia University Dissertation, 1961) also contains it.

43. Note the description of the recovery of Bible scrolls in 2 Mac. 2:14–15 and the analysis in M. H. Segal's "The Promulgation of the Authoritative Text of the Hebrew Bible," *Journal of Biblical Literature* 72 (1953): 35–47, reprinted in his *The Pentateuch: Its Composition and Its Authorship and Other Biblical Studies* (Jerusalem: Magnes, 1967), pp. 242–253. David Weiss Halivni has developed this argument much further in his *Peshat and Derash: Plain and Applied Meaning in Rabbinic Exegesis* (New York: Oxford University Press, 1991).

44. Profiat Duran, *Ma'asei Efod*, ed. Y. Friedlander and J. Cohen (Vienna: 1865; repr., Jerusalem: Makor, 1969), chap. 7.

45. *Perush Abarbanel Al Nevi'im Aharonim* (repr., Israel, n.d.).

46. *She'eilot uTeshuvot HaRashba*, Vol. 7, no. 361.

47. See further the text published by Dimitrovsky, translated here in chapter 6.

48. *Teshuvot Rabbenu Avraham ben HaRambam*, ed. A. H. Freimann and Solomon D. Goitein (Jerusalem: Mekize Nirdamim, 1937), p. 31.

49. The various rabbinic texts have been collected conveniently in Menahem M. Kasher, *Torah Shelemah*, ad loc.

50. E.g., *Tanhuma, Beshalah* (repr., Israel: Lewin-Epstein, 1961), no. 16.

51. Cf. *Aruch Completum*, ed. Alexander Kohut (Vienna: 1878–1992; repr., New York:

Pardes, 1955), Vol. 6, pp. 189–190, s.v. ʿ-ṭ-r. A possible source for some of the *Arukh* material is found in *Teshuvot HaGeonim*, ed. Abraham Harkavy (Berlin: 1887), p. 103, no. 217.

52. Kohut listed some frequently ignored data on this matter, including discussion of the accuracy of the citation from Kings. Note also that the Hebrew *raq ha-bamoṯ loʾ saru* occurs in 2 Kings 12:4, 14:4, 15:4, 15:35, while *ʾaḵ ha-bamoṯ loʾ saru* is found in 1 Kings 22:44 and 2 Chron. 20:33. The targumim for these and similar passages regularly use a form of ʿ-ṭ-r, but they are inconsistent about using *ʿṭrw* and *ʿṭrʾ* as the translation of *saru*; cf. the texts and variants published by A. Sperber, *The Bible in Aramaic* (Leiden: E. J. Brill, 1959), Vol. 2 and 4a, and by R. Le Deaut and J. Robert, *Targum des Chroniques* (Rome: Biblical Institute Press, 1971), Vol. 2. If a generalization is possible, it would be that the texts prefer *ʿṭrʾ* for phrases beginning *raq*, and *ʿṭrw* for those beginning *ʾaḵ*, but this should be irrelevant, and in any case is not true of the passage cited. In fact, *ʿṭrw* is a common form while *ʿṭrʾ* is feminine plural. See also Eliyah Levita, *Meturgeman* (Isne: 1541), s.v. ʿ-ṭ-r no. 1.

53. It is also found in BT Yom. 80a and Suk. 44a.

54. For a list of examples and discussion, see Yehudah Ratzaby, "'*Fa BeLeshon Yishmaʿel*' *BeKetuvei Miqra*'," in *Mehqarim BeIvrit uVeLeshonot Shemiyot Muqdashim LeZikhro Shel Professor Yehezkel Kutscher*, ed. Gad B. Sarfatti, Pinhas Artzi, Jonas Greenfield, and Menahem Kaddari (Ramat Gan: Bar Ilan University Press, 1980), pp. 9–17. A similar designation appears in several places in Rashi's commentaries; see Hayyim Shalom Segal, *Munahei Rashi* (Jerusalem: Ariel, 1989), p. 113, no. 26; also the treatments in Elijah Mizrahi's *Humash HaReʾem*, ed. Moshe Phillip (Petah Tiqvah: M. Phillip, 1994), *Bereishit*, Vol. 2, Index, p. 22, col. 2. On *fa* in Arabic, see Joshua Blau, "An Adverbial Construction in Hebrew and Arabic," *Proceedings of the Israel Academy of Sciences and Humanities*, Vol. 6 (1977–1982), pp. 53–65.

55. Ibn Zimra's reactions to the various Bible commentators is discussed briefly in chapter 7.

56. *Magen David* (Amsterdam: 1713), p. 15a, letter *waw*.

57. See further his *Mikhlol*, ed. Isaac Rittenberg (Lyck: 1842; repr., Jerusalem: 1966), pp. 3b–4a, and especially William Chomsky, *David Kimhi's Hebrew Grammar (Mikhlol) Systematically Presented and Critically Annotated* (New York: Bloch, 1952), p. 55, no. 16.d.a, and the important historical n. 84 on p. 75.

58. *Sheʾeilot uTeshuvot Maharit HaHadashim* [sic] (Jerusalem: Makhon Yerushalayim, 1978), no. 14.

59. Chomsky, p. 75.

60. Similar logic, attributed to Rabbi Meir Abulafia, has been applied by Maharam Al-Ashqar to a problem with the text of Rashi; *Sheʾeilot uTeshuvot Maharam Al-Ashqar*, p. 214, no. 65.

61. See Ginsburg, *Introduction*, pp. 69–71; McCarthy, pp. 131–138; and Emmanuel Tov, "*Masoret Hazal Al 'HaShinuyyim' SheHukhnesu BaTargum HaShivʿim LaTorah uSheʾeilat HaNusah HaMeqori Shel Targum Ze*," in *Sefer Yitzhaq Aryeh Zeligman*, ed. Yair Zakovitz and Alexander Rofe (Jerusalem: E. Rubenstein, 1983), pp. 371–394. The prominent display of this list on the last color page of the Lisbon Pentateuch of 1482 demonstrates its importance; *The Lisbon Bible* 1482, introduced by G. Sed-Rajna (Tel-Aviv: Nahar-Miskal, 1988), p. 183b.

62. Ben-Zion Luria, *Megillat Taʿanit* (Jerusalem: Mossad Bialik, 1964), p. 201.

63. Summarized in the appropriate sections of *Mishnat Avraham*.

64. Izhak Ben-Zvi, "The Codex of Ben Asher," *Textus* 1 (1960): 8; N. Ben-Menachem, "*Teshuvat RaDBaZ SheHipsuha*," *Studies in Bibliography and Booklore*, Vol. 3 (1957–1958), pp. 51–52; and Amnon Shamosh, *Ha-Keter: Sippuro Shel Keter Aram Tzova* (Jerusalem: Yad Ben Zvi, 1987), pp. 32–33. On copies of the scroll that remained in Egypt, see Israel Yeivin's two similarly titled articles, "*Ketav Yad Qarov Meʿod LeKeter Aram Tzova*," *Textus* 12 (1985): 1–31, and *Iyyunei Miqraʾ uFarshanut* 3 (1993): 169–193; also Nehemiah Allony, "*Heʿeteqei*

Keter Aram Tzova' BiYerushalayim uVaGolah," *Beit Miqra'* 24 (1979): 321–334, reprinted in his *Mehqerei Lashon VeSifrut*, Vol. 5 (Jerusalem: Reuben Mass, 1992), pp. 285–296.

65. The phrase *ha'ameḏ* x *'al ḥezqaṯo* is fairly common in the Talmud, but it appears not to have been applied there to a Torah scroll.

66. The possibility of an even split among the sources was seen in Abulafia's tabulations (chapter 2 of this book), and it emerges as an issue in some of the texts cited later.

67. The masoretic literature is unanimous in spelling *'tw* defective throughout the Torah, but see, chapter 2, especially pp. 46–47 and the accompanying notes.

Four. Ibn Zimra's Responsum C

1. VIII, no. 181.

2. *Midrash Rabbi Aqiva ben Yosef Al Otiot Qetanot VeTa'ameihem*, in *Battei Midrashot*, ed. Solomon Wertheimer (Jerusalem: Ketav VeSefer, 1968), Vol. 2, p. 479; Bahya ben Asher, *Perush HaTorah*, ed. Chaim Dov [Charles B.] Chavel (Jerusalem: Mossad HaRav Kook, 1966–1968), ad. loc.

3. *Teshuvot Rabbi Aqiva Eiger* (Warsaw: repr., Brooklyn: I. 2ev, 1962), Vol. 1, no. 75. Very detailed and particularly informative is the discussion of Rabbi Hayyim Moses Amarillio (1695–1748), *Devar Moshe: Yoreh De'ah, Hilkhot Sefer Torah* (Salonika: 1750), Vol. 3, no. 8. Also noteworthy are the language used by Rabbi Menahem Azariah of Fano (1548–1620), who described this *waw* and one other as *ḥaserim ke-'en yoḏ*, "deficient, like a *yod*," and the explanation of Rabbi Hayyim Ibn Attar (1696–1743), who, in *Or HaHayyim*, a.l., linked this phenomenon to the questionable *waw* of *kalloṯ*, discussed earlier in chapter 2.

4. See further *Devar Moshe*, the passage beginning on 22a.

5. The word *šalēm* is frequently used in medieval texts as a synonym for *malē'*, "plene spelling," for example in a second responsum by Ben Adret and in the Sanhedrin commentary of Rabbenu Nissim, both translated in chapter 6, and in the Zohar; this is not the intention here. It is also used in Rabbi Elijah Mizrahi's commentary to Gen. 23:9 in the sense of "full"; Phillip's note, ad loc., calls attention to the use of *šalēm* for a full mikveh in a passage near that on the "cut *waw*," BT Qid. 66b.

6. *Perush HaRitva* (repr., New York: Otzar HaSefarim, 1966), and *Hidushei HaRitva Al HaShas: Qiddushin*, ed. Abraham Dinin (Jerusalem: Mossad HaRav Kook, 1985), col. 717. See Dinin's two important notes, nos. 669 and 670. The former surveys the many halakhic discussions of this *waw*; the latter discusses two variant readings in which the penultimate word, *še-keṯuḇa (ḵe-darko)*, appears as *še-kaṯuḇ* and *še-yiḵtoḇ*. The former is a linguistic variant; the latter reverses the ruling. Whatever this latter variant's value, Ibn Zimra's version of the Ritva's commentary, like Dinin's base text, required changing any *waws* not formed according to specification. Amarillio also discussed the various versions of Ben Adret's remarks and seriously considered the possibility of omitting the part of the Ritva's comment that required changing all scrolls, because it seemed to him an unnecessary stricture and an addition; see his discussion, ad loc.

7. See further BT Shab. 103b; Ibn Zimra's responsa, I, nos. 363 and 446, and II, no. 596; Menahem M. Kasher, *Torah Shelemah*, Vol. 22 (Jerusalem: Makhon Torah Shelemah, 1967), pp. 163–166, and Vol. 29 (Jerusalem: Beit Torah Shelemah, 1978), pp. 79–80, 130–132.

8. As above, BT Qid. 66b.

9. The writings of Shem-Tov Gaon (1283–1330), a student of Ben Adret, have been studied by D. S. Loewinger in "*Rabbi Shem Tov ben Avraham Gaon,*" *Sefunot* 7 (1963): 7–40, where his masoretic activities are discussed on pp. 15–22; the article has been reprinted as the introduction to the facsimile edition of Shem-Tov's *Badei HaAron uMigdal Hananel* (Jerusalem: Mizrah uMa'arav, 1977). Shem Tov's own Bible codex is described in detail in

David Solomon Sassoon, *Ohel David* (London: 1932), the catalog of the former Sassoon collection, no. 82, pp. 2–5, though our immediate concern is not mentioned there. (According to B. Richler, *Guide to Hebrew Manuscript Collections* [Jerusalem: Israeli Academy of Sciences and Humanities, 1994], p. 244, the volume was sold, but no further information is provided.) See also the comments on "Shem-Tov" and "so called Shem-Tov" manuscripts in Paul Kahle, *The Cairo Geniza*, 2nd ed. (Oxford: Basil Blackwell, 1959), pp. 138–141, and in Norman Snaith's prolegomenon to the reprint of Christian David Ginsburg's 1867 edition and translation of *Jacob ben Chajim Ibn Adonijah's Introduction to the Rabbinic Bible* (New York: Ktav, 1968), pp. xiii and xvii, and the sources cited there.

10. Israel ben Isaac [ben Israel] the Scribe, who signed the colophon cited by Meiri in *Qiryat Sefer*, Part II, chap. 2, ed. Moshe Herschler (Jerusalem: HaMasorah, 1956), p. 48, may be the person mentioned here. He was also identified by Professor Nahum Sarna as the Rabbi Israel referred to by Isaac Abarbanel, in a discussion of a doubt over use of a *sin* or *shin*, at the end of his commentary to Amos 3:12 (cited at the end of the introduction to *Hamishah Humshei Torah: Ketav Yad Sefaradi Qadum* [Jerusalem: Makor, 1974]). He was identified by Rabbi Meir Benayahu as the Rabbi Israel referred to by Abraham Hasan, in "*Iggeret HaSofer Rabbi Abraham Hasan MiSaloniqi*," *Sefunot* 11 (1971–1978): 217, n. 48.

11. See Ginsburg, *The Massorah*, Vol. 1, p. 37, *Aleph*, no. 229, where the *waw* of *šlwm* is listed in the alphabetic chart of "Miniscule Letters" and also noted to be *qeṭuʿa*. Ginsburg's tables, Vol. 4, pp. 40–41, record that only six of the nine lists he evaluated include this *waw*. Comparison with his treatment of the other undersized letters highlights that some (e.g., Gen. 2:4, Lev. 1:1) are universally recognized, while others appear in only one or two texts. The *waw* of *šlwm* is well known, probably because of the talmudic passage about it, but the halakhic discussions of texts that lack it confirm the impression that it was not universally preserved. Ginsburg also noted the presence of undersized *waws* in other places, most noteworthy, in one witness to *šlwm* in Gen. 41:16.

Several years ago I observed a man who, when called to the Torah, asked the rabbi if the Torah scroll should be replaced because of a defect he noticed. The rabbi agreed and had the scroll removed from the reading table. Only after it became clear what had happened—that this was a case of an innocent discovery of the cut *waw* of *šalom* in Num. 25:12—was there an opportunity to point out the talmudic passage and the scribal practice of using a cut *waw* in that place. Clearly this anomaly is not well known, even today.

12. This echoes Ritva's comment cited in paragraph 5.

13. Notable exceptions include (1) the reprinted text in *Sefer Liqutei Sifrei Setam*, 3rd ed. (Jerusalem: 1981)—the third chapter of the second of two parts of the volume designated Part IV, chap. 3, which is chapter 13 of Rabbi Hayyim Joseph David Azulai's *LeDavid Emet* (republished [Jerusalem: Yahadut, 1986], p. 24); (2) Menahem Meiri, *Qiryat Sefer* 1: 36; and (3) Israel Jacob Al-Gazi (1686–1756), *Sefer Emet LeYaʿaqov: HaMishpat HaShelishi* (Livorno: 1774), the most detailed discussion, which includes reference to a manuscript of Ibn Zimra's Responsum C.

14. David L. Greenfeld and Samuel E. Granitestein, *Yalqut Tzurat HaOtiot* (Brooklyn: 1983), p. 704.

15. For a full discussion of the letter *waw* and the related rabbinic sources, as well as diagrams of its various forms, see Shelomo J. Zevin, *Intziqlopedia Talmudit*, Vol. 11 (Jerusalem: Hotza'at Intziqlopedia Talmudit, 1965), col. 393–399, which includes differing opinions as to whether the slit should be high or low on the leg of the *waw*.

16. See note 3.

17. On the Yemenite use of regular *waw* in this word, see Rabbi Benjamin Lau, "*Sefer Torah Temani BeQehillah Ashkenazit*," Tehumin 15 (1995): 447, and Uri Dasberg, "*Zihui Sefer Torah*," *Tehumin* 1 (1980): 511. On the Chinese Torah scrolls, see Michael Pollak, *The*

Torah Scrolls of the Chinese Jews: The History, Significance, and Present Whereabouts of the Sifrei Torah of the Defunct Jewish Community of Kaifeng (Dallas: Bridwell Library, 1975), pp. 98–99 and 108. For further discussion of the various halakhic positions on this letter and related bibliography, see Abraham Jaffe, *Mishnat Avraham* (Jessnitz: 1868; repr., Jerusalem: 1968), chap. 31.

Five. Ibn Zimra's Responsum D

1. *Tanakh* (Philadelphia: Jewish Publication Society, 1985), p. 197.

2. The Torah commentary of Rabbi Hizqiah ben Manoah has been edited, annotated, and introduced by Chaim Dov [Charies B.] Chavel, *Hizquni: Perushei HaTorah LeRabbenu Hizqiah bar Manoah* (Jerusalem: Mossad HaRav Kook, 1981). The passage cited below is found on page 416. Hizquni's sources have been discussed in part by Sarah Japhet, "*Perush HaHizquni LaTorah—LeDemuto Shel HaHibbur uLeMatarato*," in *Sefer HaYovel LaRav Mordechai Breuer*, ed. Moshe Bar Asher (Jerusalem: Akademon, 1992), Vol. 1, pp. 91–111.

3. I, no. 336.

4. Benjamin Kennicott, *Vetus Testamentum Hebraice cum Variis Lectionibus* (Oxford: 1776–1780), Vol. 1, ad loc.

5. Solomon Abraham Rosanes, *Divrei Yemei Yisrael BeTogarmah* (Husiatyn: Kawalek, 1907), Vol. 2, p. 181.

6. On the interchange of masculine and feminine forms, see, for example, Rashi to Gen. 15:17, Mizrahi's comment, ad loc., and the discussion in *Ariel: Rashi HaShalem*, Vol. 2 (Jerusalem: Ariel, 1988), Gen. 32:8, pp. 145–146.

7. The identity of the writer(s) to whom this notion should be attributed remains in doubt, despite persistent associations with Abraham Ibn Ezra; compare his comment on Song of Songs 1:3 and Judah L. Krinsky's added details, *Mehoqeqei Yehudah* (repr., Bene-Berak: Horev, 1961). See also the sources cited by Rabbi Malakhi Cohen in *Yad Mal'akhi* (Berlin: E. Hertz, 1857; repr., Israel: Am Olam, 1964), Part I, p. 51b, par. 308, and by Michael Wilensky in "La Source de la Proposition '*Kol Davar SheEin Bo Ruah Hayyim Zakhruhu VeNaqvuhu*,' " *Revue des Etudes Juives* 98 (1934): 66ff, translated into Hebrew in *Sinai*, vol. 12 (1949), and republished in idem, *Mehqarim BeLashon VeSifrut* (Jerusalem: HaAkademiah LaLashon HaIvrit, 1978), pp. 116–119. Wilensky's closest but admittedly imperfect parallel is Profiat Duran, *Ma'asei Efod*, p. 44; he tentatively identified the reference to Rabbenu Tam as *Sefer HaYashar* (Vienna: 1811), p. 21a, note 195.

The most thorough treatment of this matter is that of Nehemiah Allony, "*Kol Davar She-'Ein Bo Ruah Hayyim. . .* ," reprinted in his *Mehqerei Lashon VeSifrut*, Vol. 3 (Jerusalem: Makhon Ben Zvi, 1989), pp. 273–277; he also discussed briefly Ibn Zimra's use of the phrase. He abandoned the association with Ibn Ezra but saw the attempt to establish a neuter gender in Hebrew as the influence of Latin grammar.

8. This is, in fact, Hizquni's argument.

9. Passage D.5, including the accompanying list of verses, is lacking from Steinsaltz's edition of the responsum, *Perush HaMiqra' BeSifrut HaShe'eilot VeHaTeshuvot: Biblical Interpretation in the Responsa Literature: 8th—16th Centuries* (Jerusalem: Keter, 1978), p. 44. I have found no textual support for this shorter version.

10. The list begins in Lev. 19:20; the end of the section might refer to the end of the passage in chapter 18.

11. The printed text reads *hw'*, but the pattern of the other entries requires *hy'*.

12. All else aside, the word *mehaleḵet* does not appear in the Bible.

13. See further *The Massorah* (repr., New York: Ktav, 1975), Vol. 1, and Vol. 4, *Heh*, no. 89, G(3).

14. The observation that the matter is "simple" occurs at the conclusion of many of Ibn Zimra's responsa, especially the shorter ones.

Six. The Literary Background of Ibn Zimra's Responsa

1. The important essay by Moshe H. Goshen-Gottstein, "Foundations of Biblical Philology in the Seventeenth Century: Christian and Jewish Dimensions," in *Jewish Thought in the Seventeenth Century*, ed. Isadore Twersky and Bernard Septimus (Cambridge: Harvard University Press, 1987), pp. 77–94, places these efforts within their broader intellectual context and calls attention to their underdeveloped nature relative to the major text-editing projects of the day. Even so, compared with other related rabbinic efforts to edit the Bible, they were major advances. See further John F. D'Amico, *Theory and Practice in Renaissance Textual Criticism: Beatus Rhenanus Between Conjecture and History* (Berkeley: University of California Press, 1998), esp. chap. 1.

For further discussion of the history of printing in Venice, see Abraham Berliner, "*Beitraege zur hebraeischen Typographie Daniel Bombergs*," *Jahrbuch der Juedisch-Literarischen Gesellschaft*, Vol. 3 (1904), trans. in Vol. 2 of his *Ketavim Nivharim* (Jerusalem: Mossad HaRav Kook, 1969); Cecil Roth, *Venice* (Philadelphia: Jewish Publication Society, 1930), pp. 245–265; D. Amram, *The Makers of Hebrew Books in Italy* (Philadelphia: 1909; repr., London: Holland Press, 1963); idem, *The Jews in the Renaissance* (Philadelphia: Jewish Publication Society, 1964), chap. 7, "The Christian Hebraists"; and Moses A. Shulvass, *The Jews in the World of the Renaissance* (Leiden: E. J. Brill, 1973), pp. 148–155. Benjamin Ravid has shown that Jews were prohibited from printing books in Venice by 1548, not 1571, as was previously thought in "The Prohibition against Jewish Printing and Publishing in Venice and the Difficulties of Leone Modena," in *Studies in Medieval Jewish History and Literature*, ed. Isadore Twersky (Cambridge, Mass.: Harvard University Press, 1979), pp. 135–153.

2. Some of the early efforts at fixing the text have been discussed by Michael Fishbane in the first part of *Biblical Interpretation in Ancient Israel* (Oxford: Oxford University Press, 1985).

3. *She'eilot uTeshuvot HaRashba HaMeyuhasot LeHaRamban* (Warsaw: I. Goldman, 1883; repr., Bene-Berak: 1958), no. 232.

4. The discussion of the term Gemara in chapter 2 seems to apply to *sifrē ha-talmuḏ* here.

5. In BT Suk. 6a.

6. See the passage from the introduction to *Masoret Seyag LaTorah* translated in chapter 1.

7. This passage is also quoted by Baqrat, *Sefer HaZikkaron*, ed. Moshe Phillip (Petah Tikvah: M. Phillip, 1985), p. 135. The language is somewhat better than that preserved in the printed edition of Abulafia's work, but the idea is the same.

8. In addition to Ibn Zimra, IV, no. 74, and VIII, no. 141, see the following, noted according to the citations in the Bar Ilan Judaic Library on CD-ROM: *She'eilot uTeshuvot Avraham ben HaRambam*, no. 89; Rabbenu Tam, *Sefer HaYashar: Heleq HaTeshuvot*, no. 25; Rabbi Joseph Colon, *She'eilot uTeshuvot Mahariq*, no. 170, and *She'eilot uTeshuvot Mahariq HaHadashim* [sic], no. 46; Rabbi Moses of Padua, *She'eilot uTeshuvot Maharam Padua*, no. 41; Rabbi Samuel Medina, *She'eilot uTeshuvot Maharashdam: Hoshen Mishpat*, no. 54; Rabbi Solomon Luria, *She'eilot uTeshuvot Maharshal*, no. 98; Rabbi Moses Isserles, *She'eilot uTeshuvot HaRama'*, no. 7; Rabbi Elijah Mizrahi, *She'eilot uTeshuvot Rabbi Eliyahu Mizrahi*, no. 74; Rabbi Betzalel Ashkenazi, *She'eilot uTeshuvot Rabbi Betzalel Ashkenazi*, no. 23.

9. For further discussion of the *mmnw* problem, see Abraham Ibn Ezra, Commentary to Gen. 3:22, as well as the parallel citations and discussion, ad loc., by Yehudah L. Krinsky,

Mehoqeqei Yehudah, Vol. 1: *Bereshit* (repr., Jerusalem: Horev, 1961), pp. 73–74, notes 160–161; also *Gesenius' Hebrew Grammar*, ed. E. Kautzsch and A. E. Cowley (Oxford: Oxford University Press, 1930), p. 303, no. 103m.

10. See Christian David Ginsburg, *Introduction to the Massoretico-Critical Edition of the Hebrew Bible* (London: 1897; repr., New York: Ktav, 1966), p. 200, and idem, *The Massorah* (repr., New York: Ktav, 1975), Vol. 2, p. 234, *Mem*, nos. 549–550.

11. The citation from Soferim has been abridged; for the full text, see chapter 1.

12. E.g., BT Hul. 11a and Sof. 1:7.

13. See chapter 2, note 4.

14. See chapter 2, the discussion following paragraph 3 of the Responsum, and the sources listed in the footnotes.

15. Maimonides' reliance on this Ben Asher manuscript has been discussed for centuries, but an entire literature has been generated since the rescue of the Aleppo codex and its repatriation to Jerusalem. In its early years, *Textus* was devoted largely to the codex, and one of the studies of lasting worth is Jordan Penkower's "Maimonides and the Aleppo Codex," which appeared in vol. 9 (1981): 39–128. Important additional bibliographic material appears in his *Nusah HaTorah BeKeter Aram-Tzova'* (Ramat Gan: Bar Ilan University Press, 1993), including pp. 53–55, which discuss the passage in *Hilkhot Tefillin*.

16. This responsum has been published in *Iggeret HaSofer*, in *HaSegulah* no. 54 (1938), p. 5; by Meir Benayahu as "*Iggeret HaSofer Rabbi Avraham Hasan MiSaloniqi SheNishlehah El Rabbi Eliyahu Mizrahi VeRabbi Yosef Taitatzak*," *Sefunot* 11 (1971–1978): 213; and by Hayyim Zalman Dimitrovsky in *Teshuvot HaRashba* (Jerusalem: Mossad HaRav Kook, 1990), Vol. 1, p. 51, no. 14. An early comparison of the two versions of Ben Adret's responsa is found in Rabbi Hayyim Moses Amarillio, *Devar Moshe, Yoreh De'ah, Hilkhot Sefer Torah*, Vol. 3 (Salonika: 1750), no. 8, p. 24a, col. 1.

17. For examples of the types of disagreements referred to here, see Christian David Ginsburg, *The Massorah*, Vol. 1, s.v. *ḥilufim*.

18. Other responsa that also referred to Ben Asher and Ben Naftali are cited shortly.

19. Dimitrovsky, Vol. 1, introduction, pp. 10–14.

20. Baqrat, pp. 135–136.

21. An early edition of the text treated here, with a brief discussion, appeared in Simhah Assaf, *Meqorot uMehqarim BeToldot Yisrael* (Jerusalem: Mossad HaRav Kook, 1946), pp. 182–185. It has been reissued in *She'eilot uTeshuvot Maharam Halavah*, ed. Moshe and Ben-Zion Hershler (Jerusalem: Makhon Shalem, 1987), pp. 170–172.

22. On Rabbenu Nissim, see the introduction to Aryeh Feldman's edition of his commentary on the Torah (Jerusalem: Makhon Shalem, 1968). For discussion of his Torah scroll, see Solomon Z. Havlin, "*Sefer Torah SheKatav LeAtzmo Rabbenu Nissim MiGirondi*," *Alei Sefer* 12 (1986): 5–36, and Eliyahu Lichtenstein's introduction to Rabbenu Nissim's *Hidushei HaRan . . . Avodah Zarah* (Jerusalem: Mossad HaRav Kook, 1990).

23. The Hebrew says *banoṯ*, "daughters," but both Assaf and Hershler have changed it to *beriyoṯ*, "people."

24. The term *gufah šel tora* is rare in early rabbinic literature and is generally not used as Maharam has employed it here. It is found in Sifrei to Deut., no. 317; *gufē tora*, the more common term, appears in M Hag. 1:8, in both Talmudim, and in various Midrashim. Both expressions mean something like "substantial matters of Torah law," though a few refer specifically to such laws that have a strong foundation in the biblical text. The only place I have found *gufē tora* to refer to the Torah text itself is BT Hul. 60b, where it seems to mean "part of the Torah text," still not exactly as it is used here; a close parallel to Maharam's usage here is found in Jonah Landsofer's *She'eilot uTeshuvot Me'il Tzedaqah* (Prague: Gabbai, 1757), no. 55.

25. Maharam's facile observation that "everything" is from Sinai anticipated the idea expressed by Ibn Zimra in Responsum B.

26. The anonymous statement cited by Maharam is attributed to Rav in the Gemara. The same passage attributes to Samuel the observation that we do make such divisions, even if Moses did not, and without this line, the point of citing it is lost. The quotation seems to have been included only because Samuel's opinion, which contradicts Rav's, is another example of a dispute over something considered Halakhah to Moses from Sinai.

27. This line of the responsum is a dittography, copied from the line following the end of the quotation from Soferim.

28. To be discussed further.

29. *Hidushei HaRan Al HaShas* (New York: Goldman-Otzar HaSefarim, 1965), p. 2a.

30. Reading *be-maḥloqot̲* as *ke-maḥloqot̲* and *be-b̲en* as *de-b̲en*.

31. *She'eilot uTeshuvot . . . Yitzhaq bar Sheshet* (Jerusalem: Or HaMizrah, 1993), Vol. 1, p. 374, no. 284.

32. *Sefer Tashbetz* (Lemberg: U. W. Salat, 1891; repr., Tel Aviv: Gittler, n.d.), Part 3, no. 160.

33. Punning on the words *soferim*, "scribes," and *sefarim*, "scrolls." The point is taken in the extreme in order to maximize the value of scribal traditions and to minimize that of the scrolls. The formulation echoes a rule of evidence discussed in BT Yev. 31b and Git. 71a, which rejects written testimony and requires, in fulfillment of a hyperliteral reading of the biblical *'al pi . . .* (e.g., Deut. 17:6), that it be oral, *mi-pihem we-lo' mi-pi ket̲ab̲am*. Clear reference to Responsum 232 also appears in Saraval's question, discussed in chapter 1.

34. The translated passages appear in the edition of Chaim Dov [Charles B.] Chavel, *Rabbenu Bahya: Bi'ur Al HaTorah* (Jerusalem: Mossad HaRav Kook, 1966–1968), Vol. 1, p. 217, and Vol. 3, pp. 246, 281–282.

35. The Bible-related responsa published by Dimitrovsky suggest such a pattern, but it is unlikely that adjacent texts, even in the manuscripts, were originally recorded in a way that permits the transfer of attributions from one text to another in the same sequence.

36. Further discussion of this material in Bahya and in rabbinic parallels appears in Rabbi Jacob Shore's *Mishnat Ya'aqov* (Jerusalem: Mossad HaRav Kook, 1990), pp. 100–101.

37. See chapter 2.

38. Hayyim Michael, *Or HaHayyim* (Frankfort am Main: Y. Kaufmann, 1891; repr., Jerusalem: Mossad HaRav Kook, 1965), pp. 599–600.

39. D. S. Levinger, *Badei HaAron uMigdal Hannanel LeRabbi Shem Tov ben Avraham ben Gaon* (Jerusalem: Mizrah uMa'arav, 1977); it also contains the original study from *Sefunot*, vol. 7 (1963). See chapter 1, n. 25.

40. Levinger, p. 17.

41. Levinger suggested that numbers 12 and 40 of the first volume of Ben Adret's responsa were addressed to him, but the correct identification is Volume 3, as noted by Michael and by Menahem Elon in his *Mafteah HaShe'eilot VeHaTeshuvot Shel Hakhmei Sefarad uTzefon Afriqa: HaMafteah HaHistori* (Jerusalem: Magnes, 1987), Vol. 2, p. 250.

42. In the introduction to his edition of Maharam Halava's responsa (p. 15), Herschler has cited two passages that refer specifically to the personal relationship between Maharam and Ben Adret: Responsum 132, p. 137, and our text, no. 144, p. 172. A note on the latter suggests that the reference is to Judah ben Adret, but this seems incorrect.

43. Edited by Abraham Sofer, 3rd ed. (Jerusalem: A. Schreiber, 1963).

44. BT San. 4a. Meiri's commentary there does not supplement substantially the discussion of this point, though it does deal with the other related matters.

45. For other examples and discussion, see Samuel K. Mirsky "*R[abbi] Menahem HaMeiri—Hayyav, Shitato, uSefarav*," *Talpiot* 4 (1949): 1–90, esp. pp. 14–27. Note also

Moshe Halbertal, *Bein Torah LeHokhmah: Rabbi Menahem HaMeiri uVa'alei HaHalakhah HaMaimonim BeProvence* (Jerusalem: Magnes, 2000).

46. See the discussion of Abraham Hasan, noted above, and Hershler's introduction to *Qiryat Sefer*.

47. The missing piece is lacking in this text but was added by Hershler from *Iggeret Ha-Sofer*.

48. The text is translated as printed; a piece has been omitted.

49. For a list of such titles in *Qiryat Sefer*, see Hershler, pp. 97–98.

50. *Beit HaBehirah Al Masekhet Avot* (Jerusalem: Makhon HaTalmud HaYisraeli HaShalem, 1964), ad loc.

51. See chapter 2, n. 4.

52. Nahum Sarna, Supplement to *Hamishah Humshei Torah, Ketav Yad Sefaradi Qadum* (Jerusalem: Makor, 1974).

53. See, for example, the treatment by Jacob ben Hayyim in his introduction to the Rabbinic Bible of 1524.

54. Some of the evaluations of Midrash are cited in chapter 2; a good example of this treatment of the Aramaic Targumim is found in *Zikhron LaRishonim VeGam LaAharonim: She'eilot uTeshuvot HaGeonim*, ed. Abraham Harkavy (Berlin: Itzkovsky, 1887), no. 248, pp. 124–126; see also Martin McNamara, *The New Testament and the Palestinian Targum to the Pentateuch* (Rome: Pontifical Biblical Institute, 1966).

55. Nemiah Allony has dealt with the Karaite practice of reading a codex in "*Sefer HaTorah VeHaMitzhaf BeQeri'at HaTorah BeTzibbur BeAdat HaRabbanim uVeAdat HaQara'im*," *Beit Miqra'* 24 (1979): 321–334, reprinted in his *Mehqerei Lashon VeSifrut*, Vol. 5 (Jerusalem: Reuben Mass, 1992), pp. 271–284.

56. Over the years much has been said about the possibility that Ben Asher was himself a Karaite. For a summary and discussion, see Aaron Dotan, *Ben Asher's Creed: A Study of the History of the Controversy* (Missoula: Scholars Press, 1977).

57. *Iggeret HaSofer*, pp. 213–214, 226.

58. In Ginsburg's edition, this passage appears on page 41.

59. Translated anew from the Hebrew published in *The Massoreth Ha-Massoreth of Elias Levita*, ed. Christian David Ginsburg (London: 1867; repr., New York: Ktav, 1968), Introduction II, p. 94.

60. See, for example, the reproduction in Christian David Ginsburg's *Introduction to the Massoretico-Critical Edition of the Hebrew Bible*, opposite p. 625, and Mordecai Breuer's polite complaint, *HaMasorah HaGedolah LaTorah* (New York: Lehmann Foundation, 1992), pp. xix–xx. Additional reproductions are available in many works on the Bible, medieval Jewish art, and the history of Hebrew manuscripts. One relatively unknown early volume devoted to art and the Bible that contains reproductions of a number of highly ornate masoretic marginalia is *Mar'eh Miqra': Qovetz Muqdash LeItzuv Sifrei Tanakh* (Jerusalem: Misrad HaHinukh VeHaTarbut, 1976), pp. 50, 60–69.

A similar complaint can be lodged against reprinters of rabbinic Bibles (as well as the Talmud and most other rabbinic works normally accompanied by commentaries). The ability to reprint these works in ever decreasing sizes has left much of the reading public—particularly schoolchildren, who regularly use such books—unable to benefit from the almost microscopic printings of the commentaries. Readers know the commentaries are there and sense their potential contributions, but, like many owners of ornate Masorah manuscripts, benefit from their presence in ways that are best described as aesthetic.

61. *She'eilot uTeshuvot MaHaRI Mintz uMaltaRaM Padua* (Cracow: Joseph Fisher, 1882), no. 8. This remarkable statement seems to assume that Ben Asher was not an original masorete, a *ba'al ha-masoreṯ*. While Ben Asher's work was the culmination of much earlier

masoretic creativity, it hardly seems appropriate to deny his being a *ba'al ha-masoret*. However, Mintz was interested in eliminating the need to take his contribution seriously, and so he preferred to see him as something else. Presumably he took the term *ba'al ha-masoret* to mean something like "author of the Masoret" and would have applied it to Ezra or to some other ancient contributor. As one might imagine, the list of critical responses to Mintz is huge. A particularly long one, which discusses many of the other texts dealt with in this book, is Raphael Mildola's *Mayyim Rabbim, Yoreh De'ah* (Amsterdam: Joseph Dayyan, 1737), Vol. 2, no. 54, pp. 41a–47b; no. 55 continues the discussion.

62. Cited by Orlinsky in his prolegomenon to the reprint of Ginsburg's *Introduction*, p. iv.

63. See, for example, Yitzhaq Shimshon Lange, *Ta'amei Masoret HaMiqra' LeR[abbi] Yehudah HeHasid* (Jerusalem: I. S. Lange, 1981) and the similarly titled work by Rabbi Meir Rothenberg, included in *Torat Hayyim*, Vols. 1–7, ed. Mordecai Leb Katzenellenbogen (Jerusalem: Mossad HaRav Kook, 1986–1993).

64. Long Commentary to Exodus, in *Torat Hayyim: Shemot*, ed. Menahem M. Kasher (Jerusalem: Mossad HaRav Kook, 1987), Vol. 1, pp. 256–257; chapter 1 of *Yesod Mora'*, ed. Zalman Stern (Prague: Landau, 1833, repr., Israel: 197?), and by Israel Levin in *Yalqut Avraham Ibn Ezra* (New York: I. Matz, 1985), pp. 315–320.

65. *She'eilot uTeshuvot HaRashba* (Bene-Berak: 1958), Vol. 1, no. 12. Ibn Zimra rejected this notion in III, no. 945. See also Elijah Mizrahi's commentary to Ex. 20:1, 8.

66. For examples and discussion, see Ezra Zion Melammed, *Mefarshei HaMiqra', Darkheihem VeShitoteihem* (Jerusalem: Magnes, 1975); James Kugel, *The Idea of Biblical Poetry* (New Haven, Conn.: Yale University Press, 1981); and Adele Berlin, *Biblical Poetry Through Medieval Jewish Eyes* (Bloomington: Indiana University Press, 1991).

67. See the introduction to *Masoret Seyag LaTorah*, p. 3b, and the discussion in Bernard Septimus, *Hispano-Jewish Culture in Transition* (Cambridge, Mass.: Harvard University Press, 1982), p. 108.

68. These passages can be found in the first of Lange's editions of *Perushei Rabbi Yehudah HeHasid* (Jerusalem: S. Lange, 1975) but were removed in the subsequent one in deference to the feelings of Rabbi Moses Feinstein, who deemed them heretical forgeries added by someone other than their reputed author and worthy of being burned. See further *Iggerot Moshe*, Vol. 4 (New York: M. Feinstein, 1981), pp. 358–361. Among the many negative responses to this suggestion is that of Rabbi Menashe Klein, *Meshaneh Halakhot, Mador HaTeshuvot, Mahadura Tinyana* (Brooklyn: 1992), Vol. 2, pp. 136–137, no. 214, who suggested these words were added to Rabbi Feinstein's responsum by a student after his death.

69. Compare his *Torat Moshe* (repr., New York: Grossman, 1960), passim; *Derushim VeAggadot Hatam Sofer MiKetav Yad*, ed. Abraham Samuel Stern (London: E. Stern, 1998), pp. 114–116; and the responsum translated here in chapter 2.

70. See, on the one hand, *She'eilot uTeshuvot Maraham Schick, Yoreh De'ah* (repr., New York: 1961), no. 254, and, on the other, "for Moses our teacher, peace be on him, wrote [the Torah] until the poem *Ha'azinu*, and from there to the end Joshua wrote, according to one opinion," *Sefer Maharam Schick Al Taryag Mitzvot* (unidentified reprint), p. 57, no. 613.

71. See, for example, his *Pirqei Mo'adot* (Jerusalem: Horev, 1986), and the English translation of his presentation from Orthodox Forum IV, "The Study of Bible and the Primacy of the Fear of Heaven: Compatibility or Contradiction?" in *Modern Scholarship in the Study of Torah: Contributions and Limitations*, ed. Shalom Carmy (Northvale, N.J.: Jason Aronson, 1996), pp. 159–180. See also Meir Ekstein, "Rabbi Mordechai Breuer and Modern Orthodox Biblical Commentary," *Tradition* 33 (1999): 6–23.

72. Examples with explanations are available in English in Aryeh Kaplan's *Meditation and the Bible* (York Beach: Weiser, 1981); a scholarly discussion has been presented by Moshe

Idel, *Language, Torah and Hermeneutics in Abraham Abulafia* (Albany: State University of New York Press, 1989).

73. Most copies of the original edition that I have seen do not contain this page, but occasionally it does show up. The Latin has been reprinted with English translation on pp. 945–946 of Ginsburg's *Introduction*.

74. "Jacob ben Hayyim and the Rise of the Biblica Rabbinica" (Hebrew University Dissertation, 1982).

75. See, for example, chapter 2 of this book.

Seven. Ibn Zimra, Ben Adret, Ibn Adoniyah, the Masorah

1. See chapter 2, n. 76.

2. Jacob ben Hayyim ibn Adoniyah's work as editor of the first printed Masoretic Bible and his Bible edition itself have been the subject of continued interest. The most extensive analysis is J. Penkower's Hebrew University dissertation "Jacob Ben Hayyim Ibn Adoniyah and the Rise of the Rabbinic Bible" (1982). Other contributions include: J. C. Wolf, *Bibliotheca Hebraea* (Hamburg: 1715–1733), Vol. 1, pp. 366–375; B. Pick, "History of the Printed Editions of the Old Testament, Together with a Description of the Rabbinic and Polyglot Bibles," *Hebraica* 9 (1892?): 47–116; Christian David Ginsburg, *Introduction to the Masoretico-Critical Edition of the Hebrew Bible* (London: 1896; repr., New York: Ktav, 1966), pp. 956–974; Robert Gottheil, "Bible Editions," *The Jewish Encyclopedia* (New York: 1902), Vol. 3, pp. 158–162; L. Goldschmidt, *The Earliest Editions of the Hebrew Bible* (New York: 1950); Paul Kahle, *The Cairo Geniza*, 2nd ed. (Oxford: Blackwell, 1959); Moshe Goshen-Gottstein, "The Rise of the Tiberian Bible Text," in *Biblical and Other Studies*, ed. Alexander Altmann (Cambridge, Mass.: Harvard University Press, 1963); idem, Introduction to the reprinted edition of the 1524 Rabbinic Bible (Jerusalem: Makor, 1972); H. C. Zafren, "Bible Editions, Bible Study and the Early History of Hebrew Printing," *Eretz Yisrael* 16 (1982): 240*–251*; B. Barry Levy, "Rabbinic Bibles, *Mikra'ot Gedolot*, and Other Great Books," *Tradition* 25 (1991): 65–81; and Moshe H. Goshen-Gottstein, "Editions of the Hebrew Bible-Past and Future," in *Sha'arei Talmon: Studies in the Bible, Qumran, and the Ancient Near East Presented to Shemaryahu Talmon* (Winona Lake, Ind.: Eisenbrauns, 1994), pp. 221–242. See also chapter 6, n. 1.

3. Christian David Ginsburg annotated and translated it in *Jacob Ben Chajim Ibn Adonijah's Introduction to the Rabbinic Bible* (London: 1867; repr., New York: Ktav, 1968). Note also Snaith's prolegomenon and Levy's "Rabbinic Bibles . . . ."

4. Because it placed Duran before Kimhi, Ibn Adoniyah's presentation is not chronological. In my summary I have presented the writers in historical order. Parts of the statements by Kimhi and Duran are translated here in chapter 3.

5. See the full study of *Qere u-Ketib* in Robert Gordis, *The Bible Text in The Making* (Philadelphia: Dropsie College, 1937), and the brief treatment by Mordechai Breuer in Samuel HaKohen and Judah Kiel, *Da'at Miqra': Sefer Daniel* (Jerusalem: Mossad HaRav Kook, 1994), pp. 136–138. In his *Massoret HaMassoret*, ed. Christian David Ginsburg (London: 1867; repr., New York: Ktav, 1968), pp. 115–119, Eliyah Levita did a detailed comparison of the distributions of *Qere* and *Ketib* by biblical books. Modern analyses have pointed to major differences in the number of such designations found in different Bible manuscripts.

6. The text of Ben Adret's responsum, Vol. 7, no. 361, translated in chapter 3, was cited by Ibn Adoniyah in his Introduction, p. 55.

7. Indeed, this was Ibn Zimra's position in Responsum B, and it was alluded to by Maraham Halava, in the text cited in chapter 6.

8. *She'eilot uTeshuvot Ziqnei Yehudah*, ed. Shlomo Simonsohn (Jerusalem: Mossad HaRav Kook, 1957), p. 165, no. 115.

9. Whether *dk'/dkh'* in Deut. 23:2 should be spelled with a *heh* or an *aleph* is perhaps the most famous example of this type of problem, but many other variations appear in later discussions of the material: Rabbi Akiva Eiger, *Gilyon HaShas* to BT Shab. 55b (translated in chapter 8); Malachi Cohen, *Yad Mal'akhi* (Berlin: 1857; repr., Israel: Am Olam, 1964), Part I, pp. 42b–44a, no. 283, s.v. *ḥylwp*; Samuel Rosenfeld, *Mishpehot Soferim* (Vilna: 1883), "Introduction"; Jacob Bachrach, *Ishtadlut Im Shadal* (Warsaw: 1896–1897), chap. 99; and H. J. Zimmels in *Ashkenazim and Sephardim: Their Relations, Differences, and Problems as Reflected in the Rabbinical Responsa* (London: Marla, 1958), pp. 138–142.

10. Ibn Adoniyah's apostacy has been discussed at length in Ginsburg's introduction to the translation of *Jacob ben Chajim Ibn Adonijah's Introduction to the Rabbinic Bible*, pp. 11–14—one former Jew's analysis of the activities of another. It is far from clear that by this time Ibn Adoniyah intended to convert, but in any case he would have found it essential to remain on good terms with his employer and colleagues. The praise for Bomberg in his introduction to the Rabbinic Bible speaks for itself. Subsequent rabbinic writers often seemed unaware of this change in religious identity; cf. Raphael Mildola, *Mayyim Rabbim, Yoreh De'ah* (Amsterdam: Joseph Dayyan, 1737), Vol. 2, no. 55, p. 49a, col. 2.

Despite the virtually universal interpretation of Levita's comment as evidence that Ibn Adoniyah had left Judaism, one recent author has attempted to stand the argument on its head. Noting the very fine work done by Ibn Adoniyah and the questionable stands on a number of issues taken by Levita, Moshe Tzuriel has argued that the former's alleged apostacy was nothing more than the latter's attempt at slander; *Masoret Seyag LaTorah* (Bene-Berak: Yahadut HaTorah, 1990), Vol. 1, pp. 94–95.

11. Ibn Zimra has reported his interactions with Muslims and Islam in other contexts, especially in the eighth volume of his responsa, while dealing with questions related to problems in areas covered in *Yoreh De'ah*. His presentations do not clarify the problems we face here.

12. See the sources and discussion in Hava Lazarus-Yaffe, *Intertwined Worlds* (Princeton, N.J.: Princeton University Press, 1992), pp. 58, 82, 107, 137.

13. *Massoret HaMassoret*, p. 94.

14. *Massoret HaMassoret*, pp. 107–111.

15. Some aspects of this criticism are discussed in Ginsburg's introduction to *Massoret HaMassoret*.

16. *Ibid.*, p. 110.

Eight. Fixing God's Torah Since the Sixteenth Century

1. Maimonides, *Mishneh Torah, Sefer Ahavah, Hilkhot Sefer Torah* 20:1. The text has been translated from the standard editions of the *Mishneh Torah* with commentaries. The Bodleian manuscript published by Moses Hyamson, *Mishneh Torah* (Jerusalem: Boys Town, 1965), differs noticeably only in subparagraph 20, where it reads, "if he sewed the parchment sections not with the sinews of a ritually pure animal" (*še-lo' be-giḏe ṭehora*), rather than *be-lo' giḏe ṭehora*, which means the same thing.

Maimonides also penned a responsum in which he ruled that one may recite a blessing on an imperfect Torah scroll, because the blessing is associated with the contents of the text, not its spelling. This ruling has been cited, supported, debated, and challenged for the past eight centuries, and, in the process, it has spawned an entire literature. Whether or not it is consistent with reference to the passage from the *Mishneh Torah* translated above, whether it should be understood as a reversal of positions, or whether it is acceptable only post facto, the responsum has been utilized frequently to sustain the use of Torah scrolls not in keeping with the level of accuracy and conistency that Maimonides himself required; see chapter 1, n. 74.

2. I. Ta-Shema, "*Qavim LeOfyah Shel Sifrut HaHalakhah BeAshkenaz BeMe'ot XIII–XIV*," *Alei Sefer* 4 (1977): 24–29.

3. See Rabbi Hayyim Moses Amarillio, *Devar Moshe: Yoreh De'ah, Hilkhot Sefer Torah* (Salonika: 1750), Vol. 3, no. 8.

4. Thus, for example, Rabbi Elijah Mizrahi noted in his Commentary on Genesis, on the observation in Genesis Rabbah, that Efron in Gen. 23:16 is spelled defective, "to indicate his shortcoming[s]. And even though Aaron is spelled defective everywhere, Efron is always spelled with a *waw*, and the change indicates the shortcoming."

5. See the illustrations of the four sons in the many premodern and modern illuminated Passover haggadot, some of which are conveniently collected in Yosef Hayim Yerushalmi, *Haggadah and History* (Philadelphia: Jewish Publication Society, 1975), passim; also Mendel Metzger, *La Haggada Enluminee*, Vol. 1 (Leiden: E. J. Brill, 1973), pp. 138–171 and accompanying plates.

6. Menahem M. Kasher, *Haggadah Shelemah*, 3rd ed. (Jerusalem: Makhon Torah Shelemah, 1966), ad loc., has documented the variations in the talmudic and midrashic texts, as well as the Yemenite manuscript tradition of the Haggadah. H. L. Ginsberg has discussed the ancient versions in "The Dead Sea Manuscript Finds: New Light on *Eretz Yisrael* in the Greco-Roman Period," in *Israel, Its Role in Civilization*, ed. Moshe Davis (New York: Jewish Theological Seminary, 1956), p. 57. See also Yeshayahu Maori, *Midreshei Hazal KeEdut LeHilufei Nusah HaMiqra'*, in *Iyyunei Miqra' uFarshanut*, Vol. 3 (1993), trans. in *Modern Scholarship in the Study of Torah: Contributions and Limitations*, ed. Sholom Carmy (Northvale, N.J.: Jason Aronson, 1996), pp. 117–118.

7. E.g., Daniel Goldschmidt, *Haggadah Shel Pesah* (Jerusalem: Mossad Bialik, 1960), p. 29, n. 22.

8. In addition to citing the "full" passage from Menahot with the *'al tiqre* addition discussed below, *Arukh Completum*, Mem, Vol. 5, pp. 64–65, states: "and there are some who say that this entire verse reaches to the total of 100 letters."

9. *Sefer HaManhig*, ed. Isaac Raphael (Jerusalem: Mossad HaRav Kook, 1978), Vol. 1, p. 28.

10. Some texts read *R[abbi] Ya'aqov B[en] M[eir]*; others have *R[abbi] Ya'aqov M[enuhato] K[avod]*. Raphael explains both but prefers the latter, which is Yarhi's standard designation for Rabbenu Tam. The notion is cited anonymously in the Tosafot to BT Men. 43b, s.v. *šo'ēl*. See also *Mahzor Vitry*, ed. Shimon Hurvitz (Frankfort am Main: J. Kauffmann, n.d.), p. 2; *Or Zaru'a* (Zhitomer: 1862; repr., Bene-Berak: Heikhal HaSefer, n.d.), Vol. I a–b, letter k; *Orhot Hayyim: Din Me'ah Berakhot*, chapter 1. Wertheimer pointed out that the passage in question does not appear in our texts of Rabbenu Tam's *Tiqqun*, despite several references to its presence.

11. Medieval references to this abound.

12. Several commentaries on *Sefer Yetzirah* are associated with Nahmanides. Gershon Scholem has attributed to Ariel ben Menahem of Gerona the standard commentary published in Nahmanides' name, found in *Sefer Yetzirah HaMeyuhas LeAvraham Avinu* . . . with commentaries (repr., Jerusalem: M. Atia, 1962), and subsequently edited by Chaim Dov [Charles B.] Chavel, *Kitvei HaRamban* (Jerusalem: Mossad HaRav Kook, 1963), Vol. 2, pp. 451–462. That which Scholem believed to be Nahmanides' commentary, which exists in both short and long recensions, of which he preferred the former, he published in *Kiryat Sefer*, Vol. 6 (1930), pp. 385–410. As far as I can tell, the passage referred to by Norzi appears in none of these texts, nor did Scholem mention it among the many early references to Nahmanides' commentary.

13. Moses Botril's commentary to *Sefer Yetzirah* 1:1, found in the above-cited editon of *Sefer Yetzirah*, p. 17a, also refers to a commentary on *Sefer Yetzirah* by Rabbenu Yom Tov

HaMequbbal, which seems to be the book Norzi cited as *Ketem Paz*. It is described as quoting an interpretation of *Sefer Yetzirah* by Rabbi Judah HaLevi (who discussed *Sefer Yetzirah* in Book IV, 25–27, of the Kuzari), but the passage bears no relationship to the reference in Norzi.

14. *Masoret Seyag LaTorah* (Florence: Isaac Da Paz, 1750; repr., Israel: Zion, 1969), p. 68a, reads: *šʾl mʿmk*: of "and now, Israel" is written without a *waw*, and similarly *wšʾl ʾb wydʿny* (Deut. 18:11).

15. Bahya discussed the 100 blessings in detail in *Kad HaQemah*, ed. Chaim Dov [Charles B.] Chavel (Jerusalem: Mossad HaRav Kook, 1970). On page 84 he referred to the passage in BT Men. 43b, from which the notion is derived. Like many other medieval works, it cites the talmudic passage in a way that suggests it contained the *ʾal tiqrē* reading of *mh* as *mʾh*, as does Bahya's Torah commentary, ad loc., *Rabbenu Bahya: Biʾur Al HaTorah*, ed. Chaim Dov [Charles B.] Chavel (Jerusalem: Mossad HaRav Kook, 1968), Vol. 3, p. 307.

16. Several bearers of this name are known, but I have been unable to link any of them with the reference.

17. See, for example, Jacob N. Epstein, *Diqduq Aramit Bavlit* (Jerusalem: Magnes, 1960), pp. 28–29, and Mordechai Akiva Friedman, *Jewish Marriages in Palestine: A Cairo Geniza Study* (Tel Aviv: Jewish Theological Seminary, 1980), Vol. 1, p. 66.

18. Rabbi Gedaliah Felder, in his notes to Yehiel ben Yequtiel's *Sefer Tanya Rabbati* (New York: Balshon Printing, 1976), pp. 33–35, reviewed much of the pertinent literature on the talmudic text and concluded that there is no evidence that it ever contained the *ʾal tiqrē* part; he understood the medieval references that appear to contain this material as explanations, not citations. While his conclusion is appropriate for some of the materials, it may be overstated when applied universally. See further his many references and those collected by Rafael in *Sefer HaManhig*, as well as those collected by Rabbi Isaiah Berlin (Pick), perhaps best know as the author of *Masoret HaShas*, in *Haflaʾah SheBaArakhin* (Breslau: 1830, and Vienna: 1859; repr., Israel: n.d.) s.v. *mʾh*.

19. *Perush Baʿal HaTurim Al HaTorah*, ad loc.; Abudarham; *Rimzei Haftarot*, in *Perush HaRoqeah Al HaTorah*, ed. Chaim Konyevsky (Bene-Berak: J. Klugmann, 1981), Vol. 3, p. 322.

20. *Baʿal HaTurim* published with *Or HaHayyim, Nahal Qedumim, and Nahal Eshqol* (repr., Jerusalem: 1965), Vol. 5, p. 55a; Reines' edition, Vol. 2, p. 385; the Humash reprinted in the hybrid *Miqraʾot Gedolot* (New York: M. P. Press, 1959), Vol. 5, p. 65a; *Heikhal HaBerakhah* (Lemberg: P. Balaban, 1869; repr., Brooklyn: J. Weiss, n.d.), Vol. 6, p. 65a; *Torah Or* (Livorno: S. Bellporte, 1926; repr. with S. Laniado's *Keli Hemdah*, Jerusalem: Makhon HaKetav, 1984), Vol. 5, p. 15a.

21. *Perushei Rabbotenu Baʿalei HaTosafot* (Jerusalem: Lewin-Epstein, 1967), *Devarim*, p. 7b.

22. Ed. Yitzhaq Shimshon Lange (Jerusalem: I. Lange, 1981), p. 578.

23. *Perush HaRoqeah Al HaTorah*, Vol. 3, p. 200.

24. *Der Pentateuch-Kommentar des Joseph Bechor-Schor zum Fuenften Buche Moses*, ed. Alfred Zweig (Breslau: 1914; reprinted in *Peirush LeHamishah Humshei Torah MeEt R[abbi] Yosef Bekhor Shor* [Jerusalem: Makor, 1978]), p. 33. In *Perushei Rabbi Yosef Bekhor Shor Al HaTorah*, ed. Yehoshafat Nevo (Jerusalem: Mossad HaRav Kook, 1994), this passage is found in verse 13, p. 325, followed by the note, *šamaʿti*, "I heard [it]."

25. *Sefer Mitzvot Zemaniyot*, ed. J. Blau (New York: Y. Blau, 1984), p. 404.

26. *Or Zaruʿa*, Vol. 1, p. 5a, letter *kaf*.

27. *Paneah Raza*, introduced by Abba Zions (Jerusalem: Makhon Torat HaRishonim, 1998), p. 507.

28. *Megaleh Amuqot* (Lvov: 1795), p. 88b.

29. *Heikhal HaBerakhah*, Vol. 5, p. 68a.

30. *Sefer Hayyim* (Jerusalem: Yeshivat Mishmarot Kehunah, 1986), chap. 21.

31. *Sha'arei Ephraim* (Jerusalem: Makhon Yerushalayim, 1986), chap. 6.

32. *Da'at Qedoshim* (Lvov: 1896; repr., Jerusalem: 1964), pp. 39b–52a; *š'l* is discussed on p. 50a.

33. *Qeset HaSofer* (Brooklyn: Moriah Offset, 1984), p. 323.

34. *Tosefet Berakhah* (Tel Aviv: Moreshet, 1976), Vol. 5, p. 76; *Torah Temimah* (repr., New York: Otzar HaSefarim, 1962), Vol. 5, ad loc. See also his *Meqor Barukh* (New York: Goldman, 1954), Vol. 1, pp. 342–351.

35. Chaim Dov [Charles B.] Chavel, *Mishnato Shel HaGaon Rabbi Akiva Eiger BeGilyon HaShas LeMassekhtot Berakhot, Shabbat, VeEruvin* (Jerusalem: Mossad HaRav Kook, 1959), pp. 340–346. *Gilyon HaShas LeRabbenu Akiva Eiger, Me'Etzem Ketav Yad Qodsho Al Massekhet Shabbat VeSeder Qodoshim*, ed. M. Berger (Brooklyn: M. Berger, 1988), contains several corrections to the text on p. 77, many of which are not new.

36. Norzi, *Minhat Shai*, passim; Samuel Rosenfeld, *Mishpehot Soferim* (Vilna: 1883); Victor Aptowitzer, *Das Schriftwort in der Rabbinischen Literatur* (New York: Ktav, 1970); Isaiah Berlin (Pick), *Hafla'ah SheBaArakhin*, s.v. *m'h*.

37. See further Isaac Judah Yehiel Safran, *Heikhal HaBerakhah*, Vol. 1, Introduction, verso of title page; and Mordechai Breuer *Keter Aram Tzovah VeHaNusah HaMequbbal Shel HaMiqra'* (Jerusalem: Mossad HaRav Kook, 1976).

38. *Da'at Qedoshim* (repr., Jerusalem: 1964).

39. *Da'at Qedoshim*, printed with *Miqdash Me'at* and only section 15 of *Gidulei Heqdesh* (Ashdod: Makhon Binyan Simhah, 1996). Section 17 of the 1964 edition contains most of the emendations.

40. Doron Witztum, Eliahu Rips, and Yoav Rosenberg, "Equidistant Letter Sequences in the Book of Genesis," *Statistical Science* 9, no. 3 (1994): 429–438, repr. in Michael Drosnin, *The Bible Code* (New York: Simon and Shuster, 1997), is the original study in favor of decoding. Brendan McKay, Dror Bar-Natan, Maya Bar-Hillel, and Gil Kalai, "Solving the Puzzle," *Statistical Science* 14 (1999): 150–173, contains a mathematics-based refutation.

41. *Tradition* 18 (1980): 175–180.

42. "Hazon Ish on Textual Criticism and Halakhah—A Rejoinder," *Tradition* 19 (1991): 301–310.

43. I am greatly indebted to Menachem Silber, who, upon reading the rest of the present volume, provided me with the related information and numerous documents and references from various published and unpublished, handwritten, newspaper, and other sources that informed my treatment of this matter. Difficulties in acquiring full copies of these relatively obscure texts means that I have not worked through many of the details as thoroughly as I would like, but the general outline of events seems quite certain.

44. Various authorities have come out for and against the attempt to write texts according to Ben Asher, and some have allowed a variety of positions. Relevant documents include the following, in some cases, available to me only as handwritten title pages of published (or perhaps unpublished) books I have not examined: *Tiqqun Eikhah: Bar Asher* (Bene-Berak: 1988); *Tiqqun Shir HaShirim Al Pi Ben Asher* (Bene-Berak: 1989); *Tiqqun Kohelet Tzilum Ketav Ashuri Lefi Ben Asher SheMuva' BaRambam, Hilkhot Sefer Torah, P[ereq] H[et]* (Bene-Berak: 1990); *Tiqqun Rut Lefi Ben Asher, SheMuva' BaRambam, Hilkhot Sefer Torah, P[ereq] H[et], Ketav Ashuri* (Bene-Berak: 1993).

Also *Berur BeInyan HaMasoret BeNusah Torah, Neviim, uKetuvim A[l] P[i] Da'at Rabboteinu . . .* , Vol. 1 (Jerusalem: n.d.); *Qinat Soferim Odot Tiqqun Soferim Al Nakh VeArba' Megillot A[l] P[i] Keter Aram Tzova HaMeyuhas LeVen Asher* (Jerusalem: Beit HaMidrash Daat uTevunah, n.d.); Ephraim Greenblatt, *Rivevot Ephraim, Orah Hayyim*, Vol. 7 (Memphis: 1995), no. 380, pp. 342, 420–430; Vol. 8 (Memphis: 1998), no. 4, pp. 490–493.

The campaign in favor of using the Aleppo Codex has been led by, among others, David Yitzchoki; it has been criticized by, among others, Rabbi Abraham Hoffman. See, for example, David Yitzchoki, *Sefer Ashrenu: Berur Samhuto VeYihuso Shel Tanakh Keter Aram Tzova* . . . (Bene-Berak: 1995); David Yitzchoki, "*Shittot HaRishonim BeTzurat Benei Haman Shel HaMasekhet Soferim VeHaYerushalmi*," *Tzfunot* 3 (1991): 55–63; Zvi Rotenberg, "*BeInyan Parashiyyot Petuhot BeMegillat Esther Al Pi Megillat Ben Asher*," ibid., 4 (1992): 56–67; David Yitzchoki, "*Parashiyyot Petuhot uSetumot BeMegillat Esther*," ibid., pp. 100–103; Rotenberg, ibid., pp. 95–96; and Yitzchoki, ibid., pp. 96–97. Also *Quntres Daat Torah . . . shel . . . HaB[eit] D[in] Tz[edek] HaHaredit* (Jerusalem: 1995); *Tiqqun Soferim LeHamesh Megillot . . . Al Pi Tiqqun Ha[Gaon Rabbi Y. M. Zonnenfeld . . . uBerditchev, SheHu Masoret HaNahug VeHaMequbbal MiDor Dorot BeHaserot ViYeterot uFetuhot uSetumot BeHaskamat HaGeonim HaRabbanim HaBedatz* . . . (Jerusalem: 1995).

45. J. A. Sanders, *The Psalms Scroll from Qumran Cave 11 (11QPs[a])* (Oxford: Clarendon Press, 1965).

Topical Index

Pages marked with an asterisk contain translations of texts.

Abarbanel, Isaac, 78, 81, 84, 144, 148–9
Abraham Min Ha-Har, 14
Abulafia, Meir HaLevi, 9, 17–21*, 22, 27, 31, 34, 48, 59, 93*, 105–7, 112, 119–20, 123, 131, 135, 152, 161, 167, 171
aharon. *See* Ex. 29:15
Albo, Joseph, 73, 147, 151
Aleppo Codex. *See* Bible
Ali At-Tabari, 74
alphabet, Hebrew
  "cut" waw, 89–96 (*see* Num. 25:12)
  final letters, 40
  orthography, 177–8 n. 2
  Paleo-Hebrew, 42, 83–4
Al-Gazi, Israel Jacob, 47, 60*, 64
Al-Ishbili, Yom Tov, 96*
Amarillio, Hayyim Moses, 56, 59, 96
Aptowitzer, Viktor, 166
Arabic, 84
  Fa al-ʿAtf, 84, 153
Aramaic, 13, 32
Arbara, Elijah, 23
Aristeas, 16*
Arukh, 30–4, 85, 147–9, 161
Ashkenazi, Betzalel, 106
Ashkenazi, Samuel Jaffe, 50
ʿayen ("check"), 56
Azulai, Hayyim David Joseph, 60, 62–3*
bʿpwlym/ba-tehorim, 75–7, 81–2
Baʿal HaTurim, 21, 161–2
Babylonian Talmud. *See* source index
  erroneous medieval attributions to, 60–2
Bahya Ben Asher, 90, 93, 120–1*, 135, 152, 161
Baqrat, Abraham, 50, 73, 114–5*, 136
Batei Kehunah, 96
Bekhor Shor, Joseph, 162–3
Bengel, Johann Albrecht, 6
Ben Adret, Solomon, 23, 171, 102–3*, 107–8*
  on *Tiqqune Soferim*, 71–3
  responsa attributed to Nahmanides #232, 23–5, 49, 55–7, 64–5, 102–43
    alternative version of, 110–15*
    Ibn Zimra and, 137–43
    identity of correspondent, 120–30
    impact of, 115–36
Ben-Asher, Aaron, 9, 77, 87, 166
Ben Asher and Ben Naftali, 23, 55, 111, 118–9, 133, 138–9
Ben Hayyim, Jacob. *See* Ibn Adoniyah
Berlin (Pick), Isaiah, 166
Berliner, Abraham, 79
Bertinora, Ovadiah, 14
Bible
  Aleppo Codex, 9, 27, 166, 171–3
  authorship of, 77–9

Bible (*continued*)
codes, 167–73
emendations of, 38
exegesis (*see* Christian Bible exegesis, Jewish influence on)
interpretation of is highly flexible, 4–7
Kaifeng texts, 96
kitb̲e ha-qodeš, 12–3
Leningrad B 19A, 48
Lisbon, 1482, 48
multiple interpretations of, 4–7, 169
non-Jewish criticisms of, 147–8
Orthodox Jews and, 40, 223–4 nn. 23–4
Pentateuch, Spanish manuscript no. 1241, 48
text
accuracy of, 7–12; rabbinic and non-rabbinic attitudes to, 38–41; medieval reactions to inconsistencies in, 43–6; talmudic witnesses to inconsistencies in, 68–81
Christian and Muslim criticisms of transmission of, 67, 147–8
computer scanning of, 9
differences between Masorah and Talmud, 145–7
finding or establishing, 3–27
historical perspective on, 3–4
ideal, 6
in the sixteenth century, 137–155
medieval emenders of, 47–9
rabbinic changes in, 4
since the sixteenth century, 156–76
types, 11–2
use of Masorah to fix, 67–88
variants in, 27–41, 178–9; Halakhah to Moses from Sinai, 68–81; Zoharic texts of, 46–8, 53
Yemenite text of, 96
blindness, 57
Bomberg, David, 22, 147
Breuer, Mordechai, 9, 19, 27, 135
Brisker, Hayyim, 36

Calais, Judah, 51
Caro, Joseph, 15, 31*, 60, 111–2, 114, 136
Christian Bible exegesis, Jewish influence on, 207 n.30
Christianity, 86
Christianity and Islam, 67, 74, 135
circumcision, 46–7
codex, 13
history of, 8
Cohen, Simha, 35
Colon, Joseph, 106
Culi, Jacob, 14
"cut" waw. *See* Num. 25:12

Da'at Qedoshim, 167
daf, 10
Dahood, Mitchell, 40
daka'/dakah. *See* Deut. 23:2
David Ben Samuel, 61
David Joseph, 23, 55, 59, 64–5*
Dead Sea Scrolls, 3, 10, 12, 37, 40, 48, 70
Psalms Scroll, 174
decoding Bible texts, 167–73
derash, 5–6, 53
De Rossi, Johann, 27, 48
Di Modena, Aryeh, 148*
diqduq, 79
Di Trani, Joseph, 85
Di Lonzano, Menahem, 22, 52, 90, 102, 133
Dimitrovsky, Zalman, 103, 112, 114
Duran, Shimon, 14, 61–2, 119*, 136
Duran, Solomon, 89*
Duran, Profiat, 80–1*, 84, 144, 148–9

Easterners and Westerners, 55, 138–9
Eiger Guens, Akiva, 35, 90, 171
variations in Bible text, 164–6*
Eiger, Solomon, 96*
Eleazar (Eliezer) of Worms, 50*
Elijah Ben Azriel of Vilna, 61
Emet LeYa'acov, 47, 60, 64
Epstein, Baruch, 14, 163–4
Euclid, 4
Ezra, 14, 74, 81, 84

gahon. *See* Lev. 11:42
Galen, 4
Ganzfried, Solomon, 9, 48, 163
Kesset HaSofer, 9
Gaon, Shem Tov, 94–5, 121*, 121–2
Gellis, Jacob, 50
Gilyon HaShas, BT Shab, 55b. 135, 159, 164–7*
Ginat Veradim, 26*, 28*
Ginsburg, Christian David, 27, 48, 94, 101, 133

Goshen-Gottstein, Moshe H, 9, 26–7
Guens. *See* Eiger
Gunzberg, Aryeh Leib, 156*

Hagiographa, meaning of, 12–3
Hai, Gaon, 53–4
  Ibn Zimra's attitude toward, 153
Halakhah LeMoshe MiSinai, 68–9, 72, 74, 77, 80–1, 116–7, 144–51
Halava, Moses (Maharam) ben Gaon, 56, 61–2, 115–7*, 122, 130, 133, 136
  Responsum no. 145, 117*
HaLevi, Abraham ben Mordecai, 12, 25–6*, 28*
HaLevi, Judah, 33, 59*
  Ibn Zimra's attitude toward, 153
  Kuzari III:26–7, 59*
HaLevi, Shalom Isaac, 37–8
Hananel. 126
Haraz, Hayyim, 35
Harkavy, A. 79
Hasan, Abraham. 17. 59, 110–4, 119–20*, 136
Hasidei Ashkenaz, 21, 134
Hazon Ish, 173
hiluf and mahloqet, 27–9, 188 n. 77
himmol yimmol. See Gen. 17:13
Hizquni, 44, 97–8
Horowitz, Isaiah, 50
hu'/hi'. See Lev. 25:33

Ibn Adoniyah, Jacob ben Hayyim, 23, 31, 31–32*, 34, 102, 132*, 143, 148–54
  Ibn Zimra and, 148–152
  Introduction to the Rabbinic Bible, 143–152
Ibn Chiquitilla, Moses, 78
Ibn Ezra, Abraham, 20–1, 35, 49, 78, 84–5, 99, 134, 137*
  Ibn Zimra's attitude toward, 153
  Introduction to Torah Commentary, 21, 67*
Ibn Gabirol, Solomon, Ibn Zimra's attitude toward, 153
Ibn Hazam, 74
Ibn Janah, Yonah, 84, 153
Ibn Melekh, Solomon, 22, 30, 55
Ibn Yarhi, Abraham ben Nathan, 161
Ibn Zimra, David ben Solomon, 6, 7, 30, 42–66
  attitude toward Kabbalah, 65–6
  Ben Adret and, 137–43
  Ibn Adoniyah and, 148–52
  Ibn Ezra and, 153
  Magen David, 84
  Maimonides and, 71–2
  on Paleo-Hebrew, 42, 83–4
  reliance on Masorah, 100–1
  Responsa
  Book I
    146, 47
    284, 153
    336 (D), 97–101, 152–5
    344, 153
    363, 52, 62, 95
    446, 62
  Book II
    596, 62
    623, 66
    693, 153
    694, 66
    696, 56, 66
    796, 65, 66
    813, 153
    813–818, 46
  Book III
    442, 42
    549, 153
    594 (B), 47, 55, 61, 140–3, 149, 151–5
    634, 153
    643, 179 n. 7
    967, 153
    1029, 65
    1065, 84
    1066, 153
    1068, 99, 153
  Book IV
    107, 47
    1111, 54
    299, 47
    1172 (A), 42–66, 137–43, 149, 152–5
  Book V
    40, 153
    67, 153
    253, 153
  Book VI
    2006, 153
  Book VII
    33, 153

Book VIII
3, 47
6, 95
140–1, 53
171, 62
181 (C), 55, 61, 89–96, 140–3, 152–5
191, 153
inverted *nuns*, 4, 87
Israel the Scribe, 94
Isserles, Moses 31, 37, 106, 171
Ittur Soferim, 68, 71–4, 80–4, 147–8, 151. *See also* Ned. 37a–38a

Jacob Ben Asher, 21, 48, 59, 111, 134–5. *See also Ba'al HaTurim*
Jaffe, Abraham, 25
Josephus, 3, 42
Jubilees, 6
Judah Ben Eliezer (Riva), 44*, 121
Judah the Pious, 135

Kabbalah, 5–6, 135
Ibn Zimra's attitude toward, 65–6
Kagan, Israel Meir, 16
Kahle, Paul, 27
kalot. See Num. 7:1
Karaites, 79
katav/katevu, 78
Katzenellenbogen, Meir, 106
Kennicott, Benjamin, 48, 98, 163
ketav 'ivri, ketav 'ashuri, 42, 83–4
ketib. See qere u-ketib
ketib we-la' qere, 68–76, 80–1, 144–7, 154
Khazars, 33
Kimhi, David, 22, 78, 81, 84–5, 106, 144–5, 148–9, 153
Introduction to Commentary on Joshua, 80*
Kirkisani, Jacob. *See* Qirqisani
kitvei ha-qodesh, 12–15
Kook, Abraham, 28

LaGarde, Paul, 8
Landau, Yehezkel, 102*, 171
Leiman, Sid, 109, 173–4
Leiner, Gershon Hanokh, 36
leshon ha-qodesh, 183–4 n. 30, 208–9 n. 35
Letter of Aristeas, 16
letter-perfect Bible text, 3, 40–1
Levinger, David S, 121
Levita, Elijah, 14, 132*, 152–4
Masoret HaMasoret, 14, 132
Lieberman, Saul, 26
Lipschuetz, Israel, 14
Lowe, Judah, 35
Luria, Isaac, 5
Luria, Solomon, 106

ma'abirim. See 1 Sam. 2:24
Magrisso, Isaac, 14
Mahzor Vitry, 14, 30
male'/shalem, 111–3, 118–9
Maimon, Abraham ben Moses, 38
Responsum no. 91. 30*
Maimonides, Moses, 6, 37–8, 46, 71, 132–3
Hilkhot Sefer Torah, 87, 110, 117, 157*
Ibn Zimra's attitude toward, 153
Introduction to *Seder Zeraim*, 71
Margoliot, E. Z., 163
Masorah/ Masoret/*masorot*, 13–6, 19–20, 22, 26, 32–4, 36–7, 94, 120, 122, 126–9, 149–50, 190 n. 95
Masorah codices, 24, 26, 32
definition of, 13–6
medieval skepticism about, 62–4, 130–6
used to fix Bible texts, 67–88
Masoret Seyag LaTorah, 9, 23–5, 59, 93–4, 105*, 119–20, 130
matres lectionis, 3, 65
Medina, Samuel, 106
me'en bil'am. See Num. 22:14
Megaleh Amuqot, 21
Meir Rothenberg, 147
Meiri, Menahem ben Solomon, 9, 15, 25–6*, 34, 38, 48, 59, 62, 107, 119–20, 122–9, 123*, 130, 133, 136, 146, 149–50, 171
Menahem Azariah of Fano, 23
mezuzot. See Deut. 5:9
Michael, H., 121
midrashic exegesis, 4
authority of, 53–4
Mikhlol Yofi, 22, 30
Mikhlol VeShorashim, 22
mimenu. See Num. 13:31
mi-neso'. See Gen. 4:14
Minhat Kohen, 23
Minhat Shai. See Norzi
Minhat Yehudah, 121

Mintz, Judah, 132–3*
miqra', 78
Miqra' Soferim, 68, 70–4, 80–4. *See* Ned. 37a-38a
Miqra'ot Gedolot, 187 n. 55
Mishnah Berurah, 16
Mishnah manuscripts, 5–6
Mishnat Avraham, 25
mitḥakem/miteḥakemim, 47–8
Mizrahi, Elijah, 51, 106, 111, 132, 153, 165
Mordecai ben Hillel, 147
Moscatto, Menahem, 24

na'ar/na'arah, 75–6
Nahal Hever, 3
Nahmanides, Moses, 32, 37, 55, 152, 161
  Introduction to Torah Commentary, 4, 67
Nahmias, David, 23
Nathan of Rome, 79, 83, 85. *See Arukh*
Nissim ben Reuben, 115
  Commentary to BT San, 4a. 118*, 136
Norzi, Yedidiah, 9, 14, 19, 27, 30, 32–3*, 34, 48, 51, 75, 102, 112, 133, 166, 171
  Minhat Shai
    Introduction to, 21–3*
    Commentary to Gen. 25:6. 61; Deut. 10:12. 160–4*; Deut. 22:19. 76

Okhlah VeOkhlah, 76
Origen, 39, 151
Or Torah, 22, 90
'oto. See Num. 21:34 and Deut. 22:2

Palaggi, Hayyim, 163
Paltiel, Hayyim, 162
PaRDeS, 5
Passover Haggadah, 160
Penkower, Jordan, 109, 135
Perfet, Isaac, 118
Phillip, Moshe, 56
pilagshim. See Gen. 25:6
polemics, 24
Pratensis, Felix, 23, 135
printing, halakhic responses to, 178 n. 3
Ptolemy, 85–6

qarnot. See Lev. 4:5
qere u-ketib̲, 15–6, 22, 32, 68, 76–81,143–9, 151, 153–4, 174
  Are Halakhah to Moses from Sinai, 154
qere we-la' ketib̲, 68–76, 80–1, 144–7, 154, 165
Qirqisani (Kirkisani), Jacob, 74
Qiryat Sefer (Meiri), 9, 119–20, 124–5*, 126, 128–9, 136
Qumran, 3, 10
Qur'an, 6, 74, 135–6
  Muslim claims for letter-perfect text of, 152

Rabbi Joseph the Scribe, 17
Rabbinic Bible
  history of, 219 n. 2
  of 1524–5, 48
rabbinic texts, emendations of, 194–5 n. 131
Rashbam, 78
Rashi, 21, 43–4, 51, 79, 99–100, 112, 121, 133–4, 153, 171
  Masorah and, 145
  Torah Commentary
    Gen. 14:14, 62
    Gen. 24:2, 46, 50, 165
    Gen. 25:6, 44, 106*
    Ex. 13:16, 165
    Ex. 23:2, 52
    Ex. 25:22, 165
    Ex. 31:18, 62
    Num. 7:1, 106*
    Deut. 1:13, 106*
    Deut. 5:9, 44
    Deut. 33:2, 4
  Talmud Commentary
    Suk. 6b, 14
    San. 99a, 79
    Ned. 37b, 74
Recanati, Menahem, 22
remez, 5
Riva. *See* Judah ben Eliezer.
Rosenfeld, Samuel, 48, 166
Rosenmueller, E., 8
rov, 10–1, 16, 25, 33, 57–60, 115–7, 141–3

Saadiah Gaon, 78, 84
  Ibn Zimra's attitude toward, 153
Safran, Isaac Judah Yehiel, 9, 48, 163
  Heikhal HaBerakhah to Deut. 10:12. 163*
Salonika, 17, 24
Samaritan Pentateuch, 40

Samau'al Ibn Yahyaal-Maghribi, 74
Samuel HaNaggid, 54
Saraval, Yehudah Leib, 23–5, 48
Schick, Moses, 135
Schick, Solomon Zvi, 35*, 45
Scribes
  corrections of (*see Tiqqunei Soferim*)
  practices related to halakhic determinations, 27–41
Sefer, 8–10, 13, 55, 58–60, 64–5, 93, 98, 109–10, 181 note 14
Sefer HaZikkaron (Baqrat), 50, 73
  to Gen. 11:31–32, 114
  to Gen. 25:6, 114–5*
Sefer Ma'on, *Sefer Za'atutei*, and *Sefer Hi'*. *See* Sof. 6:4
Sefer Taggin, 37
Septuagint, 40, 70, 85–6, 160
Sha'agat Aryeh, 135, 156
  Hilkhot Sefer Torah #36, 156*
Shalom. *See* Num. 25:12
Sherira Gaon, 53–4
Sherwin, B., 35
Shulhan Arukh, Orah Hayyim 141:8, 15–6
Sirkes, Joel, 97*
Sodom, 70
Sofer, Moses, 35, 52–3*, 65, 135
Soloveitchik, Joseph Baer, 36, 174–5
Soloveitchik, Joseph Dov, 36–7, 174–5
Soloveitchik, Moses, 36–7, 174–5
ba-sukkot. *See* Lev. 23:42–3
Sumak, Abdullah (Ovadiah Somekh), 37

Taitatzak, Joseph, 112
Tam, Jacob, 30*, 31, 37, 44, 93, 98–9, 107, 135
Targum, 13, 32, 130
Ta-Shema, Israel, 24
Tefillin, 13, 66, 95, 110
Temple
  court of 7–12. (*see Sefer Ma'on*)
  text correctors based in, 12
Ten Commandments in scroll form, 8, 182 n. 20
tif'eret ha-lashon, 85
tif'eret ha-qeri'ah, 84–5
Tiqqunim, 25–7, 29, 33, 123–4, 127
Tiqqun Sefer Torah, 30
Tiqqun Soferim, 72–5, 81–4, 147, 151
Torah
  multiple interpretations of, 179–80 n. 18 (*see* Interpretation)
  scrolls, 3–4, 9, 10
    13 scrolls of produced by Moses, 12
    lack of vocalization in, 179 n. 7
    layout of, 73
    majority determination of text of, 10
    majority testimony, 16–8, 29–30, 57–60
    three found in the Temple court, 7–12 (*see Sefer Ma'on*)
  sefer, definition of, 13–16 (*see sefer*)
  text of (*see also* Bible text), 26–27
    contemporary fixing of, 173–6
    discovering Moses' copy, 173–6
    emending vocalization in, 97–100
    evidence about: inconsistent, 29–41; avoidance of, 35–6
    in the Second Temple Period, 11
    Joseph Dov Soloveitchik's teachings about, 35–6
    Maimonides' formulation of scribal halakhah concerning, 157–9
    Moses Isserles on, 30–1
    Ovadiah Yosef's teachings on, 37–8
    Rabbenu Tam's uncertainty about, 30–1
    using the Talmud to fix, 89–96
    waw of *shalom* in Num. 25:12, 89–96 (*see* cut waw)
    variants: in Rabbinic citations of Deut. 6:20, 159–60; in scribal manual, 167; midrashic, 44–5, 49–50; Yemenite 37–8

Tosafists, 21, 23, 30, 44, 45, 78, 121, 133, 134
Totafot. *See* Ex. 13:16, Deut. 6:3 and 11:18
Tov Elem, Joseph, 161
Trestino, Moses Aryeh, 26
Tzarfati, Ben Zion, 23, 25

u-mi-geva'ot, 45
u-ven 'ein lo. *See* Num. 27:8

Vilna Gaon, 14
Vital, Hayyim, 5
vowel signs, 4, 97–100
wa-asimem. *See* Deut. 1:13
we-ha-nose'. *See* Lev. 15:10

Wadi Murabb'at, 3
Weider, Naftali, 13
Weinberg, Yaakov, 28
Wilensky, M, 99
writing, history of, 181–2 n.18

Yehiel Mikhal of Glogau, 50
Yehudah, Zvi, 173–4
yerushalayim, 70
Yesod Morah, 137*
Yosef, Ovadiah, 36–7

Zohar, 32, 35, 46–8, 53–5, 66, 135, 150
to Num. 23:9, 45*

Source Index

Bible

Genesis
1:1, 30–1
1:21, 50
4:14, 38
7:11, 38
9:29, 38
11:31–32, 114
13:10, 70
14:14, 62
14:18, 20
17:13, 61–2, 119–20
Ch. 18, 81
18:5, 68, 83
18:12, 73
18:22, 82–3
18:23, 83
19:24, 70
24:2, 46
24:55, 68
25:6, 20, 38, 43–4, 49–51, 60–1, 63, 85, 90, 103–7, 111, 113–20, 123–25, 133, 139, 141, 165
26:5, 43, 116–7
29:22, 70
30:36, 165
31:45, 20
32:9, 99
41:22, 20

Exodus
1:10, 47
3:20, 20
10:4, 19
12:4, 20
12:26, 160
12:39, 20
13:16, 61, 108, 123–5, 138, 165
15:18, 21
16:7, 20
17:4, 20
18:2, 20
19:9, 115
20:2, 165
21:22, 20
23:2, 10, 18, 33, 49, 52, 55–6, 58, 87, 108–9, 115
23:13, 83
24:5, 56, 108, 116
24:12, 78
25:7, 19
25:22, 165
25:31, 20, 38
28:26, 38
29:15, 23–4, 48
31:18, 62, 112
32:11, 164

Leviticus
3:5, 20
Ch. 4, 125

Leviticus (*continued*)
4:7, 43, 49, 51, 56, 63, 87, 90, 103–8, 114, 118–9, 123–4, 126, 138–41, 164–5
4:25, 114
4:34, 165
8:7, 165
8:13, 100
8:15, 100
8:22, 100
8:55, 100
8:57, 100
11:42, 37, 122–3
11:47, 115
13:33, 165
15:10, 44, 52, 133, 164
19:8, 101
19:20, 100
20:14, 100
20:16, 101
20:17–23, 92, 100
21:9, 100
21:17–23, 92
22:3, 101
22:12, 100
22:42–43, 87, 108, 138–9
23:2–4, 115
23:3, 100
23:30, 100
23:36, 100
23:38, 21
23:42, 114
23:42–43, 43, 49, 51, 56, 61–6, 75, 87, 90, 108, 114, 119, 123–4, 126, 138–9, 140–1
25:6, 21
25:10–12, 100
25:30, 165
25:33, 43, 97–101
25:31–2, 98
25:34, 98–9
25:35, 98
26:9, 20
27:4, 100
Numbers
1:10, 20
1:18, 38
3:37, 20
7:1, 20, 38, 44, 49, 51, 60–1, 63, 85, 90, 103–7, 111–2, 116–9, 123–5, 133, 139, 141
10:10, 19:38
10:35–36, 87
13:31, 55–6, 108, 110, 114, 138, 141
15:13, 79
21:34, 43, 46–8, 53, 63, 88, 137–8
22:5, 38
22:14, 56, 108, 138–9
23:9, 45
24:14, 52
25:6, 87
25:12, 31, 38, 43, 59, 62–3, 89–96, 125
25:13, 91
27:8, 49, 51–2, 56, 61–3, 108, 120, 138–9
28:13, 94
28:19, 164
31:2, 68
Deuteronomy
1:13, 21, 49, 51, 60–3, 103–7, 116–7, 120, 123–6, 139
3:11, 20
5:9, 44, 120
6:1, 75
6:3, 61, 108, 123–5, 138, 165
6:20, 159–60
10:12, 160–4
11:18, 61, 70–1, 108, 123–5, 138, 165
11:19, 70–1
17:10, 36
17:11, 64–5
18:11, 161
18:13, 80
20:9, 105, 112
22:2, 43, 46–8, 53, 63, 88, 137–8
22:19, 76
22:23, 75, 99
23:2, 38
23:11, 165
23:14, 19
25:5 , 51, 123–4
27:2, 20
27:2–8, 11, 181 n. 18
28:17, 80
28:27, 75–6
28:30, 75, 80
31:34, 112
32:7, 36
32:17, 18, 33, 106
33:2, 4
33:7, 33
33:27, 56, 108, 116

Judges
16:31, 133
20:32, 85
1 Samuel
1:6, 85
2:24, 43–4, 52–3, 133
5:6, 75
5:9, 75
5:12, 75
6:4–5, 75
28:10, 85
2 Samuel
3:35, 165
8:3, 68
16:23, 69
2 Kings
5:18, 69
12:4, 83
Isaiah
2:6, 106
13:16, 75
13:17, 76
28:4, 85
58:3, 85
58:7, 165
63:19, 85
Jeremiah
3:2, 75
9:4, 85
31:37, 69
32:11, 75
50:29, 69
51:3, 69
Ezekiel
13:20, 85
17:23, 85
20:5, 85
21:15, 85
22:24, 85
27:19, 85
48:16, 69
Zechariah
14:2, 75
Psalms
22:30, 94
37:7, 68
49:14, 32
50:23, 165
68:26, 68, 83
68:27, 165
Ch. 117, 164
119:126, 30
137:1, 78
145:13–14, 175
Proverbs
25:1, 21
30:22, 21
Job
12:12, 33
23:13, 94
Song of Songs
1:2, 119
2:15, 165
Ruth
2:11, 69, 165
3:5, 69
3:12, 69
3:17, 69
Ecclesiastes
8:17, 18
Nehemiah
8:8, 14, 116
1 Chronicles
1:17, 165
2 Chronicles
33:13, 165

Hellenistic Sources
Josephus
Against Apion I, 42, 3
Septuagint
Gen. 13:10, 70
Gen. 19:24, 70
Gen. 29:22, 70,

Midrashim
Sifra
Lev. 4:7, 51
Sifre
#356, 33
Genesis Rabbah
61:6, 50
50:3, 70
59:8, 47
61:4, 43, 50, 123. *See* Gen. 25:6
Ch. 73, 165
Leviticus Rabbah
Ch. 9, 165,
22:1 (Lev. 17:3), 77

Numbers Rabbah
12:8, 123
Deuteronomy Rabbah
1:10, 123
Song of Songs Rabbah
4:1, 78
to Song of Songs 2:15, 165
Tanhuma
Emor 18, 70
Midrash Psalms
Ch. 18, 82
Megillat Taanit Batra', 86
Midrash Otiyot Ketanot, 90

Mishnah
Shabbat
16:1, 12, 13
Eruvin
10:3, 8
Yoma
7:1, 8
Megillah
1:9, 13
Mo'ed Qatan
3:4, 12
Sanhedrin
10:1 (11:1), 180 n. 12
Avot
3:11, 180 n. 12
3:13, 14, 18
Yadayim
3:2, 12
3:5, 12

Palestinian Talmud
Pe'ah
2:6, 77
Ma'aser Sheni
4:2, 115
Sheqalim
4:3, 12
5:1, 68
6:1, 4
Ta'anit
4:2, 33
Megillah
1:5, 76
1:9, 70, 86
4:1, 77
Sukkah
4:3, 165
Hagigah
1:8, 77
Yevamot
1:6, 70
Sanhedrin
4:2, 33

Babylonian Talmud
Berakhot
5a, 78
7b, 165
15b, 70
63b, 47
Shevu'ot
38b, 47
Shabbat
55b, 35, 44, 52–3, 159, 164–7
103b, 70
104a, 76, 83–4
Eruvin
13a, 42
32a, 165
Pesahim
3a, 165
112a, 32
113b, 81
117a, 78, 164
Yoma
24a, 70
Sukkah
6b, 14, 51
16b, 116
18a, 116
34b, 70
Rosh Hashanah
25a, 115
Megillah
2b, 76
3a, 83–4
9a, 86
19b, 77
22a, 116, 164
24a, 75
25b, 144, 148
Yevamot
13b, 70
Qiddushin
4a, 51, 108
30a, 28, 30, 37, 68, 103, 108, 116, 121–2, 124, 165
30b, 52, 71

38a, 116
66b, 90–3, 96
Ketubot
7b, 165
Niddah
33a, 44*, 52, 133, 164
Sotah
10b, 70
25a, 108
47b, 57
Nedarim
37a-38a, 68–74, 80–4, 116, 144, 145, 147–8, 154, 161, 165
64b, 57
Sanhedrin
4a, 60, 118, 123, 136, 164–5
4b, 60, 123
21b, 76
88b, 57
99a, 79
Baba Batra
9a, 165
14b-15a, 78
21b, 118
115a, 49, 56, 108, 123
Aboda Zarah
29b, 118
Zebahim
4a, 43
37b, 118
40a, 51
Menahot
30 , 53
27a, 70
34a, 70
35b, 70
43b, 163
Hullin
109b, 70
125b, 116

Minor Tractates
Soferim
1:7, 86
6:4, 7, 10–1, 16, 29, 33, 36–7, 55–7, 97, 108, 111, 113, 116, 118–9, 125, 138, 145, 180–1 n.13
9:8, 76
Kallah
Ch. 1, 32

Printed in the United States
63097LVS00002B/153